American Banking Through Crises and Consolidation:
How Four Banks Bought
50% of America's
Biggest Business

By Arnold G. Danielson

American Banking: Through Crises and Consolidation: *How Four Banks Bought 50% of America's Biggest Business*.

Published June, 2014

Editorial and Proofreading Services: Jenna Lloyd
Interior Layout and Cover Design: Howard Johnson, Howard Communigrafix, Inc.
Photo Credits: Depositphotos: Dramatic Sky Over New York City Skyscrapers: 31360503

 **SDP Publishing**

Published by SDP Publishing, an imprint of SDP Publishing Solutions, LLC.

For more information about this book contact Lisa Akoury-Ross by email at lross@SDPPublishing.com.

SDP Publishing
Permissions Department
PO Box 26, East Bridgewater, MA 02333
or email your request to info@SDPPublishing.com.

ISBN-13 (print): 978-0-9911597-5-8
ISBN-13 (ebook): 978-0-9911597-6-5

Library of Congress Control Number: 2014933412

Dedicated to my wife, Vivian, who played such a vital role
in the establishing of my bank consulting firm in the 1970s
and all that came later that made this book possible.

TABLE OF CONTENTS

Table of Contents

PREFACE

In 2007, when my book, *Consolidation of Banking: Or How Five Banks Bought 50% of America's Biggest Business*, went to press, it was obvious that the banking industry was headed for difficult times, but I had no idea just how bad the crisis would be–and how long it would last. It did not enter my mind that the five banks that bought half of "America's biggest business" would soon be just four with Wachovia not surviving 2008. The extent of the changes to the industry in the last five years prompted me to revise and update my earlier book and concentrate more on the impact of financial crises than on consolidation and the evolution of banking since the 1970s. It is hard to do otherwise after the events of recent years.

As one whose banking experience parallels the years when banking grew from a localized industry to one dominated by four large banks, it is somewhat disappointing to realize this experience has two major financial crises as bookends. I joined Maryland National as Vice President of Planning in late 1972, and it was only a matter of months before a market crash and rising interest rates ushered in the difficult times often just referred to as the "seventies" that lingered on until 1982. When I retired from 30 years of running Danielson Associates, a bank consulting firm, it was 2007—a year before the financial crisis that made what happened in the "seventies" look relatively small.

The intent of this book and its predecessor was and is to provide a factual history of the years that saw banking go through this extensive change. Just why the change occurred can be neatly divided into six chronological sections. These are:

- The economic crisis and double-digit inflation of the 1970s that hurt banking in general, but also bankrupted a thrift industry. All of which set in motion the changes of the 1980s that completely shifted the industry's direction;

- The savings and loan crisis and the advent of interstate banking in the 1980s that dominated business headlines for most of the decade;

- The real estate-driven recession in the late 1980s and early 1990s and thrift meltdown that resulted in more than 2,500 bank and thrift failures in four years and fueled the creation of some large regional banks.

- The spectacular rise in bank stock prices and the elimination of the barriers separating commercial banking from other financial businesses that facilitated the formation of the very large banks in the late 1990s;

- The aftermath of the 1999 deregulation, low interest rates and subprime mortgage loans in the early 2000s that created a "boom" in banking and housing that left us with five banks much larger than all others—and the ingredients for disaster;

- The financial crisis of 2008 and its aftermath that hurt national economies around the world and resulted in the failure or near-failure of such well-known financial firms as Citigroup, AIG, Lehman Brothers, Merrill Lynch, Bear Stearns, Wachovia, Washington Mutual, Fannie Mae and Freddie Mac.

This book takes the reader through each of these periods in detail, showing the impact of economic conditions; actions of individual banks; and how the industry changed over those years. For those who were not close observers of the process while it was occurring, the names of the many banks that played a part will at times be confusing, particularly since acquirers often took the name of the acquiree. This included Norwest buying Wells Fargo and taking its name and NationsBank doing the same with BankAmerica. New York-based Chemical went a step further by acquiring Chase Manhattan, taking its name and then purchasing J.P. Morgan and adopting the name JPMorgan Chase.

This is a story with an unhappy ending if the focus is primarily on the last few years, but the long view is not as negative as the daily headlines would suggest. The large American banks, for starters, have never been in as favorable a position as they are in 2014.

The book's last chapter, "What Next?" explains how the troubles in the rest of the world have hurt their banks much more than ours; and only HSBC, with most of its assets in Southeast Asia, can compare to the big four of American banking– JPMorgan, Bank of America, Citigroup and Wells Fargo. It seems likely that ten years from now, at least three of these banks will have assets of more than $4 trillion and will be the leaders from an international, as well as domestic, viewpoint with only a couple of foreign non-state banks being close to their status.

As to the small banks and thrifts, they have fallen from about 21,000 to 7,000 since the 1980s, and the numbers are going to continue to slide. With the big banks getting even larger, however, there is still room for small banks. Those that survive will focus on two models. These are urban banking boutiques that specialize in local commercial real estate and/or small business lending and country banks doing what they are doing now—filling a void in which big banks have little interest. These small banks, however, will be threatened by new technologies that take remote access banking to levels not yet seen.

The interrelationship between economic crises and consolidation that play such a big role in this book is best documented in how today's JPMorgan and Bank of America were built. JPMorgan, whose predecessor Chemical Bank broke out of its "New York only" mold with a 1987 acquisition of the second biggest bank in Texas—which was failing because of an oil crisis that eliminated nine of that state's largest banks. That same crisis saw NCNB, today's Bank of America, buying the second and third largest banks in Texas in a federally-assisted deal. Fast forward to the national economic crisis of 1989 to 2002, and Chemical struck again by acquiring Manufacturers Hanover in the most expensive bank deal in history until that time. This record lasted a little less than a month before NCNB paid twice as much for C&S/Sovran. Its later purchases of Chase Manhattan and JPMorgan were not crisis driven, but NCNB's (by then NationsBank) move to the top came from the purchase of California-based BankAmerica that had not fully recovered from the hard times in California in the early 1990s.

Then comes 2008 and the worst economic and banking crisis since the Great Depression, and who were the winners? Chemical, by then JPMorgan, was handed one of the five largest investment banks, Bear Stearns, and the largest thrift, Washington Mutual, by the regulators. NCNB, now Bank of America, bought the largest securities brokerage, which was also an investment bank, Merrill Lynch, as it was close to failure. The latter also, much to its eventual dismay, bought the biggest mortgage banker, Countrywide, and proved that its universal banking model was strong enough to absorb more than $50 billion in mortgage-related losses, albeit with some anxious moments in 2011 and at a great cost to investors.

I was fortunate enough to have a front row seat for these forty years of crises and consolidation. First at Maryland National for five years and then for more than 30 years at my own firm, Danielson Associates, which specialized in helping banks adjust to the constantly changing environment. At the latter, I wrote quarterly banking reports that were helpful in preparing for the two books. In 2007, I retired to spend more time at my home in southern France and benefited from a global perspective on the excitement, if I dare use that word, which began toward the end of that year, and hit its peak in late 2008 and early 2009.

SURPRISE OR BUSINESS AS USUAL?

I t was early September 2008, and my wife and I had just arrived at our home in southern France for a few weeks of rest and relaxation. It had been a year since I finished my book, *Consolidation of Banking: Or How Five Banks Bought 50% of America's Biggest Business*, and about the same amount time since banking and the American economy had moved into one of their periodic downturns. With the overheating of the housing market in 2005 and 2006, concerns about subprime mortgages and declining home prices, this downturn had not come as a surprise. Nevertheless, even with the fall in bank stock prices in the second half of 2007, the big trading losses for Citigroup and other large banks and the failure of Bear Stearns in early 2008, I (like most industry observers) was unprepared for the extent of what happened in those fateful days of September 2008. I had no idea that I would spend most of that month glued to the television watching international CNBC.

Things were obviously bad when on Labor Day weekend, Fannie Mae and Freddie Mac were nationalized and then a week later the Federal Reserve called together the leaders of the nation's largest banks in an attempt to avoid a possible bankruptcy of one of the biggest investment banks, Lehman Brothers. In the midst of the closing days of a presidential election, there was suddenly a very real fear that if something was not done to save Lehman, much of the financial services industry would follow it into oblivion. There was concern that if Lehman went, Merrill Lynch might not be far behind and liquidity problems could add Citigroup, Morgan Stanley and Goldman Sachs to the list. It sounded like a financial Armageddon just waiting to happen.

Five years after those six crucial weeks in the early autumn of 2008 when the nation's financial system seemed so close to collapse, the extent of the damage incurred was still far from certain, but the industry had survived, albeit in a much different form. A financial reform bill, the Dodd-Frank Wall Street Reform Act ("Dodd-Frank") that supposedly would solve the ills that surfaced in 2008 was passed in the late spring of 2010, but it did little to make people feel "it could not happen again"–or put aside a national anger at bankers and the banking industry. This negative feeling was further inflamed by the alleged actions of one of the most revered of financial institutions, Goldman Sachs, that had become the poster child for all that was wrong with banking, along with the continued losses of Bank of America stemming primarily from its ill-advised Countrywide acquisition. In this environment, it was hard to remember that little more than a generation ago, banking was a local, decentralized business in which most bankers were beloved leaders in their communities, yet it was quite easy to recall that the responses to the many banking crises since the mid-1970s had done little to prevent the future ones.

Despite all the concerns after the problems of 2008, bank consolidation not only continued to move forward, but this time with more help from the regulators than usual. As recently as 2000, no American bank had assets above $1 trillion, but by 2009, there were three—Bank of America, JPMorgan and Citigroup—over $2 trillion, and a fourth, Wells Fargo, was headed in that direction. In addition, as recently as 1990, the four largest banks had held just 14 percent of bank assets. By 2000, this percentage had risen to almost 30 percent, and ten years later, after the debacle of 2008 with so many losers and so few winners, the four banks' asset share had risen to about 50 percent.

In these days of giant banks, it strains the imagination to look back to the 1970s when banks—big or small—were not allowed to open deposit-gathering offices across state lines. At the time, there was a lingering national concern about bank size that reflected memories of the banking excesses of the 1920s that had led to the Great Depression. In the 1970s, these excesses were still viewed as having been caused primarily by distant New York City bankers, and years after the Great Depression had ended, banking outside of New York City was still a Main Street business and Wall Street seemed far away.

What happened? How did banking move from the relatively benign days of the early 1970s to the turbulence that began in 2007 and by late 2008 was threatening to take down banks and economies worldwide? Most of the blame was laid at the feet, rightly or wrongly, of the country's big commercial and investment banks, with no distinguishing between the two, or Wall Street as they, collectively and derogatively, were referred to no matter where they were domiciled.

It may be that the economic collapse and banking crisis that began in 2007, and was only starting to dissipate by 2012 will eventually be viewed as just another step in the rising dominance of a handful of banks—a process that began in a banking crisis in the 1970s, but that was not the near-term perspective. There is no forgetting how close events of 2008 had come to taking down much of the world's economy and how, without massive government assistance, it could have been a lot worse.

Even with government help, three of the five largest investment banks— Merrill Lynch, Lehman and Bear Stearns; the country's fourth largest commercial bank, Wachovia; the biggest thrift, Washington Mutual; the largest originator and servicer of commercial loans, Countrywide; and the government-sponsored enterprises that held or guaranteed most of the nation's residential mortgages, Fannie Mae and Freddie Mac, either failed, were rescued by acquisition or were nationalized. Citigroup, the country's largest bank in 2007, and AIG, one of the largest insurance companies, were quasi-nationalized and in all likelihood would have failed if this had not occurred. It was also possible that the two remaining large investment banks, Goldman Sachs and Morgan Stanley, although healthy, could have been victims of fatal customer "runs" without government intervention.

As dramatic as these events were and how large their economic impact was, this was not the nation's first major banking crisis, and in terms of bank failures, not even close to being the worst. From 2009 through 2012, there were 441 bank and thrift failures. From 1985 through 1992, there had been more than 3,000 such failures, or an average of almost 400 per year—and 710 failed in 1990 alone. The size and importance of many of those that failed or were rescued just short of failure, though, were much more significant this time around.

The concern about banks being too big to fail in the aftermath of events in 2008 was a prime political concern, but it was not a new concern, just one that was getting a lot more attention than in the past. Concerns about bank size and banks being "too big to fail" surfaced in the 1980s, but the dramatic events in 2008 and 2009 moved beyond the worries of a few and created a national anti-bank furor that threatened a return to post-Great Depression bank regulations. Some of the concern may have been misplaced, but there was no denying that America's financial services companies, collectively, created serious problems that spread an economic malaise across most of the industrialized world.

The "too big to fail" concern primarily reflected the immense size of four banks, but, perhaps, it should have been focused more on the increased disparity in the size between these four and all others. Not only had their share of bank assets risen from 14 percent in 1990 to about 50 percent in 2012, but the fourth largest, Wells Fargo, was more than four times the size of number five, U.S. Bancorp. This placed a lot of banking "clout" and a lot of risk in very few hands.

What gave these events of 2008 and 2009 such a large impact on bank and financial services consolidation was that only three financial services companies—Bank of America, JPMorgan and Wells Fargo—had the size and balance sheet strength to absorb the largest of the failed or failing financial institutions. Thus, as was invariably the case in previous banking crises as well, the biggest banks were the ones capable of taking over the large troubled financial institutions, and this time they were larger than ever, even before events started downhill in 2007. Therefore, when these big banks became even bigger in 2008 and 2009, they had become "much too big to fail."

Bank of America and JPMorgan were the primary recipients of a federally assisted redistribution of bank assets in 2008 and surpassed Citigroup in asset size. Even before this crisis-induced expansion, Bank of America had taken LaSalle Bank out of the 2007 ABN AMRO dismantling in Europe. LaSalle was Chicago's second largest bank and a major factor in Detroit. In early 2008, Bank of America would buy a failing Countrywide, the largest originator and servicer of residential mortgages. This was followed by the purchase of a deeply troubled Merrill Lynch, one of the nation's largest investment banks—and one with a large international franchise. JPMorgan came to the regulators' aid with the federally-assisted purchases of Bear Stearns and Washington Mutual.

When all was said and done, by 2012, Bank of America accounted for 12 percent of bank assets and more than 13 percent of domestic deposits—and this was only a start.[1] It was already one of the three largest issuers of credit cards, and with the purchase of Merrill Lynch, became one of the world's largest managers of assets and one of the two biggest securities brokerages. JPMorgan had an even larger share of bank assets at almost 15 percent and had increased its share of domestic deposits to almost 11 percent. There was little doubt that if Bank of America and JPMorgan were not previously too big to fail, they certainly were now.

The much-increased disparity in the relative size of American banks after 2008 was statistically impacted even more by the purchase of a troubled Wachovia by Wells Fargo. This was the fifth largest commercial bank buying number four and creating another bank with more than $1 trillion assets—*and* widening the gap between the largest banks and all others. In 2010, Wells Fargo had assets of about $1.3 trillion, which was not only more than four times the size of the fifth largest bank, but it was also nearly as big as all of the banks ranked fifth through tenth combined.

The leading American banks maintained their status relative to other privately-held banks worldwide. Measured by similar assets in 2012, Bank of America, JPMorgan and Citigroup were closely grouped with HSBC as the largest privately-owned banks in the world—ahead of BNP Paribas, Mitsubishi UJF, Crédit Agricole and Deutsche Bank—with Wells Fargo just a step behind them.

Goldman Sachs and Morgan Stanley, investment banks that are frequently grouped with the above as "big banks" and certainly under the "Wall Street" label, are also world banking powers, but much smaller than the large commercial banks. In 2012, they had assets and normalized earnings potential equal to only about half those of JPMorgan, Bank of America, Citigroup and Wells Fargo.

Since that week in early September 2008, banking had been shaken to its roots and irrevocably changed, but this was the culmination of 40 years of dramatic change—much of which was the result of earlier economic crises. In the 1970s, it would have been hard to imagine that a large New York bank, let alone NCNB, the North Carolina predecessor of Bank of America with assets in 1970 of less than $2 billion, could have assets of $2 trillion in 2012. Such numbers were totally beyond imagination as interstate banking was not yet a reality. At that time, someone working in Washington, D.C. could not use a downtown bank and have an office convenient to his or her suburban home, or even one of their automated teller machines, or ATMs, as they are commonly called. This was the case in New York, Philadelphia, Chicago and St. Louis or any city close to a state line. Banking then was truly a local business, and interstate banking was always at least "a couple of years away." It was not only nonexistent, but also not something that interested consumers or politicians with the country in the midst of a recession.

How banking could move from the local nature of the business in the 1970s would have been hard to imagine at the time. Speculation then was not about a bank with $2 trillion in assets or a bank that was too big to fail, but rather about whether a New York City bank might be able to put a branch in Connecticut or New Jersey.

Banking did get from where it was then to where it is today, but it is now a very different business. The more than 13,000 banks of 1970 had been reduced to less than 6,000, and populous states such as New Jersey, North Carolina, Washington and Maryland have fewer than 80 banks domiciled within their borders.

In addition, by 2012, three of the large banks—Bank of America, JPMorgan and Wells Fargo—were dominant in every corner of the nation and no longer just big city or regional institutions. JPMorgan and Bank of America had the largest deposit shares in the Northeast; Wells Fargo and Bank of America were first and second in the South; and the same duo were the leaders in the Far West. Only in the Midwest was there a semblance of local control, and even there, Wells Fargo and JPMorgan had the largest deposit shares.

As for the local leaders in the 1970s, they are mostly memories today. This was as true nationwide as it was for five large states listed below.

- In Florida and Virginia, the 15 largest banks of the 1970s are long gone.

- In Pennsylvania, only PNC remains out of the 30 largest banks in the state 35 years ago.

- Two of the most storied bank names in California—Bank of America and Wells Fargo—live on, but only because their acquirers (out of Charlotte and Minneapolis) chose to keep their names. All other big banks in the state from the 1970s are gone.

- In Illinois, which resisted interstate banking, branching and any attempt to join the modern banking world, the results were the same. Because of its prohibition on branching, the state's only large banks in the 1970s were in Chicago, and all that is left of those is Northern Trust, a trust and asset management specialist.

Among the missing are some of the most familiar bank names of the past. Chase Manhattan, Bankers Trust, Morgan Guaranty, Manufacturers Hanover, Security Pacific, First Chicago, Continental, Wachovia, Bank of Boston, Barnett, Mellon, National City and Riggs are only a few of the once revered bank names that had become historical footnotes.

The massive, forced mergers of 2008 that made four banks so much larger than all others were not isolated events, but rather a culmination of almost 40 years of consolidation driven by economic crises, government pursuit of minimizing losses in disposing of troubled banks and aggressive bankers. In all banking crises since 1980, the usual outcome was to make the big banks even bigger.

Banking in the United States, of course, did not begin in 1970 or 1980 or end in 2014 and is a story far bigger than the four largest banks. To understand just how it got from the 1970s to where it is today, it is necessary to understand what happened earlier, and why consolidation went on "hold" from the 1930s to the 1970s. Since the first domestic banks were started in the late 18th century, this is a long time, but it is not a complicated story. It can be told in a single chapter as a prelude to the chapter-by-chapter account of the industry's continuing struggles with economic crises and consolidation culminating in, but certainly not ending with, the dark days of 2008 and 2009.

CHAPTER

THE EARLY YEARS

U nderstanding the early years of American banking is simplified by the fact that for at least the first hundred years, size and expansion into new states was not an issue. The lack of modern transportation and communications meant that all banks were local, whether it was mandated or not and, as late as 1870, there were less than 2,000 banks in the country.

By 1870, regulations had arrived and banks were already dealing with a dual regulatory system in which some banks were regulated by a federal agency, the Office of the Comptroller of the Currency ("OCC"), and others by state banking agencies. This meant different rules for different banks, but at the time, federal rules were far more important since federally-chartered banks outnumbered those in the state system by a five-to-one ratio.

Between 1870 and 1910, the number of banks in the country rose rapidly, and the balance between federal- and state-chartered banks was greatly altered. In 1870, there were 1,963 banks.[1] Forty years later, there were almost 25,000 banks, and the vast majority of these, more than 17,000, were state-chartered. With the improvements in communications and growth of a more industrialized society, there was an obvious need for increased coordination among banks.

An early response to this need was the Federal Reserve Act of 1913 that created the Federal Reserve System and its Board of Governors ("Federal Reserve"). This was to be an important step in time, but its initial impact on the regulation of banks was limited as it required only national banks to become members.

The establishment of the Federal Reserve did nothing to slow the growth of the banking system. There was an addition of about 6,000 banks between 1910 and 1921, when the total number of banks reached 31,076. This would be the historic peak for the number of banks and about five times as many as there were in 2013.[2]

With so many banks operating under different types of supervision, the need for some degree of unification of bank supervision was increasingly necessary. A major step in this direction was the McFadden Act of 1927 ("McFadden Act").

This Act had many provisions, but its most important impact on the future of banking was limiting the expansion of the federally-regulated, or national, banks, to the same as what was allowed for state banks. This meant that if state banks could not go beyond city, county or state boundaries, then the national banks in the same state could not do so either. This ended almost all interstate banking until the 1980s.

An even more important event in determining the future banking structure was the stock market crash of 1929 and ensuing Great Depression. The number of banks, which had been declining steadily since 1921, fell by over 12,000 between year-ends 1928 and 1933.[3] To make matters worse, most of the decline came from failed institutions as more than 9,000 banks failed in the four years after 1929.[4]

Banking problems caused by the poor economic conditions during this period led to two pieces of legislation in 1933 that, along with the McFadden Act, were major reasons why bank expansion was put on hold for such a long period of time. These were the Federal Deposit Insurance Act and Glass-Steagall Act ("Glass-Steagall").

The Federal Deposit Insurance Act created the Federal Deposit Insurance Corporation ("FDIC") that would provide insurance coverage for bank depositors. The benefits of federally-insured deposits were so obvious that almost all banks became FDIC members. Thus, although most banks remained state-chartered, they also now had a *de facto* federal regulator that had a strong interest in the safety and soundness of the institutions whose deposits it was insuring.

Glass-Steagall was a response to a belief held by many at the time that the destabilization of the banking system was at least partly the result of the conflict of interest caused by big banks being both major sellers of corporate securities and lenders to the same corporations. It was intended to separate lending from the power to issue most types of securities, and it was the primary reason banks thereafter could do little more than gather deposits, make loans and invest surplus funds in securities until Glass-Steagall was, in effect, repealed by the Gramm-Leach-Bliley Act of 1999 ("Gramm-Leach-Bliley").

Consolidation by Subtraction

Since there was a dramatic drop in the number of banks during the 1920s and 1930s, we could also argue that this was the beginning of domestic bank consolidation. The early 1920s were the high point in numbers of banks, and at that time, not only were there more than 30,000 banks with about 1,300 branches, but the ten biggest banks held less than 10 percent of all deposits. In 1940, there were less than half that number of banks, 13,442 at year-end, and the ten largest held a little over 26 percent of deposits. Even with the opening of more than 1,000 branches during these years, the number of banking offices, both main offices and branches, declined by more than 14,000 in twenty years.

Banks, Branches and Deposit Share of Ten Largest Banks, 1920 to 1970

	Banks	Branches	Offices No.	Offices Change	Deposit Share of Ten Largest*
1970	13,511	21,839	35,350	11,668	18.8%
1960	13,126	10,556	23,682	5,404**	19.9
1950	13,446	4,832	18,278	1,347	18.9
1940	13,442	3,489	16,931	(10,252)	26.4
1930	23,679	3,522	27,201	(4,371)	16.4
1920	30,291	1,281	31,572	-	9.7

*A year close to 1930, 1950 and 1960
**4,013 occurred since Dec. 31, 1954
Source: FDIC: Historical Statistics on Banking and Federal Regulation of Banking 1981, Golembe Associates, Inc., Washington, D.C

Much of this twenty-year decline in number of banks took place in the first five years of the Great Depression. Between year-ends 1928 and 1933, the number of banks fell by about 10,500, a decline of 44 percent. There was an increase of about 1,000 banks in 1934 as failed banks were reconstituted. Thereafter, there were modest annual declines until almost the end of World War II.

The big increase in large bank deposit share after the Great Depression was surprising. It might have been expected that bad times of that magnitude and a national distrust of banking, in general, would reduce the number of banks, but not dramatically increase the deposit shares of the banks that had supposedly caused the problems.

This sharp drop in bank numbers, though, was not a consolidation trend like what would occur after 1990, but rather a passive deposit share growth by a few large banks that flowed primarily from the disappearance of so many small banks across the country. The result could be described as a "last man standing" outcome, but it was an early reminder that in down times, large banks usually benefit at the expense of smaller banks. This would be played out over and over again in banking in later years.

That this early consolidation was the by-product of an economic depression, and not the beginning of a long-term industry trend, became evident over the next twenty years. The number of banks in the country fell by about 300 between 1940 and 1960, but there was no further gain in the share of deposits held by the ten largest banks. In fact, their share dropped from a little more than 26 percent in 1940 to less than 20 percent by 1950.

A.P. GIANNINI

The reduced bank consolidation in the 1940s and 1950s was in spite of the efforts of Amadeo Peter Giannini, more commonly known as A.P. Giannini, the founder of the original Bank of America in California. In 1904, he opened Bank of America's predecessor, Bank of Italy, in San Francisco and then took full advantage of California removing its restrictions on statewide branching in 1909. He built a pre-1930s retail banking franchise that remained unmatched until the late 1950s. By 1918, Bank of Italy had 24 branches in 18 California communities. Eight years later, the number of branches had risen to 300, and Bank of Italy's assets were $750 million—a big number for the time.[5]

The growth of Giannini's banking empire was aided by California's rapid growth, but like the builders of large branch networks in the 1960s and 1970s, he did not want to be confined by state lines. When he bought Bank of America of New York in 1928, he formed a holding company, Transamerica Corporation, to hold the shares of Bank of America of New York, Bank of Italy and his other California banks that had not been consolidated into Bank of Italy. After 1928, Transamerica began buying banks in other western states, and in 1930, the name of Bank of Italy was changed to Bank of America.

Giannini did not get a "pass" from the regulators after the Great Depression when anti-bank feelings were running high. In 1940, Transamerica, which also had a large insurance business, was forced to spin-off Bank of America. After being divested in 1940, Bank of America continued to grow. By 1945, it was the nation's largest bank, and as the 1950s began, it had assets of $6.3 billion and 525 banking offices, far more offices than any other bank. Its closest competitor was Security

First, another California bank that had about 130 branches. Through most of the 1950s, 1960s and 1970s, it was the country's biggest bank, and it remained near the top until bought by NationsBank in 1998. Even then, its name lived on as the acquirer chose to call itself Bank of America rather than NationsBank.

It was not until 1958 that Transamerica was forced to divest its remaining 23 banks in eleven western states into another holding company, First America, which eventually became First Interstate—a bank that would be acquired by Wells Fargo in 1996. As a result, major parts of two of today's four biggest banks, Wells Fargo and Bank of America, can be traced back to the early efforts of Giannini. There, however, would be no other Gianninis in banking until the 1960s.

1940S AND 1950S

As economic conditions improved after the 1930s, the animosity toward large banks that had curtailed the expansion of the original Bank of America began to fade and was replaced by a gradual renewal of trust in the banking system. This was reflected in the growth of local banks, not so much in number of banks, but in the number of banking offices and amount of deposits they held. From the 1940s through the 1970s, the major change in banking was the growth of banks with extensive branch networks, some of which would become the large regional banks that led the industry consolidation that had its beginnings in the 1970s.

Thus, the story of banking from the Great Depression until the 1970s was one of minimal turmoil and little consolidation, at least on a national level, but it was an industry that was changing. The change, though, was primarily building local branch networks that, in some cases, turned single-office community banks into large statewide branch networks. By the 1970s, these banking networks were ready to move well beyond local markets and traditional products.

This emphasis on expansion by branching saw the number of bank branches grow from about 3,500 in 1940 to more than 10,000 in 1960, and in this twenty-year period, the deposits, other than those held by the ten largest banks, almost quadrupled from $47 billion to almost $185 billion. The deposits of the ten largest banks grew rapidly as well, but not as fast as those of smaller banks. The big bank deposits only a little more than doubled during this period.[6]

As long as banks were in a single state, and usually in a single market, the urge to get larger was constrained by the size of the state and/or market. Banks in places like New York, Chicago and Boston could think on a large scale and even consider lending beyond their home areas. For most banks, though, their customer potential was generally defined by how far a customer was willing to drive, be driven or, in many cases, walk.

It was not only regulatory constraints that made large branch networks a relatively recent phenomenon, as most of the 1940s and 1950s increase in bank size took place in the 1950s when shopping patterns underwent major changes. In the 1940s, there was a net gain of only about 1,300 branches nationally. In the 1950s, the increase was more than 5,000, and most of that occurred in the latter half of the decade.

The primary reason branching became an important element of bank growth in the 1950s and the primary *modus operandi* of so many banks in the 1960s was a demographic shift, particularly relative to changing shopping patterns. The growth of suburbs at the expense of the central cities; the coming of suburban shopping centers; and a greater use of cars for shopping activities, created a retail revolution that went far beyond banking.

Until the 1950s, retail banking was almost entirely a Main Street event, and a common urban experience growing up in the 1940s was the weekly trip downtown on a bus or trolley with one of the stops being at the bank. By the 1950s, the same trip to the bank was likely combined with a car ride to a suburban grocery store.

With the spread of retail activity from downtown to the suburbs, it was only natural that bankers would want to follow their customers. If they did not, they would lose them to banks that opened in or near the suburban shopping centers. Since in most states, California and North Carolina being major exceptions, there were laws keeping banks from putting branches near these shopping centers, bank regulators were pressured by the more aggressive banks to remove these restrictions. Doing so though, was further complicated by lingering memories of the Great Depression and the problems it brought to banking along with the natural reaction of some, if not most, small banks to resist any move toward geographic expansion. This resistance was frequently supported by a majority of a population that seldom likes change.

The outcome of efforts to remove branching restrictions varied from state to state with major ramifications on how banking developed and responded to consolidation within those states. The efforts typically met with the most success on the two coasts, where change was not viewed quite as negatively. It was partly because of the early elimination of in-state branching restrictions in North Carolina that one of the world's biggest banks is now based there and because of the prohibition of branching well into the 1980s in Illinois that no large retail bank calls Chicago home.

With interstate banking eliminated for all but a few banks that were in multiple states before the Great Depression, it was not surprising that only a few banks had interstate banking operations. California-based Western Bancorporation was by far the largest of these "grandfathered" banks operating in eleven western states. Other such banks that had branches beyond their home state were two Minneapolis-based bank holding companies, Northwest Bancorp and First Bank System, and this helped both adjust to the changing banking environment of the latter part of the twentieth century. Northwest is the predecessor of today's Wells Fargo, and First Bank System lives on as U.S. Bancorp. Even these multi-state banks, though, had to abide by the branching laws of the states in which they operated in during the 1940s and 1950s.

In the 1950s, these state branching laws came in four basic variations:

- *Unrestricted statewide branching* that only applied to North Carolina, California and a few other states, most of which were quite small;

- *Unrestricted countywide branching* that was common along the East Coast, and most of the larger coastal states had at least this much branching freedom;

- *County or statewide branching* with home office protection that allowed banks to branch within their own community and in any other community in the county or state that did not have its own bank. This was New England's approach, and it did not leave much room for branching beyond the home city, but if the city was as big as Boston, or even Hartford, it allowed a bank to become much larger than other banks in the state;

- *Unit banking* prohibited branching entirely, and it was the reality in almost every state in the country's mid-section in 1950. In the 1970s, and even later, Colorado, Illinois, Missouri, Texas and less populated Midwest states still had unit banking, but by then, many permitted holding company ownership of multiple banks within a state.

As the 1950s progressed, there was a continual movement toward relaxed branching restrictions, but despite the obvious market needs for more flexibility, the pace of change was slow. Maryland, Washington and a few others had joined California and North Carolina in having almost unfettered statewide branching, but they were the exceptions.

Legislative relaxation of branching restrictions would take many intermediate forms that eventually paved the way for more branching flexibility. Pennsylvania went from allowing branching countywide to permitting it in contiguous counties, which, in effect, meant branching was allowed throughout the Philadelphia area west of the Delaware River and in metropolitan Pittsburgh. New Jersey and New York, in gradual moves toward statewide banking, first set up regions within which banks could buy other banks and open branches. These regions were scheduled to be phased out in favor of statewide branching in a relatively short period.

Because of market needs and relaxed in-state branching rules, a number of large branch networks had been developed by 1960. The largest were in California, where there had been no statewide branching constraints for years, and in New York City, which was large enough to support many branches without banks going beyond single or contiguous counties.

The growth of retail bank branch networks outside of New York and California, though, did little to change the dominance of New York and California banks when banks were measured by asset size. In 1960, eight of the country's fifteen largest banks were in New York—Chase Manhattan, First National City, Chemical, Morgan Guaranty, Manufacturers Trust, Bankers Trust, Hanover Bank and Irving Trust, and four were in California—Bank of America, Security First, Western Bancorporation and Wells Fargo. The only interlopers were two large single office banks in Chicago—First National Bank of Chicago and Continental, and Pittsburgh-based Mellon.

There were large banks at that time in other big cities as well, but only four of them—Philadelphia, Detroit, Boston and Cleveland—were represented in the top twenty. These banks were First Pennsylvania in Philadelphia, National Bank of Detroit, First National Bank of Boston and Cleveland Trust.

THE THRIFT FACTOR

Banking—from a deposit gathering and mortgage lending perspective—was, and is, more than just commercial banks. Thrifts, both savings and loans ("S&Ls") and savings banks, were relatively small factors outside of the Northeast until the 1950s, but the pent-up demand for housing after the war and the movement of people from the cities to the suburbs created a much-increased demand for home mortgages. This was the *raison d'etre* for S&Ls and the primary lending orientation of savings banks.

With the post-war housing boom, S&Ls joined the branching boom and lifted their share of deposits nationally from a little over 8 percent to almost 19 percent during the 1950s. This reduced the commercial bank deposit share from about 81 percent to less than 70 percent. It also meant that while the deposit share held by the ten largest banks may have stabilized in the 1950s relative to other banks after a sharp decline in the 1940s, it continued to slide relative to all depository institutions.

Deposit Share by Type of Institution, 1950 to 1970

	Percent of Deposits			
	Commercial Banks	S&Ls	Savings Banks	Credit Unions
1970	68%	21%	9%	2%
1960	69	19	11	1
1950	81	8	11	-*

*Share was .5%.
Source: United States League of Savings Institutions, '77 Savings and Loan Fact Book.

The S&L growth was a counter-consolidation movement. S&Ls had a federally-guaranteed interest rate advantage on savings accounts of .25 percent over banks that were not allowed to pay more than 3 percent interest on these accounts. S&Ls could pay as high as 3.25 percent on savings accounts—and the expectation was that S&Ls, and savings banks, albeit to a lesser extent for the latter, would grow in perpetuity with the housing industry. In so doing, they would increase deposits at the expense of banks.

In the 1960s and early 1970s, the rapid thrift growth became a major concern for state and national bank associations. They responded by urging members to write their congressional representatives about what they considered the unfair rate advantages of the thrifts, much as they were later urged to do regarding credit union membership rules and their tax-free status.

Unfortunately, for thrifts, perpetual growth and the continued diminishing of commercial bank dominance was not to be. Erratic interest rate movements in the 1970s and the early 1980s and a near total reliance on long-term fixed-rate home mortgages for revenues combined to not only reverse the thrift growth pattern, but resulted in a massive shift of deposits and loans to banks as a result of thrift acquisitions and failures.

Credit unions were relatively inconsequential during the 1940s and 1950s, but were showing strong growth. In 1950, they held less than 1 percent of the nation's deposits. They approximately tripled their share in the 1950s, but that was still well below 2 percent of all deposits.

1960s' BRANCHING EXPLOSION

It was in the 1960s when branching really came into its own. There were more than 11,000 bank branches added in these years raising the number of branches nationwide to over 21,000. This was more than twice what had existed a decade earlier. With a net gain of 385 banks, the total increase in banking offices was about 11,700.

The immediate effect of these new branches on concentration was muted nationally by historic prohibitions against banks crossing state lines and the persistence of unit banking in most of the Midwest and Southwest. None of the 11,000 plus new branches was in Illinois, and the few in Texas were drive-up facilities within several hundred yards of a bank's main office. Thus, any consolidation in the 1960s was limited to individual states and generally focused on the two coasts.

More branches, though, meant larger banks even if the branches were limited to one state. The largest single state banks and those few that had the benefit of "grandfathered" interstate branch networks were in as good, if not better, position to take advantage of restored interstate banking than the money center banks in New York and Chicago that were focused primarily on lending to large companies and governments. Fifty years ago, it would have been hard to believe that decisions made in Charlotte or Minneapolis would have a greater impact on the future structure of American banking than those made in Chicago and, perhaps, almost as much as decisions made in New York, but that is what happened.

In the 1960s, Charlotte's NCNB and First Union were among the few banks that aggressively took advantage of the growing importance of bank branches and favorable state rules to move beyond their hometowns and begin their march toward state and then national prominence. NCNB increased its assets from $526 million in 1960 to $1.5 billion in 1970, and its number of banking offices rose from 12 to 162. First Union was slightly smaller with assets of $1.1 billion in 1970, but this was up from $204 million in 1960. Its 180 offices were more than NCNB had and a big increase from just twenty offices ten years earlier. As far and as fast as NCNB and First Union had risen by 1970, they were still the second and third largest banks in North Carolina. Wachovia with $1.8 billion in assets and 185 branches was not only the biggest bank in North Carolina, but also the largest in the Southeast and one of the most respected banks in the country.

The long-term successes of NCNB and First Union were likely helped by their cross-town rivalry, and this may have played a role in Minneapolis as well. That city's two large bank holding companies, First Bank System and Northwest Bancorp, did not have the benefit of the unfettered statewide branching of North Carolina, but having been formed in the late 1920s as "protectors" of their region's troubled banks, they early on had subsidiary banks in multiple states. Thus, when the prohibition on interstate banking became nearly ironclad after 1933, they were already operating in multiple states and became experts in running multi-bank operations. This was an expertise they used effectively.

NCNB, First Union, First Bank System and Northwest may have had the most lasting success of the regional banks that grew to prominence in the 1950s and 1960s, but they were not the only major players in the statewide consolidation process occurring at the time. Among the banks that operated more than 100 banking offices in 1970 were Marine Midland in New York, which would become the core of HSBC's American banking network until most of those branches were sold in 2010; BancOhio that was later acquired by National City of Cleveland; Virginia National that would change its name to Sovran; and Maryland National.

Even when county or contiguous county branching limitations or the small size of a state kept a bank from reaching 100 branches, the 1960s saw dramatic growth by some of the other future leaders in the consolidation process. Besides the above-mentioned banks, prominent among the trailblazers were Pittsburgh National that was initially dwarfed by neighboring Mellon Bank, but under the shortened name of PNC, eventually surpassed Mellon in size; First Pennsylvania, a Philadelphia "shooting star" of the 1970s; a bank in little Rhode Island, whose Industrial National name did little to suggest its dynamic future as Fleet; and two Albany banks, State National and National Commerce, that would show what cross-town competition could do. The latter duo, like Industrial National, opted for more marketable names by becoming Norstar and KeyCorp, respectively, in the 1980s.

The growth of regional branch networks in the 1960s had not yet altered the national banking leadership picture. The biggest banks looked nearly the same as they had a decade earlier with New York and California banks in most of the top spots. Bank of America was still the nation's largest bank with assets over $29 billion. Other banks with assets over $20 billion were Chase Manhattan and First National City. Six other New York banks—Manufacturers Hanover, Morgan Guaranty, Chemical, Bankers Trust, Marine Midland and Charter; and four from California—Security Pacific, Wells Fargo, Western Bancorporation and Crocker-Citizens—ranked among the fifteen largest. As was the case ten years earlier, two Chicago banks—Continental and First National Bank of Chicago—were also in the top fifteen.

The nation's largest banks may have remained the same, but the recognition of the benefits of branching had spread well beyond California and New York. Nevertheless, in 1970, Bank of America with its 955 branches and Western Bancorporation with 654, still had far more branches than any other banks, and five of the six banks with more than 200 branches were in California. In New York, four of its six biggest banks had more than 100 retail banking offices, and a fifth had more than ninety. Only Morgan Guaranty had stayed out of the branching game. Most of the big New York City banks' branches were in the metropolitan area, but these banks had used holding companies to buy banking presences in the largest upstate cities—Buffalo, Rochester, Syracuse and Albany.

New York also was in the forefront of the development of retail banking operations in which the branches were more important than the main office with its money center-type activities. Buffalo-based Marine Midland had banking offices throughout Upstate New York, as well as in the New York City area, and it was the only bank outside of California with more than 200 branches. The ill-fated Franklin National Bank—it would fail in 1972—went a step further by making it into the top twenty with 96 offices *and* did so without having a big city base. Its headquarters was in Mineola, a small Long Island town.

The largest thrifts were much smaller than the big banks in 1970, but the influence of the liberal branching laws of California was readily apparent with them as well. The five savings and loans with assets above $1 billion were all in California.

It was not, though, the California or New York banks or thrifts that would lead the consolidation charge. This leadership came from banks in cities such as Charlotte, Minneapolis, Columbus, Albany and Providence.

Product Impact

The branching boom of the 1950s and 1960s and the growth of large branch networks were key contributors to future structural change in the industry, but changes in product mix also played a role in consolidation and in making banking more vulnerable to economic crises. This was evident in deposits where the introduction of certificates of deposits, or CDs, in 1962 by First National City, as Citibank was called then, was revolutionary in its impact. The credit card was a slightly earlier Bank of America creation—a card that started as BankAmericard and eventually carried the Visa name. It had a major impact on consumer lending, but that impact was slower to develop than that of CDs on deposits and affected only one part of a bank's loan portfolio.

Up through the 1960s, bank deposits were almost all checking and passbook savings accounts, and deposits funded about 90 percent of bank assets. By the early 1960s, however, checking accounts had fallen from more than 75 percent of deposits twenty years earlier to about two-thirds, but this was still a long way from the 9 percent in 2006, or even the 17 percent of 2012 when extremely low interest rates had investors leaving money in the most flexible deposit type for later movement. In 1961, deposits that could not be classified as checking or savings accounts were only about 7 percent of total deposits.

CDs, with their reflection of market rates, at least upon issuance, represented a major industry transformation. It allowed banks to circumvent the guaranteed rate advantage held by thrifts on savings deposits and provided considerable flexibility in the cost of funds when interest rates fluctuated. By 1970, almost 28 percent of all bank deposits were CDs.

Bank Deposit Mix by Type, 1940 to 1970

	Deposits				Deposits/ Assets
	Demand	Savings	CDs	Total	
1970	51%	21%	28%	100%	85%
1961	67	26	7	100	89
1950	76	24	n/a	100	92
1940	75	21	4	100	90

Source: FDIC: Historical Statistics on Banking.

The introduction of CDs and a modest reduction in the dependence on deposits were initially a competitive advantage for banks vis-a-vis thrifts and a tool to manage earnings in times of interest rate change, but they also proved to be consolidation stimulants. The most aggressive banks, the ones building statewide branch networks, were quick to introduce CDs and promote them vigorously. The money center banks went even further by finding alternatives to deposits to fund their lending and investments. Most local banks, on the other hand, felt that CDs and the use of borrowed funds in general—instead of more traditional deposits—introduced risks reminiscent of the 1930s and, as a result, were slow to respond. Not surprisingly, many of them experienced a substantial loss of customers.

The bank credit card introduced in 1959 by Bank of America did not have the immediate impact of CDs. At the end of 1969, bank credit card loans were less than

$4 billion, or about 6 percent of all personal loans. The credit card was expanding rapidly, but it struggled with state regulatory constraints, specifically ceilings on the rates that customers could be charged.

The big lending change in the 1950s and 1960s was that banks actually *began* to make loans. As late as the early 1950s, loans represented only about 30 percent of all bank assets and a little over 35 percent of deposits.

Lending increased steadily in the 1950s and 1960s, reaching 52 percent of assets by 1970, but businesses remained the primary borrowers. Commercial banks lived up to their name as 35 percent to 40 percent of bank loans were commercial loans not secured by real estate. Personal loans, usually around 20 percent of the total, were a distant second in emphasis.

Bank Loan Mix by Type, 1942 to 1970

Loans					
Year	1-4 Family	Other Real Estate	Commercial*	Consumer	Loans/ Assets
1970	14%	10%	38%	22%	52%
1960	17	7	36	22	47
1950	20	6	42	19	31
1942	17	7	41	12	26

*Not secured by real estate.
Source: FDIC: Historical Statistics on Banking.

In the 1960s, real estate lending, both residential and commercial, was a secondary source of revenues for commercial banks, partly because it was the domain of the thrifts. By 1970, real estate loans accounted for about 24 percent of all bank loans, which was unchanged since 1940, but far less than the 50 percent plus they accounted for in recent years.

Banking as it was in the 1960s would continue into the early 1970s, but this was the calm before a storm. Interstate banking, much bigger banks and expanded banking powers were inevitable in a world where state or national borders were no longer sacred and technology would soon make geographic constraints irrelevant, but for banking, moving into the modern world did not come gently. By 1973, the country was headed into an economic downturn that would last until 1982. For banking, this was clearly a tumultuous dividing point between two eras followed by an environment that created giant banks and the opportunity for high profits and rapid growth for all banks, but with greatly enhanced risk.

UNCHARTED WATERS

Just saying "the seventies" brings thoughts of bad times and the worst economic conditions since the Great Depression and with good reason, but this was not true of the entire decade. The stock market did not begin its downward slide until January 1973; the country did not fall into recession until November of that year; and it was the summer of 1974 before the stock market fell significantly below the 1973 peak. What began in 1973, though, was more than eight years of economic stagnation running all the way to 1982, but the three years from 1970 to 1972 were for banks a period of experimentation and strong efforts to put aside regulatory and geographic constraints.

As banks entered the 1970s, their interest in both product and geographic expansion was rapidly increasing as the extensive branching in the 1960s had taken many of them fully across their own states, and the more aggressive of these banks were finding the state line barriers to be an irritating growth constraint. By the late 1960s the geographic barriers were forcing them to look in new directions for growth and profits, and there were only two real alternatives—expand into other countries or circumvent interstate banking restraints by using the holding company concept to acquire bank-related businesses, often referred to as nonbanks, in other states. The international route was only feasible for the big New York and California banks, but using holding companies to acquire nonbank businesses beyond state lines was possible for banks of all sizes.

Thus, interstate acquisitions via bank holding companies was a phenomenon that began in the late 1960s and became so widely utilized that it raised regulatory concerns and led to new legislation, the Bank Holding Company Act Amendments of 1970. This Act did not put an end to bank holding companies making interstate nonbank acquisitions, but it established the rules under which they could be made. The rules, though, were not that definitive and a decade long battle ensued between the Federal Reserve and certain banks over just what was allowable. The only hard and fast rule was that any acquired institution could not offer checking accounts, which were most bank deposits at the time, in operations across state lines. Thus, it was clearly "uncharted waters" for the industry.

This 1970 legislation left enough leeway for Citibank and other large banks to shift their expansion emphasis away from branching and toward interstate nonbank acquisitions, and they were joined in doing so by many mid-sized banks. This nontraditional expansion beyond state lines coincided with, and was reinforced by, an expanded use of credit cards. The credit card did not require the proximity of a branch and was another way to move across state lines, albeit more true for the 1980s than 1970s.

This use of the holding company for interstate expansion and new sources of income had a strong real estate orientation. As a result, entering new businesses, some of which were far from the home market, may have potentially been a good source of additional revenues and profits, but in times of economic turbulence, they brought with them considerable risk. As it turned out, risk and the 1970s were closely intertwined when in 1973 the economy slipped into an economic downturn that continued over the next eight years.

That increased risk played out when twelve banks with deposits in excess of $100 million either failed or required regulatory assistance to avert failure in the six years from 1973 through 1978. Prior to 1970, the FDIC, which began operating in 1934, had never dealt with a troubled bank with deposits in excess of $100 million. The combined deposits of these troubled banks in the 1970s were over $6 billion and included one of the nation's twenty largest financial institutions.[1]

BANK HOLDING COMPANY ACT AMENDMENTS OF 1970

In 1970, bankers did not know the problems that lay ahead as they made expansion plans that were often based on circumventing interstate banking restrictions through holding company acquisitions. The Bank Holding Company Act of 1956 was enacted to extend the McFadden Act interstate constraints to holding companies, particularly relative to branching across state lines, but this prohibition was interpreted as not applying to one-bank holding companies—holding companies formed to include only a single bank.

The support for this circumvention was not universal even within the industry as most small banks saw any move by large banks across state lines as a threat. By the weight of their numbers, small banks usually controlled the state banking associations, and, as a result, had considerable political clout. Regulators and many legislators, whatever their views, pro or con, also saw the circumvention of the interstate banking prohibitions by holding companies as something that should be within their purview if it was to happen.

The result was the passage of new legislation that would bring the one-bank holding company under the regulatory authority of the Federal Reserve. This legislation, the Bank Holding Company Act Amendments of 1970, was signed into law on the last day of that year, and these amendments extended the coverage of that earlier legislation to one-bank holding companies.

The amendments specifically gave the Federal Reserve the power to permit one-bank and multi-bank holding companies to engage in nonbanking activities that were "determined to be so closely related to banking … as to be a proper incident thereto" and that "can reasonably be expected to produce benefits to the public, such as greater convenience, increased competition, or gains in efficiency, that outweigh possible adverse effects, such as undue concentration of resources, decreased or unfair competition, conflicts of interest or unsound banking practices."[2] This was a lot of legal terminology, but it clearly made the Federal Reserve the deciding factor as to what could and could not be done relative to banks crossing state lines using holding companies.

Since there had been many nonbank acquisitions by bank holding companies preceding this legislation, rules relative to these acquisitions were also included. If the acquisition was made after June 30, 1968, and most were made after that date, then it was retroactively subject to the provisions of the amendments and needed Federal Reserve approval. If approval was not forthcoming, then the acquisition had to be divested prior to the end of 1980. Acquisitions before June 30, 1968, as long as they were not dormant at any time subsequent to that date, were allowable and, in effect, "grandfathered."

This legislation directed the Federal Reserve to determine which financial services that banks were not presently allowed to perform would be allowable as separate subsidiaries of a holding company. These services, though, had to be "closely related" to financial services that were already permissible to banks.

The major impact of the legislation was not so much that it added to what banks could do, but rather that it reflected a legislative and regulatory acceptance of an expansion of banking services, including offering them beyond state lines, as long as they conformed to the guidelines of the new legislation as interpreted by the Federal Reserve. The McFadden Act, however, still applied, so even if approved, the new subsidiary could not offer checking accounts at a facility in another state.

Banks had always made loans across state lines, particularly when the state lines divided metropolitan areas with the New York, Chicago, Philadelphia and Washington, D.C. metropolitan areas being prime examples, but prior to the late 1960s, there had been little effort to lend across state lines through subsidiaries and offices located in other states. Many banks had loan production offices in other states, but this format did not work well except for big banks lending to large borrowers.

The introduction of regulatory oversight with the Amendments to the Bank Holding Company Act in 1970 did not lessen the interest of banks in using holding companies to go beyond their traditional business. As would be expected, though, the oversight set up some legal battles as banks tried to push beyond the limits of these guidelines.

In the early 1970s, most banks were prepared to live within the guidelines as they provided ample room for expansion. Banks of all sizes wanted to have holding company subsidiaries that specialized in such traditional bank lending areas as mortgage, personal and commercial loans, and be able to operate them with offices across state lines. Many of them jumped at the opportunity to get into financial advisory and consulting services, data processing for other financial services companies and other businesses that were deemed "closely related" to banking by the Federal Reserve.

This eventually led to banks advising, and assuming responsibility for, Real Estate Investment Trusts ("REITs"), which made construction loans primarily for commercial properties. REITs, like other real estate-related activities, were susceptible to economic swings, particularly since the rationale behind them was that real estate values always go up. Since this was not true in the 1970s any more than it was in recent years, REITs became a problem for banks during the difficult economic conditions that prevailed as the 1970s progressed.

The move by banks to diversify into new businesses and take traditional bank lending activities across state lines affected the bank consolidation process in two ways. It was a trend that was far more likely to be used by large banks, and, when successful, it added to their overall size and marketing power. Perhaps, more importantly, as it took banks across state lines, it made them even more eager to cross those borders with traditional full-service banking offices that accepted all types of deposits.

The most aggressive large bank in pursuing these new businesses was initially Citibank, and its holding company Citicorp, and its efforts raised concern among banks outside of New York. Its purchase of Nationwide Financial with its personal loan offices in multiple states raised the specter of Citibank having an overwhelming advantage when interstate banking was allowed. This proved to be a false alarm, but in the 1970s, that was not the thinking.

Two of the most aggressive mid-sized banks using holding companies for interstate expansion in the early 1970s were NCNB and First Pennsylvania, but they were far from alone. First Union, Wachovia, Citizens & Southern, Virginia National, Maryland National, Pittsburgh National, National Bank of Detroit, Security Pacific, Northwest, Wells Fargo and many others made significant moves in this direction.

The plans for many of these banks were to have "one of each" of the most important, allowable financial services businesses operating as a subsidiary of their holding company with the freedom to go beyond their home state. The most common starting points were mortgage banking, consumer finance and leasing, as they were businesses with large volume potential. For some, interstate expansion also extended to REITs, and all-to-frequently with disappointing results.

CITICORP–THE INITIATOR[3]

If there is any consistency in the evolution of America's leading banks, it was Citicorp, or as it was later called, Citigroup. Its name has changed over time, but always with City, or Citi, as part of it. As far back as rankings go, it was either the nation's first, second or third largest bank. Citicorp was one of only three large New York City banks, Chemical and Bank of New York, being the others, that would adapt to the major industry changes following the 1970s and maintain a national leadership position. In both the real estate-driven recession of the late 1980s and early 1990s and the most recent financial debacle, though, it came close to failing.

Citicorp's roots go back to 1812 when it opened its doors as the City Bank of New York, and it rose to national prominence as National City Bank, a name it adopted in 1865. By 1894, National City was the largest bank in the country, and in the early 1900s, it was thought of as the "Rockefeller bank" when National City and J.P. Morgan and Company were the main bankers for the cartels of the "robber baron" era. Its leader, James Stillman, was among the most powerful bankers of his time. By 1929, it was the largest bank in the world. After the Great Depression,

National City kept a low profile, but in many of those years, it was still the nation's biggest bank.

In 1955, in one of many mergers among the large New York banks in that decade, National City bought another of the big names of New York banking, First National Bank of New York. By 1955, First National was much smaller than National City, but it was a high prestige operation. This was the impetus for another name change, as National City became First National City.

The "low profile" disappeared in 1967 when the first of its CEOs to play a major role in the consolidation process, Walter Wriston, assumed leadership. In 1974, the holding company name was changed to Citicorp, and two years later the bank name was changed to Citibank.

During Wriston's 17 years at the helm, Citibank and Citicorp were at the leading edge of virtually everything that was going on in banking, and when he retired, Citibank was not only the country's biggest bank, but was also the only American bank with a significant international presence. He led the way in the 1970s in using holding companies to move across state lines, albeit without full-service banking.

Along the way, though, there were some difficult times with foreign loans, and Wriston was forever at odds with the regulators, but he was one of the three bankers that did the most to change the face of American banking during the 40 years after 1970—Hugh McColl and Sandy Weill being the others. This was despite being a CEO for only three of the years after 1980 when the consolidation process moved into high gear.

In the 1970s, Citicorp acquired one of the nation's largest mortgage bankers, Advance Mortgage in the Detroit area, with the intent of it being the focal point of a national mortgage business. "Largest" in mortgage banking in 1970, however, was not quite what it sounded like since mortgage banking was a fragmented business. It was unlikely the biggest mortgage banking firm had as much as 2 percent of the business nationally, but Advance Mortgage was a start toward a national mortgage banking operation for an owner with "deep pockets," a description that certainly fit Citicorp.

Citicorp was also in negotiations to acquire an insurance company. This would have gone well beyond what was later defined as "closely related" to banking, but this transaction was never finalized.[4]

In 1973, Citicorp took a big step with its nonbank geographic expansion when it acquired Acceptance Finance Corporation in St. Louis that operated under the Nationwide Financial Services name. It was a small personal loan company with assets of a little over $30 million, but it had 85 loan offices in 14 states. The Federal Reserve approved this acquisition in 1973, and in the next two years, Nationwide Financial opened 87 additional offices in seven new states. By the end of 1975, it had assets of $304 million and 172 offices in 21 states.

In Phillip Zweig's biography of Citicorp chairman, Walter Wriston, he quoted Wriston as saying that the strategy behind this purchase was "blanketing the country with store-front 'person-to-person' offices that would sell all sorts of consumer financial services and establish *de facto* interstate banking." Wriston went on to say that this "moves us closer toward the long-range goal of becoming a truly national financial service corporation."[5] In effect, by simply changing the signs above the doors, the finance offices could be converted overnight to branches of Citibank.

The intent was to use Nationwide Financial to acquire consumer finance companies throughout the country and become truly national. This did not happen as concerns about the size and geographic reach of Citicorp were widespread, and the relationship between Citicorp and the Federal Reserve had become adversarial.

The latter became apparent when, after approving the Citicorp purchase of Nationwide Financial in 1973, the Federal Reserve then rejected its request for approval of its 1970 acquisition of Advance Mortgage. The rationale was the anticompetitive effect of the nation's largest commercial bank buying the second largest mortgage banking company. Citicorp did not divest Advance Mortgage until 1980, but it did not make any other nonbank acquisitions for a long time after the disapproval by the Federal Reserve in 1973.

Citicorp had many other options and concerns, and its temporarily losing interest in domestic geographic expansion was based on more than just Federal Reserve opposition. In the 1970s, it was expanding around the world, and, as a result, it experienced one of the major big bank problems of this era—loans to developing countries. This would become a bigger problem in the 1980s, but it was already a concern in the 1970s, and one further complicated by the slippage in the domestic economy in 1973.

Even though it suspended its interstate nonbank expansion after 1973, to other banks, Citicorp still presented an ominous picture of the future. The fears of smaller banks may have been unduly exaggerated, but if interstate banking had become a reality in the 1970s, Citicorp might have been able to use Nationwide Financial to instantaneously provide a national banking branch network. In the end, the thrift crisis would provide Citicorp with an even better way of moving across state lines in 1982.

NCNB–THE COUNTRY RIVAL[6]

The origins of NCNB, which was the predecessor bank of today's Bank of America, were as far from the Wall Street connotation that is commonly associated with the large banks as possible. Its roots go back to American Trust, a small bank in Charlotte, North Carolina that was founded in 1908 and in the 1950s had assets of less than $200 million. At that time, American Trust brought in a CEO, Addison Reese, who had big ideas on a statewide basis. Thereafter, the climb to the top never ceased.

Under Reese, American Trust took its first big step in 1957 when it bought another Charlotte bank, Commercial National. This purchase made American Trust Charlotte's biggest bank and began a history of name changes. The names of the two banks were combined, and the surviving entity was called American Commercial.

In the early 1960s, Reese's next step was to merge American Commercial with a Greensboro bank, Security National. This created a $500 million asset bank, which may not sound like much today, but at the time, this put it among the largest banks in the South. In North Carolina, only Wachovia was bigger. This merger was the impetus for changing the name to North Carolina National Bank. When its holding company was formed in 1968, it used the initials, NCNB, which became synonymous with aggressive bank growth. The initials were soon used for the bank as well as for the holding company.

In the 1970s, Tom Storrs replaced Reese as CEO and not only continued to expand the banking franchise in North Carolina, but he also made NCNB one of the most successful holding companies by going across state lines with nonbank businesses. At that time, though, it was far from being a Citicorp. It was not even the biggest bank in North Carolina, but it, along with Citicorp, was one of two banks at the forefront of change of American banking.

Soon after forming its holding company in 1968, NCNB established an insurance subsidiary and two real estate subsidiaries, the most prominent of which was NCNB Mortgage. It followed this with the purchase of a finance company, which had 65 consumer finance offices throughout the Carolinas and Georgia. It also bought a factoring company that year, which was an accounts receivable financing business servicing the textile industry. In 1972 and 1973, NCNB stepped up its real estate commitment by acquiring mortgage banking firms in South Carolina and Georgia. Also during this period, it joined forces with banks in Georgia and Virginia to establish an Atlanta-based REIT.

By 1974, with its expansion in both traditional and nontraditional banking, NCNB had become the 26th largest bank holding company in the country with $3.6 billion in assets. This included nonbank businesses that had 250 offices in six states and two foreign countries.

By the end of 1974, though, NCNB was no longer celebrating this seeming success as its rapid expansion in the real estate business ran into high interest rates, a recession and declining values. Unfortunately, for NCNB, the greatest negative impact of the down economy of the mid-1970s was in the Southeast, particularly Atlanta and the Carolinas, which were the focus of its activities. Losses from the REIT and mortgage banking and increasing non-performing assets, temporarily removed the glitter surrounding NCNB; caused some anxious moments; curtailed its nonbank expansion; and reduced its commercial real estate exposure.

The strength of traditional banking business carried the day for NCNB, and despite reduced earnings in the mid-1970s, it did not spend much time looking back. It had become a regional rather than a state bank, and a minor acquisition in 1974 of a non-depository trust company in Florida would be one of the most important steps in opening the door to interstate banking. The notoriety and high stock price that NCNB enjoyed in the early 1970s was a major plus in its bank acquisition activities during that period. Most importantly though, its management team had seen the world outside of North Carolina, and for them, there was no going back to the quiet life of small town bankers.

FIRST PENNSYLVANIA–THE NOT SO SUCCESSFUL FOLLOWER

While in retrospect, NCNB may be the most remembered of the regional banks for its aggressive use of nonbank acquisitions in the early 1970s to further its cause, at the start of that decade, much of the attention was focused on First Pennsylvania. When the decade began, it was the 20th largest bank in the country compared to NCNB's 46th place ranking; it was in the Northeast and, thus, nearer the centers of the national media; and its president, John Bunting, seemed to revel in publicity.

In 1968, Bunting became president of this staid old Philadelphia bank that opened in 1812 and immediately began the nonbank expansion. In that year, First Pennsylvania joined the parade of banks forming one-bank holding companies, and a year later, it made its first out-of-state purchase, Associated Mortgage Company, which was renamed PENNAMCO. Over the next three years, it added four finance company acquisitions to the mix in such diverse places as Colorado, Louisiana, Maryland and Puerto Rico.

In 1970, it entered the REIT business with the formation of Associated Advisers, which was the advisor to the newly-formed First Pennsylvania Mortgage Trust. For First Pennsylvania, this was a major misstep as the REIT stumbled badly when interest rates rose sharply in 1974. In fiscal 1975, which included half of 1974, the REIT lost about $19 million. This was half of First Pennsylvania's total earnings in its last good year. First Pennsylvania never recovered from this disaster. Bunting was forced to resign in 1979; the bank had fallen from 20th in size in 1970 to 40th in 1980; and by that time, might have failed without federal assistance.

In March 1980, the regulators had to decide between closing it, arranging a federally-assisted sale to another bank or giving it the finances to continue. The favored choice was a sale, but under the laws of the time, this would have required the buyer to be a Pennsylvania bank. Mellon was the only bank in the state large enough to absorb First Pennsylvania, and the FDIC was reluctant to put so much of one state's banking resources in a single institution. Ruling out a sale, the FDIC was left to choose between closing the bank and giving it the funding to proceed, and it chose the latter.[7]

As part of this bailout, First Pennsylvania reduced its exposure to non-traditional bank activities. It packaged PENNAMCO, which by then was the country's third largest mortgage bank—a place ahead of Citicorp's Advance Mortgage—with its consumer finance subsidiary, and then sold the entire package to Manufacturers Hanover for $106.5 million.

First Pennsylvania's performance improved when it got back to the basics, and it was able to pay back the FDIC, but it was no longer Philadelphia's pre-eminent bank. It had experienced a near failure, and its assets had fallen from $9 billion in 1980 to less than $7 billion in 1989. It had passed the mantle of local leadership to Philadelphia National Bank, and in 1989, it was acquired by that bank for less than $1 billion. This was about 40 percent of what Georgia's Citizens & Southern sold for in the same year, which was 80 percent of First Pennsylvania's size in 1980.

MARYLAND NATIONAL—A CLOSE-UP VIEW

During the1970s, I was in charge of planning at Maryland National, another bank in the NCNB mold that had followed a similar growth pattern and gave me a good insight on the banking events of that decade. In 1960, its primary subsidiary was a Baltimore bank with 28 branches in the immediate Baltimore area, and its name, Fidelity-Baltimore National, reflected its single city orientation. In the 1960s, it made a series of acquisitions across the state and, to reflect its broader coverage, changed the name to Maryland National and formed a holding company.

By 1970, Maryland National was the largest bank in Maryland with assets of $1.2 billion, and in order to continue growing rapidly, it had to either intensify its coverage in the Washington, D.C., suburbs or go beyond traditional banking. It decided to do both, and its experience with nonbank expansion in the 1970s was typical of most mid-sized banks.

At Maryland National, as well as at NCNB, First Pennsylvania and the other banks choosing this path, there was little concern about buying businesses better than banking. If there had been such a concern, there would have been very few nonbank acquisitions since there were few businesses better than banking.

A representative of another Baltimore financial company, Commercial Credit, expressed his amazement to me at the interest of banks in getting into its business, which was commercial finance. Commercial Credit's management would have traded their operation for a banking franchise without a moment's thought. This is what happened 14 years later when Sandy Weill became CEO of the then failing Commercial Credit and used it to trade up until he was where he wanted to be—buying and then running Citicorp.

Nonbank expansion, though, was the 1970's "new, new thing" and logic was not to get in the way. Maryland National, like the others, wanted "one of each," and off it went. While its primary interests may have been reaching the same level of branch coverage in the Maryland suburbs of Washington as it had in the Baltimore area and taking a unique credit card opportunity as far as it could, nonbank expansion was also high on the "to do" list. Real estate *seemed* to be the area that met the criteria of "good as or better than" what Maryland National already had. Real estate, unfortunately, also included REITs.

In 1973, Maryland National began its nonbank expansion by establishing two de novo nonbank subsidiaries—a mortgage bank, and a leasing operation; acquiring a consumer finance company with 18 offices in eastern and central Pennsylvania; and entering into a joint venture with a Florida-based mortgage bank to establish Commonwealth National Advisers. The latter was to be the advisor to Commonwealth National Realty Trust, a REIT. A year later, Maryland National opened two more nonbank subsidiaries. The first was an asset-based lender. The second was an investment advisory firm.

It was also in 1974 when interest rates hit their first historic high; real estate loan risk escalated dramatically; and Maryland National learned the hazards of operating a real estate business far from home. The joint venture partner advising

Commonwealth National Realty Trust was a Florida-based mortgage banking firm that did the on-site managing. Maryland National's primary role was warehousing the loans. On top of all the other real estate problems at the time, one Friday in early 1974, the partner borrowed funds from the REIT for needs within its own mortgage banking business. By Monday, interest rates had moved so quickly that it could not repay the borrowed funds, and the mortgage bank and the REIT were in deep trouble from which neither would recover.

As the solvent partner, Maryland National had to accept total responsibility, which included a $5 million loss. Fortunately, as Maryland's leading commercial lender, the rising interest rates were a plus for its traditional business, and the loss did not stand in the way of a strong year-to-year earnings gain.

Maryland National did not maintain the unbroken earnings gain throughout the turbulent 1970s as the real estate problems spread beyond the REIT in 1976 and 1977, but by the end of the decade, nonbank activities contributed 11 percent of earnings. In 1980, there was no more REIT in the mix, but Maryland National still had nine nonbank subsidiaries.

Its 11 percent of earnings from nonbank activity did not accomplish much for Maryland National's overall growth. From 1960 to 1972, when its emphasis was on branching and buying banks, it rose in the national asset rankings from 76th to 59th. In the rest of the 1970s, when nonbank expansion was a high priority, it moved up only three places.

For all of its nonbank activities in the 1970s, Maryland National's major success would be its credit card, which was a new activity, and had it been included with the nonbank activities, then Maryland National's nonbank record changes dramatically. It was the largest credit card bank in the state in the 1970s, and by the late 1980s, it had become the nation's fifth largest bank-owned credit card operating as a Delaware-based subsidiary under the name of MBNA. It was spun-off in 1990 to "pay some bills" when Maryland National was sinking under the weight of excessive nonperforming assets, and the rest is history. Before being acquired by Bank of America in 2005, MBNA had joined Citigroup and JPMorgan in consolidating the credit card business into a big three that left all others far behind.

Nonbank Expansion Impact

The time and effort commercial banks spent on expanding through holding company nonbank subsidiaries, both organically-developed and acquired, could be dismissed as "much ado about nothing" if measured only by what it added to commercial bank earnings, assets and market capital. These ventures were not nearly as profitable as anticipated, and First Pennsylvania was not the only bank to be badly hurt by such expansion.

The impact, though, was significant even if it could not be readily defined in dollar and cents. It took banks across state lines; separated those that were adept at operating away from home from those that were not; set the stage for the sweeping inter-industry consolidation that began in the 1990s; and had a major impact on the consolidation process.

During the 1970s, however, banks had successfully used their market clout in at least one nonbank industry, mortgage banking. As the decade ended, seven of the ten largest mortgage banking firms were owned by banks. The leader, Lomas & Nettleton, was still independent, but the mortgage banks ranked second through sixth in 1979 were subsidiaries of Philadelphia National, First Pennsylvania, Citicorp, Norwest and Wells Fargo. Pittsburgh National and First Union also had subsidiaries among the top ten.[8]

Despite seven of the top ten mortgage banks being part of bank holding companies, this did not create a large national market share, as this was a very fragmented industry. The largest mortgage bank, Lomas & Nettleton, serviced a little less than $7 billion in mortgage loans and, even factoring in inflation, this was a long way from the $1 trillion plus being serviced by the 2012 leader, Wells Fargo.

First Pennsylvania sold its consumer finance—and its number three spot in mortgage banking in 1980—to a larger bank, Manufacturers Hanover. For a brief time in the 1980s, Manufacturers Hanover, which would be acquired by Chemical in 1991 and eventually became part of JPMorgan, was the largest mortgage banker in the country.

Specialty consumer finance was the second most pursued target for nonbank and out-of-state expansion, but this business was dominated, much more than it is today, by the captive finance companies of the auto and appliance companies and large independents. The latter included Household Finance, Beneficial Finance, Associates and C.I.T., which remained independent until the 1990s, or in the case of Household Finance, even later. The only banks with holding company subsidiaries ranked among the fifty largest non-captive finance companies in 1979 were First Pennsylvania, NCNB, Security Pacific and Chemical.

These nonbank acquisitions did not directly have much impact on bank consolidation, partly because adverse economic conditions, beginning in 1973 and running through 1982, put most of their plans on hold, but it was the proverbial "camel's nose under the tent." Some very aggressive banks had gotten a taste of going beyond their home markets, and they liked the expanded opportunities.

ECONOMIC TURMOIL AND BANKING

It is easy today to forget just how bad the 1970s were, in general, and for banking in particular, and it is impossible to understand what happened in banking starting in 1973 and running through the early 1980s without understanding the economic conditions of the time. For those who lived through these years, the most vivid memories are Watergate and long lines at the gas pumps, but not far behind were inflation-driven record high interest rates and a dismal, extended stock market performance. For commercial banks, the outflow of deposits resulting from high rates paid by others that they initially could not match on deposits because of rate caps was high on the list of bad memories. As for thrifts, they do not even want to think back on those days.

The rising rate of inflation in the 1970s began even before 1973 and was generally attributed to successive administrations incurring the expense of fighting a costly war in Vietnam while also paying for the new social programs of the 1960s, particularly Medicare. With tax rates already at extraordinarily high levels from World War II, there was no easy way to add revenues, and in those days, the Federal Reserve was not into "quantitative easing." This resulted in inflationary conditions that were intensified by oil shortages caused by Mideast turmoil that drove gas prices to rise to previously unimagined heights.

The average rate of inflation during the 1970s was 7.1 percent, and in 1974, and again in 1979, the annual rate reached 11 percent. Inflation spilled over into the 1980s when the annual rate reached 13.5 percent in 1982 before starting down. This was in stark contrast to the 1960s when the average inflation rate was 2.4 percent and did not exceed 2 percent until 1966.[1]

As is the normal course of events when inflation goes out of control, interest rates follow a similar upward pattern, and this forced the Federal Reserve to raise its discount rate—the rate it charges banks to borrow funds—to 8 percent in 1974, 12 percent in 1979 and 14 percent in 1981. Commercial banks were partially able to offset this with loan rates charged to commercial customers that normally did not have fixed rate loans. The corresponding banking industry prime rates—the rate banks charge their best commercial loan customers—were 10.25 percent, 15.25 percent and 20.50 percent in those years.

With a mandated "cap" on rates paid on savings accounts and no interest paid on demand deposits in checking accounts—the primary source of funding for commercial banks in those days—these high loan rates had a positive effect on margins, but they came with a price. Asset quality deteriorated as many borrowers were unable to pay the increased rates, and deposits flowed out of banks seeking higher rates paid by non-regulated institutions, particularly money market funds.

The latter problem was addressed in 1980 for banks and thrifts with the passing of the Depository Institutions Deregulation and Monetary Control Act, which removed the cap on rates paid on deposits. For commercial banks, this was a net plus, but for thrifts that were generally limited in their lending to long-term home mortgages that were almost invariably fixed rates, it was a disaster. In order to fund their loans they had to pay competitive rates for deposits, and by 1981, most thrifts were losing money as the cost of their funding was much higher than the yields on their loans.

As would be expected in such unsettled times, stocks in general, and bank stocks in particular, did not perform well. The Dow Jones Industrial average hit a peak of 1,052 on January 11, 1973 and then, over a two-year period, it fell to 578, a 45 percent decline. The Index would not surpass that January 1973 high until late in 1982, or stay above that level until 1984. Put that in terms of the latest downturn where stocks peaked in October 2007, this would be the equivalent of not reaching the 2007 high until the middle of 2016—and not staying above that level until 2018.

The downswing began early in Nixon's second term; lasted through the entire presidencies of Ford and Carter; and through the first two years of Reagan's first term. It included a triple dip recession with the first starting in November 1973 and lasting 16 months. This touched the Nixon and Ford administrations. The second came in 1980 and only lasted six months, but it was enough to put an end to the struggles of the Carter presidency. The last of these recessions began in July 1981 with Reagan in office and was another 16-month event.

These last two recessions were at least partially triggered by the drastic steps taken by a newly appointed Chairman of the Federal Reserve, Paul Volcker, in 1979. He raised the interest rates to extremely high levels to force the country into such a severe recession that interest rates would return to more normal 3 percent to 4 percent levels and create a better growth environment. These actions were bitterly criticized by the incoming Reagan administration, but the results set the stage for tax cuts and military spending that put the economy in high gear for at least a few years.

Two oil-driven interest rate spikes were key economic events in this lengthy economic downturn, and each had a different impact on the banking industry. The first interest rate spike followed the Mideast's Yom Kippur War in 1973. The war threatened the oil supply, came with little warning and had a much more negative impact on bank earnings, asset quality and stock prices than the second increase, despite its much lower peak. It put an end to most holding company expansion and had banks talking about getting back to the basics.

The second oil price induced rise in interest rates began in 1977 and was made worse in 1979 by the Iranian Revolution. While the ascent was much more dramatic, the banks were better situated the second time around. Asset quality was not a problem and margins improved as loan yields rose faster than deposit costs. By then, bank stock prices had been down so long that low multiples of earnings or capital, much as the high rates of inflation, had gained a disappointing acceptance. For thrifts, though, it was the beginning of the end.

The problems spanning the 1970s and early 1980s are often referred to as similar to what occurred in 2007 through at least 2012, but there were a couple of very big differences. The recent downturn was not accompanied by high inflation rates and the banks in the 1970s economic turmoil were not blamed for the problems.

NON-ECONOMIC CONCERNS

Beyond the economic concerns of the 1970s, bankers felt that not only had expansion been put on "hold," but it also started to appear that when, and if, expansion moved forward it might not be dominated by the banks. Persistent fears among bankers were that ATMs would make branches obsolete and that interest would be permitted to be paid on checking accounts with a devastating impact on bank earnings.

There were reasons to consider banks under siege in the 1970s and that regulations were making banks compete with "one arm tied behind their backs" in the pursuit of deposits. This mentality was a major reason banks spent so much time trying to cross state lines even if the businesses they were entering were not as profitable as banking. In addition to the geographic expansion, banks wanted the right to compete with a wider range of financial services, but at that time, the expansion of powers and coverage seemed to be a one-way street favoring thrifts and brokerage firms. The emergence of the ATM raised the specter of various types of retailers taking a backdoor route into banking at the expense of bank branches.

Thrift competition, particularly from S&Ls, was a big concern to banks in the 1970s. Historically, thrifts had not competed directly with banks for deposits since they could not issue checking accounts, which was the primary bank deposit prior to 1970. Thrifts were also required by regulation to limit their lending to home mortgages. The *quid pro quo* for thrifts was that they could pay a rate of 3.25 percent on savings accounts, while banks were not allowed to pay more than 3 percent. This was not an issue in a low interest rate environment when market-determined rates were below 3 percent, but it became a big disadvantage for banks as they became more dependent on non-checking deposits as interest rates were rising in the 1970s.

The difficult economic environment from 1973 on added to these myriad of concerns, particularly the extreme volatility of interest rates. It was the interest rate increase more than anything else that made the 1970s so threatening to banks. Ironically, it also was these high interest rates at the end of the decade that resulted in legislation in the 1980s that shifted the balance of power back in favor of banks. These changes, including bankrupting the thrift industry, were unimaginable a few years earlier.

While banks were better prepared for the second interest rate spike in 1977 and the dramatic increase in rates, this was not the case for thrifts, whose loans were primarily long-term fixed-rate home mortgages. With cheap deposits replaced by rising rates on savings accounts and high cost CDs, many of the thrifts were dealing with funding costs that were higher than their yields— frequently much higher. This was the origin of the S&L crisis that dominated banking headlines in the 1980s.

Even commercial banks had to face a nearly forgotten reality in the 1970s— that even large banks could fail. An inevitable result of difficult economies are that they bring with them higher risk and, if the risk is combined with banks reaching beyond their traditional skills and experience, the results can be disastrous. This was apparent in the REIT problems of the mid-1970s that hurt the earnings of several banks and was a major reason why the FDIC had to step in and rescue First Pennsylvania.

First Pennsylvania was the last of four large banks to either fail or require government assistance during this period, and its rescue sent far fewer shock waves through the industry than the near failure of Detroit's Bank of Commonwealth in 1971, the failures of United States National Bank in San Diego in 1973 and Long Island's Franklin National in 1974. By the time First Pennsylvania was rescued by the FDIC, the S&L crisis had surfaced and the rapid rise in interest rates had many banks taking unusually large securities losses. Thus, its rescue was consistent with the times. The early 1970s, however, followed almost 40 years of banking stability and a large, or even a medium-size, bank failing was a totally unanticipated event—and one of these failures, Bank of Commonwealth, occurred even before the hard times arrived in 1973.

BANK OF COMMONWEALTH[2]

Bank of Commonwealth's problems did not occur overnight. It had been acquired in a highly-leveraged proxy fight in the mid-1960s, but because Michigan was neither branching "friendly" nor permitted bank acquisitions statewide, its new owners used a system referred to as "chain banking" to expand. In other words, to cross county lines, they would buy control of several banks, but had to operate the banks independently. The problem was not the "chain banking" concept, but a dangerous mixture of leveraging that flowed from this ownership mode and operating plans oriented toward playing the rate game with securities rather than making loans.

Interest rates increased slowly in the late 1960s and early 1970s, but Bank of Commonwealth's management bet on interest rates declining. This structuring of the securities portfolio to make money only if interest rates declined became an acute problem in 1969 as interest rates and the unrealized losses on the securities portfolio not only continued to rise, but the gamble was increased to try to solve the problem. Highly leveraged and without the capital to absorb unrealized securities losses, Bank of Commonwealth was at the mercy of its creditors and regulators.

A few years later, a solution to Bank of Commonwealth's problems might have been a quick, assisted sale to a larger bank. With $1.2 billion assets and being in a market in which the three largest banks held 77 percent of the deposits a sale to any them had serious anti-trust implications at the time. A sale also was further complicated by it being in a state whose laws barred the entry of banks from another in-state market, and the concept of an "emergency" lifting of legal barriers had not yet surfaced. Thus, a sale was not an option due to legal constraints. The regulators were not ready to let the fourth biggest bank in Michigan become the first large bank failure since the 1930s, and in 1972, they took a third approach—a bailout. This was short-hand for the government providing the money needed to allow a company to continue to operate.

Bank of Commonwealth was the reintroduction of regulators to large troubled banks since it was almost 40 years since the last large bank failure. As a result, it was not surprising that the outcome of the Bank of Commonwealth bailout was disappointing.

Irvine H. Sprague, one of the FDIC Commissioners involved, in his book, *Bailout*, said, "One vital ingredient was missing—confidence. That was the biggest mistake we made—thinking we could cure the bank simply by putting enough money into it. The fact was that government money seemed to have made the bank suspect in the eyes of the depositors and private investors. Rather than restoring confidence among the public, the federal assistance seemed to have had the opposite effect."[3]

This loss in confidence not only slowed Bank of Commonwealth's growth and ability to absorb its debt, but the bank actually got smaller. When it was sold a dozen years later, its assets were $300 million less than in 1972, and assistance was needed to complete its sale to Comerica, one of the Detroit banks that a decade earlier was considered "off limits" as an acquirer because of its negative impact on concentration in the Detroit banking market.

THE OTHERS

Bank of Commonwealth was noteworthy because it was the first big bank since the Great Depression to need regulatory assistance to avert its failure, but it did not have the "shock" effect of the 1974 failure of Long Island-based Franklin National Bank. Franklin National was not only much larger—it was the country's 20th largest bank—but also next door to one of the world's financial centers and took place as the country was heading into an economic recession. In addition, in 1972, it had been bought by Michele Sindona, "an Italian financier with reputed connections to the Mafia and Vatican banking."[4] Thus, its failure raised concerns about the stability of worldwide banking in a year when interest rates, inflation and asset quality were all moving in the wrong direction.

The negative impact of Franklin National's failure was further magnified by the failure of a mid-sized German bank, Herrstatt, a few months earlier. Its failure was caused by miscalculations in trading foreign currencies and its funding included large loans from other banks. This raised the specter of a "domino effect" with international implications. Despite being on Long Island, Franklin National, through ownership and sources of business, raised the same fear on a larger scale.

New York was more amenable to a bank sale solution than Michigan, and although Franklin National was allowed to fail, most of its assets and liabilities were assumed by a consortium of European banks—Deutsche Bank, Societe Generale of Belgium, ABN AMRO and Midland Bank—through a New York-based joint venture, EAB Bank. EAB received less than the $3.7 billion assets of Franklin National prior to its failure, but it was the start of a wave of foreign entry into retail banking in America—even before interstate banking was allowed for domestic banks.

The failure of the $1.3 billion United States National Bank in San Diego in 1973 did not get the attention of Bank of Commonwealth and Franklin National. It was not the first big bank in the decade to either fail or need assistance to avoid failing and was considerably smaller than Franklin National. It was another sign, though, of an increasingly difficult banking environment.

There were no other large bank failures throughout the rest of the 1970s, but the list of banks labeled as "troubled" was growing. This would be a major ingredient in the acceleration of the consolidation process.

BANK STOCK PRICES

Beginning in 1973, banks were plagued by falling stock prices that were a long time in recovering. The reappearance of troubled banks and money center banks receiving very negative press for loans to emerging countries that were not really "emerging," and investor aversion to financial stocks when interest rates were rising and the economy was slipping was not good for bank stocks. The 45 percent drop in the Dow Jones Industrial Index in 1973 and 1974 did not exempt banks nor were bank stocks quick to recover.

Maryland National, where I was at the time, was typical of banks in stock price movement. In the early 1970s, investors liked its growth and the potential of its nonbank subsidiaries. In those "good days," its stock sold at 14 to 15 times earnings and for more than two times capital, or book as it is commonly called.

Maryland National's stock continued to show good earnings per share ("EPS") gains through 1975—earnings went from $2.02 per share in 1972 to $2.86 per share in 1975—and this seemed sufficient to maintain existing price levels, but in 1973, its stock followed the market down. In 1974, the average of its high and low for the year was only 8.5 times earnings and 121 percent of book. A year later, Maryland National's stock price was 6.8 times earnings and 114 percent of book, but by then, real estate loan problems provided some justification for a reduced value.

Maryland National Stock Price, 1970 to 1980

Year	Stock Price*	Times Earnings	Percent of Book**	EPS
1980	$16.50	3.9X	54%	$4.29
1979	16.88	4.8	61	3.49
1978	17.38	5.9	69	2.96
1977	18.00	6.8	75	2.63
1976	21.88	9.8	102	2.24
1975	19.50	6.8	114	2.86
1974	21.50	8.5	121	2.52
1973	29.50	12.6	185	2.34
1972	31.00	15.3	216	2.02
1971	28.50	14.9	219	1.91
1970	24.00	12.5	205	1.92

*Average of high and low.
**Average book value per share.
Source: Maryland National Corporation annual reports.

By the mid-1970s, investors' love affair with banks was clearly over. Maryland National's EPS rose from $2.24 in 1976 to $4.29 in 1980, a double-digit annual percentage increase, but despite this, the average of its annual high and low stock prices from 1978 through 1980 did not exceed six times earnings or 70 percent of book. In 1980, the average price was 3.9 times earnings and 54 percent of book. The net result was that by the end of the decade, its stock was selling at less than $17 per share, or about $7 per share less than in 1970, despite doubling its EPS during that period.

This type of bank stock performance was the norm in the late 1970s, and it contributed greatly to putting traditional bank consolidation "on hold" after 1973. It is not easy to acquire banks with a stock selling at 50 percent to 60 percent of book.

OPENING AGAINST THE GRAIN

Despite these difficult times, new banks were opening at rates well beyond preceding decades; mergers were still occurring, albeit not with high premiums, and usually among banks in the same market; and failures among small banks were not near what they would be ten years later despite the troubled times. Many more banks opened in the 1970s than were sold or closed. This was marginally the case in the 1960s, but this relationship was in stark contrast with other ten-year intervals since 1920.

The 2,224 new banks in the 1970s was a continuation of the 1960s' trend of banks following retail activities into the suburbs, particularly in states where they were not allowed to branch out. The flow of banking activities to the suburbs was an acute problem for existing banks in unit banking states, as they could not branch anywhere, let alone in the fast-growing suburbs. This was quite a change from the 1940s and 1950s, when the memories of the Great Depression were still fresh in people's minds and the move to the suburbs had just begun.

New Banks, Mergers and Failed Banks, 1940 to 1999

Period	New Banks	Mergers	Failed Banks
1990-99	1,315	5,047	455
1980-89	2,700	3,465	1,030
1970-79	2,224	1,316	73
1960-69	1,552	1,375	43
1950-59	763	1,416	24
1940-49	621	698	87

Source: FDIC: Historical Statistics on Banking

The 1980s would see more banks opened than in the 1970s, but because of an increased number of mergers and failures, this did not result in a net gain in the number of banks. In the 1970s, there were about 800 more banks opened than were merged out of existence or failed. Conversely, in the 1980s, there were almost 1,800 *more* bank mergers and failures than openings. Merger activity was constrained in the 1970s by loan quality concerns throughout much of the decade and the low bank stock prices that made it difficult for banks wanting to buy other banks to pay a price that would induce them to sell.

CONTINUING BRANCH GROWTH

Since these were hard times without large numbers of banks and thrifts failing, as was the case in the Great Depression, the real estate-driven recession of the early 1990s and the 2008 to 2009 debacle, it was no surprise that there was a decline in the deposit share of the large banks between 1970 and 1980. It did not mean that the big banks were losing strength, but it reflected that their primary business, corporate lending, was not growing as fast as retail banking. Also, in the 1950s and 1960s, the money center banks in New York and Chicago that lent primarily to large multi-state and multi-national corporations and governments, were reluctant participants in going from downtown to the suburbs, and there was little reason to expect that reluctance to disappear in the 1970s.

The big banks in New York and Chicago, along with three or four retail banks in what had become the most populous state, California, were still by far the largest banks in the country in 1980. Their customers were big companies and governments, and they were as ready to do business in Buenos Aires and Madrid as in Buffalo and Peoria. The big New York banks' branches were primarily in markets experiencing a population outflow, and the Chicago banks were held back by Illinois' reluctance to allow in-state branching. Thus, it was inevitable that the big New York and Chicago banks would be losing domestic deposit and retail lending share.

Banks, Branches and Large Bank Deposit Share, 1970 and 1980

Year	No. of Banks	Branches	All Offices		Ten Largest Deposit Share
			Number	Change	
1980	14,434	38,738	53,172	17,822	17.2%
1970	13,511	21,839	35,350	11,668*	18.8

*Since 1960.

Source: FDIC: Historical Statistics on Banking and Report of Condition data as of December 31, 1980.

This loss of deposit share by the big money center banks to local retail banks reflected the bank branching mania of the 1960s continuing into the 1970s, to which was added an unusual increase in the number of banks. The net increase in full-service banking offices had not doubled as it did in the previous decade, but the almost 18,000 net new banking offices in the 1970s was about 50 percent more in absolute numbers.

The greater emphasis on branching was universal except in those states that clung to unit banking laws, and leading the way was a new breed of banks that accumulated substantial bulk, but whose growth was constrained by state lines. They were not part of the industry's upper echelon in the 1970s, but they were better prepared than the money center banks to be winners when interstate banking arrived. The 1980s and 1990s would belong to NCNB, First Union, Norwest, First Bank System, Bank One, Fleet, KeyCorp, PNC, SunTrust, Sovran and a few others that would be referred to as superregionals, but that was unimaginable in 1970 and only slightly more so in 1979.

THRIFTS

The competitive impact of thrifts, and particularly S&Ls, was a major bank concern in the 1970s. Savings and loans had been around for a long time, but it was not until after World War II that they became major bank competitors in the pursuit of deposits. In the 1950s, S&Ls had spectacular growth and increased their share of deposits from a little over 7 percent to almost 19 percent. This share increase was produced primarily by single office institutions as the 6,320 S&Ls operating in 1960 had less than 2,000 branches.

S&L Branch Growth, 1960 to 1980

Year	No. of S&Ls	Branches	All Offices	
			No.	Change
1980	4,613	16,733	21,346	11,359
1970	5,669	4,318	9,987	2,056
1960	6,320	1,611	7,931	-

Source: United States League of Savings Institutions, Chicago, Illinois, '83 Savings and Loan Source Book.

The S&Ls continued to increase their overall share of deposits in the 1960s, but unlike in the previous decade, it was by only a modest two percentage points. The slowdown in the deposit share gain reflected the delay in joining banks in the proliferation of branches. In the 1960s, the number of branches more than doubled, but with a decline of more than 600 S&Ls, the total increase in offices was only a little over 2,000. Collectively, there was still less than one branch per S&L.

This conservative approach to branching by S&Ls was reversed in the 1970s. Thrift branches almost quadrupled during that decade, and even with almost 1,000 fewer S&Ls, there was a net S&L gain of more than 11,000 offices. This was an increase from less than one to almost four branches per S&L.

This branching binge and aggressive deposit pricing in the high interest rate environment rekindled the S&L's rise in deposit share. Even with about a 1,600 reduction in numbers by the end of the decade, S&Ls increased their share of depository institution assets from less than 21 percent to almost 25 percent between 1970 and 1980. More than half the increase came at the expense of banks whose collective share declined from almost 68 percent to 61 percent.

Deposit Share by Type of Institution, 1970 and 1980

Percent of Deposits				
Year	Comm. Banks	Savings & Loans	Savings Banks	Credit Unions
1980	66.1%	24.5%	6.6%	2.8%
1970	67.9	20.7	9.3	2.1

Source: United States League of Savings Institutions, '83 Savings and Loan SourceBook.

Their fellow thrifts, the mutual savings banks, which differed from S&Ls primarily by being insured by the FDIC, rather than FSLIC, did not share the S&L gain and had an even steeper asset share loss than banks. The savings banks' share of depository institution assets fell from a little over 9 percent to less than 7 percent in the 1970s. This partly reflected the slow growth of the markets they served since most savings banks were in the Northeast.

Credit unions grew rapidly with their asset share rising from 2.1 percent to 3.4 percent during the 1970s. They were still, though, minor players in the overall banking mix.

PRODUCT CHANGE

There was minimal change in the traditional banking product mix on the loan side in the 1970s, but the transformation of the deposit mix away from checking accounts was dramatic. Noninterest-bearing demand deposits, or checking accounts, fell from a little over half of bank deposits in 1970 to 36 percent in 1980. This was a long-term downward trend that would continue for years to come, but the 1970s slippage was accelerated by high interest rates that shifted funds of all types into high priced CDs. This increased the CD share from 28 percent to 47 percent of bank deposits. The bank savings account share was not down as much as demand deposits, but the impact of not being competitive in rates with S&Ls and the movement to CDs was apparent.

Bank Deposit Mix by Type, 1970 and 1980

Year	Deposits			Deposits/ Assets
	Demand	Savings	CDs	
1980	36%	17%	47%	80%
1970	51	21	28	85

[[TBL SRC]]Source: FDIC: Historical Statistics on Banking.

Along with the shift to CDs as interest rates went into double-digits, there was a movement of money to brokerage firm-run money market funds. Between 1978 and 1980, cash in money market funds grew from $10 billion to $76 billion, and would reach $150 billion in 1981 before leveling off.[5] This contributed to banks relying less on deposits for their funding, as deposits fell from 85 percent to 80 percent of assets in the 1970s. The major reason for a lesser use of deposits was large banks finding alternative, and often cheaper, sources of funding, such as commercial paper, which were short-term, unsecured promissory notes issued by bank holding companies.

It was also in the 1970s that the ATM became a standard part of the banking delivery system. The number of ATMs grew from only about 100 in 1970 to almost 14,000 in 1979, and as the decade wound down, the question was no longer whether ATMs could be cost-justified, but whether a bank could be competitive without them.[6]

STRUCTURAL STABILITY

Despite the many commercial bank concerns that existed as the 1970s came to an end, particularly relative to S&Ls, the flow of funds out of the banking system and being unable to cross state lines, their problems were far less than those of other depository institutions. The high interest rates were not only hurting S&Ls, but they were about to set them adrift in a "sea of red ink." This emerging thrift disaster provided a major impetus for interstate banking and with it a big step forward in the consolidation process. The investment banks and their money market funds would remain a competitive factor, but be more of a nuisance than a concern.

The negative impact of stock prices, as well as state line constraints, kept the large banks from enhancing their position in the industry while everyone else was much smaller and kept aggressive regional banks from gaining ground on the money center banks, even though the money center banks were losing deposit share against the all-bank universe. In fact, this deposit share loss of the big banks was a little misleading as they used funding other than deposits and looked to other countries for lending opportunities. If market share was measured by assets instead of deposits, the big banks actually gained ground in the 1970s.

This stability at the top, collectively, was seen in the national rankings of banks or bank holding companies during the 1970s. There was little change in the positions of the largest banks between 1970 and 1980. There were few signs of upward momentum for mid-sized banks except in Texas, and these were not gains for regional retail banks since Texas banks were not allowed to branch. They, in effect, had become regional money center banks serving the oil-and-gas industry.

The static structural situation is seen in the lack of change among the nation's nine largest banks. In 1970, the top nine included six banks from New York City, two from California. Ten years later, the nine largest banks were the same. Citicorp had moved ahead of BankAmerica at the very top, but only Continental had significant upward momentum, moving from ninth to sixth place. It was, though, an ill-conceived momentum that Continental would pay for in 1984 when it became the biggest corporate bailout prior to 2008. Losing ground was First Interstate that fell from fifth to ninth despite the benefit of being one of the very few banks "grandfathered" into multi-state operations and having most of its branches in fast-growing California. Chase Manhattan, Manufacturers Hanover, Chemical and Bankers Trust held the same positions in 1980 that they had in 1970, and J.P. Morgan moved up just one spot.

Further down in the rankings, where more position changes were expected because of less size disparity, the bank holding companies ranked tenth through 16th were unchanged from 1970 to 1980. These seven banks included three from California—Security Pacific, Wells Fargo and Crocker National—and four regional money center banks—First Chicago, Marine Midland, Mellon and First National Boston. There was some change within the seven, though, as Wells Fargo and Crocker National used their retail orientation in a large, rapidly-growing state to move up a couple of places.

Rounding out the 1980 top twenty were the two Minneapolis banks, Norwest and First Bank System, and the only new entrant, Dallas-based InterFirst. Norwest and First Bank System changed little in ranking from a decade earlier, but InterFirst jumped from 31st to 19th with more than a six-fold asset increase. Most banks had large asset gains because of the high inflation rates in the 1970s, but only Continental, among the very largest banks, came close to matching InterFirst's percentage increase.

To put this continuing structural stability between 1970 and 1980 in the broader context of what would happen later, of the twenty largest banks in 1980, only Citicorp, Chemical and the two Minneapolis banks are still around. This assumes Travelers acquisition of Citicorp was more of a management change than a true acquisition. The big banks with the most momentum in the 1970s, Continental and InterFirst, did not even make it through the 1980s, as they were casualties of the oil patch meltdown. They were joined on the sidelines by Crocker National, Charter and Marine Midland that were acquired in the 1980s.

The rapid growth of InterFirst in the 1970s followed by disaster was mirrored by other large Texas banks. Republic, Texas Commerce and First City were just outside the national top twenty in 1980, ranking 21st through 23rd, and Texas Commerce and First City were not even in the top fifty in 1970. They either failed or were sold in the late 1980s, when financial meltdowns seemed imminent.

Among the superregionals that would have leading roles in the 1990s consolidation process, only NCNB and PNC were even close to being among the banking leaders in 1980. NCNB had assets of about $7 billion at that time, and it had risen from 46th place in 1970 to 28th in 1980. PNC had a little over $6 billion in assets as the 1980s began and was 31st in the rankings.

Fleet, First Union and Bank One were still local banks with assets in the $3 billion to $4 billion range when the 1970s ended, and were not even among the sixty largest in the country. Bank One, though, while still a local bank, had come a long way. In 1970, it had assets of about $500 million and was nowhere to be found in the national rankings.

The 1970s also did not have the mergers that would result in immediate jumps in national, or even regional, concentration, and when a large bank was sold, the buyer was usually a foreign bank. Franklin National, a top twenty bank, failed in 1974 and was sold by the FDIC to a consortium of European banks. Union Bank in Los Angeles and National Bank of North America, which ranked 22nd and 28th, respectively, in 1970, were sold to British banks. The regulators, when faced with the failures of Bank of Commonwealth and First Pennsylvania, chose to "bail" them out with government funds rather than let buyers cross state lines or in-state buyers greatly increase their local market shares.

The biggest bank acquired by another domestic bank in the 1970s was Security National on Long Island. It had assets of about $2 billion when acquired by Chemical in 1975.

1980S: A NEW ERA

Bankers were glad to see the 1970s end, as they were hard, frustration-filled years. Overly restrictive regulations limited growth, and at the time, it appeared that banks were losing ground to competitors that were either not regulated, or at least had the benefit of more favorable regulations. While asset size increased rapidly for most, this was a bit deceptive because of the impact of an unusually high inflation rate—real growth was much less than what was reported—and asset growth did not always correlate with increased earnings. To add insult to injury, investors appeared to have written off banks as "not worth the effort" and having a good position in bank management had more prestige than wealth impact.

The arrival of 1980 did not suggest much improvement or even a meaningful change in direction. Interest rates were high and still rising, and, although high rates helped earnings at a time when noninterest-bearing checking accounts were more than one-third of bank deposits, money that would normally be put into bank deposits was going into the brokerage-managed money market funds. There was no reason to believe that investor interest in bank stocks would improve any time soon.

Even the rising thrift losses, instead of being a competitive plus for banks, were a major nuisance. A need for thrifts to pay-up for deposits to support their long-term fixed-rate loans was making deposits more costly for everyone. This was a problem that prevailed throughout the 1980s.

No matter what it looked like to bankers at the time, though, 1980 would be a year that signaled a new era in banking. Earlier, banking was evolving rapidly, particularly with ATMs and the growing importance of credit cards and CDs, but there had been little change in who was delivering banking services. Regulations limited competition between banks and other types of financial institutions, and they were still not allowed to cross state lines. Things would begin to change as legislation in 1980 was the first in a series of laws and court decisions that began the erosion of the industry's constraints, and by the mid-1980s, the erosion had turned into a landslide.

The changes beginning in1980 were prompted by a series of regional and industry crises, some of which were caused by the double-digit interest rates in 1980 and 1981. These high rates had put thrifts in a much more tenuous position than anyone could have anticipated and were the cause of a farm crisis that plagued the Plains states. High rates did not cause the oil-and-gas industry collapse that devastated banking in the oil patch states of Texas and Oklahoma, but the dramatic rise in oil prices in the 1970s had created a false long-term optimism as to the future of that industry.

The first of the many laws and court decisions responding to the problems within the banking industry was one passed in 1980 removing the cap on rates paid on savings accounts to help stem the flow of money out of banks and thrifts into unregulated investment alternatives. This law, the Depository Institutions Deregulation and Monetary Control Act, put thrifts more directly in competition with banks in the pursuit of deposits, not only by doing away with pricing constraints, but also by their being allowed to offer checking accounts. Coming when interest rates were at record heights, however, paying more for deposits contributed to the decline of an independent thrift industry with its low-yield fixed-rate home loans.

In 1982, there was additional legislation, the Garn-St. Germain Act, which further narrowed the difference between banks and thrifts. This Act and its impact are discussed in the next chapter, but what it did was create an environment that encouraged rapid thrift growth in areas in which they had little expertise—with disastrous results. This was an era of a strong belief in deregulation, and the thrifts and their regulators, unfortunately, bought into deregulation in a big way.

In addition, there were four interstate acquisitions in 1982 that would help set the stage for the acceptance of interstate banking. These acquisitions were either very small or the result of a bank or thrift failure, and, by themselves, did not amount to much, but the size and nature of the buyers—Citicorp, NCNB and BankAmerica—helped change the thinking relative to interstate banking.

A third governmental action that made the 1980s different from the 1970s was aimed directly at interstate banking. In June 1985, the Supreme Court ruled that the regional interstate compacts in the Southeast and New England were legal. Interstate banking had already become legally permissible if a state explicitly let out-of-state banks buy banks in their state, but until the early 1980s, only Maine had done this, and even in Maine, it necessitated the acquiring bank's state to have similar banking laws.

A primary interstate deterrent was the fear of domination by banks in large states, particularly New York, but, in the early 1980s, states in New England and the Southeast passed reciprocal interstate banking laws—you can buy banks in my state if our banks can buy banks in your state—with geographic constraints that excluded New York. This was challenged in the courts by Citicorp, and with the 1985 approval of these exclusionary constraints by the Supreme Court, interstate banking had cleared a major hurdle.

Another piece of legislation in the 1980s that was to play a major role in the consolidation of the once highly differentiated thrift and commercial bank businesses was the Financial Institutions Reform, Recovery and Enforcement Act of 1989, or as it is was better known, FIRREA. It was a response to the disastrous second stage of the thrift crisis and, among other things, it abolished the Federal Home Loan Bank Board ("Bank Board") and FSLIC; put all thrifts under the regulatory authority of the Treasury Department; and shifted their deposit insurance authority to the FDIC. With the same regulators and insurers as commercial banks, "turf" impediments to banks buying thrifts, and vice versa, even under non-emergency situations, would disappear.

The role that the regional economic downturns, particularly in the north central states and then the oil producing states, played in the 1980s relative to consolidation was immense, and they greatly contributed to the passage of the three major pieces of banking legislation. The 1980s are often considered to have been good years, particularly when compared to the economic turbulence of the 1970s, but being good years did not apply to the entire country or all industries. There were the aforementioned severe regional recessions in the 1980s, two of which were caused by problems in a specific industry that was a primary source of income. These regional recessions had a negative impact on banks.

The first regional economic downturn in the 1980s was a farm crisis resulting from the combination of low prices for agricultural products and high rates on farm loans dictated by the interest rate environment. The negative impact of the farm crisis on banking was limited primarily to small banks in rural areas, but it slowed the growth of the two large Minneapolis banks, Norwest and First Bank System, albeit only temporarily, as they were on their way to becoming the Wells Fargo and U.S. Bancorp of today.

A more serious regional banking problem had its genesis in the oil price increases in the 1970s, which ultimately peaked in 1981. When prices collapsed in the mid-1980s, the oil-and-gas industry as well as the economies of the states that were dependent on it, primarily Texas and Oklahoma, went from robust to "bust." The region's banking industry was ill-prepared to adapt to this changed economic climate, and one direct result was eight of the forty largest banks in the country disappeared.

At the end of the 1980s, a softening economy and excess real estate capacity became a serious banking problem in the Northeast and California. This was more of a 1990s than a 1980s problem, and by then, the radical structural change of the 1980s within the banking industry had made major strides, but this real estate-driven bank disaster resulted in more than 1,000 bank and thrift failures.

There were also some bank problems in the 1980s that came from outside the United States. In the mid-1980s, many less-developed countries in the world, particularly in Latin America, were forced to default on their loans and among the major holders of what were referred to as Less-Developed Country or LDC loans, were America's biggest banks. The losses from these loans were so severe that there was concern that a big New York City money center bank would collapse under the burden.

No money center bank failed because of the LDC loans, but they stopped the growth of what had been the country's biggest bank, BankAmerica, and it was not the only big bank that never really recovered from the losses incurred. By the mid-1980s, BankAmerica and most of the big money center banks were limited because of earnings problems in their ability to make large acquisitions, and their plight worsened when large commercial real estate losses in the Northeast and California came on the heels of their LDC problems.

The number of failing financial institutions resulting from the 1980s regional and thrift crises was so substantial that the small banks' concerns over the possible loss of local control were easily put aside by the regulators because of need. There were not always in-state buyers for the large thrifts that failed, and when Texas banking collapsed, the impact was so widespread regionally that the rescuing banks had to come from states in other parts of the country. Regulators could only ignore McFadden Act prohibitions against pre-empting state laws on out-of-state bank entry in emergency situations, but in the 1980s, there were many "emergencies."

If national and state prohibitions against out-of-state bank takeovers could be put aside to the benefit of the country's biggest banks, then it was also an easier task for regional banks that were so disposed to get state laws changed to allow them to cross state lines as well, even if it was not an "emergency" situation. This process became even easier when the Supreme Court ruled in 1985 that state legislation that allowed interstate banking could set geographic limits as to the states that could participate in buying healthy out-of-state banks.

Because of these crises and the arrival of interstate banking, by the end of the 1980s, the banking industry looked quite different from what it was in the 1970s. The money center banks were tottering, and a new breed of regional banks, the superregionals, was moving forward with great haste. Two of the four banks that now dominate banking—Bank of America and Wells Fargo—came from the ranks of the superregionals of the 1980s.

The impact of these crisis-driven changes on the banking structure in the 1980s was not immediately apparent in the upper echelons of American banking. Citicorp, BankAmerica and Chase Manhattan and most of the leading New York and Chicago money center banks started out so far ahead of everyone else in size that they could not lose their high rankings in just ten years. Except for Citicorp, though, the gap between the 1980 leaders, and the fast-growing superregionals would be greatly reduced. BankAmerica had fewer assets in 1990 than it did in 1980, and Chase Manhattan's assets grew by only 25 percent in ten years. Meanwhile, Security Pacific almost tripled its assets and moved from eleventh to fifth place nationally, and North Carolina's NCNB had a nine-fold asset increase as it rose from 28th to seventh in the national rankings.

The money center banks were losing ground in the 1980s because they were culturally not well-suited to benefit from either branch or interstate growth and were almost universally crippled by LDC loans and then commercial real estate lending at the end of the decade. BankAmerica, Chase Manhattan, Manufacturers Hanover and Continental were in dire straits or had been a few years earlier. BankAmerica had to fend off an unfriendly takeover; Manufacturers Hanover would give up the fight and sell to Chemical in 1991, a fate that awaited Chase Manhattan a few years later; and Continental was sold in 1994. BankAmerica would last only four years longer.

In the 1980s, interstate banking, concerns about future viability by many banks and almost all thrifts and high bank stock prices—something that seemed to be little more than a dream as the decade began—resulted in a merger explosion that was new to banking. Despite this, asset and deposit share of the largest banks actually declined during those ten years as the gains of NCNB, Security Pacific, First Union, Fleet and other superregionals were more than cancelled out by share losses of California's BankAmerica and the New York and Chicago money center banks. The ten largest banks held almost 31 percent of bank assets going into the 1980s, and that was down to about 25 percent at the end of the decade.

What the 1980s would do, though, was to bring a different banking culture to the forefront; create regional banks with this new culture that were large enough to undertake big interstate mergers; and set the stage for the mega-mergers and consolidation of the next fifteen years. During these years, banking consolidation would show up in the numbers in a big way.

How the shift from the largest banks, almost all having a money center culture, to most of the national leaders being superregionals with a retail culture occurred in the 1980s, and its later impact on bank consolidation that created banks too big to fail, is a story with many parts and variations. It includes a thrift crisis, troubles in Texas and Oklahoma, the impact of LDC loans on the money center banks, high stock prices and, most of all, interstate banking, all of which are discussed in the next few chapters. The proliferation of branches that built the pressures for going beyond state lines in the 1960s and 1970s did not continue at as high a rate in the 1980s, but it had become, in any event, a secondary issue with interstate banking emerging as the primary impetus for bank expansion and consolidation.

THRIFT CRISIS: EARLY STAGES

Of all the structure-changing events in the 1980s, the thrift crisis attracted the most attention, and deservedly so. It devastated an industry that was intended to be the underpinning of an American dream—home ownership for the masses. It coincidentally got the consolidation process rolling in the early 1980s and provided an impetus for interstate banking being permitted sooner than it might have been otherwise.

The thrift crisis was a story that moved beyond the business pages. Not only did it eliminate thrifts as major bank competitors in many parts of the country, with the Northeast and West Coast being the exceptions, but the financial impact on taxpayers of solving the crisis is estimated to have been more than $300 billion—a big number in the 1980s.

To understand the thrift crisis and how it impacted the overall banking structure, it helps to divide it into two parts: a) damage done to the thrift industry, as it existed before 1980 and b) the inflating of the industry after 1982 in response to misguided legislation and regulation. A major impact on bank consolidation came from the failure of so many large thrifts that had solid and locally generated deposit bases. These were S&Ls and savings banks that were increasingly competing with commercial banks, and, in many cases, gaining deposit share at the banks' expense. It was the new and/or high growth thrifts of the post-1982 era with "bought" deposits that were the focus of the media coverage and primary source of much of the more than $300 billion in government outlay coming from this thrift crisis.

The two segments of the thrift crisis are seen in the changing number of S&Ls and their assets. In 1980, there were more than 4,200 federally-insured S&Ls in the country with a combined $604 billion assets. In the next two years, these S&Ls had combined losses of about $9 billion, and the number of federally-insured S&Ls fell by about 700, or 18 percent of the total; and the collective tangible capital of the survivors was less than 1 percent of assets by the end of 1981.

Despite the industry being virtually devoid of capital, S&Ls took advantage of reduced capital standards and lax regulation to raise total assets from $604 billion in 1980 to more than $1.3 trillion in 1988. This was more than a doubling in size, and it significantly increased the S&L share of total deposits.

FSLIC and FDIC Insured Thrift Assets, 1980 to 1989

Savings & Loans			Savings Banks	
Year	Number	Assets (In billions)	Number	Assets (In billions)
1989	2,878	$1,252	489	$280
1988	2,949	1,349	492	284
1987	3,147	1,249	484	262
1986	3,220	1,162	472	237
1985	3,246	1,068	394	217
1984	3,139	976	373	206
1983	3,146	814	391	194
1982	3,287	686	428	174
1981	3,751	640	442	176
1980	3,993	604	460	172

Source: *History of the Eighties–Lessons for the Future*, FDIC and 1990 Factbook of Savings Associations, National Council of Savings Associations.

In Texas alone, S&L assets rose from $28 to $84 billion between 1980 and 1988[1], but much of that growth came from S&Ls that rose from near obscurity when investors took advantage of the easy access to banking these S&Ls provided through the lax regulations and low capital requirements. This would be the source of many "headline grabbing" stories of Texas rogue thrifts filling their loan portfolios with commercial real estate, which became a centerpiece of a second, and even more disastrous, phase of the thrift crisis. The Texas S&Ls' $84 billion in assets, though, pale next to their California counterparts' $373 billion in the latter year.

There were another 590 state-insured S&Ls in 1980 with assets of $12.2 billion in Maryland, Massachusetts, North Carolina, Ohio and Pennsylvania.[2] They were a small part of the industry, but the limited resources of the states standing behind them resulted in mini-crises in Maryland and Ohio in 1985 that foreshadowed what was to come a year later nationwide.

Most of the post-1982 S&L assets increase took place in California, Texas and Florida, and it is a story well chronicled in other books, one of the best of which is Martin Mayer's *The Thrift Crisis*. This rise and fall of the rogue thrifts, however, did not have the same impact on bank consolidation as the failure of long-established, large S&Ls and savings banks.

This thrift crisis stretched over more than a dozen years, but it was only in the late 1980s that it produced front page headlines. Being of this duration, the crisis began before interstate banking and was not resolved until interstate banking had become a national reality. Thus, to put the decline of the thrifts in its proper perspective, it needs to be interspersed among other industry changing, and often interrelated, events.

AN INDUSTRY OF THE PAST

The thrift crisis was a disaster waiting to happen. S&Ls and savings banks were a good idea whose time had passed, but like countless good ideas that outlive their usefulness, many of the people who were involved did not want to give up or make the necessary changes—until it was too late.

S&Ls and savings banks were initially cooperative community endeavors. The overwhelming majority did not issue stock and were technically owned by depositors and operated with minimal capital. Their business model was to take in savings deposits at low customer-acceptable rates, and then lend that money out to finance the purchase of homes. Historically, they did not compete directly with banks since they did not offer checking accounts until the early 1980s, and banks did not become highly interested in savings accounts and home mortgages until the 1960s. Without equity ownership, thrifts did not have to make a profit, and if they did, it was often distributed to depositors, and throughout most of their history, thrifts were not taxed.

The first thrifts date back to the early 1800s and operated successfully using this simple business model until the 1930s and the Great Depression, when millions of depositors lost their savings and about 2,000 thrifts, mostly S&Ls, failed.[3] This, however, was not a failure of the model, but rather a lack of capital and the stresses of the time. Like bank customers, beleaguered Great Depression thrift customers withdrew much-needed funds and many defaulted on their mortgages.

With the thrift model not in question, the government response to their failures in the 1930s was to impose more regulatory oversight and offer deposit insurance. For most S&Ls, this came with the establishment of the Bank Board for regulation and the FSLIC for deposit insurance. Some states, most notably Maryland, Massachusetts and Ohio, established their own supervisory and insurance systems. The savings banks shared regulators with commercial banks, and they were insured by the FDIC.

While there were many similarities between savings banks and S&Ls, there were some important differences. The savings banks were not tied exclusively to home mortgage lending, and the large ones in New York City tended to be more oriented toward commercial real estate and multi-family mortgage loans rather than single-family home loans. From a regulatory perspective, there were higher capital standards for savings banks than for S&Ls, which reflected their more diverse lending and the shared regulation with commercial banks.

Better regulation and deposit insurance after the Great Depression may have been good ideas at the time, but they also contributed to what proved to be a faulty business model in a high interest rate environment. In the 1960s, this regulatory assistance included the interest rate that thrifts could pay on savings deposits capped at .25 percent higher than the 3 percent rate at which banks were capped. This was a competitive advantage for thrifts, but it removed rate flexibility for their entire deposit base. For banks, a cap on deposit rates was less of a flexibility problem since most of their deposits were noninterest-bearing checking accounts that were less sensitive to interest rate changes.

S&Ls were restricted in their lending to only fixed-rate home mortgages, and most savings banks, even though not similarly restricted, had the same loan concentration. Capped deposits supporting long-term fixed-rate home loan portfolios worked fine for thrifts as long as interest rates stayed low, which was the case for more than 30 years, but those days ended in the mid-1970s.

There was an attempt after the Great Depression to have S&Ls and savings banks maintain more capital as a cushion against future problems, but since home mortgages were not considered high risk loans, capital was never required to be at the same level as banks. The target was 5 percent of assets, but even that was not rigidly enforced, particularly with the S&Ls.

As interest rates began to climb in the late 1960s, it became harder for thrifts to attract funds with a 3.25 percent interest rate cap on savings deposits. The addition of CDs eventually provided the rate flexibility necessary to attract funds even as interest rates increased, but while CDs made it easier for thrifts to attract deposits, they also increased the overall cost of funds and reduced the spread between loan yields and money costs.

Fortunately, the first interest rate peak in the 1970s was neither so high nor of sufficient length to create serious margin-related earnings problems. Thrift lending still was almost entirely oriented toward long-term fixed-rate home mortgages, but at least the new mortgages booked were made at higher, market-determined rates.

In 1976, when interest rates started up again, the rate levels went so high, and stayed there so long, that it was disastrous for thrifts. By 1980, interest rates were in the double-digits, and as might be expected, new high-yielding home mortgages were far-and-few between, and to support existing long-term fixed-rate mortgages, thrifts were forced to pay high rates on their CDs. For many of them, buying money to meet existing loan obligations meant an average cost of funds that was higher than the average yield on loans. The result was that the thrift business model was broken, and a thrift crisis was on its way.

DISASTROUS 1981 AND 1982

The mismatch between the average cost of funds and average yield wiped out almost all S&L earnings in 1980, and then in 1981 and 1982, resulted in a collective loss of almost $9 billion for the federally-insured S&Ls. This reduced industry tangible capital from 5.3 percent of assets in 1979 to less than 1 percent in 1981. If all S&Ls were viewed as a single firm, the industry had, in effect, failed. In 1981, 28 S&Ls with total assets of $11.5 billion actually did fail, and in 1982, the number of failures grew to 74 with combined assets of $20.2 billion.[4] To put this in context, the assets of all banks that had failed from 1934 through 1979 was $9.2 billion.[5]

From 1980 to 1982, there were 493 voluntary mergers and 259 supervisory mergers of S&Ls.[6] These were technically failures in which the government loss was deferred by providing the acquirer with assistance in making the acquisition. In other words, the negative impact on the deposit insurance funds was pushed into the future.

The S&L failures from 1981 through 1983 included some of the country's largest thrifts. The failed First Federal Savings & Loan of Chicago was the nation's ninth largest S&L; Fidelity in San Francisco was 19th; and Miami's Biscayne Federal was in the top fifty.

The savings banks did not fare much better than the S&Ls, but they were helped by higher capitalization. Between 1980 and 1982, they lost about $3 billion.

This was a slightly higher percentage of assets than for the S&Ls, but with equity capital at 7.1 percent in 1979, and adequate tangible capital, the losses still left the savings banks, collectively, in a much sounder condition. Failures were fewer than for the S&Ls, but the FDIC still had to deal with 12 failed savings banks in 1981 and 1982 with combined assets of $14.8 billion.[7]

Thrift Income and Expense, 1979 to 1983

Year	Net Income (In millions)	Return on Avg. Assets	Capital*/ Assets
S&Ls			
1983	$1,969	.26%	.3%
1982	(4,270)	(.64)	.4
1981	(4,632)	(.73)	.5
1980	765	.13	4.0
1979	3,619	.67	5.3
Savings Banks			
1983	$ (125)	(.07)%	5.1%
1982	(1,263)	(.72)	5.0
1981	(1,438)	(.83)	5.5
1980	(207)	(.12)	6.4
1979	741	.46	6.8

*Tangible capital for S&Ls.
Source: 1988 Factbook of Savings Institutions, National Council of Savings Institutions.

In some respects, the early stages of the thrift crisis looked even worse for the savings banks than the S&Ls, based on near-term results. Four of the 13 largest saving banks—New York Bank for Savings, Western Savings Fund of Philadelphia, Dry Dock Savings Bank and Greenwich Savings Bank—failed between 1981 and 1983 and were sold by the FDIC in federally-assisted transactions. Five others among the fifty largest met a similar fate. Seven of the nine biggest assisted savings banks sales in this first round of the thrift crisis involved New York savings banks.[8]

The FDIC took a much harder line relative to the savings banks than the Bank Board and the FSLIC did toward S&Ls. They dealt immediately with the most troubled institutions, and, unlike the S&L regulators, did not push most of the problems into the future.

There were some successes among the federally-assisted thrift sales, but, in many cases, it was merely putting a failed thrift into a bigger, but still troubled, thrift that would later become a casualty in the next round of failures. Two of the seven largest failed savings banks in New York were sold in federally-assisted transactions to Buffalo Savings, which would change its name to Goldome, switch to an S&L charter and then turn several years of rapid growth into one of the largest S&L failures. The purchase of Western Savings of Philadelphia had a similar result as part of PSFS, which is discussed in detail later in this chapter.

Massive losses and thrift failures in 1981 and 1982, however, were just the tip of the iceberg. Neither legislators nor regulators wanted to see many more thrift failures, and they played games with the accounting rules to buy time for struggling thrifts to recover. The thinking was that lower interest rates and expanded lending powers would restore margins and profitability to levels that would allow troubled thrifts to work their way out of their predicament. It was an understandable reaction, but interest rates did not cooperate, and relaxed accounting rules and expanded lending powers led to other problems.

LEGISLATIVE REACTION

The need for changes in the laws governing thrifts and commercial banks was obvious in 1980, not only because of the thrift losses, but also because of the flow of funds out of banks and thrifts. With the prevailing high interest rates, money was shifting from deposits, particularly deposits constrained by caps, into money market funds run by brokerage firms and other investments.

The initial legislation was the Depository Institutions Deregulation and Monetary Control Act of 1980. It phased out the caps on rates paid on deposits; raised the amount of coverage on insured deposits from $40,000 to $100,000 per account; and expanded deposit powers to include checking accounts for all thrifts.

Passed in 1980, this legislation came before the full extent of the thrift loss problem had materialized. Thus, while the removal of deposit rate caps may have been a much-needed move to help banks and thrifts compete with the money market funds, it was a mixed blessing for the thrifts. They were better able to compete for money, but competing meant paying market rates for deposits while almost all of their loans were long-term fixed-rate mortgages with yields far below market deposit rates.

The increase in insured deposit coverage from $40,000 to $100,000 per account had its drawbacks. It made deposits safer and increased customer confidence in banks and thrifts, but if a bank or thrift failed, it greatly increased the financial exposure of the deposit insurance funds. That concern in aggregate, though, seemed minimal in 1980.

The Garn-St. Germain Depository Institutions Act of 1982 was aimed specifically at the thrift problems. It expanded the lending powers of all thrifts by allowing 30 percent of their assets to be in commercial loans and to write loans at 100 percent of appraised value. It gave states the authority to provide additional incentives to S&Ls and savings banks, including investing in real estate projects. The latter proved to be particularly damaging as California, Texas and Florida, in particular, made it legal for S&Ls, and in these states almost all thrifts were S&Ls, to invest in real estate developments of various types and in other high risk businesses. The intent of this Act was to reduce thrift dependence on long-term fixed-rate mortgages, but diversification into high-risk investments and loans only made a bad problem worse.

CAPITAL DILEMMA

For thrifts and their regulators, a lack of capital became a major problem in 1982. After two years of large losses and a substantial erosion of capital, the industry, in general, and a majority of individual thrifts needed more capital. Conversely, if capital requirements were enforced as they were for banks, the number of failed thrifts would greatly increase. Thus, the regulators had a dilemma, and in their efforts to solve it, they tried to have it both ways. They encouraged thrifts to raise capital by converting to a stock form of organization and selling assets, but, at the same time, the minimum allowable capital was reduced to 3 percent of assets for S&Ls. This reduced the margin for error while encouraging growth. The savings banks, because of their sharing of regulators and deposit insurers with banks were held to higher capital standards, but even then, it was frequently not high enough.

The capital level for all thrifts was further "softened" by allowing them to operate outside of the standard generally acceptable accounting principles. The two most notable exceptions to these standards were deferring losses on loans and accompanying intangibles, particularly the "goodwill" generated by an acquisition of a failing thrift, with regulatory capital notes that would count as additional capital from a regulatory perspective.

Goodwill contributing to capital was turning the accounting rules upside down. Goodwill is an accounting term for the approximate difference between the price paid for an acquisition and the capital of that acquired company. It was supposed to be a deduction from equity capital, but under thrift regulatory accounting practices, or "RAP accounting," the goodwill, indirectly, was an addition to capital. The goodwill still had to be written off against earnings over a set period of time, but to make this less of a burden, the time was extended from ten to forty years.

It was not anticipated in 1982 that virtually every aspect of the thrift capital problem and supposed solutions eventually would contribute to a cost to taxpayers of more than $300 billion and increase banking concentration, but that is exactly what happened. Shifting from a mutual to a stock form of organization made converting thrifts easier to acquire, and, in fact, it had made their acquisition a probability. Counting goodwill-related capital notes as capital not only promoted acquisitions, but was also a method for regulators to sell failing thrifts rather than liquidate them. The relaxed capital standards were less direct in their concentration effect, but, at best, all they did was delay the day of reckoning for a large portion of the thrift industry—and increase the eventual cost to taxpayers.

MANAGEMENT AND BOARD WEAKNESSES

What legislators, regulators and trade association lobbyists did not take into account when they passed these laws and reduced accounting and capital standards, was the inability of most thrift managements and boards to handle major changes while under duress. What looks good on paper often does not relate to the real world. The new laws also made it easier for the less scrupulous to abuse the system.

It is human nature to think it is "greener on the other side of the fence," but in the 1980s, for thrifts, it was. Thrift managements and boards understandably were envious of the favorable position banks had because the majority of bank deposits were interest-free checking accounts that help earnings when loan yields rise in high interest rate environments, and that most bank loans had yields that adjusted with changes in interest rates. Banks that suffered in 1980 and 1981 were primarily those with large fixed-rate securities portfolios that were "underwater" because of the rapid increase in interest rates.

Operating in "greener pastures," though, requires an understanding of how business is done "over there," and even if allowed, asset and loan portfolios cannot be changed overnight. The industrial conglomerates of the 1960s had learned the pitfalls of businesses they did not understand, and their managements and boards generally had better business acumen than those of most thrifts.

The inadequacy of the boards of directors of most thrifts may have been a bigger problem than management shortcomings. Management at least could be, and frequently was, changed or enhanced by knowledgeable outsiders, but boards were turf-oriented, susceptible to bad advice and frequently far overestimated their banking capabilities.

The origin of the board problem was another good idea of the past outliving its usefulness. Most thrifts in 1980 were non-stock mutual organizations, and, as a result, the directors did not have a financial stake in the business. Their mutual status did not attract the most skilled executives as directors. A typical thrift board was composed of politicians, doctors, lawyers, hospital and school executives, pharmacists and the like. They were well-intentioned, community-oriented individuals, but they were often lacking in sophisticated business skills. It was common for representatives of the law firm that handled the thrift's real estate transactions to sit on the board, and they were usually among the more powerful board members.

To make matters worse, few thrift boards had a mandatory retirement age. Since most thrift directors were not wealthy and enjoyed the board meetings, there was no incentive to leave the board because of increasing age. In addition, after retiring from their regular jobs, they had more time for meetings and the monthly check looked bigger. Unfortunately, as people age they do not become more receptive to change.

One of my first acquaintances with a thrift board in the early 1980s was a prime example of the lack of receptiveness to change. Prior to meeting with the board of this $1 billion Midwest thrift to discuss strategy options, it was stressed by management that the word "association" rather than "bank" should be used. The directors were proud of their thrift heritage <u>and</u> did not like to be referred to as a bank, even though the intent was to become more like a bank. Clearly, change was not something that board really wanted.

The sophistication of thrift boards varied by size and proximity to major cities, but there were elements of the above in even the largest thrifts. The bigger the thrift often meant the less likely the directors would feel that they had to listen to outsiders. When the directors of thrifts of all sizes did listen, the advice they often took was what they wanted to hear, not what they really needed to do.

It was inevitable that thrifts would get bad advice mixed in with the good, but what was particularly damaging was that so much of it came from their regulators. The common regulatory theme in advising thrifts in the early stages of the thrift crisis was to grow rapidly with loans and investments other than fixed-rate home mortgages and, in so doing, not to worry about reducing capital as a percent of assets.

I experienced this type of regulatory advice with another Midwestern thrift, while sitting through a presentation by a representative of the Bank Board. The advice was the common Bank Board theme at the time, to grow rapidly to reduce the amount of low-yielding fixed-rate home mortgages as a percent of total loans and assets. The Bank Board representative was telling the board of this $400 million thrift with no lending skills beyond home mortgages to make loans they did not understand and further reduce capital relative to assets.

This advice not only had the stamp of approval of the regulators, but it was what most thrift directors and managements wanted to hear. Going slow and cutting costs, which would have meant firing employees, was not nearly as pleasant a thought as growth. This board, like many others, felt they <u>had</u> to listen to their regulators, and many of the thrifts had passed the point where they could do anything else.

CONVERSION PROCESS

Conversion from a mutual to stock form of organization was one of the more interesting side effects of the response to the financial problems of thrifts in the early 1980s. It provided new capital to replace lost capital; helped support rapid growth; and was a process chosen by a much higher percentage of large thrifts than small ones. It created merger potential that was profit-driven—an incentive that did not exist as a mutual.

Conversion to a stock organization also subverted the principle that thrifts were owned by their depositors. This caused considerable legal and regulatory machinations since few depositors had any idea that they were "owners," and it was an outdated concept. Depositors were constantly changing, and a depositor of fifty years was technically no more of an owner than the customer that made his initial deposit that very day.

Since the need for capital was so strong for thrifts, regulators approved most conversion applications. The *quid pro quo* was that depositors were given the first opportunity to buy the stock. This began a new investment game of potential investors putting deposits in thrifts they think will convert so that they are assured of being able to buy the stock in the initial public offering.

The conversion process was virtually nonexistent in the 1970s and started slowly in 1980, but by the mid-1980s, it had become a mini-industry for lawyers and investment bankers. In the 1970s, the total gross proceeds from public equity offerings were less than $300 million. From 1980 to 1982, a similar amount was raised by converting thrifts in a difficult market. Then from 1983 through 1987 the conversion business exploded and about $7.8 billion was raised, of which $5.4 billion was raised in just two years—1983 and 1986.[9]

Converting to a stock organization, though, did not change the board composition and management. The result was stock thrifts with a mutual mentality and investors taking a far greater risk than they imagined. It also meant more mergers and more costly thrift failures.

PSFS

There was no better illustration of the extent of the thrift problem and the solutions tried in the early 1980s, than the saga of the nation's oldest thrift, the Philadelphia Savings Fund Society, or PSFS as it was commonly-known. It was the largest banking organization in Philadelphia when measured by deposits, biggest savings bank in the country and the fourth largest thrift of any type. At the end of 1980, it had assets of about $7 billion; capital of $424 million, or a healthy 6 percent of assets; was profitable; and, presumably, had been profitable in most previous years. There were many previous years, since PSFS was founded in 1816.

When interest rates rose sharply and the industry-wide mismatch in the cost of funds and yields occurred, all that history did little for PSFS. It lost about $40 million in 1981 and $124 million in 1982, and its capital had fallen to about 4 percent of assets.

With the assistance of its regulators, PSFS improved its capital base, but at a high price. In 1982, it acquired the failed Western Savings Fund, which prior to its demise, was Philadelphia's second largest thrift with assets of about $2 billion. It added $796 million of goodwill to the PSFS balance sheet that was accompanied by $500 million in capital notes that counted as regulatory capital. By standard accounting practices, the goodwill incurred from the Western Savings Fund's purchase had technically made PSFS a failed institution as its goodwill exceeded equity capital, other than the FDIC-issued capital notes, by more than $300 million. This goodwill would be a future earnings burden, as it had to be written off over forty years in equal annual payments that began immediately.

In September 1983, PSFS converted from a mutual to a stock form of organization. This added another $335 million to its capital base and made PSFS marginally solvent by lifting real equity capital above the amount of goodwill on its books. With these moves, PSFS increased its capital as reported in its annual reports from $424 million in 1980 to $970 million in 1986.

The capital increase was a positive step, but PSFS also followed the thrift growth pattern espoused by the regulators. Between 1980 and 1986, it increased its assets from $7 billion to more than $18 billion, and two years later, its assets were $19 billion. PSFS reported profits between 1983 and 1986, but these were accounting profits that deferred actual losses. It also tried to bury the past by changing its name to Meritor.

This was the thrift rescue game played at the highest level with one of the nation's largest thrifts, and in the immediate post-1982 period, it looked like it might succeed. PSFS was Philadelphia's biggest bank or thrift in 1980 when its troubles started, and by 1986, as Meritor, it was far larger than any local banking organizations. It was also profitable using RAP accounting.

PSFS's Financial History, 1980 to 1992

Year	Assets	Capital*	Net Income	
			Call Report	As Reported
		(In millions)		
	(In billions)	(In millions)		
1992*	$ 5.0	-	$ (93)	$ (145)
1991	6.0	$ 146	(103)	(61)
1990	6.5	191	(106)	(209)
1989	12.6	304	(91)	(56)
1988	17.2	359	(227)	(210)
1987	19.0	569	(74)	(396)
1986	18.4	970	(18)	23
1985	17.1	954	(13)	65
1984	13.7	894	(12)	72
1983	11.9	823	(22)	26
1982	10.1	428	(124)	(174)
1981	7.4	389	(40)	(33)
1980	7.1	424	12	21

*September 30, 1992.
Source: Meritor call reports and annual reports.

Unfortunately, the PSFS story did not end in 1986. Interest rates rose in 1987 making its deferred losses harder to defer and the goodwill repayments overwhelming. In 1987, it restructured its balance sheet and wrote off much of its goodwill and, in so doing, reported a loss of almost $400 million. From 1987 through 1992, PSFS, or Meritor, lost almost $1.1 billion. The losses included the goodwill write-offs, but they also were net of income received from selling assets as it reduced assets from $19 billion at the end of 1987 to $5 billion in 1992.

What happened after 1986 goes beyond the thrift crisis' early stages, but the losses that led to the FDIC closing Meritor in 1992 were partly caused by loan quality problems that accompanied the rapid asset expansion. At the quarter-end prior to being closed, almost 10 percent of Meritor's assets were not performing.[10]

Meritor's demise also contributed to the consolidation process. It began as the biggest bank or thrift in the Philadelphia area, and in the end, Mellon, one of Pennsylvania's largest banks, acquired its branches. These branches eventually were sold to a subsidiary of the Royal Bank of Scotland.

Short-term Industry Recovery

Meritor's temporarily improved earnings performance from 1983 through 1986 was typical of the thrift industry, and by 1986, the surface numbers looked good industry-wide. From 1983 through 1985, S&Ls were profitable as a group, albeit using dubious accounting methodologies, and in 1985, the industry earnings reached $2.6 billion. This was only .26 percent of average assets, but it was a profit. Again looking at 1983 to 1985, S&L assets grew from $686 billion to almost $1.1 trillion, and about 300 new S&Ls were chartered.

Thrift Income and Expense, 1983 to 1987

Year	Net Income (In billions)	Return on Avg. Assets	Tangible Capital/Assets
S&Ls			
1987	$(7.1)	(.59)%	.7%
1986	(1.5)	(.13)	1.2
1985	2.6	.26	.8
1984	1.0	.11	.3
1983	2.0	.26	.4
Savings Banks			
1987	$1.9	.79%	7.6%
1986	2.3	1.00	7.3
1985	1.3	.60	5.6
1984	.0	-	4.9
1983	(.1)	(.07)	5.1

Source: 1988 Factbook of Savings Institutions, National Council of Savings Institutions.

S&L tangible capital was still less than 1 percent of assets, and the worst was yet to come. In 1987, the industry lost $7.1 billion, and in the next two years, the total loss was $31 billion, but that is a story for a later chapter.[11]

The deteriorating situation had outrun the ability of the insuring agency to solve the problem without outside assistance. At year-end 1984, the FSLIC had reserves of only $5.4 billion to pay off the depositors when an S&L failed, while the number of insolvent S&Ls, even under phony RAP accounting, had assets of almost $15 billion. A year later, the assets of insolvent thrifts were $68 billion.[12]

The savings banks, because of the less forgiving approach of its regulators did better. Their renewed profitability continued through 1987, and in 1985, had reached 1 percent of average assets. With an abundance of capital, it seemed likely that these mostly-Northeast institutions would weather round two of the thrift crisis, but they would be exchanging one crisis for another. With a heavy orientation toward real estate and a much expanded exposure to commercial real estate, the savings banks were among the biggest losers in the real estate-driven recession of 1989 through 1992 that devastated thrifts as well as banks.

THRIFT CRISIS AND INTERSTATE BANKING

A collateral effect of the initial stages of the thrift crisis was to help banks accomplish what they had been trying to do for so many years—crossing state lines with full-service banking. With an entire thrift industry suffering from the mismatch between cost of funds and loan yields, it was extremely difficult, if not impossible, to find thrift buyers for all large failed thrifts, even using capital notes for capital relief, as was done when PSFS bought Western Savings Fund. The only alternative to a costly liquidation, in some cases, was a sale to a bank, even if this meant a violation of McFadden Act prohibitions against crossing state lines with full-service banking, or at least nearly full-service banking.

The regulators took this step in 1982, and the recipient of their largesse was Citicorp. It not only assumed the liabilities and good assets of a $2.9 billion failed S&L, but that S&L, Fidelity, was located in one of the country's most attractive banking markets, San Francisco. What Citicorp had been trying to do for fifteen years, cross state lines with traditional banking, became a reality—and this was just the beginning.

Citicorp acquired three more failed thrifts in 1984 through federally-assisted transactions that had combined assets of about $4 billion in other large, attractive markets. In March 1984, it took over Biscayne Federal in Miami and First Federal

Savings & Loan of Chicago. In August 1984, it added National Permanent in Washington, DC to its trophy case. In a little over two years, Citicorp had added branch networks in California, Florida, Illinois and the District of Columbia to its New York base.

These assisted thrift acquisitions by Citicorp revived the concerns of the early 1970s of a New York domination of American banking. Small banks and state bank associations had to accept the *fait accompli*, but the early 1980s' thrift acquisitions by Citicorp had the dual effect of making large regional banks in other states want the same opportunity to cross state lines, yet they also wanted to limit further expansion by big New York banks.

The primary impact of the early stages of the thrift crisis on consolidation was the sale of these four S&Ls to Citicorp and the incentive that it provided for interstate banking. Three of those four S&Ls were among the 35 largest in the country in 1980, and First Federal Savings & Loan of Chicago was the ninth largest.

Countervailing these Citicorp acquisitions was the rapid growth of the S&Ls after 1982 that temporarily had reduced the bank share of total deposits. The increased S&L deposit share, though, was a "bubble" and only the beginning of the thrift crisis. The worst was yet to come at a high cost in taxpayer money.

TROUBLE IN THE OIL PATCH

The thrift crisis and interstate banking were the headline stories of the 1980s, but for impact on consolidation, they had to share the stage with the troubles in the oil patch states of Texas and Oklahoma. During these years, a sharp drop in oil prices and a small rogue bank in Oklahoma City were catalysts that forced eight of the country's forty largest banks to sell. Of these eight, four are now part of Bank of America; three were bought directly, or indirectly, by JPMorgan; and the eighth is Wells Fargo's Texas franchise. Of today's "big four," only Citigroup was not a beneficiary.

The problems in the oil patch, though, were far more than just a big bank problem. In Texas, 425 banks failed in the 1980s, and, in the latter part of the decade, nine of its ten largest banks either failed or were sold in anticipation of possible failure. In 1988 alone, 175 Texas banks failed with assets of $47.3 billion, which was 25 percent of the state's banking assets at the end of the preceding year.[1]

This was in stark contrast to the 1970s and early 1980s when there seemed to be no limits as to how high the Texas banks could go and oil was a source of wealth, not disaster. When most banks were worrying about the negative impact of oil-driven high interest rates on deposit inflow, banks in Texas, and throughout the Southwest, were prospering. They may have been held back by state laws that prohibited branching, but when an economy does well, banks will benefit, and the high oil prices that drove up the interest rates in the late 1970s and into the early 1980s, created a strong economic environment in markets dominated by the oil-and-gas industry.

Texas and its two largest cities, Dallas and Houston, were the major beneficiaries of this "oil boom," but times were also good in Denver, Tulsa, Oklahoma City and other oil-and-gas centers. Oil patch millionaires were seemingly created overnight; their status embellished by two top-rated TV shows; and the region's banks, particularly those in Texas, were rapidly rising among the ranks of the largest. At the time, there seemed to be no end in sight for the oil patch, its millionaires or its banks.

This "go-go" reputation was something Texas and Oklahoma bankers relished. It was a different world, and just how different was hard for those who did not live or work there to imagine. My first taste of this go-go attitude came in 1979 with a call from a small bank in suburban Houston. Its CEO wanted to meet soon, and he was thinking about lunch the next day. He did not see why I could not catch a morning flight at his expense and fly back that night. With this "have to get it done fast" attitude at a very conservative, small Texas bank, it was not hard to envision the Texas lending culture of that era.

Unfortunately, a go-go attitude cannot totally change business cycle patterns, and it may be a bit of cliché to say "what goes up must come down," but much to the dismay of the oil patch, this applied to oil prices, the local economy and the fortunes of local banks. Oil prices rose from $2.75 per barrel in 1973 to almost $37 per barrel in 1981 and then fell to $10 in 1986.[2] The oil patch economy and bank profits followed the oil prices in the downward slide.

When oil prices were at their peak in 1980, there were 1,467 Texas banks that, collectively, were highly profitable, and they only had to make modest contributions of just over $300 million to loan loss reserves. These were good times for the oil-and-gas industry and Texas banks, and over the next five years, the number of banks increased by about 500.

Texas Banking Statistics, 1980 to 1990

	Number of Banks	Pre-tax Operating Income	Contribution to Reserves
		(In billions)	
1990	1,184	$ .8	$.9
1989	1,318	(.6)	2.3
1988	1,501	(2.0)	2.7
1987	1,772	(2.8)	3.6
1986	1,972	(1.7)	3.5
1985	1,936	.9	1.9
1984	1,854	1.5	1.3
1980	1,467	N/A	.3

Source: FDIC: Historical Banking Statistics.

In 1986, when oil prices hit bottom, the number of banks in Texas peaked, and the earnings and loan loss contributions were telling a different story. The annual $318 million loan loss reserve contribution in 1980 grew to almost $3.5 billion, and the combined pretax net operating loss was $1.7 billion. In the next three years, Texas banks would lose over $5 billion on a pretax basis, and by 1990, the number of banks was reduced by about 800, or 40 percent. These were not the expectations of the Texas bankers.

The extent of this banking disaster in Texas and Oklahoma with some carryover into the contiguous states of Arkansas, Louisiana and New Mexico was well-documented and succinctly summarized in the FDIC's *History of the Eighties: Lessons for the Future.* At the beginning of its chapter on *Banking Problems in the Southwest* it stated that "of the total failure-resolution costs borne by the FDIC from 1986 to 1994, half ($15.3 billion) was accounted for by southwestern bank failures. This included losses of nearly $6.3 billion in 1988 and $5.1 billion in 1989—91.1 percent and 82 percent, respectively, of total FDIC failure-resolution costs for those two years. From 1987 through 1989, 71 percent of the banks that failed in the United States were southwestern banks (491 out of 689), and so were some of the most significant failures such as banks within the First City Bancorporation, First Republic Bank Corporation and M-Corp holding companies."[3]

The area's banking problems went beyond the banks. The Southwest was one of the areas hit hardest by the S&L crisis, which is chronicled in chapter nine. Texas, alone, accounted for almost 30 percent of federal expenditures for solving the S&L crisis.[4]

REPUBLIC BANK

The rapid rise, and subsequent fall, of the large Texas banks was epitomized by the fortunes of one of its biggest, Republic. This Dallas-based institution was founded in 1920 and had become the largest bank in the state by 1954, but it was small by national standards. In 1960, it barely made it into the top 100 nationwide, but it was helped by being in a rapidly growing state. Even though Republic could not open branches because of Texas banking laws, by 1970, it had become one of the fifty biggest banks in the nation. By 1980, it had formed a holding company, and, in that year, Republic took advantage of a change in Texas banking law that allowed the intrastate acquisition of banks by acquiring Houston National Bank.[5]

With this acquisition, Republic had become a force in both of Texas' largest cities, Dallas and Houston, and by the 1984, it was the 19th largest bank holding company in the country, and the fifth largest not based in New York, California or Illinois. The aura of invincibility, though, was gone, and four years later Republic was part of one of the largest failures in American banking history.

Even as its fortunes diminished, Republic would continue to rise in the rankings. A desperation-driven merger in 1987 with the second largest Texas bank, InterFirst, to form First Republic Bank Corporation would make it the country's 13th largest bank holding company. This, though, was the combining of banks with similar problems in a deteriorating economy, and it was the end for both banks. Republic is best remembered as the federally-assisted sale to NCNB, which highlighted the disappearance of big-time Texas banks *and* the vehicle that allowed NCNB, today's Bank of America, to become more than a regional bank.

PENN SQUARE BANK

The oil patch did not have to wait for the price of oil to drop sharply to create problems for the banking industry, nor did all the problems start in Texas. Oil was still king when little Penn Square Bank in Oklahoma City was sowing the seeds that would lead to the failures of two large banks far removed from the area and threaten the viability of one of New York City's largest, Chase Manhattan. Its failure in 1982 took place a few years before the oil-and-gas industry collapsed and there was widespread concern about the viability of the big Texas banks, but it was a reminder of the downside of the oil-and-gas industry—a downside that had brought us the Teapot Dome scandal in the 1920s and gave us Enron in 2002.

The Penn Square saga began quietly enough in 1972 when William Jennings bought a small bank in Oklahoma City's Penn Square Shopping Center. At the time, the bank had assets of about $30 million and capital of $4 million, and even at its peak in 1981, its assets were only $436 million. Size, however, did not constrain its lending.

What Jennings did with Penn Square was sell the glamour and high yields of its speculative oil-and-gas industry loans to banks in other parts of the country that were starved for high-yielding loans in an environment that had seen the cost of funds reach record levels. Its strategy was to make loans to oil-and-gas companies far beyond its legal lending limit and then participate those loans out to large banks around the country. The large banks included Continental in Chicago, SeaFirst in Seattle and Chase Manhattan, and the reputation of the participating banks, particularly Continental, became an endorsement of the quality of the loans. The other participating banks did little checking on their own.[6]

In the late 1970s, Penn Square accelerated its lending, and it did not have to do much marketing. As a source of much-desired high yielding loans, it could off-load virtually every loan it made. This reduced the incentive for Penn Square loan officers to do their homework and paperwork on the loans they were making. This style of lending could only go on so long, and in 1982, Penn Square collapsed.

Without its many loan participants, the collapse of a still small bank in Oklahoma would have been a local story. It became a major story when some of the upstream banks had losses relating to Penn Square that ran into the hundreds of millions of dollars. Chase Manhattan, Continental and Seafirst were hit the hardest, and, in the case of Continental, it had about $1 billion in Penn Square-originated loans.[7]

Chase Manhattan was large enough to survive with only its reputation impaired, but SeaFirst and Continental were not so fortunate. The Seattle-based Seafirst was the largest bank in Washington and 28th largest in the country, but the Penn Square-related losses were sufficient to force its sale to BankAmerica. Continental, the sixth largest bank in the country and the largest in the Midwest, did not immediately succumb to its Penn Square problems, but the damage to its reputation was more than it could handle, and in 1984, the FDIC was forced to rescue it with a $5 billion bailout. This was the nation's most expensive bank rescue up to that time.[8]

Continental, like Bank of Commonwealth and First Pennsylvania before it, never recovered from its FDIC bailout. It was eclipsed in the Chicago market by its longtime rival, First National Bank of Chicago, and by 1990, it was not only no longer one of the ten largest banks in the country—it did not even make the top twenty-five. In 1994, Continental, like SeaFirst before it, was bought by BankAmerica.

Penn Square may have done more to further bank consolidation than any bank, big or small, in the country, and it can be argued that its impact on consolidation rivaled that of the thrift crisis. Bringing down the biggest banks in Illinois and Washington and causing each to become part of BankAmerica was no small feat.

CONTINENTAL

The failure and subsequent FDIC bailout of Continental was a result of the Penn Square loans, but it also reflected the aggressive attitude of Continental, and a general laxness of the regulatory system at the time. Continental was looking for Penn Square as much as Penn Square was looking for Continental.

In the late 1970s, Continental had become an extremely aggressive lender. Between 1976 and 1981, commercial loans not secured by real estate grew from about $5 billion to more than $14 billion. This made it the nation's largest commercial lender and helped lift its assets from $21 to $45 billion. By more than doubling its size in five years, its growth was much faster than that of any of the other national banking leaders.

Ten Largest Bank Asset and Loan Growth, 1976 to 1981

	Bank	Assets		C&I Loans*		Annual Asset Growth
		1981	1976	1981	1976	1976-1981
		(In billions)				
1.	BankAmerica	$119	$73	$12	$7	10.6%
2.	Citibank	105	62	13	8	11.3
3.	Chase Manhattan	77	45	10	9	11.4
4.	Manufacturers Hanover	55	30	10	4	12.8
5.	Morgan Guaranty	54	29	6	3	13.5
6.	Continental	45	21	14	5	16.1
7.	Chemical	45	26	11	5	11.6
8.	Bankers Trust	33	22	5	3	8.7
9.	First Nat'l.-Chicago	33	19	6	4	11.8
10.	Security Pacific	31	16	6	3	13.5

*Commercial and Industrial loans not secured by real estate.
Source: History of the Eighties–Lessons for the Future, FDIC, page 237.

As is so often the case, rapid growth was greeted with more praise than concern, which can add to the desire to grow rapidly. In response to a question asked relative to how he anticipated where the next big bank problem might occur—William J. Seidman, who headed the FDIC for a tumultuous seven years starting in 1985—answered all too correctly in words to the effect of "I would just check to see who was last year's banker of the year."

Continental fit this role. According to the FDIC's *History of the Eighties-Lessons for the Future*, "Continental's management, the bank's aggressive growth strategy and its returns were lauded both by the market and by industry analysts. A 1978 article in Duns Review pronounced the bank one of the top five companies in the nation; and analyst at First Boston Corp praised Continental, noting that it had 'superior management at the top, and its management is very deep'; in 1981, a Salomon Brothers analyst echoed this sentiment, calling Continental 'one of the finest money-center banks going.'" [9]

By late 1981, Continental's luster had started to erode. Its second quarter earnings declined, and some large credit gambles had gone awry. Among others, it had a $200 million loan to a nearly bankrupt International Harvester. It was also a major participant in lending to developing countries, the infamous LDCs, which were a major problem for money center and large California banks in the 1970s and 1980s. [10]

Continental's slide had begun, and with $1 billion in loans from Penn Square, which failed in July 1982, it was no longer an investor favorite. Its stock price dropped by more than 60 percent the month Penn Square's failure was announced.

A bigger problem, though, were the depositors. As a money center bank in a state that did not allow branching, Continental's local core deposits were only a small part of its deposit base. It had to buy deposits across the country and even in foreign countries. This was "bought" money with above-average costs, and, with the lack of confidence instilled by the Penn Square failure, Continental's ability to find new funding was made more difficult and the cost of funds increased significantly. As its troubles mounted, it was only a matter of time before there would be a "run" on deposits. This threat was increased by the type of depositors it had and their ability to use electronic transfers to withdraw deposits. [11]

The "run" began in earnest in the spring of 1984, and the FDIC had to find a buyer, put in sufficient federal funds to keep Continental operating or let it fail. Continental's problems were so severe that there were no buyers, and its salability was hindered by its lack of a branch network. The only options were a bailout or failure, and Continental was deemed "too big to fail," a concept that was to stir a lot of controversy. This left only the bailout option, and in 1984, the FDIC bought its bad loans and inserted new capital at a total cost of about $5 billion. [12]

Texas Bank Collapse

Penn Square and Continental were precursors of things to come in the oil country. The go-go banking Penn Square carried to an extreme was still in effect after Penn Square failed, and it had spread beyond the oil-and-gas industry. Dallas, Houston and a host of other cities in the Southwest were growing at a rapid pace, and one result was that commercial real estate loans became a major lending emphasis of the area's big banks, a focus reinforced by the still-existing prohibition against branching.

The problems of the big Texas banks were also complicated by some typical board reactions. Bank boards do not like to lose market share, and for Dallas and Houston banks, a natural response was to push their lenders to make more oil-and-gas and commercial real estate loans. Much of this pressure was based on a widely held belief that the price of oil would go as high as $60 per barrel.[13]

A $60 per barrel price was excessive at the time, but this was an economic "boom" built on oil price expectations, and when prices fell, an economic collapse was inevitable. Oil-and-gas may have been a great business in 1981 when the price of oil was close to $37 per barrel, but it was a disaster at $10 in 1986. As went oil, so went commercial real estate and banking. Between 1980 and 1987, office vacancy rates in Dallas rose from 8 percent to 17 percent, and in Houston they went from 11 percent to 37 percent.[14]

Largest Texas Banks, 1984

	Bank	Assets (In billions)	National Rank	Outcome	Eventual Owner
1.	InterFirst*	$22	18	Failed	Bank of America
2.	Republic*	22	19	Failed	Bank of America
3.	Texas Commerce	21	21	Sold	JPMorgan
4.	M-Corp	21	22	Failed	Bank of America
5.	First City	17	24	Failed	JPMorgan
6.	Allied	10	36	Sold	Wells Fargo
7.	Texas American	6	63	Failed	JPMorgan
8.	Cullen Frost	4	-	As is	Cullen Frost
9.	National Bankshares	3	-	Failed	Bank of America
10.	BancTexas	2	-	Failed	Various

[[TBL FTN]]* Republic and InterFirst merged in 1987.
[[TBL SRC]]Source: American Banker, March 19, 1985

Republic was not alone in riding this wave of oil prosperity and the resulting optimism into the upper ranks of American banking. In 1984, Republic and four other Texas bank holding companies—Texas Commerce, InterFirst, M-Corp (the holding company name for Houston's Mercantile Bank) and First City—were the nation's fastest growing large banks and ranked among the country's 25 largest. They were larger than NCNB, Bank One or any of the superregionals that were to become such familiar names in ensuing years. Even Allied Bank, the sixth largest Texas bank, was bigger than Bank One.

At the time, it seemed as if nothing could stop these Texas banks, and that interstate banking was likely to spread their reach throughout the South and West. With the close links between banks in Texas and Chicago, a move in that direction also seemed possible.

A year later, the Texas economy collapsed, dousing the dreams of the state's banks in a torrent of nonperforming loans and red ink. Republic and InterFirst tried to survive through the cost savings of an ill-fated equal merger. Texas Commerce and Allied were sold to large out-of-state banks while they were still technically viable organizations. Texas Commerce was bought by Chemical and Allied by California-based First Interstate. M-Corp and First City waited too long and would join the Republic-InterFirst combination as wards of the government.

Despite the collapse, out-of-state banks were still enamored with the long-term potential of Texas, and the FDIC initially did not lack for buyers for the failed banking leaders. Chemical and First Interstate took their chances early-on with the 1987 and 1988 acquisitions of Texas Commerce and Allied Bank, respectively, without federal assistance and, for a while, they may have questioned their wisdom in doing so. Time, though, proved their acquisitions to have been good ones. NCNB made the biggest move by acquiring Republic from the FDIC in a tax incentive-laden 1989 deal that cost taxpayers $3.8 billion. Bank One would follow suit later that year with its assisted purchase of M-Corp, which, although only half the size of First Republic, resulted in a public outlay of $2.8 billion.[15]

First City, which was the fifth largest bank in Texas when the deluge began, was the last large Texas bank to go, albeit not through any wisdom of its own. It went into government receivership in 1990, but was not sold until 1993, as asset quality problems elsewhere had reduced the pool of potential buyers. When the national banking climate improved in 1993, First City was sold in parts, and its largest parts, including its Houston and Dallas banks, were acquired by Chemical and integrated into its Texas Commerce operation.

BankAmerica did not acquire any of the leading banks in Texas as it had its own problems with LDC loans, but it was not completely left out of the Texas sell-off. By 1990, its financial condition had improved, and it added $3.7 billion in assets in the assisted purchase of Sunbelt Savings. In 1993, it added $6.9 billion in assets when it acquired First Gibraltar, the largest Texas S&L. First Gibraltar, or Gibraltar as it was then called, also was the largest thrift in Texas in 1982, and was merged with the third largest, First Texas, in the mid-1980s.

NCNB-REPUBLIC

The NCNB federally-assisted takeover of the bank subsidiaries of First Republic Bank, or Republic as it usually referred to in deference to one of its lead banks, was particularly noteworthy in that it was the first large assisted bank transaction done with tax incentives. It also moved Hugh McColl and NCNB into the top tier of American banks. Prior to this deal, NCNB was the nation's 18th largest bank with assets of $28.6 billion. It was smaller than Shawmut and First Fidelity and only slightly larger than First Union, Sovran and its Texas target, First Republic Bank. After the deal closed, NCNB became the seventh biggest bank in the country.

NCNB was one of the most aggressive regional banks. In the 1970s, it was a leader in crossing state lines with nonbank acquisitions. Then, when limited interstate banking was permitted in the 1980s, its expansion focused on the Southeast, particularly Florida. NCNB increased its assets from $7.2 billion in 1980 to almost $29 billion in 1988 through a series of mid-level Florida bank acquisitions—Ellis Banking, Pan American Banks, Exchange Banking and Gulfstream Banks—and the purchase of South Carolina's second largest bank, Bankers Trust.

These acquisitions made NCNB the biggest bank in the Southeast, but it did not have the capacity to easily absorb the purchase of a failed bank the size of Republic. Citicorp and Wells Fargo were on the short list of likely buyers. BankAmerica would have been on that list as well, if it was not temporarily sidelined by LDC problems.

The appeal of Texas and its growing list of troubled banks had caught the attention of NCNB management as early as 1986, but it was not likely that they were thinking as big as Republic at that time. In 1986, NCNB had invested $6 million in Charter Bank of Houston and had used the Charter base to acquire a failed Houston Bank, which gave it a 40 percent ownership of a $500 million Texas bank. This small acquisition put NCNB in Texas and gave it a familiarity with the FDIC sale process.

Going from a $500 million acquisition to the purchase of a $20 billion bank not much smaller than itself was a big step, and NCNB had neither the capital nor ability to raise the funds to pull off such a transaction. These were obstacles, but they did not prove to be insurmountable.

NCNB, and its CEO, Hugh McColl, in particular, saw Republic as a unique opportunity and were determined to give it a try. Giving it a try meant selling the FDIC on NCNB providing it the best of all worlds in solving one of its biggest headaches—the expertise to handle the bad loans and running Republic at the least cost for the FDIC. Because of its size, this would require the FDIC to become a partner and let NCNB buy Republic on a "pay as you go" basis with a key element being able to use the accumulated losses as future tax deductions against bank earnings.[16]

What NCNB was proposing was to acquire 20 percent of about $20 billion in acceptable assets for $210 million and manage a pool of about $5 billion in bad assets that technically would still belong to the FDIC. It would buy the other 80 percent over time, out of the tax loss carry-forwards that Republic had accumulated; would legally be protected from suits or damages connected with Republic's past; and would get a small percentage on any gains realized in the reduction of the pool of bad assets.

Acquiring $20 billion of good banking assets in Texas for about $1 billion of which all but $210 million could come out of tax credits sounded too good to be true. The tax credits, though, would only materialize if the restructured Texas bank made money, which considering the status of the local economy, was no sure thing. The FDIC did not jump at this arrangement and was discussing other rescue opportunities with Citicorp, Wells Fargo and a Republic management group. It presumably had internal doubt as to whether NCNB could really make this work.[17]

In the end, those concerns did not deter the FDIC, and in July 1988, it accepted the NCNB proposal as being the least costly to the taxpayers, and, in no small part, this was the result of the sales effort by McColl and others in the NCNB team as to their ability to make this work. It proved to be a correct call on the FDIC's part, and NCNB, overnight, had become the biggest bank in Texas and one of the ten largest in the country.

THE OIL PATCH LEGACY

The impact of the problems in the oil patch on the consolidation of banking and its contribution to interstate banking are impressive. Of the forty largest banks in 1982, eight were forced to sell or were sold by the FDIC because of oil patch-related problems.

Penn Square's collapse alone took down two of them. The largest bank in the state of Washington, SeaFirst, was sold to BankAmerica in a 1983 assisted transaction. Continental was bailed out by the government in 1984, and in 1994, it was also acquired by BankAmerica.

The other six were casualties of the decline in oil prices in the mid-1980s and the resulting collapse of Texas real estate values. The two largest Texas banks, Republic and InterFirst, after their merger and subsequent failure, became part of NCNB. Chemical bought Texas Commerce and First City, numbers three and five; Bank One acquired M-Corp from the FDIC; and First Interstate bought Allied Bank.

Two of the three failed top ten Texas banks that ranked between seventh and tenth, Texas American and National Bancshares, also ended up as part of major out-of-state acquirers. Texas American's franchise was sold to Bank One, and, as a result, ended up as part of JPMorgan. Nine of the twelve National Bancshares banks were sold to NCNB, and today are part of Bank of America. Cullen Frost in San Antonio, the ninth largest bank in Texas in 1986, was the only one of the ten largest banks in the state to survive.

Although not of the same importance to the consolidation process as the disappearance of eight of the forty largest banks in the country, the three Texas S&Ls that ranked among the country's forty largest S&Ls in 1982 were also sold during this period. As will be described in more detail in chapter nine, the 22nd ranked Gibraltar acquired the 40th ranked First Texas in 1987 and changed its name to First Gibraltar, and was subsequently bought by BankAmerica in 1993. The 31st ranked University Savings failed in 1989, and its branches were acquired by NCNB.

These sales made Bank of America and JPMorgan the big winners in the oil patch banking disaster and gave Wells Fargo a big stake in Texas. Directly or indirectly, Bank of America ended up with the two largest banks in Texas, Republic and InterFirst; the ninth largest, National Bancshares; and the state's three largest thrifts. JPMorgan, or Chemical as it was called then, on its own bought the state's third largest bank, Texas Commerce, and most of the fourth largest, First City, and then through the acquisition of Bank One, ended up with the fifth and seventh largest Texas banks, M-Corp and Texas American as well. When the original Wells Fargo bought First Interstate in 1996, it also bought the Allied Bank franchise.

The impact of these moves on consolidation went beyond just what was acquired. Republic, InterFirst and Texas Commerce were likely to have become major players in interstate expansion, and their forced sale eliminated potential rivals to the four banks that now dominate American banking. In 1984, in fact, the three leading Texas banks were as likely, or even more likely, to be major players in the interstate banking expansion and consolidation than NCNB, Bank One or Norwest.

INTERSTATE BANKING GATHERS MOMENTUM

B y the late 1970s, even before there were thrift and oil patch crises, there was a growing sense of the inevitability of interstate banking, but "inevitability" always was at least a couple of years away and without good answers as to how the protectionist attitude of small banks would be overcome. As technology improved and ATMs proliferated, it was illogical that in a business as important as banking, a state line would decide whether a bank could maximize its ability to provide optimum service. Logic, though, often comes in a distant second when the protection of local businesses is the prime obstacle—whether it is banking, steel or the benefits of free trade.

For one living in the Washington, D.C., area, the state line constraints seemed particularly ludicrous as the central city and its two main suburban areas, the Maryland suburbs and Northern Virginia, were three different banking markets, each with its own set of banks. A customer working in Washington and living in the suburbs could not use the same bank where he or she worked and lived. Even the area's one-bank holding company with "grandfathered" multi-state coverage, First American, had to operate its banks completely independent of each other in the different political jurisdictions.

Prior to 1982, the inevitability of interstate banking was more of an intellectual argument than part of any actual movement. The large New York banks, particularly Citicorp, and regional banks such as NCNB were pushing the concept, but there was little support in most state legislatures or state banking associations. There was a real concern at the time that interstate banking would lead to the takeover of banking in small states by the big banks in New York and California and, to a lesser extent, Texas.

In this hostile environment, if interstate banking was to become a reality, it was going to have to take a backdoor approach and probably with the courts playing a major role. It was a classic "David versus Goliath" battle, and the votes in this battle were, at least initially, for the combatants with the slingshots.

By 1982, three areas of vulnerability to the interstate banking barriers had surfaced, and each was to play a major role in its undoing. The most obvious was a growing thrift crisis accompanied by large thrift failures that would force their regulators to look to out-of-state banks and/or thrifts as buyers to minimize the negative impact on the deposit insurance funds. This happened in December 1982, when Citicorp was permitted to buy a large, failed thrift in San Francisco. Not so obvious, but also destined to play major roles were NCNB's mid-1970s acquisition of a Florida trust company and Maine opening its doors to out-of-state bank acquisitions in 1975.

The oil patch problems in the Southwest had some interstate banking implications as early as 1982, but their impact was muted by geography. The regulators had little choice but to approve the sale of a failing SeaFirst, the largest bank in the state of Washington and a Penn Square casualty, to BankAmerica on an "emergency" basis. With both seller and buyer being West Coast banks, though, these acquisitions did not have the same impact on the interstate banking battle that was playing out on the East Coast of a Citicorp buying out-of-state thrifts.

Citicorp was the source of most local bank fears, and it was on the East Coast that the initial interstate banking battles were fought. The West Coast was receptive from the beginning, and in much of the Midwest, banks were still battling to get in-state branching and not very concerned about interstate banking.

NCNB's Florida Incursion

If one event stood out above all others in pushing aside the interstate barriers in 1982, it was NCNB using a previously acquired trust company to buy its way into traditional banking in Florida. This unforeseen fortuitous circumstance changed the direction of an industry. Without NCNB's early 1970s acquisition of a small trust company in Florida, interstate banking might have been delayed for several years in the Southeast and elsewhere.

If interstate banking had been delayed, NCNB would not have had the size to buy the failed Republic and InterFirst banks in Texas, and without those purchases, it is unlikely that there would be a Bank of America based in Charlotte today. NCNB might have found other stepping stones, but the path would have been more difficult and the end result might have looked more like today's U.S. Bancorp than the $2 trillion assets plus Bank of America.

In the 1970s, NCNB, however, <u>did</u> buy the Trust Company of Florida as part of its effort to cross state lines with nonbank acquisitions. It would have liked to expand across state lines with traditional banking as well, but this was long before that type of expansion was possible. A trust company, though, was a natural extension of a nonbank strategy even if the trust company technically had to have a bank charter to operate.

How much of a role chance can play in an industry altering event was evidenced by this trust company acquisition. In his biography of Hugh McColl, Ross Yockey provided some relevant dialogue to this point as this acquisition took place even without the chairman and CEO at the time, Tom Storrs, being there. According to Yockey:

> "Hugh McColl (an EVP at the time) was in the middle of a discussion in Luther Hodge's office when Bill Dougherty (NCNB's president) came in and told them about the Orlando opportunity. Dougherty had just got off the telephone with a former associate who was now CEO of Pittsburgh National Bank. He told them, 'This guy wants to know if we are interested in buying a little trust company down in Florida.'
>
> 'How much money is it losing?' McColl wanted to know.
>
> 'No, no, it's not that,' Dougherty protested. 'It seems he forgot to ask his board if he could buy it and now they want him to get rid of it. He says he will sell it to us at cost. And Mr. Storrs (NCNB's chairman) is out of town.'
>
> McColl and Hodge (also an EVP) looked at each other.
>
> 'Why not?' asked McColl.
>
> 'Sure,' Hodge agreed. 'Go ahead and buy it.'
>
> So Dougherty bought it. The Trust Company of Florida had only $35 million in assets, pocket change to a bank like theirs, but it might get larger someday, especially with Walt Disney building that new tourist attraction down there."[1]

For better or worse, NCNB had acquired an entry vehicle into Florida banking, but it is unlikely in 1972 that anyone fully realized the magnitude of this possibility. In fact, a couple of years later when NCNB was struggling with real estate problems, some of its executives suggested selling the trust company.[2]

Trust Company of Florida may not have been a traditional bank, but even in 1972, its purchase by an out-of-state bank raised a few hackles down in Florida, and legislation was subsequently passed to keep other out-of-state banks from doing the same thing. As time would show, though, this did not keep out-of-state banks already there from expanding in Florida via traditional bank mergers.

In 1981, NCNB decided to see if it could take advantage of this legal opening and use its trust company presence to buy one of Florida's bigger banks. It talked to most, if not all, large banks in the state and was most enthused about the possibility of buying the $2.5 billion Florida National Bank in Jacksonville. The major impediment was getting this bank, and presumably other large banks as well, to agree to a merger not knowing if the legislative loophole that NCNB was counting on to get a merger approved would materialize.[3]

To remove this uncertainty, NCNB reached an agreement with the owners of First National Bank of Lake City, Florida, a bank with assets of about $30 million. This was to be NCNB's test case to see if it could get Federal Reserve approval of a bank acquisition in Florida based on its trust operation. In December 1981, the Lake City acquisition was approved and the deal was closed on January 8, 1982. NCNB was in the banking business in Florida and able to buy other Florida banks.

Even with this approval, NCNB was unable to convince any of the larger Florida banks to accept an acquisition offer; but before 1982 was over, it had bought two mid-sized banks, Gulfstream Banks in Boca Raton and Exchange Banking in Tampa. By year-end 1982, NCNB had Florida assets of almost $2 billion and had become the state's seventh largest bank; and this was only the beginning. It was a major player in Florida and had at least a couple of years' head start on other out-of-state banks.

NCNB's success in Florida could have been an isolated event with minimal effect on the consolidation process, but it had an impact on the thinking of other banks that went far beyond its increased size in the state. The leading banks in the Southeast were both delighted with and envious of NCNB's Florida moves, and, as a result, they became much more proactive in supporting legislative change in favor of interstate banking. It was a "breach in the dike," and the urgency of going further was building.

THE MAINE EVENT

Meanwhile, at the far other end of the East Coast in Maine, a second 1982 interstate merger announcement would open the door to interstate banking even further. Maine was an unlikely place for a major interstate event to occur, since unlike California and Florida where Citicorp and NCNB had made their moves, it was not on the wish list of many banks. Maine's primary interest to bank acquirers was more likely to have been the scenery and second homes rather than banking. The old political saying of "as Maine goes, so goes Vermont" would pretty much sum up the out-of-state banking interest.

In fact, Maine had opened its doors to out-of-state banks as early as 1975 when it passed a law allowing out-of-state banks the right to buy banks in Maine if the partner's home state extended similar privileges to Maine banks—a process known as reciprocity. This opening for interstate mergers received so little attention that even banks in Maine had not given it much thought.

The low level of concern in Maine about being inundated by out-of-state banks was evident in a 1982 planning meeting of one of the state's largest bank holding companies, Northeast Bankshares, a bank holding company I was working with at the time. The primary subject of discussion was statewide expansion by Northeast, not the possible entry into the state by out-of-state banks. The only person at that meeting even thinking about the ramifications of the 1975 legislation was Northeast's inside counsel.

The counsel reminded attendees that New York had just passed reciprocal legislation, and that the structure of Maine banking could be in for big changes. His comments were not ignored, but neither did they raise much concern. There was not much Northeast could do about it, in any event, and selling the bank was not a consideration, or at least it was not thought to be a consideration, at that meeting.

A few months later, a telephone call from the Northeast president, Roger Castonguay, presented a very different picture. Peter Kiernan, the president and CEO of Norstar, an Upstate New York regional bank based in Albany, had visited with Castonguay and made an offer of 135 percent of book—a good price at the time—to buy the bank, which Castonguay felt might be too good to refuse. The price did not seem "too good to refuse" to me, but interstate banking in northeastern United States was on its way.

The pricing was of little importance relative to the impact of the sale of this bank on the bank consolidation process, but it is an interesting sidelight as to just how low bank sale prices were at the time. My response to Castonguay was that the bank was worth at least 150 percent of book, and he asked me to make that case in writing. This was done as requested, and in a conversation I will long remember, Castonguay called and said, "You and I are not too smart. I showed your memo to Kiernan. He took a quick look and said, 'Will you shake on this?' I guess we should have asked for more."

Whether or not it was a good price, Northeast had agreed to sell to Norstar. Regulatory approval was forthcoming, and by June 1983, the first true interstate bank acquisition in the United States since the 1930s was a done deal. A few months later, a second Maine bank, Depositors, would be acquired by KeyCorp—another Albany bank.

As in Florida, the importance of the initial interstate acquisitions in Maine was not the impact of the actual purchases, but the response they evoked. Maine may not have been a large, or even an attractive, banking market, but it did not sit well in the bank boardrooms in Boston to see New York bank holding companies buying banks in what they considered their own backyard.

REGIONAL COMPACTS

The responses to NCNB's acquisition in Florida and Norstar's in Maine were the same—regional interstate banking compacts. These were agreements between states to allow interstate banking on a reciprocal basis within a specified geographic area. What had happened in Florida and Maine, as well as Citicorp's acquisition of a failed thrift in California—followed by similar thrift acquisitions in Florida, Illinois and the District of Columbia—would make interstate banking a reality and move the inevitability of interstate banking from an intellectual discussion to, "What was the proper strategic response?" The challenge for states and banks was no longer how to stop interstate banking, but how to use it to their benefit.

Two underlying and interrelated concerns that shaped the general response to the arrival of interstate banking were the fear of domination by the large New York banks and the time needed for regional banks to build the necessary mass to compete with them, which was thought by some to be as long as ten to fifteen years. Banks in California and Texas were also a concern because of size, but on the East Coast, their proximity made them less likely threats than the large New York banks, particularly Citicorp. An answer to these concerns was a regional compact that excluded banks in New York, California and Texas.

Regional banking compacts were not new considerations. NCNB had proposed legislation in North Carolina in 1979 that would permit interstate mergers between banks in North Carolina and southeastern states on a reciprocal basis, and similar legislation was considered in Florida. The proposed legislation, though, did not garner support from the state banking agencies and other leading banks in either state and, as a result, never even made it to a vote.[4]

Five years later, it was a completely different banking environment, and NCNB did not have much trouble making the Southeast banking compact a reality. In 1984, Florida, Georgia, North Carolina and South Carolina all signed on, albeit with a one-year waiting period. It would only be a matter of time before other states in the region would join.

The same process played out in New England with Boston and Hartford banks taking the lead. In 1984, banking legislation passed in Connecticut, Massachusetts and Rhode Island to form a New England banking compact that allowed mergers between banks in the participating states. Since Maine had full interstate banking already on its books as long as the other state had reciprocity, banks in any of the southern New England states could merge with banks in Maine. Rhode Island also included a "trigger date" that would take reciprocal interstate banking nationwide in 1987.

In both regions, some large banking combinations were announced fairly soon after the regional compacts were in place. The biggest proposed merger in the Southeast was the original Wachovia and First Atlanta, a combination that would create a bank larger than NCNB. In New England, Boston-based Bank of New England announced its intention to merge with CBT, Connecticut's largest bank, and Bank of Boston agreed to buy Casco Northern in Maine, RIHT Financial—the initials stand for Rhode Island Hospital Trust—in Rhode Island and Colonial Bancorp in Connecticut. Interstate banking and consolidation in the Southeast and New England were off and running.

There was one problem, New York was excluded from both of the regional compacts and this did not sit well with the large New York banks. Not only would the compacts allow the largest Florida banks to be acquired by out-of-state interests without New York banks being able to participate, but also nearby Connecticut, whose southwest corner is part of the New York metropolitan area, would also be off-limits. Citicorp, the primary target of the exclusion responded by filing suit to stop the exclusionary legislation.

Citicorp's suit put interstate banking on hold, and the case made it all the way up to the Supreme Court. This was a much anticipated court ruling without an overwhelming consensus as to what the outcome would be. It is an open question as to what the states involved would have done if the Supreme Court had ruled against regional compacts, but they did not have to face that decision. In June 1985, the Supreme Court ruled in favor of the regional compacts, and with that approval, interstate banking was not only permissible, but an irresistible force.

In New England, which is separated from the rest of the United States by New York, the geographic limits to the New England compact were near their final form right from the start. New Hampshire and Vermont opted out initially as they did not want to have their banking dominated by the big Boston banks, but they are a small part of the New England banking market. Banks in Connecticut, Maine, Massachusetts and Rhode Island were free to merge, and merge they did.

In the Southeast, the Supreme Court's approval of regional interstate banking had a geographic broadening effect. In 1985, Maryland and Virginia joined the original four states—Florida, Georgia, North Carolina and South Carolina—in the Southeast regional banking compact. The District of Columbia had technically become a member that year by permitting interstate banking nationwide, but its banks were only of interest to neighboring states. By 1987 Alabama, Mississippi and Tennessee were also members of the Southeast compact.

North Carolina Domination

Looking back, it is easy to view the Southeast compact as a one-sided agreement that allowed North Carolina banks to dominate banking in the region and to eventually become national banking powers. This was not the intention, and despite the intense early merger activity of NCNB and the Wachovia-First Atlanta merger, it was not that one-sided at the beginning.

In 1984, and prior to the Supreme Court decision, NCNB had used its early entry into Florida to become the biggest bank in the Southeast with assets of $15.7 billion. The only other bank in the area with assets of more than $10 billion was Barnett in Florida with $12.5 billion. This was a good start for NCNB, but three years later, it was still just barely first among near-equals.

By the end of 1987, NCNB had almost doubled in size to $28.9 billion assets with more Florida mergers and the acquisition of Bankers Trust, the second biggest bank in South Carolina, but it was only slightly larger than First Union, another North Carolina bank, and SunTrust. First Union had been active in the interim with the acquisition of First Railroad & Banking in Georgia, Northwestern Bank in its home state and Florida's Atlantic Bank. These deals had lifted its assets from $7 billion in 1984 to $28 billion three years later. SunTrust, an Atlanta-based combination of Trust Company of Georgia and SunBanks in Florida, had 1987 assets of $27 billion.

Largest Southeast Banks, 1987

	Bank	Assets		1984 Rank	Eventual Owner
		1987	1984		
		(In billions)			
1.	NCNB	$29	$16	1	Bank of America
2.	First Union	28	7	8	Wells Fargo
3.	SunTrust	27	9	11	SunTrust
4.	Barnett	24	13	2	Bank of America
5.	Sovran	21	8	6	Bank of America
6.	C&S	20	8	7	Bank of America
7.	First Wachovia	19	9	5	Wells Fargo
8.	MNC	17	7	9	Bank of America
9.	Southeast Banking	13	10	3	Wells Fargo
10.	Signet	11	4	19	Wells Fargo

Source: American Banker, March 29, 1985 and March 29, 1988.

There were three other banks—Barnett, Norfolk-based Sovran and C&S in Atlanta—that had 1987 assets in excess of $20 billion, and First Wachovia, the combination of First Atlanta and the original Wachovia, had just missed that cut-off with assets of $19 billion. Maryland's MNC, the holding company for Maryland National, had assets of $17 billion, and with its inclusion, there were eight Southeast banks with the size and momentum to be candidates for regional leadership.

It was during this period that the term "superregional" was first used to describe banks that were regional in scope, but of substantial size. When it came to superregionals, the Southeast had more than its fair share.

In 1987, though, it would have been hard to believe that of the ten largest banks in the Southeast, only two would be left 22 years later. Five are now part of Bank of America, and four are major components of Wells Fargo. Other than NCNB, only SunTrust managed to maintain its independence.

NEW ENGLAND IMPACT

New England was a much smaller region than the Southeast, and the elimination of state line restrictions in four of the six New England states led to a much greater degree of local concentration with four Boston banks—Bank of Boston, Bank of

New England, Fleet and Shawmut—and two in Connecticut, CBT and Hartford National, leading the way. Bank of Boston was by far the largest bank in New England in 1984, but despite its initial position and several interstate acquisitions, it could not maintain its earlier dominance. Others used their newly gained geographic freedom to close much of the size gap.

Bank of New England, the name taken in 1982 by what had been New England Merchants, was initially the most aggressive of the New England banks using the regional compact to its advantage. It increased its assets from $6.8 billion to $29.6 billion between 1984 and 1987, most of which came from a supposedly "equal" merger with CBT. Equal, in this case, meant that the headquarters was in Boston; management came from CBT; and a new name was utilized. Being the most aggressive initially, though, did not lead to success as four years later Bank of New England would become one of the largest failures in banking history.

Largest New England Banks, 1987

	Bank	Assets		1984 Rank	Eventual Owner
		1987	1984		
		(In billions)			
1.	Bank of Boston	$34	$22	1	Bank of America
2.	Bank of New England	30	7	3	Bank of America
3.	Fleet	25	6	6	Bank of America
4.	Hartford National	16	6	5	Bank of America
5.	Shawmut	11	7	4	Bank of America
6.	BayBanks	9	5	7	Bank of America

Source: American Banker, March 29, 1985 and March 29, 1988.

Another Boston-Hartford equal bank merger, Shawmut and Hartford National in 1988, would create a major player in the region. It would also take away Hartford's last bank of any size.

The key player in New England bank consolidations would be Fleet, or Fleet/Norstar as it was temporarily called. It was the product of still another supposedly equal merger in 1987 when Rhode Island's national trigger "kicked in" and mergers between New York and Rhode Island banks were allowed. This one was between Rhode Island's biggest bank, Fleet, and Norstar, the upstate New York bank that had put the interstate process in New England in motion when it acquired a bank in Maine in 1983.

Fleet, a bank holding company whose origins go back to 1791 was the dominant partner from the beginning, with the headquarters staying in Providence even though Norstar's Peter Kiernan was named Chairman and CEO. The Fleet dominance was made even more so when Kiernan died within a year of the merger.

After Kiernan's passing, Fleet, which would subsequently drop the Norstar name, increased its assets from $6 billion in 1984 to $27 billion by the end of 1987. Its new CEO, Terry Murray, would be one of the most successful of the new breed of superregional leaders, and over the next twelve years, he would make Fleet pre-eminent in the region. The six biggest banks in New England in 1987, starting with the failed Bank of New England, would become part of Fleet by 1999, and subsequently part of Bank of America when Fleet took that larger bank's $49 billion offer in 2004.

LDC CRISIS

Interstate banking and the rise of the superregionals began in earnest with the approval of the regional banking compacts in June 1985. By the end of 1987, several East Coast banks had tripled in size and were on their way to becoming much bigger banks. This, though, was only part of the story in the mid-1980s, as the largest banks in the country were not enjoying those years. While NCNB, First Union, Fleet and others were moving toward bigger and better things, the money center banks were struggling to survive. In fact, they were struggling so much that it may not have made much difference to the future industry structure if the New York banks had been included in the regional compacts.

The problem for these banks were the previously discussed loans to the less-developed-countries, or as it was commonly called, the LDC debt crisis. This crisis began in August 1982 when Mexico announced that it would be unable to meet its obligations to service an $80 billion debt. By October 1983, there were 27 countries owing $239 billion that had rescheduled their debts. The largest portion of this debt was in Latin America, an area in which American money center banks were the primary lenders. The eight largest banks in the United States were major holders, and LDC loans constituted 147 percent of their combined capital and reserves at the time.[5]

There was no "quick fix" to the LDC problem, and in 1987, Citicorp, Chase Manhattan, BankAmerica, Chemical and Manufacturers Hanover had a combined loss of almost $5 billion. It was not just a BankAmerica and big

New York bank problem either, as California-based First Interstate and First Chicago added another $1.1 billion to the 1987 losses. Continental, Mellon, Marine Midland and Charter also had big losses.

Largest American Banks, 1987

	Banks	Assets		Net Income	Long-Term Debt Rating*
		1987	1984		
		(In billions)			
1.	Citicorp	$204	$151	$(1.1)	A1
2.	Chase Manhattan	99	87	(.9)	Baa1
3.	BankAmerica	93	118	(1.0)	Ba3
4.	Chemical	78	52	(.9)	Baa1
5.	J.P. Morgan	75	64	.1	Aa1
6.	Manufacturers Hanover	73	77	(1.1)	Baa3
7.	Security Pacific	73	46	.0	NA
8.	Bankers Trust	57	45	.0	A1
9.	First Interstate	51	46	(.6)	NA
10.	First Chicago	44	40	(.6)	A3

*Moody's ratings.
Source: American Banker, March 29, 1985 and March 29, 1988.

Concern about the health of these large banks severely impacted their credit ratings. In the late 1970s, they were all triple-A credit banks, but in 1987, only J.P. Morgan had even a double-A rating. BankAmerica, Chase Manhattan, Chemical and Manufacturers Hanover were B-rated, which was just above junk bond status.

The LDC problem greatly slowed the growth of these banks. Between 1984 and 1987, BankAmerica and Manufacturers Hanover had their asset size decline, and Chase Manhattan, J.P. Morgan, Bankers Trust, First Interstate and First Chicago had only modest gains.

Citicorp went against the slow growth trend with a $53 billion asset gain during these three years, some of which came from its multiple thrift purchases. This made it more than twice as big as the second largest bank, Chase Manhattan, but it was not a sign of good things to come as Citicorp would be only slightly larger in 1990; still losing money; and would drop out of the world's twenty largest banks as measured by assets. Ten years earlier, it was one-two with BankAmerica in the world rankings.

With these problems, the ability of the money center banks to play a major role in the early years of interstate banking would have been severely limited even if they had been included in the regional compacts, and they were not alone on the sidelines. The LDC crisis coincided with, and was aggravated by, the sharp decline in oil prices that devastated the big Texas banks. As a result, the money center banks were forced to watch smaller regional banks close the size gap. The Texas banks did not even last long enough to watch.

Even with their problems, size alone allowed some New York and California banks to participate in interstate expansion in areas other than New England and the Southeast, but they were limited to rescuing seriously troubled or failed banks and thrifts. In 1982, BankAmerica crossed state lines to buy a failed SeaFirst in Seattle under the "emergency rules" that permitted interstate acquisitions if there were no in-state buyers; Citicorp bought failed thrifts in three different states and the District of Columbia in 1982 and 1984; and, in 1987, Chemical rescued a near failing Texas Commerce. When a buyer was desperately needed, the regulators would look the other way if there were no better alternatives, but healthy banks were usually not interested in selling to a bank with poor bond ratings.

MIDWEST REACTION

The leading Midwest banks, except First Chicago and Continental, were not hobbled by the LDC crisis, but they were latecomers to interstate banking. In a region where many states had not removed the barriers to statewide branching, enthusiasm over interstate banking was generally quite low.

By 1987, though, the most easterly of the Midwest states—Ohio, Indiana, Michigan and Wisconsin—had passed reciprocal interstate banking laws that had no regional restrictions. This meant that banks in these states could merge with one another and with banks in Kentucky to the immediate south of Ohio and Indiana, which by then had joined the interstate banking parade. In 1988, an adjoining state, Pennsylvania, would opt-in to interstate banking leaving Illinois as the only major holdout among large states in the Midwest or geographically close to the Midwest.

This was about a two-year delay in interstate banking in the eastern part of the Midwest relative to New England and the Southeast, and since it did not include all of the Midwest, the regional impact in the initial years was far less than in those other regions. The different starting dates for interstate banking for the states within the Midwest shifted the balance of power in favor of the banks in states like Ohio and Michigan, vis-à-vis banks in states further west, particularly Illinois and Minnesota.

The Midwest banks quickest to take advantage of interstate banking were Bank One and National City in Ohio. Bank One acquired one of the biggest banks in Indiana, American Fletcher, in 1987. A year later, it bought one of Wisconsin's largest banks, Marine. In so doing, it increased its assets from $13 billion in 1986 to $25 billion in 1988 and moved from seventh to third in asset size in the Midwest. National City did not improve its area ranking immediately, but its acquisition of First Kentucky, the biggest bank in Kentucky, was the major reason its assets went from $14 to almost $22 billion during this period. This gave National City near parity in size with all of the leading Midwest banks except First Chicago.

Largest Midwest Banks, 1988

	Bank	Assets		Rank 1986	Eventual Owner
		1988	1986		
		(in billions)			
1.	First Chicago	$44	$39	1	JPMorgan
2.	Continental	31	33	2	Bank of America
3.	Bank One	25	13	7	JPMorgan
4.	First Bank System	24	21	3	U.S. Bancorp
5.	NBD	24	21	5	JPMorgan
6.	Norwest	22	22	4	Wells Fargo
7.	National City	22	14	6	PNC
8.	Boatmen's	15	10	11	Bank of America
9.	Harris	11	10	9	Bank of Montreal
10.	Comerica	11	10	10	Comerica

Source: American Banker, April 16, 1987 and April 11, 1990.

Even with only modest growth, First Chicago was still much larger than other Midwest banks in 1988. Its $44 billion assets were about 45 percent more than any other bank in the region despite being in a state that still prohibited branching and interstate banking.

Its cross-town rival, Continental, and the Minnesota banks were not as fortunate and lost some of their edge in the immediate years after interstate banking was allowed. Continental, which had its customer "confidence" problem after being bailed-out by the FDIC, as well as unfriendly Illinois banking laws, had it assets fall by about $2 billion. It was still number two in the region in assets in 1988, but within two years, it would be passed by Bank One and Norwest and be only slightly ahead of Detroit's NBD. First Bank System, with an unusually large asset decline between 1986 and 1988 that would continue into 1990, fell from third to fourth place and would eventually slide all the way to seventh before reversing its momentum.

More important than the individual bank performance in the Midwest, relative to consolidation, was that in this large geographic area there were only seven banks in 1988 with assets over $15 billion. This included the two banks in Chicago that were still constrained in their growth by state laws. This slowed consolidation in the Midwest in comparison to the Southeast and New England, and regionally it stacked the deck in favor of Ohio and Michigan banks, particularly Bank One, NBD and National City. Not much later, though, the economic problems in other parts of the country in the post-1989 era eventually would work to the advantage of Midwest banks relative to comparative growth, and particularly favor those banks in the states with an interstate banking head start.

MIDDLE ATLANTIC DILEMMA

Caught in a "no man's land" in interstate banking were banks in New Jersey and Pennsylvania. These states were slower than other East Coast states to enact interstate banking legislation, primarily because they did not fit geographically into either the Southeast or New England regional banking compacts, and for these two states to accept interstate banking would be an open invitation to New York dominance of their local banking. Using the "contiguous state" wording to limit the interstate banking geographic area did not accomplish anything since New York was a contiguous state. The big New York City banks may have been limited in what they could do in the mid-1980s because of the LDC loans, but that did not lessen the fear in nearby states of a New York takeover if interstate banking was allowed.

Nevertheless, Pennsylvania and New Jersey had interstate legislation on their books by 1987. This included New York, but except for a couple of mid-sized acquisitions by Chemical in New Jersey, the New York banks, troubled by LDC loans, stayed home.

Largest Middle Atlantic Banks, 1988

		Assets		Rank	Eventual
	Bank	1989	1986	1986	Owner
		(in billions)			
1.	PNC	$41	$22	2	PNC
2.	Mellon	31	34	1	Mellon*
3.	First Fidelity	30	15	3	Wells Fargo
4.	Midlantic	20	12	5	PNC
5.	CoreStates	16	15	4	Wells Fargo

*Sold all retail branches to Royal Bank of Scotland.
Source: American Banker, April 16, 1987 and April 11, 1990.

The only Pennsylvania bank that took advantage of the introduction of interstate banking in the late 1980s was Pittsburgh's PNC. It used proximity to the Midwest to move into Kentucky and Ohio in 1987 and 1988. This lifted its assets from $22 billion in 1986 to almost $41 billion in 1988, which made PNC, by far, the biggest bank in Pennsylvania. It was also much larger than any bank in the Midwest except First Chicago, and for PNC with its Pittsburgh base, the Midwest was as natural an expansion area as eastern Pennsylvania and New Jersey from a geographic perspective.

Starting from a smaller base, two New Jersey banks, First Fidelity and Midlantic, used interstate acquisitions to improve their regional status. First Fidelity's acquisition of one of Philadelphia's largest bank holding companies, Fidelcor, helped to almost double its assets from just over $15 billion in 1986 to almost $30 billion in 1988. Midlantic, with a series of smaller mergers, had a similar percentage increase going from nearly $12 billion to almost $20 billion with much of the increase coming from the acquisition of four Upstate New York banks from Bank of New York.

Sitting on the sidelines in the early years of interstate banking were the largest banks in Pittsburgh and Philadelphia, Mellon and CoreStates. Mellon, which was in a battle for survival with an overdose of LDC loans, saw cross-town rival PNC, not only go past it in size, but leave it far behind as Mellon's assets fell by $3 billion between 1986 and 1988. CoreStates also lost ground between 1986 and 1988, but it would make up for lost time in 1990 with the in-market purchase of First Pennsylvania. The latter had not recovered from its problems in the 1970s that led to its bailout by the FDIC.

THE WEST

Interstate banking in the western part of the country had little in the way of resistance and, in fact, had become a necessity in parts of the region because of the oil patch problems. As noted earlier, BankAmerica had acquired the biggest bank in Washington, SeaFirst, in 1982 under "emergency" conditions after the latter's overdose of Penn Square's oil-and-gas loans, and Texas had no choice but to endorse the concept to facilitate exits for its largest banks when its economy collapsed in 1986. First Interstate was already in many western states as a result of its "grandfathered" status when it was spun off from A. P. Giannini's Transamerica in 1958.

The openness of the West to interstate banking worked primarily to the benefit of banks in California after the biggest Texas banks had been eliminated. BankAmerica had made its move into Washington before stumbling; First Interstate was among the out-of-state acquirers of the failed or failing Texas bank leaders; and Security Pacific had bought the second largest bank in Washington, Rainier Bancorporation.

The original Wells Fargo stayed home, but it was by no means silent. It greatly increased its size in the 1980s with the purchase of a struggling cross-town rival, Crocker National, which in 1980 had been the nation's 13th biggest bank.

Largest Western Banks, 1988*

		Assets		National Rank	Eventual Owner
	Bank	1988	1984	Rank	
		(in billions)			
1.	BankAmerica	$95	$104	3	Bank of America
2.	Security Pacific	78	63	5	Bank of America
3.	First Interstate	58	56	9	Wells Fargo
4.	Wells Fargo	47	45	12	Wells Fargo
5.	Valley National (AZ)	12	11	57	JPMorgan

* Includes Southwest and Rocky Mountain states.
Source: American Banker, March 29, 1985 and April 11, 1990.

In fact, as the 1980s were coming to a close, it was not a stretch to think of the largest California banks as future leaders internationally as well as nationally, notwithstanding BankAmerica's problems. These were the years when Japan was riding high, and being located on the Pacific Rim was considered to be a stroke of good fortune. First Interstate, Wells Fargo, Security Pacific and a recovering BankAmerica stood to be the beneficiaries. At the end of 1988, they were the third, fifth, eighth and eleventh largest banks in the country. The next largest bank in the West was Valley National in Phoenix, and it had assets of a little under $12 billion and was not among the forty largest banks nationwide.

Unfortunately, neither the Japanese nor the West Coast economies were able to maintain their momentum into the 1990s, and, in fact, both went into reverse. As a result, a California banking collapse, and not a national bank ascendancy, became the big banking story out of the West in the early 1990s and a major contributor to the consolidation process—a story told in a later chapter.

GOING NATIONAL

This seemingly imminent interstate potential of the big California banks in the late 1980s and the rise of superregionals in the Southeast, New England and parts of the Midwest had created a banking environment far different from what had existed in 1980. Less than five years after the 1985 Supreme Court approval of the regional compacts that took interstate banking beyond emergency situations, most states had either accepted national interstate banking or were about to do so.

As the 1990s began, the stage had been set for American banks to follow the course of industries that had not been segmented by artificial barriers. Interstate banking's impact on consolidation, though, would be muted from 1989 through 1992 because of the most serious crisis banking had faced since the Great Depression. Banks and thrifts had been far too eager to lend to developers, and the result was a crash in real estate values, particularly commercial real estate, with disastrous results throughout much of the country.

Many of the problems that were to come, however, had their roots in the thrift crisis and the regulatory response to the massive thrift losses of the early 1980s. It is easy to say that banks and thrifts had been far too eager to lend to developers, but the thrifts were encouraged to do so by the regulators and, in many cases, banks were either responding in order to remain competitive or were just swept up in the real estate hysteria of the late 1980s. As the 1980s progressed, the thrift crisis, interstate banking and the regulatory response would be increasingly interrelated.

THRIFT CRISIS: CHANGING THE LANDSCAPE

By the time interstate banking had moved into its national phase, the thrift crisis had entered its second stage, and a very painful second stage it was to be. In this stage, the focus moves almost entirely to S&Ls as the number of insolvent S&Ls ratcheted upward dramatically, particularly in the Southwest. By 1987, the FSLIC had exhausted all of its reserves, and in 1989, the situation would deteriorate to the point that legislation was passed that eliminated FSLIC; shifted the insuring of S&L deposits to the FDIC; and took S&L regulation away from the Bank Board and placed it in a new agency, the Office of Thrift Supervision, or OTS, that would report to the Treasury Department.

Savings banks also struggled in the late 1980s, but most remained viable until at least 1989 when real estate values in the Northeast, particularly commercial real estate, declined as a result of overbuilding and a softening of the national economy. By then, it was difficult to sort out just what was a continuation of the 1980's thrift crisis or part of a new, and in many ways even more devastating, banking problem when measured by the number of both bank and thrift failures.

What happened to undo the post-1982 progress seemingly made by thrifts? For a while, it looked like the gamble the regulators and legislators had taken in trying to prop up the S&L industry with phony accounting, relaxed capital standards and diversification had succeeded. In 1983 and 1984, the "Band-Aids" seemed to be working, as most S&Ls were profitable, busy diversifying assets and raising capital. It was a high-risk period, but a couple of years of profitability and the willingness of investors to literally throw money at thrifts through stock conversions created a false sense of optimism.

For the regulatory and legislative gamble to work, though, three things had to happen. Interest rates had to go down sharply, and stay down; there had to be an extended period of economic stability; and thrifts had to avoid the temptation to abuse the relaxed supervision and capital standards. This was asking a lot, but at least there was a sharp drop in interest rates between 1981 and 1986 with only modest increases in the next couple of years. If lower interest rates were all that was needed, then the gamble might have worked.

An extended period of economic stability was a lot to expect after the turbulence of the 1970s. Optimists could dream about the years after World War II through the mid-1960s, and even all the way to 1972, as to what was possible, but that was a different era. The collapse of the economy in Texas and other oil patch states in 1986 would put an end to those dreams.

As to the good behavior on the part of S&Ls, there were too many of them and too much temptation in a go-go era for there to be little in the way of corporate malfeasance. Most S&Ls and savings banks made a sincere effort to adjust to a changed environment without going across the line, and some of those that did were doing so at the urging of the regulators. The introduction of stock ownership brought with it incentives to take advantage of the relaxed supervision and the low cost of buying S&Ls for personal gain. The result was too many rogue thrifts that made a bad situation even worse and contributed to giving S&Ls, in general, a bad name.

Thus, in 1983 and 1984 whatever optimism there was about limiting the damage to the thrift industry would prove to be false. The first sign of this came in March 1985. A "run" on the Home State Savings in Cincinnati occurred, followed shortly by a run on Baltimore's Old Court Savings & Loan. They were state-insured thrifts, but their actions and the effect on their state insurance funds were precursors of what would happen nationally a year later.

HOME STATE AND OLD COURT

Home State Savings was not the first S&L closed in the 1980s, nor even the first one since 1983, but it holds a special place in the annals of the thrift crisis. Prospects, as noted above, were looking better for thrifts as interest rates declined, profits returned and investors re-capitalized almost any sizeable thrift that was willing to convert from a mutual to a stock form of organization. Then, in March 1985, came the Home State fiasco.

The $1.4 billion Home State was the largest S&L in a state-insured banking system, and, as such, it took down the entire Ohio deposit insurance fund with it.

To make matters worse, its failure was preceded by a highly publicized depositors' run that was based on fraudulent behavior. Its owner, Marvin Warner, and nine others connected with Home State went to jail as the result of its failure.[1]

Home State's collapse was caused by its investments, not by bad loans or a margin-overhead mismatch. The trigger was the failure of ESM Government Securities, Inc., a firm with a long-time, close relationship with Home State. The Florida-based ESM was deeply in debt, a fact it had been hiding with misleading reports, and in March 1985, it was closed after being charged with fraud. When it was revealed that Home State was a big holder of ESM bonds, its depositors rushed to get their money. After a deposit withdrawal of $150 million, which was twice the amount of the reserves of the Ohio deposit insurance fund, the state had no choice but to step in and close it.[2]

This, unfortunately, was not the end, though, as deposit runs began at five other Ohio-insured S&Ls, and nine days after Home State failed, the governor of Ohio felt compelled to call a "thrift holiday" on March 15 and closed all state-insured thrifts for a day. On the following Monday, the dollar fell relative to other currencies and the value of gold rose $50 in a day, which made Home State more than just a local problem.[3]

The only good news in the Home State story is that recoveries made by the state repaid the initial cost of the bailout that was about $130 million. The recovery process, though, took more than fifteen years to complete.[4]

Two months later, the Home State story was rerun in Maryland as another state-insured S&L, Old Court Savings & Loan in Baltimore, started down the same path. As early as 1978, its owner, Jeffrey Levitt, had been accused of diverting funds for his own use, but again the triggering event for its demise was not a direct theft of funds, but rather the failure of a bond seller. When news of the negative impact of the Old Court's bond losses became known in May 1985, as with Home State, a run on deposits began that spread from Old Court to other Maryland-insured S&Ls, and it nearly caused a collapse of the Maryland deposit insurance fund. It was almost two years before Old Court's depositors got all of their money back.[5]

Old Court was the second widely publicized case in 1985 of management misdeeds at an S&L. Besides investing badly, Levitt was also convicted of stealing $14.7 million of Old Court's depositors' money, and spent seven years in prison.[6]

Problems at just two S&Ls were enough to bankrupt the state deposit insurance funds, and put 121 state-insured S&Ls in Maryland and 71 more in Ohio at risk. Most of Ohio's and Maryland's state-insured S&Ls survived and qualified for federal deposit insurance, but these crises exposed the potential for problems elsewhere. Home State and Old Court were the public's first exposure to thrifts playing fast and loose with depositor money, but they were far from the last.

At the time, though, the statewide thrift crises in Maryland and Ohio were generally dismissed as special situations that occurred only because they did not have the weight of the federal government behind them. Many on the inside knew better, but they were still hoping for the best.

POST-1985 SLIDE

However, the "best" was not to be, and with the collapse in 1985 and 1986 of the economy in Texas and other oil patch states, any hopes of a "soft landing" disappeared. Nationally, S&L profits fell from $3.7 billion to a little more than breakeven in 1986, and the S&Ls that failed in 1986 were large enough to wipe out all existing FSLIC reserves. Two years later, the FSLIC's reserve deficiency had reached $75 billion.

S&L Decline, 1985 to 1989

	No. of S&Ls*	Net Income	Assets of Failed Thrifts	FSLIC Reserves
			(In billions)	
1989	2,878	$(18)	-	-
1988	2,949	(13)	$143	$(75)
1987	3,147	(8)	21	(14)
1986	3,220	0	16	(6)
1985	3,246	4	6	5

*FSLIC-insured only.
Source: *History of the Eighties–Lessons for the Future*, FDIC.

The number of S&Ls began to decline, including even those kept open under government receivership, and the assets of failed thrifts were rising rapidly. From 1985 to the end of 1989, the number of FSLIC-insured S&Ls fell from 3,246 to 2,878, and in 1988, assets of failed S&Ls had reached $143 billion. These were not good times for S&Ls or those who regulated and insured them.

FIRREA

By 1989, the S&L portion of the thrift crisis had reached such a serious state that a radical restructuring of the industry and its oversight was needed resulting in the passage of Financial Institutions Reform, Recovery and Enforcement Act, or FIRREA, in February of that year. This legislation shifted the supervision of S&Ls from the Bank Board to the OTS that would report to the Treasury

Department, which also had authority over national banks. FIRREA abolished the S&L insurance fund, FSLIC, as well and replaced it with the FDIC-administered Savings Association Insurance Fund, and created the Resolution Trust Company, or RTC, under the management of the FDIC to handle insolvent S&Ls. FIRREA also imposed stricter accounting, capital and lending standards.

FIRREA was the end of the long-time autonomy of the S&Ls. Their supervision and deposit insurance had been placed under the same federal authorities that handled banks, which made inter-industry mergers inevitable even for healthy thrifts. FIRREA required thrift capital, loans and investments to meet the much stricter bank requirements, which immediately reduced the survivability potential of many S&Ls, including some of the largest, and it sped up the closing of failed thrifts.

REGIONAL PROGRESSION

Despite the dire circumstances of the FSLIC in 1988 and 1989, the second stage of the thrift crisis had not reached all parts of the country even though the overreaching and inadequate capital was fairly universal within the industry. In the Ohio and Maryland mini-crises, the state-insured coverage was such that the misdeeds of a couple thrifts could take down the local thrift insurance funds, but the panic had not spread to the federally-insured thrifts in those states. In most states, Texas being an exception, it took a sharp downturn of the local commercial real estate market in the late 1980s to push the local thrift industry over the edge.

Selected States Thrift Industry Income, 1984 to 1992

	Texas	Florida	Pennsylvania	New York	California
	(In billions)				
1992	$.7	$.3	$.3	$.8	$.6
1991	.2	.1	.1	(.7)	.3
1990	.1	(.4)	(.2)	(.6)	(1.1)
1989	(.5)	(.7)	(.5)	(1.4)	(.7)
1988	(4.4)	(.4)	(.2)	.7	.7
1987	(7.1)	(.1)	.2	1.3	.1
1986	(3.2)	.1	.3	1.5	1.0
1985	.5	.2	.3	.8	1.3
1984	.3	.0	.1	(.2)	(.1)

Source: FDIC: Historical Statistics on Banking.

Thrifts in the other big states had problems as well, but they generally trailed Texas by two to three years in maximum impact. The Florida thrifts would have a dip in earnings in 1986, but their peak loss year was 1989. In Pennsylvania, the thrift losses would start in 1988 and peak in 1989. The California and New York thrifts generally remained profitable until 1989 when those states also began to suffer from overbuilt real estate markets.

TEXAS S&L DEBACLE

The catalyst for FIRREA, the legislation that was intended to bring closure to the S&L portion of the thrift crisis, was Texas. Its S&Ls carried to an extreme the "grow and diversify" mantra preached by regulators and, collectively, lifted assets from $35 billion in 1980 to $111 billion in 1988. Texas was not only first out of the gate in the second stage of the crisis with large losses and widespread failures, but its S&L losses, alone, were enough to bankrupt the FSLIC. These S&Ls were part of the go-go attitude of the state that accompanied the oil boom of the 1970s and early 1980s, and when that boom ended and the economy collapsed, like the Texas banks, the state's S&Ls were stuck with overwhelming amounts of bad loans.

Texas S&L Decline, 1985 to 1991

	No. of S&LS	Assets	Net Income	Equity Capital	Noncurrent Loans
		(In billions)			
1991	68	$49	$.2	$2.4	$.3
1990	80	59	.1	2.1	.3
1989	116	69	(.5)	1.4	7.3
1988	205	111	(4.4)	(4.1)	10.7
1987	279	99	(7.1)	(7.8)	14.0
1986	281	96	(3.2)	(1.0)	11.3
1985	273	91	.5	3.0	3.7

Source: FDIC: Historical Statistics on Banking.

By the end of 1986, Texas noncurrent S&L loans were $11.3 billion, and a year later, they were $14 billion. This resulted in a collective loss of about $15 billion from 1986 through 1989, and in 1987, the total capital of all Texas S&Ls was a negative $7.8 billion. By year-end 1987, Texas S&Ls accounted for 62 percent of all S&L losses nationwide, and it was not surprising that the number of S&Ls in the state would fall from 281 in 1986 to 68 in 1991.[7]

Also helping to make Texas the centerpiece of a controversial second round of phony accounting was the 1988 Southwest Plan. This was an effort by an already bankrupt FSLIC to conserve its cash by consolidating failed thrifts into clusters, and then selling them with capital notes, future loss coverage guarantees and tax credits. This was a rushed rescue project because the law that allowed S&L losses to offset other taxable gains, which was the key attraction to buyers, was to expire at the end of that year.

By being the first state to have widespread S&L failures and the focus of the Southwest Plan, Texas became forever linked with the worst abuses of the thrift or S&L crisis, which was somewhat unfair. The popular books written about the crisis at the time put a lot of emphasis on how the Texas S&Ls had robbed the taxpayers, but those who argued that what happened to the S&Ls in 1986 was no different than the simultaneous collapse of the Texas banks were not wrong. The Texas S&L failures were part of the oil patch meltdown, but these S&Ls had more than their fair share of shady characters and many were not from Texas.

With the oil patch economy still booming in the 1980 to 1982 period, Texas S&Ls actually had come through the first part of the thrift crisis in better condition than thrifts elsewhere and believed, like the banks, that there was no stopping the Texas economy. Their subsequent rapid growth was facilitated by the relaxed capital and lending standards, but those growing rapidly did not expect to fail, and most of their owners took large personal losses when an S&L did fail. There were exotic investments that make good reading and look bad in retrospect, but what brought the Texas S&Ls down was the same decision that hurt the local banks—lending on commercial real estate in Dallas, Houston and other large Texas cities.

Something else different about the S&Ls in Texas that contributed to their spectacular growth from 1982 to 1985 and their equally spectacular fall after 1985, was that so many of its thrifts were already stock organizations in 1980, including most of the large ones. Thus, when rules were relaxed relative to capital required and acquiring new capital, many Texas S&Ls did not have to convert from mutual to stock in a process that required regulatory oversight and kept individuals from gaining control. These S&Ls were ready for immediate sale, and, unfortunately, their buyers included some of the more notorious corporate raiders of the day using the junk bond financing of Michael Milken of Drexel Burnham & Lambert.

GIBRALTAR

Gibraltar Savings, the largest thrift in Texas with about $3.3 billion assets in 1980, was typical of what happened and why there were so many bad headlines. It was a stock thrift before the S&L crisis began, and, in the early 1980s was acquired by Saul Steinberg, a well-known corporate raider and long-time beneficiary of the Michael Milken-Drexel Burnham junk bond financing.[8]

Steinberg was one of many characters involved in Texas S&Ls that liked the headlines. He was a big-time art collector and spender, and a Liz Smith *New York Magazine* column in 1989 lends flavor to his life and the times. She describes a party Steinberg's wife threw for his 50th birthday for which it "was reported that she spent her own money (estimated at from $250,000 to $1 million) to impress her husband and some 250 guests." She went on to note that "the Steinberg beach house overlooking the Atlantic rocked and rolled with hundreds of flickering terra cotta pots, identical twins posing as mermaids in the pool, dancers in seventeenth century garb, heralds and banner wavers.... He [Steinberg] joked that his wife had done a lot for the economy and 'anyone who is talking about recession—well, forget it!'"[9] This was in 1989 when concerns over the cost of the thrift crisis were at their peak.

Steinberg, though, had been smart enough to sell Gibraltar in 1984 to a holding company that controlled the state's third largest thrift, First Texas. He and the other owners of Gibraltar were allowed to take out $268 million in cash as part of the sale.[10] This was not the only source of wealth that made his 1989 birthday party possible, nor was Gibraltar the investment most associated with him—that would be Reliance Insurance—but this was the type of story that added so much to the luster of the Texas portion of the S&L crisis. As was so frequently the case, the person adding the luster, Steinberg, was not from Texas.

After the sale to the holding company, Gibraltar and First Texas were operated separately, but by 1988, both had failed. At that time, Gibraltar, First Texas and a few other insolvent thrifts, in the words of Martin Mayer in his book, *Greatest-Ever Bank Robbery*, "were stitched into one $12 billion S&L by the FSLIC in 1988 [part of the Southwest Plan] and sold to Milken's friend Ron Perelman of Revlon [for $315 million]. To make the deal satisfactory to Perelman, the FSLIC had to provide a subsidy that has been estimated as high as $5 billion, some of it in the form of notes guaranteeing as much as ten years of high return on loans that were actually in default, some of it in the form of tax credits." Mayer went on to say that "for $315 million (of which $240 million was borrowed) ... he [Perelman] got tax deductions valued at $897.3 million. For calendar 1989, Perelman's new First

Gibraltar reported payments from the government of $461 million and net profits to Perelman [all tax-free] of $129 million."[11] In 1993, Perelman sold First Gibraltar to BankAmerica for $110 million.

Perelman, another New Yorker dabbling in Texas S&Ls, was colorful and seemed to enjoy publicity as much as Steinberg did. His bald head, ever-present cigar and the beautiful women at his side, four of whom he married, were frequently on display in the society pages including this billionaire's ex-wife, the actress Ellen Barkin.

The notoriety of—and financial gains by—investors like Steinberg and Perelman gained more attention as the cost of resolving the S&L crisis rose, which added to the public concern. The cost, excluding interest payments, of the failures of Gibraltar and First Texas was $5.4 billion. Add in Vernon S&L, which was also in the Southwest Plan's First Gibraltar package, and the cost goes up to $6.4 billion.[12]

The stories of a couple of others among the five largest Texas S&Ls, University Savings and Sunbelt, only vary from those of Gibraltar and First Texas in that they did not merge with another large S&L prior to their 1987 or 1988 failure. They were put into RTC receivership, and then sold by the RTC—University as branches to NCNB and SunBelt to BankAmerica. The total pre-interest cost of resolution was $3.8 billion for SunBelt and $2.5 billion for University.[13]

The differences between the failures of the large oil patch S&Ls and those of the big Texas banks were more in how they were handled by their regulators than the actual monetary cost to the insurance funds. The FDIC moved a lot quicker, but its cost of selling First Republic to NCNB and M-Corp to Bank One was a hefty $5.6 billion. From a consolidation perspective, the end result was similar, with Gibraltar, First Texas, Sunbelt, University Savings and First Republic all ending up as part of Bank of America.

BEYOND TEXAS

Texas accounted for 14 of the 25 largest RTC bailouts, but it was far from alone in costing the taxpayers billions of dollars. California had four of the 25 largest RTC bailouts, including the most expensive, American Savings and Loan in Stockton, which had a resolution cost of $5.7 billion, as well as one the most famous of the S&L failures, Lincoln Savings and Loan. Lincoln was owned primarily by Charles Keating, and it gained particular notoriety when the names of five U.S. senators, including John McCain and John Glenn, were bandied about as having possibly provided assistance in keeping the regulators at bay. They became known as the Keating Five, but it appeared that they did little more than make the normal inquiries that congressional representatives make on behalf of constituents.

Among the other states, Arizona had two of the 25 costliest S&L bailouts; and New Jersey, Arkansas, New York, Louisiana, Colorado and Florida had one each. The Arkansas S&L was not Madison Guaranty of Whitewater fame, but the one that failed in Colorado was Silverado whose board included Neil Bush, son of the first George Bush, who was president at the time. The cost of closing and selling Silverado was estimated to be $1.3 billion.

New York's contribution to the list, Buffalo-based Empire FSB, is of particular interest in that it started as a mutual savings bank, and then after going public and being allowed to buy two failed savings banks, Empire switched to what it considered a more favorable S&L charter. As an S&L, it was closed by the RTC and sold to various buyers at a cost of about $1.6 billion.

WINDING DOWN

The passage of FIRREA in early 1989 marked the beginning of the end of a thrift crisis distinct from an overall banking problem. The RTC would be selling failed S&Ls and S&L assets for several more years, but by the end of 1991, the extent of the damage was measurable. The damage that was done, and in terms of money and what it did to the S&L industry, it was mind-boggling.

From 1981 through 1991, the FSLIC and the RTC sold 891 S&Ls with federal assistance and closed another 242. This was 1,133 failed S&Ls with combined assets of $463 billion, and at the end of 1991, the RTC still had 46 S&Ls in receivership with assets of $15.2 billion. This was almost one-third of the total number of thrifts that existed in 1980, and more than three-fourths of 1980 S&L assets.

The assisted mergers and closings per year from 1981 through 1989, see table on page 123, showed just how the regulators had delayed solving the problem before the economic collapse in the oil patch turned a serious situation into a crisis. From 1981 through 1985, there were just 27 S&Ls closed and 141 merged with federal assistance. This was not a lot of closings and assisted-mergers compared to what was coming. The assets involved were not much more than 10 percent of what would eventually be sold or closed by FSLIC and the RTC.

By 1987, it was obvious that the "Band-Aids" had not solved the problem and the economic collapse in the Southwest had become a major complication, but the FSLIC did have the funds to deal with the situation. In 1986 and 1987, the S&Ls closed or merged with federal assistance were still a relatively modest 127 with combined assets of $37 billion.

S&L Assisted Mergers and Closings, 1981 to 1991

	Assisted Mergers	Closings	Total	Assets Involved (In billions)
1991	153	78	231	$89
1990	246	68	314	113
1989	54	6	60	31
1988	207	26	233	143
1987	56	17	73	22
1986	34	20	54	16
1985	22	10	32	6
1984	17	9	26	6
1983	33	6	39	17
1982	46	1	47	20
1981	23	1	24	N/A
Total	891*	242	1,133	$463

* Did not include 46 S&Ls still in RTC receivership with assets of $15.2 billion as of December 31, 1991.
Source: Sheshunoff S&L Quarterly, December 1986 and 1991.

Going slow ended in 1988, but with the FSLIC still short of funds, it had to find methods other than closing an insolvent thrift, and the next attempt to delay the inevitable was to use federally-assisted mergers with notes, margin guarantees and tax benefits–the infamous Southwest Plan. This was once again pushing the problem into the future, but the FSLIC managed to sell off 207 S&Ls holding total assets of about $140 million with a minimal immediate cash outlay. There were 26 S&Ls closed in 1988, but these were mostly small and had combined assets of only a little over $3 billion.

In 1989, FIRREA and a well-funded RTC replaced the FSLIC, but it took time for the RTC to become fully functional. As a result, it was a year of insolvent S&Ls being taken over by the RTC, but not many were closed or sold. There were only 60 S&Ls with total assets of about $31 billion that were put out of their misery in 1989.

In 1990 and 1991, the RTC was fully operative, and it sold or closed 545 S&Ls with assets of more than $200 million. The primary type of assistance was the RTC keeping the bad assets, and by 1992, it had moved from being the manager of troubled S&Ls to being a manager of troubled assets.

The cost of the S&L portion of the thrift crisis has been estimated to be anywhere from $200 billion to more than $300 billion, with the difference between the high and low estimates normally being the interest paid on the initial cost. It is likely that the direct cost was over $200 billion, but that does not begin to cover the cost of the problems created by S&Ls and savings banks liberally supplying developers with funds to build offices, malls and hotels that were not needed. This led to large real estate losses for banks, thrifts and investors that put the country into an economic downturn that lasted from 1989 to 1992. Thus, while it is impossible to measure definitively the real cost of the thrift crisis, $300 billion is a modest estimate.

The savings banks contributed to the overbuilding in the late 1980s, but with almost all of them being in the Northeast, there were few savings bank failures between 1983 and 1990. Syracuse Savings was the only one with assets in excess of $1 billion to be closed and sold by the FDIC during this period.

RTC Sales

With FSLIC replaced by the FDIC and the RTC in 1989, all constraints about selling failed S&Ls to commercial banks disappeared, and in the massive sell-off in 1990 and 1991, banks were the primary buyers. As a result, a large part of what was once an independent S&L industry was taken-over by acquisition by banks, and much of it went to BankAmerica and the superregionals.

BankAmerica, which had survived its LDC loan problems and moved away from its flirtation with money center bank activities, was the most aggressive acquirer of failed S&Ls. It bought nine, large failed S&Ls with collective assets at the time of assumption of $32 billion. This understates its total gain from RTC sales as it acquired Security Pacific and First Gibraltar in 1992 that between them had bought five failed S&Ls with combined assets of about $22 billion. Total assets bought from the RTC, direct and indirect, was about $53 billion.

Bank One, NCNB, First Union and Meridian in Pennsylvania were other bank buyers of multiple large S&Ls from the RTC. Each had S&L asset purchases in excess of $5 billion.

The most active S&L on the buyer's side of the RTC sales was Great Western, one of several big California S&Ls that came through the thrift crisis in relatively good shape. It bought five S&Ls from the RTC with combined assets of $20 billion. Other large S&Ls on the buyer's side were Texas-based Bank United with four purchases with combined assets of $7 billion, and a California holding company, H.F. Ahmanson, with three large acquisitions that had combined assets of almost $5 billion.

Large RTC S&L Sales*

Acquirer	No. of Transactions	Assets (in bill.)	Eventual Owner
Banks			
BankAmerica	9**	$32	Bank of America
Security Pacific	3	18	Bank of America
Bank One	3	8	JPMorgan
NCNB	2	6	Bank of America
First Union	2	6	Wells Fargo
Meridian	3	5	Wells Fargo
Thrifts			
Great Western	5	$20	JPMorgan
Bank United	4	7	JPMorgan
H.F Ahmanson	3	5	JPMorgan
First Gibraltar	2	4	Bank of America
Sunbelt Savings	2	2	Bank of America

*Assets at time of assumption over $500 million.
**Includes Sunbelt Savings.
Source: SNL Financial, Charlottesville, Virginia.

The eventual big winners from the RTC sales were Bank of America and JPMorgan. Among the deals in which buyers of S&Ls added total assets of $2 billion or more from purchasing S&Ls with assets in excess of $500 million, about $62 billion is part of Bank of America's franchise and almost $42 billion is in the JPMorgan network. Wells Fargo is a distant third with $13 billion of such RTC assets finding their way into its hands.

That Bank of America and JPMorgan ended up with more RTC sales than the other big banks was at least partially because of location. Bank of America's two main components, BankAmerica and NCNB, and Washington Mutual and Bank One, which were bought by JPMorgan, had much stronger interests than other buyers at the time in the areas where the largest failed thrifts were—Texas and California.

SUMMARY

The impact of the thrift crisis on consolidation had as much to do with how it changed the banking landscape, as the increased size provided by the thrift assets acquired by big commercial banks, directly or indirectly. From a consolidation perspective, what the thrift crisis had done beyond these acquisitions was:

- Help pave the way for interstate banking, primarily through the impact of Citicorp's early 1980 acquisitions;

- Reverse the upward momentum of thrifts;

- Bring on the consolidation of the regulatory and insurance agencies of both thrifts and banks under the Treasury Department and the FDIC to create a more unified banking industry; and

- Create more expansion opportunities for superregionals than for the once dominant money center banks.

The FDIC's *History of the Eighties—Lessons for the Future*, which is good reading for anyone who wants an objective and detailed view of the bank and thrift problems of the eighties, summed up the second stage of the thrift crisis, or S&L crisis as the FDIC preferred to call it, in a thoughtful and concise two paragraphs:

"The S&L crisis overlapped several regional banking crises in the 1980s and at first was similar to the crisis involving mutual savings banks (MSBs). However, in contrast to the FSLIC, the FDIC had both the money to close failing MSBs and the regulatory will to put others on a tight leash, while allowing some forbearance in the form of the Net Worth Certificate Program. To be sure, some MSBs later got into trouble with poor investments and failed, but the cost of those failures pales in comparison with the costs of the failures in the S&L industry, which was encouraged to grow and engage in risky activities with little supervision. When the Bank Board realized that its strategies had failed, it attempted to correct the problems through regulation. In contrast, federal bank regulators used supervisory tools and enforcement actions to limit growth and raise capital levels at commercial banks and mutual savings banks. However, both banks and S&Ls, and their regulators, got caught up in boom-to-bust real estate cycles.

In the 1980s, a 'go-go' mentality prevailed, along with the belief in many regions that the economies in those regions were recession proof. In both the Southwest and New England, the high growth strategies pursued by many S&Ls increased the competition for deposits and therefore raised the interest expense for both banks and thrifts. This situation persisted and worsened as deeply insolvent

S&Ls remained open because the FSLIC lacked reserves. Banks also faced competitive pressures from the thrifts that aggressively entered commercial mortgage lending markets and aggravated the risk taking already present in commercial banking."[14]

In retrospect, there is little doubt that once the damage had been done in 1980 through 1982 to thrift viability, the thrift crisis, particularly the S&L portion, was a series of mistakes by the regulators made worse by regional recessions and a "go-go mentality" that made sure the "Band-Aids" did not work. Those thrifts most severely damaged in the early 1980s' sea of red ink would not survive, and few of the thrifts that were insolvent in 1982 were around a dozen years later.

The thrift crisis caused problems for other banking organizations. As noted in the FDIC analysis, the desperate effort by so many thrifts to grow rapidly and diversify had them bidding aggressively for deposits that drove the cost of funds up for all banking organizations, and they made funding too available for developers that seldom saw a vacant lot that could not use a building. Much of the real estate overbuilding on the two coasts and in the Southwest could be traced to unwise lending by thrifts and the competitive need of the banks not wanting to be left behind.

The FDIC, in its comments, was a bit self-serving in exonerating itself. Meritor was the biggest savings bank insured by the FDIC and it used the phony accounting, relaxed capital standards and rapid growth as eagerly as any S&L, albeit there did not appear to be any management chicanery involved. Also, to blame S&Ls for excesses in New England is wrong considering the predominance and actions of savings banks in the region. The primary differences between the Bank Board, FSLIC and the regulators and insurers of the savings banks was that the latter *did* have the reserves to cover the losses of failed institutions and were under less industry pressure to look the other way when things went wrong.

CHAPTER

THE 1980S

The 1980s were a period of dramatic change in banking led by the arrival and spread of interstate banking. It would have been hard to imagine as the decade began that in just ten years a bank based in North Carolina would be among the leaders in states as large and as far away as Florida and Texas or that Bank of Boston would be among the most common signage in Connecticut, Maine and Rhode Island. By 1990, it was hard to recall that a few years earlier customers in the suburbs of New York, Washington and the other cities that straddled state lines had to use different banks if they wanted to use a banking office near their home <u>and</u> downtown. This was one of many changes, and even increased customer convenience was not universal as Illinois still had very few branches. For most of the nation, though, it was a vastly different banking environment in 1990 than what had existed ten years earlier.

A period of change in how a product is delivered, almost by definition, results in more structural change within an industry than in a period of calm. When accompanied by an event such as extremely high interest rates that favor one section of an industry over another, the amount of change is magnified. The 1980s favored a retail banking culture over a money center culture and also favored the depository institutions that had the most flexibility in product pricing. Thus, superregionals and banks that were able to follow their customers with offices had improved their competitive status while banks with money center cultures, or in states with limited branching and thrifts were disadvantaged. These disadvantages were further exacerbated by the LDC debt crisis and collapse of the oil-and-gas industry greatly impacting the banks without retail cultures, which in many cases were in hostile branching environments like Texas and Illinois. Thrifts with a business model that required stable or declining interest rates had little chance of keeping pace with more favorably situated banks.

With much of the country moving into a recession in 1989 and almost 500 banks failing in the next three years, the 1980 losers were not alone in questioning the benefits of change. The bottom line, however, was that no matter what happened negatively from 1989 to 1992 in banking, the winners in the 1980s would be in better shape to move forward when the economy improved than those that had not fared as well.

In retrospect, interstate banking was clearly the change in the 1980s that made the biggest difference, but there were other, often interrelated changes that played major roles in the transformation and increasing level of consolidation. Among the most important of these were:

- The rise of superregionals with a retail culture and seemingly endless desire to expand;
- The reversal of the thrift momentum of the 1960s and 1970s;
- Slowdown in the opening of branches;
- The diminished importance of checking accounts; and
- The growth of loan securitization.

Except for the rise of the superregionals and the thrift reversal of fortune, these changes were not headline grabbers, but when viewed over time, they were dramatic in their own right. Checking accounts, which were more than 50 percent of bank deposits in 1970 and 36 percent in 1980, were only 20 percent of deposits by 1990, and this was with deposits of all types declining as a source of bank funding. The securitization and sale to third parties of home mortgages that represented more than half of the nation's private debt rose from 12 percent of home mortgages in 1980 to 37 percent in 1990. The decline in checking accounts' importance raised questions about the need for branches, and the big increase in the securitization of home mortgages did the same about the need for thrifts. The growth of securitization would be the conduit for the subprime home loan debacle that led to the 2008 financial crisis.

RISE OF THE SUPERREGIONALS

The usurping of center stage by the superregionals in the 1980s was an outgrowth of interstate banking, but their rise was greatly assisted by the problems of others. Playing major roles in the growth of regional banks based outside of New York were acquisition opportunities that came with the collapse of the Texas banking system; the inactivity of the money center banks throughout most of the decade because of the LDC problems; and the diminished position of thrifts.

Largest American Banks, 1990

	Assets		Asset Share		Banking Offices
	1990	1980	1990	1980	
	(in billions)				
Money Center Banks					
1. Citicorp	$217	$115	5.6%	5.7%	322
2. BankAmerica	111	112	3.4	5.9	1,295
3. Chase Manhattan	98	76	2.9	4.1	344
4. J.P. Morgan	93	52	2.2	2.7	5
5. Chemical	73	41	2.2	2.2	369
6. Bankers Trust	64	34	1.7	1.8	4
7. Manufacturers Hanover	62	56	1.7	2.8	220
8. First Chicago	51	29	1.4	1.5	1
9. Bank of New York	46	10	1.4	.6	243
10. Bank of Boston	33	16	.9	.8	264
Subtotal	$848	$541	23.4%	28.1%	3,070
Superregionals					
1. Security Pacific	$85	$28	2.2%	1.4%	1,001
2. NCNB	65	7	1.9	.4	924
3. Wells Fargo	56	24	1.6	1.3	575
4. First Interstate	51	32	1.5	1.7	1,057
5. C&S/Sovran	51	3	1.5	.1	1,009
6. PNC	46	6	1.4	.3	511
7. First Union	41	3	1.2	.2	767
8. SunTrust	33	3	1.0	.2	625
9. Fleet	33	4	1.0	.2	538
10. Barnett	32	5	1.0	.2	598
Subtotal	$493	$115	16.8%	6.0%	7,605
Total	$1,341	$656	40.2%	34.1%	10,675

* Excludes substantial Citicorp and Fleet thrift assets.

Source: American Banker, April 20, 1982 and February 8, 1991.

In 1990, the ten largest superregionals had combined assets of almost $500 billion, and about 17 percent of bank assets. This was more than a fourfold increase in assets in ten years, and almost a tripling in asset share. NCNB, C&S/Sovran, First Union, SunTrust and Fleet had ten year asset gains in excess of 900 percent, and the largest superregionals—Security Pacific, NCNB and Wells Fargo—moved into 1990's top ten in asset size nationwide, ranking fifth, seventh and tenth, respectively.

The superregional growth came primarily from buying smaller banks, but their share gains were facilitated by the slowed growth of money center banks. While the ten biggest superregionals were recording more than a 400 percent increase in assets in the 1980s, the ten largest money center banks had a collective gain of just 56 percent. As a result, the money center share of all bank assets fell from about 28 percent to a little over 23 percent between 1980 and 1990.

The nation's second largest bank, BankAmerica, was the big loser as it struggled with an internal culture conflict. It had long been the country's largest retail bank, but in the late 1970s, it began acting like a money center bank and, as a result, was severely hurt by the LDC debt crisis. Despite being in rapidly-growing California, BankAmerica sat on the merger sidelines from 1982 through 1990 and was almost acquired in the mid-1980s in a hostile takeover attempt by the much smaller First Interstate. It had an asset decline between 1980 and 1990, failing to grow with inflation.

BankAmerica would put its focus back on retail banking, but there was no making up for the ground lost in the 1980s. If it had not strayed from its retail roots, it would have had substantial in-state growth and most likely would have been a major buyer of banks in Texas during the oil patch crisis. In this mode, it almost certainly would have been by far the biggest of the superregionals in 1990—probably with $200 billion plus assets instead of $111 billion. Considering how acquisitive it became after 1990, if it had started from this larger base in 1990, BankAmerica would not have been as vulnerable to a less than equal merger eight years later that kept the name, but moved the headquarters and control from San Francisco to Charlotte.

While BankAmerica was the most illustrious of the big bank losers in the 1980s, it was far from alone in its ill fortune. Continental was no longer in the top ten; Manufacturers Hanover had annual asset gains of only 1 percent per annum; and Chase Manhattan did not do much better at about 3 percent annually. They all would be gone by the mid-1990s.

It was not all bad for the money center banks in the 1980s. Citicorp, despite being stung by LDC losses and falling out of the top twenty in the world in earnings and assets for the first time in 1990, increased its domestic dominance. With $217 billion assets in 1990, it was almost twice as large as its closest rival, BankAmerica. Chemical did well holding its market share and becoming a leading player in Texas.

Two of the smaller money center banks, Bank of New York and Bank of Boston, improved their status by moving away from the traditional money center mode of operation. Bank of New York began a strategy of abetting money center banking with processing activities that generate large amounts of fee income, a strategy that continues to serve it well. Bank of Boston benefited from the New England interstate banking compact and took a page out of the superregional playbook by acquiring banks in Connecticut, Maine and Rhode Island.

The isolated money center bank successes, though, would not slow the changing of the guard, an occurrence that became particularly noticeable in terms of numbers of banking offices. Security Pacific, First Interstate and C&S/Sovran had more than 1,000 banking offices in 1990, and each of the ten biggest superregionals had at least 500 offices. BankAmerica had more than 1,000 branches, but each of the New York money center banks had fewer than 400 branches. This was a cultural variance that favored superregionals in a national interstate banking environment.

Despite the dramatic increase in asset share of the superregionals in the 1980s, the overall share numbers obscured the ongoing consolidation of banking. The share of the ten largest banks fell between 1980 and 1990, but this reflected the fortunes of the money center banks that dominated the top ten in both years. The consolidation that really counted, and a forerunner of what was to happen in the 1990s, was the rise from 6 percent to almost 17 percent of bank assets by the ten largest superregionals.

Merger Mania

Interstate banking had set in motion a quest for size led by superregionals that triggered an unprecedented merger spree in the 1980s. From 1980 to 1989, there were 4,271 bank acquisitions. This was more than three times the number of bank mergers in the 1970s, and slightly more than the number of sales that took place in the twenty years from 1950 through 1979. Unfortunately, about 800 of those mergers were assisted transactions involving failed banks.

Merger activity increased steadily as the 1980s progressed with 1987 and 1988 being by far the busiest years. The decade began with 133 bank mergers in 1980, but by 1985, there were more than 400 in a single year. That number jumped to 679 in 1987, and then peaked in 1988 at 771 before slowing due to deteriorating economic conditions. Some of the increase in merger activity in the mid-1980s is attributed to interstate banking, but a rise in bank stock prices was also a big contributor.

Bank Mergers in the 1980s

Year	Mergers			New Charters
	Unassisted	Assisted	Total	
1989	413	175	588	192
1988	598	173	771	229
1987	543	136	679	219
1986	341	101	442	257
1985	336	87	423	331
1984	330	62	392	391
1983	314	33	347	361
1982	256	25	281	317
1981	210	5	215	198
1980	126	7	133	205
Total	3,467	804	4,271	2,700
1970-79	1,316	50	1,366	2,224

Note: There were 226 banks closed in the 1980s and 50 closed in the 1970s.
Source: FDIC: Historical Statistics on Banking.

Most mergers in the 1980s used pooling accounting, which is an exchange of stock that combines the balance sheets and income statements of the two merging entities as if they had always been together and without punitive accounting adjustments. With pooling, a bank could buy another bank at a price times the seller's earnings plus after-tax cost savings equal to its existing market price times earnings without incurring any earnings per share, or EPS, dilution. If a selling bank's earnings were increased by 50 percent because of cost savings, then a buyer with stock selling at 14 times earnings could pay 21 times earnings without EPS dilution. If a bank's stock price went up, it could pay more, and if the price went up significantly, then it often could pay a price that could not easily be refused.

When the 1980s began, bank stock prices were low, and it was hard for a bank to buy another bank using pooling accounting for much over book value without sustaining excessive EPS dilution. As a result, there were few bank mergers, and those that occurred were often cash purchases rather than an exchange of stock that required the use of purchase rather than pooling accounting.

In purchase accounting, the acquirer does not keep the seller's equity and has to put the approximate difference between the price paid and capital of the seller on its books as a non-earning asset commonly referred to as goodwill, which was discussed briefly in the chapter on the early stages of the thrift crisis. As a result, purchase accounting not only lowered the price that could be paid, but it usually required the buyer to be much bigger than the seller because of capital constraints. Not being able to include the seller's capital in a cash transaction usually reduced the buyer's capital-to-asset ratio, often below acceptable regulatory levels.

STOCK PRICE GAINS

In 1982, the prices of stocks, in general, and bank stock prices, in particular, began a six-year rise after almost a decade of being in the doldrums. This was a necessary ingredient in the merger spree of the mid-1980s that contributed so heavily to the rapid growth of superregionals.

Good bank stock indices were not readily available in the 1980s, but the movement of the stock of one high-flyer of that decade, Fleet, or Fleet/Norstar as it was called from 1988 to 1992, was indicative of the stock price trends of this period. Its major difference from the stock movements of other large Northeast banks was that Fleet's value lasted through 1989 since it was not overwhelmed by commercial real estate problems quite as early as most others.

In the early 1980s, Fleet's stock, like most bank stocks, struggled to get above six times earnings and 100 percent of book. It was not until 1983 that it was able to finish a year above both those levels—and even then, a stock priced at 6.8 times earnings and 117 percent of book was not making anyone rich. This type of pricing made it difficult for banks to pay a high price for an acquisition in an exchange of stock, and, if cash was available, it usually was a better alternative as acquisition currency. At that time, there was a lot of acquiring done using debt instruments, and, in some cases, giving the seller the securities behind the debt as partial payment.

It was in 1986 that bank stock prices really took off, and Fleet's stock almost doubled in value between year-ends 1985 and 1986, reaching $23.25 per share. By mid-1987, the price was above $27 per share. This was 10.4 times earnings and 187 percent of book, which were high multiples for the time, albeit well below what would come a decade later.

This was the high point for bank stock prices in the 1980s, and it lifted the median prices paid for banks above two times book. After years of stock prices below book, this type of pricing was a strong inducement to sell, and higher stock prices coinciding with the advent of interstate banking led to the surge in unassisted mergers in 1987 and 1988.

Fleet Stock Price, 1980 to 1990

Year-End	Stock Price*	Times Earnings	Percent of Book	EPS
1990	$11.00	-	62%	$(.51)
1989	26.13	7.9X	131	3.30
1988	25.50	8.5	143	3.01
1987**	27.13	10.4	187	2.62
1986	23.25	9.7	179	2.50
1985	13.72	6.3	-	2.17
1984	14.28	7.1	125	2.03
1983	11.94	6.8	117	1.80
1982	8.95	5.6	101	1.60
1981	7.28	5.5	91	1.33
1980	5.83	5.1	82	1.15

*Adjusted for all stock splits through 1990.
**June 30, 1987 or six months ended June 30, 1987.
Source: Moody's Financials, various editions.

Bank stock prices fell along with all other stock prices in the October 1987 market crash, but bank acquisition activity stayed at a high level for a year after the stock price peak. This reflected deals in the planning stage prior to a fall-off in stock prices and some sellers wanting to sell before prices fell even further.

Fleet's stock price ended 1989 only slightly below its June 1987 high, but the impact on multiples of earnings and book was not as favorable. Its EPS and capital continued their upward movement, and, as a result, its year-end 1989 stock price was only 7.9 times earnings and 131 percent of book. This was not much above where it was in 1983 and 1984.

A year later, Fleet would be caught up in the regional collapse of the real estate markets, and its stock would be back at 1983 levels and selling at only 62 percent of book—and even that was better than many bank stocks. This, however, was the beginning of the 1990s, and part of a New England banking debacle that will be discussed in the next chapter.

Branch Growth

Surprisingly, even as large branch networks became more important to a bank's success and market value, the branch explosion of the 1960s and 1970s did not carry over into the 1980s. There were many reasons for this including so many existing branches that there was no longer the same customer need for additional offices, growing concern that the proliferation of ATMs would eventually make branches obsolete and the poor financial condition of so many banks and thrifts. Mergers also played a role as some included overlapping offices that would be closed. In the 1960s and 1970s, there were few branch closings to offset the branches being opened.

There were still, however, a lot of branches opened in the 1980s, but the net increase in banking offices of 9,611 was only about half the net increase in the 1970s—about 2,000 fewer than in the 1960s. The slowdown was more pronounced when the increase in number of branches is viewed as a percent. The net gain in banking offices in the 1980s was just under 12 percent compared to a 50 percent increase in both the 1960s and 1970s.

The change in the number of offices for the troubled S&Ls was more dramatic. In the 1970s, S&L offices grew from just under 10,000 to 21,346, a gain of 114 percent, even as the number of S&Ls fell by about 1,000. However, between 1980 and 1984 there was a slight decline in number of offices.

Bank and Thrift Branches, 1970 to 1990

Year	No. of Institutions	Branches	All Number	All Change*
Banks				
1990	12,347	50,406	62,763	9,611
1980	14,434	37,738	53,152	17,822
1970	13,511	21,839	35,350	11,668
Thrifts**				
1990	2,815	18,815	21,630	(3,901)
1987	3,622	21,909	25,531	1,593
1984	3,418	20,520	23,938	-
S&Ls Only				
1984	3,391	17,949	21,340	(6)
1980	4,613	16,733	21,346	11,359
1970	5,669	4,318	9,987	2,056

*Preceding ten years for banks and for S&Ls in 1970 and 1980; preceding three years for thrifts; preceding four years for S&Ls only in 1984.

**Federally-insured and increase between 1984 and 1987 is primarily shift of state-insured S&Ls to federal charters. Total thrifts in 1984 was 3,993.

Source: FDIC: Historical Statistics on Banking and S&L Factbook-1985.

In the mid-1980s, changes in the reporting of numbers of thrifts and thrift branches created some "apples and oranges" in comparing the early 1980s with the latter part of the decade. The FDIC took over the insuring of S&Ls in 1989 and only takes its historic thrift data back to 1984, and then between 1984 and 1987, the state-insured thrifts either disappeared or joined the FDIC system. As a result, the FDIC undercounts S&Ls and all thrifts in 1984 and had an unusual increase between 1984 and 1987 as state-insured thrifts moved into its system.

From 1987 through 1990, without the "apples and oranges" problem, the decline of thrifts and thrift branches was substantial. In those three years, there was a reduction in S&Ls and savings banks of about 800 and a decline in the number of thrift offices of almost 4,000. Some of the disappearing branches found their way into the bank numbers because of bank acquisitions of thrifts, but this did not change the net impact on all banking offices.

Bank/Thrift Mix

The decline of the thrifts in the 1980s was more apparent in fewer branches, S&L failures and reported losses than in lost market share. After having increased their share of deposits from 7.3 percent in 1950 to 25.7 percent in 1985, the S&L upward momentum ended. The slippage in the latter part of the 1980s, though, was not of seismic proportions.

Share of Depository Institution Assets, 1980 to 1990

	Banks	S&Ls	Savings Banks	Credit Unions
1990	68.3%	22.5%	4.7%	4.5%
1985	65.8	25.7	5.2	3.3
1980	68.1	23.1	6.3	2.5

Sources: FDIC: Historical Statistics on Banking; 1988 Factbook of Savings Institutions; and 1990 Credit Union Report.

The S&L share of depository institution assets in 1980 was 23.1 percent; in 1985, they were up to 25.7 percent; and then in 1990, the S&L asset share slipped to 22.5 percent. Thus, the S&Ls ended the decade pretty much where they began in terms of asset share as the crisis ended.

There was slippage, though, if their thrift brethren, the savings banks, were combined with S&Ls. During the 1980s, savings banks did not place nearly the same emphasis on growth as did the S&Ls, and their share of depository institution assets fell from 6.3 percent in 1980 to 4.7 percent in 1990. This slippage reflected their problems, but it also reflected the low growth in the Northeast where most of the savings banks were located as well as some of them choosing to adopt a more lenient S&L charter. In so doing, their assets moved from the savings banks to S&L universe.

The commercial banks had little change in asset share in the 1980s as they mirrored the S&Ls in reverse. The banks started the 1980s with a 68 percent asset share; fell to 65 percent in 1985 as S&Ls went on their desperation growth binge; and then were back at 68 percent in 1990.

The credit unions were the big gainers as they rose from an asset share of 2.5 percent in 1980 to 4.5 percent in 1990—nearly overtaking the savings banks. In many respects, they filled a void left by the decline of thrifts, particularly mutual savings banks, which like credit unions had a competitive advantage relative to pricing by not needing to produce bank-like earnings.

The shift from deposits to assets in measuring share growth partly reflects a lack of good asset data on thrifts prior to 1984, but it also reflects the large banks reducing their dependence on deposits for funding. Asset share is not a perfect measure of relative status, but deposit shares understate the position of the big banks, including the superregionals, that were gaining the upper hand in the battle for supremacy among financial institutions.

PRODUCT MIX

The shift away from deposits for funding indicated a lesser importance of noninterest-bearing checking accounts. In 1950, they were 76 percent of all bank deposits; by 1970, they had fallen to 51 percent; ten years later they were 36 percent; and by 1990, a mere 20 percent. As a majority of funding shifted to interest-bearing funding, the big banks weighed the relative cost of deposits against borrowings. The overall decline in deposits as a percent of assets was modest, but it was much larger for the big bank segment.

Bank Deposit Mix by Type, 1970 to 1990

	Percent of Deposits			Deposits Assets
	Demand	Savings*	CDs	
1990	20%	34%	46%	78%
1980	36	17	47	80
1970	51	21	28	85

* Includes MMDAs, NOW accounts and regular savings.
Source: FDIC: Historical Statistics on Banking.

The 1980s saw a broad customer acceptance of money market demand accounts, or MMDAs. Passbook savings were becoming a thing of the past, and in the 1970s, the combination of all interest-bearing accounts other than CDs fell from 21 percent to 17 percent of all deposits. In the 1980s, instead of declining, these deposit types doubled their share to 34 percent of all deposits with most of the increase reflecting the growth of MMDAs.

CDs, which had grown rapidly when interest rates were in double-digits in 1980 and 1981, held their status well throughout the rest of the decade. The CD share of all deposits jumped from 28 percent in 1970 to 47 percent in 1980, and in 1990, they were still 46 percent of deposits.

The shift in bank loan mix was equally dramatic in the 1980s and a clear break with the past. The major changes were a greater commitment to lending overall; a shift away from unsecured commercial loans toward real estate-secured lending of all types, albeit the shift had as much to do with an increase in real estate lending than an actual decline in commercial lending not secured by real estate; and the rise of the credit card.

Using real estate as a vehicle to increase loans as a percent of assets was symbolic of banking in the 1980s and the source of many of the bank problems. Loans went from 55 percent of assets in 1980 to 62 percent in 1990, and commercial real estate jumped from 11 percent to 19 percent of loans. Too many of these were nonperforming commercial real estate loans in California, Texas and the Northeast, and by 1990, the banking industry was already paying for this increased commercial real estate orientation and the poor credit standards associated with so many of those loans.

Bank Loan Mix by Type, 1970 to 1990

	Percent of Loans					
				Consumer		
	Home Mtg.	Other Real Estate	Comm-ercial	Credit Card	Other	Loans/Assets
1990	19%	19%	29%	6%	14%	62%
1980	14	11	38	3	19	55
1970	14	10	38	2	16	52

Source: FDIC: Historical Statistics on Banking

The impact of the credit card was not that noticeable in percent of all loans, but these numbers understate the reality. In the 1980s, credit cards grew from 3 percent to 6 percent of loans, but credit cards were much more important than this by 1990.

Credit card loans held in bank portfolios were only a little more than half of all credit card debt, and about 20 percent of credit card loans were securitized.

Securitization, the packaging of loans to be sold as securities, came into its own in the 1980s. Being able to make loans, but not having to hold them, meant that the number of loans a bank could make was no longer limited by capital and locally-generated deposits. A bank could generate as many conforming mortgage loans as its lenders could produce and sell them to third parties—primarily Fannie Mae, Freddie Mac and Ginnie Mae—that packaged them and sold as securities.

This radically changed the residential mortgage market in the 1980s as the mortgage pools replaced thrifts as the primary holder of mortgage loans. When the 1980s started, thrifts held almost 50 percent of all home mortgages in their portfolios. By 1990, their share was down to 28 percent. Conversely, the mortgage pools' share had jumped from 12 percent to 37 percent. Not only did thrifts have earnings and capital problems in the 1980s, but also their reason for existing had been undermined.

Holders of Residential Mortgage Debt, 1980 to 1990

	Mortgage Pools*	Thrifts	Banks	Govt. Agency	Others**
1990	37%	28%	16%	5%	14%
1985	26	38	15	8	13
1980	12	49	16	6	17

*Includes Federal National Mortgage Association, Federal Home Loan Mortgage Association and Government National Mortgage Association.
**Includes individuals, credit unions, mortgage companies, REITs, pension funds and life insurance companies.
Source: Federal Reserve Bulletins.

Securitization is an often-overlooked factor in the consolidation of banking, but in the 1980s, it played a major role. The relationship that went with holding a mortgage or owning the credit card in a customer's pocket was an important element of small bank and thrift success, a benefit that securitization was taking away as it was no longer necessary for the lender to have the funding on hand to support the loans it made. In the 1990s, almost all fixed-rate mortgages were sold to third parties, and credit cards outstanding were headed in this direction as well.

NEW ENGLAND "MIRACLE" ENDS

The 1980s took banks from the dark ages into the modern era in the midst of a national thrift crisis, a near meltdown of the money center banks and problems in the oil patch that devastated local banking industries, but it was 1989 to 1992 that would decide which banks fell by the wayside and which ones might prevail in the consolidation process. During these years, a national real estate-driven recession would contribute to the failure of more than 1,500 banks and thrifts; push many of the emerging superregionals of the 1980s to the brink of failure— sending one, Bank of New England, over the brink; and add to the woes of the already staggering money center banks. These were difficult years for banks and thrifts, and by the time the dust had cleared, the direction of the consolidation process was irrevocably altered.

During these years, the problems were no longer just happening with the big banks that the local bankers did not like very much anyhow; with thrifts that banks felt were unfairly poaching on their territory; or far away in Texas, which was "far away" for everyone not living in Texas, Arkansas, Oklahoma or Louisiana. Nationwide, but particularly on the East Coast from Maine to Florida and in California, asset quality was deteriorating and being a banker was no longer the safe, pleasant occupation it had once been.

This was a shock to most banks because the 1980s, other than for the money center and Texas banks, had been good years until 1989. High interest rates in the early 1980s may have been a disaster for thrifts, but they sent money rolling into banks, widened margins and benefited earnings. Interstate banking had become a reality, bank stock prices were once again moving up and bank salaries were rising as well. For most bankers, the 1980s really were Reagan's "morning in America," and the bad days of the 1970s were a fading memory.

It is easy to look back at the 1980s and realize that it may have been too much of a good thing in much the same way that the oil boom was in Texas in the years preceding 1985. These good times revived the investor interest in bank stocks, but at the same time, producing double-digit earnings gains to keep stock prices rising began to override other considerations. The only way to do this seemed to be to lend, lend and lend some more, and with the optimism that existed throughout most of the decade, there always seemed to be a need for another office building or condominium. If banks did not make the loans, there were plenty of thrifts that would and customers would be lost. The real estate lending fever had reached the stage in one small "hot" state, New Hampshire, that if the employment gains in banking and construction were removed, there was no growth at all.

By 1987 and 1988, however, there was a growing concern about the future and the "bubbles" that were appearing in parts of the economy. Most of the concern was about rising home prices and excess commercial and retail space, but much like in the late 1990s' technology bubble, even the "bears" were not expecting anything more than a period of modest adjustment. If there were asset quality problems on the horizon, the feeling was that it was still primarily a thrift problem.

The full extent of the adverse banking trends in 1989 was not widely recognized at first, and even as the clouds darkened as the year moved on, it was easy to rationalize that it was just another regional problem—New England and Florida falling into the Texas trap of overbuilding based on false optimism. Concerns that loan quality problems would spread to New Jersey, the Washington area, North Carolina's Research Triangle and then on to California was a year away. The 1989 to 1992 banking crisis would hit the hardest in the "boom" areas where overbuilding was easy to justify, but in the search for double-digit earnings gains, banks from all over the country were putting money into these areas.

The impact of these four years, from the beginning of 1989 through 1992, or from 1990 to 1993 in California, on the future structure of banking went far beyond what anyone could have imagined at the time. In New England, these were the years when Fleet moved away from the crowd and Royal Bank of Scotland gave its recently acquired Citizens subsidiary the backing to go from being a fringe competitor to an emerging powerhouse. Elsewhere on the East Coast, NCNB and First Union took advantage of the problems of others to build the bulk needed to become the Bank of America and Wachovia of a later date. On the

West Coast, BankAmerica and Washington Mutual were the main beneficiaries of the consolidation that was to result from these difficult years. In New York City, the woes of the money center banks went from bad to worse as lingering international loan problems were compounded by delinquent commercial real estate loans.

The idiosyncrasies of the structural changes in the four most affected regions—New England, the Southeast, California and the New York area—are such that each deserves its own chapter. New England was the first to see its economy and banking industry falter during this national recession, and it is the logical place to start.

New England Overview

In the 1980s, New England was home to the "Massachusetts miracle" that launched the presidential candidacy of its governor, Michael Dukakis, and had made Route 128, the highway that encircles Boston, synonymous with "high tech." New Hampshire, with its proximity to the Massachusetts technology base and lack of an income tax, was growing even faster than Massachusetts. Digital and Wang were the "hot" high tech companies; the Reagan military build-up had revitalized Raytheon and a host of small defense industry suppliers; and Harvard and MIT were a source of endless management and technological skills. At least in 1988 that was what everyone thought.

The region's largest banks, particularly Bank of New England, were caught up in the euphoria and went on acquisition binges which—with the arrival of interstate banking—greatly increased their size, but along with the enhanced size, came much greater risk. Shortly after the Supreme Court blessed the New England interstate banking compact in 1985, Boston-based Bank of New England completed an "equal" merger with Connecticut's largest bank, CBT. Two years later, another Boston bank, Shawmut, went the same route with Hartford National, Connecticut's second largest bank. That same year Fleet in nearby Providence took advantage of Rhode Island's 1987 "trigger" opening the state up for national interstate banking to move into upstate New York and Maine with another so-called "equal" merger—this one with the Albany-based Norstar. In each case, the surviving holding company was headquartered in either Boston or Providence.

Bank of Boston was too big for an "equal" merger within the confines of New England, and unlike Rhode Island, Massachusetts was several years away from letting its banks expand beyond New England. Bank of Boston did what it could, though, to expand and, in the mid- and late 1980s, bought the largest banks available in Connecticut, Maine and Rhode Island.

In 1989, the "miracle" started to unravel in Massachusetts and throughout New England. Digital and Wang were making yesterday's products, a common ailment in the high tech business, and the fall of the Berlin Wall spelled the end of the defense spending boom. Suddenly, instead of wondering where they would find workers, companies in New England were letting people go, and the abundance of new office space and luxury condominiums went from a sign of prosperity to a drag on the economy. This economic slowdown hit first in the Merrimac Valley in Massachusetts and southeastern New Hampshire, home to Wang and so many of the high tech and defense companies, but within a year, it had spread to all of New England. Digital, in particular, seemed to have a plant in almost every corner of the region.

New England Bank Asset Quality, 1988 to 1992

	CT	ME	MA	NH	RI	VT
	NPAs/Assets					
	Banks					
1992	3.78%	2.02%	2.37%	2.82%	3.60%	2.85%
1991	5.89	3.79	3.55	4.27	5.99	3.64
1990	8.95	3.85	6.62	5.65	6.25	2.93
1989	4.53	2.12	3.81	3.06	2.58	1.77
1988	1.35	.75	1.57	1.15	1.53	1.12
	Thrifts					
1992	5.60%	3.42%	3.25%	3.09%	5.54%	4.46%
1991	6.96	4.55	5.22	4.51	8.03	5.91
1990	6.98	5.76	5.95	8.55	6.62	4.27
1989	3.34	4.26	4.99	5.17	3.87	2.93
1988	1.45	2.38	2.92	2.13	2.68	2.04

Source: FDIC: Historical Statistics on Banking.

By the end of 1989, nonperforming assets (NPAs) had become a big banking problem throughout New England. Between year-ends 1988 and 1989, bank NPAs in Massachusetts had jumped from 1.57 percent of assets to 3.81 percent. In Connecticut, they went from 1.35 percent of assets in 1988 to 4.53 percent in 1989.

In each state, Bank of New England was a major contributor to the decline in asset quality. In New Hampshire, even without a Bank of New England contribution, the amount of assets not performing increased from 1.15 percent of all assets in 1988 to 3.06 percent in 1989. A year later, NPAs were 6.62 percent, 8.95 percent and 5.65 percent of all bank assets, respectively, in Massachusetts, Connecticut and New Hampshire.

As 1990 came to an end, NPAs exceeded tangible capital for banks in Connecticut, Massachusetts, New Hampshire and Rhode Island and had a similar negative relationship with thrifts in Connecticut, Maine, New Hampshire and Rhode Island. NPAs for Connecticut banks and New Hampshire thrifts were more than 200 percent of tangible capital. In general, the negative impact on banks and thrifts was similar with the major variances coming from two things. These were the negative effect of Bank of New England on the Connecticut and Massachusetts bank numbers in 1989 and 1990 and the positive effect of the abundance of capital that thrifts in Massachusetts had going into the period as a result of the stock conversions of so many of the state's largest thrifts.

Statewide totals, of course, are just that—totals—and many banks and thrifts were doing much worse. As a result, banks and thrifts began failing in large numbers in 1990, but it was 1991 that was the year of reckoning with more than 50 New England bank and thrift failures. In 1991, failed banks were 25 percent of the prior year-end banking assets in New Hampshire, 18 percent in Connecticut, 15 percent in Maine and 12 percent in Massachusetts.[1] These 1991 failures included Bank of New England and New Hampshire's five largest banking organizations.

In one of my *New England Banking Reports* at the time, I wrote "New England banking hit its low point in the first quarter of 1991 when the Bank of New England was seized and nonperforming assets climbed above 7 percent of total assets. At that time, New Hampshire's banking leadership was on its 'last legs,' and obituaries were being written for Bank of Boston, Shawmut and BayBanks."[2]

The opening line of that winter's *New England Banking Report* was "Somebody said things couldn't get worse, but they did." Those were bleak days for New England banking, and before the year (1991) ended, 53 banking organizations with more than $40 billion in deposits had failed.[3]

From a bank consolidation perspective, the big New England stories in these troubled times were the failure of Bank of New England, the demise of New Hampshire's banking leaders, the rise of Fleet to preeminence and the opportunism of a Rhode Island thrift, Citizens, with foreign ownership. Superior management may have been the main reason that Fleet and the Royal Bank of Scotland's subsidiary, Citizens, benefited from the problems of others, but they were helped by banks in New York and New Jersey having their own problems and not being able to take advantage of the opportunities in New England.

Bank of New England

The biggest banking story in New England in the 1980s was Bank of New England. It was a rags-to-riches saga with a disastrous ending that was played out in less than a decade. In May 1982, Boston's $3.8 billion New England Merchants announced its biggest acquisition up to that point, T.N.B. Financial in the western part of the state, and then changed its name to Bank of New England. It was eager to be something more than a second-tier bank in Massachusetts and by the end of 1988, Bank of New England was no longer second-tier. Its assets had topped $32 billion, and it was almost as large as Bank of Boston. The dream was to end two years and six days later when Bank of New England went into FDIC receivership.

The big step for Bank of New England in moving from $3.8 billion to over $32 billion in assets was its equal merger with CBT, the largest bank in Connecticut. This deal was announced in 1984, but delayed by Citicorp's legal objection to its being excluded from buying New England banks until the Supreme Court ruled in June 1985 that states could exclude New York, and thereby Citicorp, from their interstate banking legislation. Three months later the merger was consummated. As part of the merger agreement, the Bank of New England name was retained and the headquarters stayed in Boston. Leadership from CBT led by Walter Connolly, however, assumed management of the combined banks—whether that was the original intent or not. Within a year of this merger, Bank of New England acquired mid-sized banks in Maine and Rhode Island.

As a result of these acquisitions, Bank of New England raised its assets from $3.8 billion in 1981 to $22.6 billion by 1986. It was already second only to Bank of Boston in New England, and it was rapidly closing the gap between the two.

In 1987, Bank of New England received a "gift" from Fleet that would contribute to its sudden decline. Fleet made an unsolicited offer in late 1986 to the Conifer Group, Inc., a bank holding company in Worcester with assets of almost $4 billion and bank subsidiaries stretching from Cape Cod to the Berkshires. Conifer angrily felt this offer had "put it in play" and looked for buyers other than Fleet. Bank of New England was a logical alternative, and it outbid Fleet with what at the time was considered an astounding price at 18.6 times earnings and 303 percent of book.

Conifer proved to be a bad deal for both Bank of New England and the Conifer shareholders. One of Conifer's banks, Union National, was in the heart of the high tech country and would be a major source of bad loans. As for the Conifer shareholders, they would soon wish they were holding Fleet rather than Bank of New England stock.

In early 1989, the first bad vibes about Bank of New England began to surface. It was one of several banks with loans to William Stoecker and his Chicago-based Grabill Corporation, a leveraged buyout that was in danger of defaulting on its loans.[4] Bank of New England's exposure was not that big, but the Grabill loans raised questions about its lending habits as this was a long way from home.

In December 1989, Bank of New England sent shock waves across New England and beyond when it announced, under pressure from the FDIC, that it was increasing loan loss reserves by more than $700 million. It put much of the blame on the loan portfolio of Union National even though Union National did not even have assets of $700 million. Bank of New England would report a loss for the fourth quarter of 1989 of $1.1 billion, and in early 1990, its CEO, Walter Connolly, was forced to resign. He would be replaced a few months later by Larry Fish, who would later prove to be one of the country's most capable bank CEOs, but by then it was too late for Bank of New England.

Bank of New England's losses caused the regulators grief as well, and in Phillip Zweig's book on Wriston and Citicorp, he stated that "under the gun for their belated handling of BNE [Bank of New England], regulators came down like gangbusters on institutions throughout the country, virtually cutting off bank credit for real estate transactions." He quoted Citicorp's then president, John Reed as saying "That just killed the market.... From then on you couldn't sell buildings for love or money." According to Zweig, "If the credit crunch and the recession that it triggered needed a starting date, the 1989 examination of Bank of New England was it."[5]

Zweig and Reed were not alone in blaming the regulators for the real estate loan quality problems of the banks and thrifts in the post-1980 era. The regulators, though, had a tough choice. They could do what they did in the early 1980s with the thrifts, which was "close their eyes and hope for the best," or "get tough." The former approach had been a costly mistake, and it is hard to blame the regulators for not wanting a re-run of the thrift crisis.

Whatever its effect on the rest of the banking industry, Bank of New England was finished. It spent 1990 trying to find a partner and selling assets to maintain its capital adequacy, but by the end of the year, its time had run out. On January 6,

1991, its banks in Massachusetts, Connecticut and Maine were declared insolvent and went into FDIC receivership. The FDIC had to find a buyer on the best terms possible. One possible buyer was Citicorp, and BankAmerica was believed to have a strong interest.

In April 1991, the FDIC made its decision and decided to stay local, accepting a Fleet offer for all three banks. A deal that was partially financed by the leverage buyout specialist, Kohlberg, Kravis, Roberts & Co. (KKR) of *Barbarians at the Gate* fame—a best-selling book that told the story of how, in 1988, KKR won a widely-publicized hostile takeover of American Tobacco. This time around, KKR provided $283 million of the $683 million capitalization increase that Fleet had promised in order to obtain regulatory approval of the Bank of New England acquisition. Fleet would later repay KKR and have sole control of Bank of New England. The total cost to the FDIC was $889 million.[6]

With this transaction consummated, the big banks in New England banking were down from four to three, and Fleet had become the largest bank in the region. At the end of 1991, it had assets of $45.6 billion compared to $32.7 billion for Bank of Boston and $22.8 billion for Shawmut.

New Hampshire Impact

Bank of New England was the headliner in New England's early 1990s' banking disaster, but what happened in New Hampshire was more devastating in its local impact. Much like the economic collapse in Texas a few years earlier, this banking crisis completely annihilated the largest New Hampshire banks and thrifts and let out-of-state banks gain preeminence in this small, but attractive, banking market. Most of this out-of-state takeover occurred on a single day in October 1991.

Like Texas, New Hampshire is a state with a strong independent streak, and in the 1980s, it was growing rapidly and prospering. The state's lack of an income tax along with a business friendly environment, attractive lifestyle and proximity to a Boston-centered high tech and defense industry boom had attracted businesses, second homes and retirees. As in Texas, prior to 1986, there was a strong feeling of invulnerability in New Hampshire.

New Hampshire did not join Massachusetts, Connecticut, Rhode Island and Maine in their early endorsement of interstate banking. The out-of-state takeover of banking that occurred in Maine was viewed as inevitable in New Hampshire under similar circumstances, and the state legislators resisted opening its doors to out-of-state banks until 1988, when it felt it had no other choice. When the doors opened, two of its three largest banks, First New Hampshire and Indian Head, were sold to Bank of Ireland and Fleet, respectively. They were the only ones thinking "sell," and they proved to be the smart ones.

In 1989, New Hampshire still had five local banks and thrifts with assets in excess of $1 billion—Amoskeag, New Hampshire Savings, United Savers, BankEast and Numerica. While historically reluctant to sell, they were in a race against the clock in a rapidly declining economy, but asset quality uncertainties had eliminated the possibility of a sale. Thus, it was a race, unfortunately, that they were destined to lose, and on October 10, 1991, the FDIC took over all five. Amoskeag and BankEast had the most attractive franchises and were packaged together and sold to the Bank of Ireland. The others—New Hampshire Savings, United Savers and Numerica—were also sold as a package, but to an investor group as there were no bids from banking organizations. The investor group, New Dartmouth, contributed $38 million and the FDIC contributed $61 million to insure that there was adequate capital. The investors sold this package to Shawmut in 1993. The total cost to the FDIC for all five banks and thrifts was $891 million.[7]

These closings and sales dramatically altered the New Hampshire banking structure. Of the seven biggest banking organizations in the state when the economic downturn began, four became part of Bank of Ireland, two were acquired by Shawmut and one was bought by Fleet. A couple of years later, Royal Bank of Scotland, through its Rhode Island-based affiliate, Citizens, would purchase majority ownership of the Bank of Ireland's New Hampshire operation and Fleet would purchase Shawmut. Thus, by 1996, Fleet and Royal Bank of Scotland had, directly or indirectly, acquired all of New Hampshire's largest banks and thrifts.

FLEET

Fleet's success in New Hampshire was only a small part of one of the more remarkable success stories in American banking. The bank's origins go back to 1791 with the founding of Providence Bank. In 1951, it became the Providence Union bank following a local merger, and in 1954, it merged with Industrial Trust Company and became Industrial National. In the 1970s and early 1980s, Industrial National was an active buyer of mortgage banks and other nonbank financial companies, and by 1982, it had assets in excess of $5 billion. In that year, it also changed its name to Fleet.

When interstate banking was allowed, Fleet responded quickly with some small bank acquisitions in Connecticut, but its big move came when it was allowed to go beyond New England in 1987 and announced an equal merger with Norstar. This merger took Fleet into Upstate New York and Maine; made it one of New England's big four; and temporarily resulted in the cumbersome Fleet/Norstar name. In the late 1980s, few would have anticipated that the Providence-based Fleet, rather than one of the leading Boston banks—Bank of Boston, Bank of New England or Shawmut—would be the last big bank standing in New England; have the largest retail deposit share in the Northeast; and then sell to Bank of America for an imposing $49 billion in 2004.

The Norstar merger was a big step in Fleet's ascendancy, but equally important was how Fleet navigated the treacherous waters from 1989 to 1992, particularly having the courage to undertake the Bank of New England acquisition. Fleet was not immune to asset quality deterioration—in 1991, its NPAs were almost 5 percent of assets—but it did not slip as far as Bank of Boston, Shawmut or Bank of New England—and apparently it impressed the FDIC with how it was dealing with its problems. That Fleet was willing to take on Bank of New England in 1991 was a surprise, but perhaps even more surprising was the FDIC's willingness to let it do so.

Fleet's purchase of Bank of New England in 1991 instantaneously made it the largest bank in New England and kept a large competitor out of the region. Neither Bank of Boston nor Shawmut were in a position to assume what was left of Bank of New England, and if Fleet had not come up with a creative acquisition proposal, the FDIC almost certainly would have turned to BankAmerica or some other out-of-state bank. If they had done so, Fleet might not have been able to afford Shawmut and then Bank of Boston, and even if it could, it would have had to outbid a much larger potential acquirer.

CITIZENS

The other bank that benefited greatly from the troubles of others in New England during this period was Royal Bank of Scotland, which in 1988 acquired Citizens Financial Group, a Rhode Island holding company whose primary subsidiary was a Providence-based savings bank with assets of $2.6 billion. Citizens was one of many New England thrifts in 1988 in the $1 to $4 billion asset range and did not seem to be nearly as good an entry vehicle as First New Hampshire, which had been acquired by Bank of Ireland. They were about the same size, but First New Hampshire was a commercial bank in a much more dynamic market. A less dynamic market, though, was a plus as Citizens, unlike First New Hampshire, was profitable every year from 1989 through 1992 and had relatively modest asset quality concerns.

Thus, Citizens was not an embarrassment to its foreign parent, Royal Bank of Scotland, and with the parent's muscle behind it, Citizens was able to buy when others were on the sidelines. In 1990, it bought the $1.2 billion Old Colony Trust Company in Rhode Island from Bank of New England prior to BNE's failure. In 1992, it moved into Massachusetts with the acquisition of a failed savings bank in Plymouth.

In 1992, Citizens made a management change that would give it the leadership to move to the next level. Larry Fish, a top executive at Bank of Boston and the man who tried to save Bank of New England in its dying days, knew the New England banking market well and became Royal Bank of Scotland's "man in America."

Fish kept the Citizens acquisition machine rolling. In the next two years, it bought three more thrifts from the FDIC with combined assets of $2.5 billion, two of which were in Connecticut. The recession was over in 1993, but there were few buyers with an appetite for New England thrifts still struggling with the scars of the previous years. In 1993 and 1994, Citizens acquired three Boston area savings banks with combined assets in excess of $3 billion. By 1996, Bank of Ireland had enough of New England and sold a majority interest in First New Hampshire to Citizens.

By the time Royal Bank of Scotland integrated First New Hampshire into its system, it had become a major New England player. Its regional assets were in excess of $15 billion; it had significant presences in Rhode Island, Massachusetts, Connecticut and New Hampshire; and it was third in New England deposit share behind Fleet and Bank of Boston.

AFTERMATH

In 1993, New England bankers could breathe a sigh of relief as the economy and asset quality improved, but it was a badly shaken local banking industry. In the preceding four years, about 100 New England banks and thrifts with combined assets in excess of $55 billion had failed, and this was only the assets at the time of failure. Counting what the failed institutions' assets were a couple of years earlier, the assets involved would have been at least $75 billion. In addition to Bank of New England, the 1989 to 1992 casualties included at least a dozen banking organizations with assets in excess of $1 billion.

If the recession had lasted another six months, there would have been several more large failures as recapitalizing troubled banks required investor confidence. This was something that would only come when a turnaround was in sight, and there were a lot of banks and thrifts just barely making it.

The "near death" experience also had a psychological impact on the willingness to remain independent, particularly among stock thrifts. Because of asset quality problems for both buyers and sellers in 1990 and 1991, there were no unassisted thrift sales in New England, and there was only one in 1992, albeit a big one—Society for Savings in Hartford. When the recession began, it was the ninth largest banking organization in New England with assets of $4 billion and was acquired by Bank of Boston in 1992. It was a different story in 1993 and 1994 when 21 stock thrifts were sold, including seven of Massachusetts' ten largest with Fleet and Citizens buying five of the seven.

Of the four big banks in New England when 1989 began, Bank of Boston, Fleet and Shawmut were still there in 1993, but the order had changed. Fleet had replaced Bank of Boston as the leader, and Fleet's going forward while the Bank of Boston and Shawmut stagnated had ramifications that went far beyond 1993. Fleet had the momentum and would soon have the market capital and investor support to acquire Shawmut in 1995 and Bank of Boston three years later.

State Street and BayBanks did not have the size of New England's big three, but they were much larger than all other banks in the region in 1988 and 1993. State Street more than doubled in size during those five years with assets reaching almost $19 billion by the end of 1993, but even before 1988, it was exiting traditional banking, concentrating instead on asset management and selling its trust servicing capabilities to other financial institutions. State Street's much increased size

Largest New England Banks, 1993

	Assets		1988 Rank	Eventual Owner
	1993	1988		
	(In billions)			
1. Fleet	$48	$29	3	Bank of America
2. Bank of Boston	41	36	1	Bank of America
3. Shawmut	27	29	4	Bank of America
4. State Street	19	8	6	State Street
5. BayBanks	10	10	5	Bank of America
6. Citizens	7	3	-	Royal Bk.- Scotland

Source: SNL Financial Services, Inc., Charlottesville, Virginia.

reflected its trust and trust-related businesses. The consumer-oriented BayBanks slipped badly during the early 1990s and was acquired by Bank of Boston in 1995.

The rest of the top ten banking organizations in New England in 1993 were thrifts—Citizens, People's, Northeast Savings, Peoples Heritage and NBB—two of which, Citizens and Peoples Heritage, would successfully make the transformation from thrift to bank and become Fleet's primary competition throughout most of New England. Peoples Heritage would do so under a name it took from one of its acquisitions, Banknorth. Within two years, Northeast Savings, a Hartford-based S&L, sold to Shawmut, and NBB, a New Bedford savings bank, were acquired by Fleet. People's, a Bridgeport savings bank, was still around in 2014, and although it had been slow to move much beyond its southwest Connecticut base, it had become one of the 25 largest banking organizations in the country under the slightly changed People's United name.

The ultimate beneficiary of the consolidation in New England that was triggered by the real estate-driven recession from 1989 to 1992 would be Bank of America. The five largest banking franchises in 1988 and seven of the ten largest would be part of Fleet ten years later and delivered to Bank of America in 2004 when it acquired Fleet.

CHAPTER

CHARLOTTE'S WEB

The negative effect of the real estate-driven recession that began in 1989 and stretched through the early 1990's was not nearly as damaging to banking in the Southeast as it was in New England, or for that matter in California, the subject of the next chapter. As a result, the impact on bank consolidation was more positive than in those other areas, particularly in North Carolina. It was during these years that NCNB and First Union, later to be Wachovia, took advantage of problems elsewhere to become more than just a couple of ambitious southern banks.

In 1989, if one had been asked to name the banks most likely to be among the banks that would dominate the domestic industry in fifteen or twenty years, few would have put NCNB on the short list even after its purchase of the Republic and InterFirst banks in Texas, and it is unlikely anyone would have included First Union. The obvious choices were the traditional leaders—Citigroup, BankAmerica and Chase Manhattan. Despite their recent problems, these banks held the top three spots over most of the last sixty years and were still the three biggest. Its money center culture may have been working against Chase Manhattan, if not Citigroup, but it was reasonable to assume that it would solve that problem by buying a large superregional when it had its finances back in order. Beyond these three long-time leaders, Security Pacific and First Chicago were much more likely to have been mentioned than NCNB as a future dominant bank. First Interstate, PNC and Bank One were others that would have been considered.

Security Pacific was the most obvious choice beyond the big three to be among the dominant banks of the future. It was the largest bank in Los Angeles; a likely beneficiary of the booming Pacific Rim fueled by strong growth in

Japan; and had jumped from 11th to fifth in asset size since 1980. There was no indication then that the California economy would soon be reeling and Security Pacific would have such serious asset quality problems that its sale would be a matter of survival as early as 1992.

First Chicago, or a successor, was another strong candidate to join the big three at the top, based on location. Illinois banking laws still did not allow branching and interstate banking, which limited First Chicago's ability to grow, but despite being smaller than NCNB, it seemed logical that when national interstate banking laws superseded state laws that some large bank would want to be headquartered in the Midwest's commercial center. This theory looked prescient in 1995 when NBD, the alphabetized name for what used to be National Bank of Detroit, acquired First Chicago in one of those equal, but not really equal, mergers and took its management and holding company name to Chicago. Three years later Bank One in Columbus, Ohio made the same move after acquiring First Chicago/NBD. In 2003, when there were six, rather than four, banks with about 50 percent of the banking assets, one of those six was a Chicago-based Bank One.

Why not NCNB after what it had accomplished in the 1980s. It had been a primary force in breaking down interstate barriers and had increased its assets from $7.2 billion to $66 billion in just nine years. In so doing, it had moved from 28th to seventh in size among the nation's banks and moving up a couple of more places would have been a normal progression. Nevertheless, NCNB had its doubters.

There were many reasons for not believing totally in NCNB in those days. One of the most common criticisms was that it was better at buying banks than running them. In 1989, the rumblings out of Texas were that NCNB was driving away customers by the droves, and it was jokingly said that its initials really meant "no credit for nobody." There was some truth to this as its Texas loans were less than 40 percent of its assets in 1990. Time would show, however, that NCNB was right to worry more about the bottom line than market share in the early 1990s, and by the end of 1994, its Texas bank loans were in excess of 70 percent of assets.

NCNB's acquisition activity was primarily buying smaller banks and failed institutions auctioned by the regulators. It was a bold and ready acquirer, but the banks it most wanted to buy usually chose another option. The three biggest banks sold in Florida in the 1980s—the primary target state for NCNB—chose someone other than NCNB. A much courted First Atlanta picked Wachovia over NCNB, and in 1989, an unsolicited offer to Citizens & Southern, Georgia's largest bank, was rebuffed with bitter words. An exception was Bankers Trust in South Carolina that had close board ties to NCNB, but it was only number three in a relatively small state.

A major reason why NCNB was not a buyer of choice was its CEO, Hugh McColl. NCNB owed its recent success to McColl's leadership and determination, but his determination had a dark side that did not win over everyone. He had a reputation for being bold, arrogant and abrasive. He was an ex-marine, and proud of it, and he liked to use military terms when talking about acquisitions, which did not always go over well with potential partners. Unsolicited public offers to buy banks were not a common, or popular, banking practice, particularly in the South.

In the process of taking over C&S/Sovran, McColl had asked his head of human resources to provide a profile of the CEO of C&S/Sovran, Bennett Brown. In response, he also received an internal profile on himself that stated that from Brown's vantage point "McColl was arrogant, crude and ungentlemanly. Moreover, Brown was turned off by McColl's use of words suggesting power."[1]

What may have seemed like weaknesses in 1989, however, would serve McColl and NCNB well in the difficult banking environment that lay ahead. NCNB *did* know how to run banks, as well as buy them, and it was ready to exploit opportunities in a down economy while others were worried about adding risk. In the difficult environment of the early 1990s, NCNB's most desired merger candidates frequently had limited, if any, other options.

First Union, with its more congenial leader, Ed Crutchfield, was able to fill the role of "buyer of choice" better than NCNB, although neither could match a third North Carolina bank, Wachovia, in that role. Congeniality and money, though, helped First Union acquire banks in Florida and Georgia that put it ahead of NCNB in those states. Its Texas acquisitions, however, put NCNB far ahead of First Union in overall size, which was to be a trump card in the days to come.

Southeast Banking Environment

It was the debilitating impact of commercial real estate lending gone awry in the early 1990s that reshaped the East Coast banking structure from Maine to Florida and provided the opportunity for NCNB and First Union to become more than just large southern regionals. Outside of New England, the degree of the loan quality problems varied greatly, and the fortunes of banks striving for regional leadership were influenced heavily by location. New York City and its New Jersey suburbs looked a lot like New England from a loan quality perspective, but going south and west from that densely populated area, the problems were much more scattered, and, ironically, the problems reflected an area's growth dynamics. The better the market seemed to be for commercial real estate, the worse the loan problems.

In a Southeast that included all of the coastal states that were part of the southern interstate banking compact—from the Mason-Dixon Line south—the areas hardest hit were Washington and southern Florida. Like New England, these areas had been hot markets that seemed invulnerable to a serious downturn. As the nation's capital, Washington, historically, kept growing in good and bad times as the latter usually resulted in expanded government programs. Southern Florida, with growth fueled by sunshine and retirement homes, seemed equally immune to normal economic cycles.

Another "hot" market that bred builder over-optimism was North Carolina's Research Triangle. The state capital and three large universities—Duke, University of North Carolina and North Carolina State—created a strong growth environment, but being a much smaller market than either Washington or southern Florida, limited the damage it could inflict on North Carolina banks.

In cities with low commercial real estate demand like Baltimore and most of the ones in the Midwest, locally-generated loan quality concerns were more of a nuisance than a concern. If there was little need for the first large office building or new mall, then there would not be multiple developers trying to meet that need.

Atlanta also missed this round of overbuilding, and this may reflect its earlier experience. In the mid-1970s, it was the focus of a real estate debacle with an emphasis on excess hotels. At that time, Atlanta was emerging as a major airline and convention center with a need for more hotel space. With little going on in most of the country, this need was met with too much developer enthusiasm, and a few hotels too many were built with bank loans. It is hard to generate the same lending enthusiasm a second time around.

These regional loan quality variations coming at a time when banks were in a race for size and able to move across state lines had a tremendous effect on how that race played out. The real-estate driven recession of the early 1990s favored banks in Charlotte and Atlanta over banks in the Washington and Miami areas. Banks in Baltimore, as well as in southeast and central Virginia, would also suffer because most of the larger banks in those areas had substantial subsidiaries in the Washington market.

NCNB may have done well under any set of circumstances, but if the playing field had been level or tilted the other way in the early 1990s, Sovran and MNC instead of NCNB and First Union might have been the ones that became national banking powers. Real estate woes, unfortunately for Sovran and MNC, Maryland National's holding company, are fickle in geographic orientation. In the mid-1970s, it was Atlanta and the Carolinas that were the main sources of bad loans in the region. This time around, it was Washington and southern Florida.

The unevenness of the asset quality in the Southeast in the early 1990s was seen in the percent of assets not performing. At one extreme, banks in the District of Columbia had NPAs rise from less than 1 percent of total assets at year-end 1988 to more than 7 percent two years later and then move above 10 percent at the end of 1991. This was higher than in any New England state. Conversely, even at the peak of the crisis, in Georgia, North Carolina and South Carolina, bank NPAs were less than 2 percent of all assets.

Southeast Bank Asset Quality, 1988 to 1992

	NPA/Assets				
	1992	1991	1990	1989	1988
District of Columbia	7.00%	10.06%	7.09%	1.08%	.86%
Maryland	3.05	3.59	3.42	1.01	.71
Virginia	2.34	3.45	2.34	.68	.65
Florida	2.21	2.82	2.95	1.83	1.82
South Carolina	1.74	1.95	1.36	.77	.63
Georgia	1.34	1.90	1.68	1.12	.97
North Carolina	1.17	1.80	1.50	.70	.48

Source: FDIC: Historical Statistics on Banking.

Banks in Maryland, Virginia and Florida did not have as many bad assets when measured as a percent of all assets as the District of Columbia or the New England states, but their statewide numbers do not reflect the depth of the problem in parts of these states. Banks in the Maryland and Virginia suburbs of Washington and in southern Florida may not have reached double-digits percentage in NPAs, but they were at least in the 5 percent to 7 percent of assets range of the New England states.

Since the extent of the asset quality concerns of the large Southeast banks during this recession reflected its commitment to the most troubled markets, Southeast Banking and MNC were the most vulnerable big banks. Southeast Banking was Miami-based and had the biggest commercial real estate commitment in southern Florida. MNC, despite being based in Baltimore, was not much better off since it owned one of the two largest banks in the District of Columbia, American Security, and its Baltimore-based flagship bank, Maryland National, had almost 100 branches in the Maryland suburbs of Washington. MNC was second behind Sovran in Washington area deposit share.

Sovran, which would soon be C&S/Sovran, was the area's largest bank and vulnerable as well, but its Washington area assets were a smaller part of its overall asset base than for MNC. Its asset quality deterioration might have been little more than a bad memory, if it had been given time to work through its loan problems. Its problems, though, would be NCNB's opportunity.

First American, Washington's largest locally-based bank, would also be hit hard. Its troubles, however, went far beyond the local economy due to its ties to an overseas criminal banking organization, BCCI, discussed later in this chapter.

For banks in Georgia and the Carolinas to have troubled loans rise above 1 percent of assets, let alone 2 percent, was not something they were accustomed to, or liked, but relatively speaking, they did not have asset quality concerns. For the bigger banks in these states, other than NCNB and First Union, the response to even a modest increase in bad loans was one of extreme conservatism. Wachovia and SunTrust were risk-adverse even when it meant forsaking better loan yields, and that was also the attitude of Citizens & Southern before being pushed into a merger with Sovran in late 1989.

SOUTHERN BANKING IN 1989

Entering these troubled times, NCNB had a big size advantage over other banks in the South stemming from its acquisition of the Republic and InterFirst banks in Texas in 1988, but not an advantage that assured its position as a market leader. These purchases had made NCNB more than just first among near-equals in the South, but the Texas banks were outside NCNB's home area, the Southeast. A merger between two of the other large Southeast banks could create a bank that would rival NCNB. As for First Union, it was still part of the crowd and had temporarily lost its number two position in asset size to SunTrust.

The differences between banking in Texas and the Southeast alluded to above reflect a regionalization that prevailed in the South in 1989. Interstate banking was only four years old, and the initial step for a bank in crossing state lines was usually to buy a bank in a neighboring state. The southern interstate banking compact stretched from Maryland to Texas, but there were four distinct banking markets within a broadly defined South. These were a true Southeast composed of Florida, Georgia and the Carolinas; the lower Middle Atlantic states of Maryland and Virginia plus the District of Columbia; a Mid-South grouping of Alabama, Louisiana, Mississippi and Tennessee; and Texas, whose oil patch problems had thrown its banking open to all.

North Carolina's NCNB and First Union were an integral part of a four-state "true" Southeast that not only had common geography, but was also bound together by the common objective of the area's largest banks to expand into Florida because of its size and growth potential or, if already there, concentrate on in-state expansion. NCNB's interest in Florida had been an impetus for interstate banking in the South, and by 1989, NCNB and First Union were among the five largest banks in that state, measured by deposit share. Citizens & Southern and Trust Company of Georgia (two of Georgia's big three), also had extensive Florida coverage. Trust Company's merger with Florida's third largest bank, Sun, created SunTrust, which despite the semblance of equality in the name was headquartered in Atlanta. The biggest remaining independent Florida banks, Barnett and Southeast Banking, had neither the need nor desire to move north into slower growing states.

In 1989, Florida's banking structure had undergone a major change when First Union announced the acquisition of Florida National. It was one of the largest banks headquartered in the state; the primary target for NCNB when it entered Florida in 1982; and for a while, it had an agreement to sell to Chemical contingent on New York banks being allowed entry into Florida, which was not to be in the 1980s. The Florida National acquisition put First Union in second place in Florida deposit share behind Barnett.

The fourth state in the Southeast, South Carolina, was much smaller than the other three, and its banking was destined to go the way of banking in most small states—absorption by big banks in bordering states. Wachovia acquired the state's largest bank, South Carolina National, in 1991. Prior to 1989, Citizens & Southern, NCNB and First Union had bought the next three in size.

The intertwining of banking in the four "true" Southeast states was further enhanced by inter-region mergers that tied North Carolina and Georgia together. In 1985, First Atlanta had spurned the overtures of NCNB and announced an equal merger with Wachovia to form First Wachovia—with dual headquarters in Atlanta and Winston-Salem. A year later, First Union acquired Georgia's fourth largest bank, First Railroad.

Thus, NCNB may have greatly increased its size by its acquisitions in Texas, but it was falling behind in its home market. Wachovia, which would drop the

"First" that had come with the First Atlanta merger, was the most respected bank in North Carolina; had the second largest deposit share in Georgia; would soon become the leader in South Carolina; and was the area's buyer of choice. First Union was number two in Florida; number four in Georgia; and had a solid presence in South Carolina. NCNB was only number three in South Carolina; falling behind in Florida; and just a fringe player in Georgia. This was not what NCNB had in mind when it opened the door in the South for interstate banking.

In fact, it appeared that NCNB had misplayed its hand close to home in 1989, and that its Texas acquisitions had merely given it size, while others were building better franchises. A heavy-handed and hostile approach to a merger with Citizens & Southern, Georgia's largest bank, would drive that bank into a marriage of convenience with Virginia's biggest bank, Sovran. This created a bank almost as large as NCNB and with a far more cohesive franchise, or at least, so it seemed.

The formation of C&S/Sovran was 1989's big merger—nationally as well as in the South—but it was not the only Southeast merger to affect the regional balance of power. First Union's purchase of Florida National had made it the second biggest bank in Florida. Further north, MNC bought one of its chief Maryland rivals, Equitable, and with that transaction had moved far ahead of all banks, other than Sovran, in an area that had better growth potential than the Carolinas.

Thus, as the 1990s began, NCNB may have greatly increased its size with its Texas acquisitions, but it was still stuck with the rest of the pack in a regional big nine. This would change over the next three years as not only did fortune favor NCNB, but it also had a leader in McColl who was not one to pass up the opportunities presented to him.

In the early 1990s, NCNB became the pre-eminent bank in the South with its purchases of C&S/Sovran and MNC, and First Union became a solid number two acquiring what remained—Southeast Banking in Florida, Dominion Bankshares in Virginia; the Washington-based First American; and several large thrifts. Of the region's nine largest banks in 1989, Citizens & Southern, Sovran, MNC and Southeast Banking were gone by 1993, and Barnett, SunTrust and Wachovia were left to play catch-up in an environment in which "catch-up" would be no easy task.

NCNB–CITIZENS & SOUTHERN

NCNB's transition from being one-of-many in the Southeast to the dominant force in the entire South in just four years came neither easily nor without a lot of effort on its part. As would be the case in this and any other consolidation process, one move tended to beget another. Crossing state lines in the 1970s had brought NCNB into Florida with a small trust company, the vehicle it then used to be the first out-of-state bank to make a real bank acquisition in that state. Then the size and experience gained from its Florida ventures gave NCNB the credibility to accomplish the acquisition of two failed banking leaders in Texas in 1988. With Texas came size and the ability to make an unsolicited offer to buy a bank that had a year earlier been its equal, Citizens & Southern. When it finally succeeded in that endeavor in 1991, MNC would be "easy pickings" a year later.

The "one step begets another" sequence was severely tested in 1989 when NCNB tried to use its size to force an acquisition that would make it the largest bank in the Southeast. Its target, Citizens & Southern, was the largest bank in Georgia—an obvious gap in NCNB's coverage—and also had a sizeable presence in Florida and South Carolina. It was an ideal fit, and McColl began the pursuit by calling Citizens & Southern president, Bennett Brown, to arrange for merger discussions.[2] When that failed, NCNB made an unsolicited offer of $2.4 billion, which would have been the highest price ever paid for a bank up to that time.

What seemed logical and desirable to NCNB did not meet with a favorable reception at Citizens & Southern. A war of words began, which was accompanied by both sides hiring some of the top law firms and investment bankers in the country. Three weeks later, NCNB recognized the inevitable and withdrew the offer, but this was only the beginning.

The history of hostile takeovers in banking did not favor NCNB in its first use of this tactic. McColl's belief that he had a chance to succeed may have reflected his having beaten strong odds in convincing the regulators to sell him failed banks in Texas that, collectively, were almost as large as NCNB. Hostile takeovers, however, usually only succeed when three key factors are in alignment—the aggressor is strong and competent; the target is underperforming; and there are no comparable alternatives, or "white knights," available. NCNB was a strong, competent bank, but Citizens & Southern was not underperforming; and it had "white knights." These "white knights" may not have been able to top the NCNB price, but they possibly could have been sold to investors as better long-term alternatives, even if this may have been a stretch.

Hostile transactions, although far-and-few-between in banking, have been part of the consolidation process. Norstar, the Upstate New York bank that had made the first interstate acquisition in Maine and was later to merge with Fleet to form Fleet/Norstar, had one of the more notable hostile merger successes in its pursuit of Security New York in Rochester in 1983. This was the city I had left when I first got into banking, and when I was asked to participate, my initial reaction was that Rochester takes care of its own, and that Norstar and its CEO, Peter Kiernan, were wasting their time.

In 1968, Taylor Instruments, one of Rochester's larger firms, was recipient of a hostile tender offer from a Latin American-based holding company. The Rochester firm for which I was working at the time, Ritter Pfaudler, was the successful "white knight" in a spirited acquisition battle that preserved the Rochester roots of Taylor Instruments. After the merger, the name of the firm changed to Sybron as Ritter Pfaudler Taylor seemed a bit much. A visit with Kiernan, however, convinced me that my experience did not apply here and made a believer out of me.

In Norstar-Security New York, unlike NCNB-Citizens & Southern, the conditions for a successful hostile takeover were there. Norstar was a strong bank with a highly respected CEO; Security New York was an underperformer with limited investor support; and there were no better buyer alternatives. There were other buyers, but even within Security New York, the thinking was that if a sale was necessary, Norstar was the lesser of evils—and the best outcome for shareholders.

Despite not having matched Norstar's success, NCNB's aborted hostile takeover was not the end of its efforts to buy Citizens & Southern, and if a mistake had been made, it was not NCNB's hostile bid, but Citizens & Southern seeking a partner in order to survive. In September 1989, it announced a merger with Sovran, Virginia's largest bank. Sovran was a good choice based on 1989 circumstances, but the timing could not have been worse.

Sovran had become Virginia's number one bank after a merger of Virginia National and First & Merchants, the market leaders in Norfolk and Richmond, respectively. It subsequently acquired the largest bank in the Maryland suburbs of Washington, Suburban Trust, and then in 1987, it purchased Commerce Union, the third largest bank in Nashville, Tennessee. Sovran had also bought a small bank in the District of Columbia. By 1989, it was by far the biggest bank in the Middle Atlantic States south of the Mason-Dixon Line as well as being a factor in adjoining Tennessee's best market, Nashville.

The merger of Sovran and Citizens & Southern created a bank almost as large as NCNB, and it had a more cohesive franchise. The combined banks were number one in Virginia and Georgia and among the top six in Florida, Maryland, South Carolina, Tennessee and the District of Columbia. Its less abrasive leadership also made it appear more suited than NCNB to make the next big acquisition in the area.

There were two flaws, however, in the "live happily ever after scenario" for the newly-formed C&S/Sovran. The economy did not cooperate, and the terms of the deal let the economy be a bigger weakness than it should have been. On the plus side, it quickly abandoned its initial name of Avantor in favor of the longer, but more meaningful, C&S/Sovran.

Sovran was the dominant partner getting 15 board seats to 14 seats for Citizens & Southern, but there was to be dual headquarters in Norfolk and Atlanta, and, although the CEO was initially Citizens & Southern's Brown, upon his retirement at the end of 1991, the position would shift to Sovran's president, Dennis Bottorf. Bottorf was in his late forties, which suggested he would be around for a long time. The normal sequence in this type of an equal transaction is that the equality disappears with the retirement of the first CEO, and the new CEO's home base, in this case Norfolk, becomes the de facto, if not the legal, headquarters.

Any good feelings related to this merger began to dissipate in 1990 as the economic problems that had surfaced in New England and Florida a year earlier were now hurting other areas—none worse than Washington. By the end of 1990, the NPAs of District of Columbia banks had risen from less than 1 percent of assets two years earlier to more than 7 percent, and the problems were far more acute in the Washington suburbs than in the city, particularly in a part of northern Virginia referred to as the Dulles Corridor. The excessive optimism of the mid- and late 1980s had resulted in a glut of empty office buildings financed by bank loans, and the large banks in the area, including C&S/Sovran, were major holders of these loans.

With its geographic diversity, C&S/Sovran, was far from the hardest hit by the loan quality crisis in the area, but its NPAs had increased from less than 1 percent of assets at the end of 1989 to 2 percent of assets a year later and were still rising. In 1991, the Virginia portion of C&S/Sovran alone had an increase from 2.23 percent to 5.87 percent of assets not performing. This was less than some other banks in the area, but it was enough to send the stock price plummeting. When the merger was announced in September 1989, Sovran's stock, which C&S shareholders were receiving in exchange for their stock, was selling at about $42.00 per share. By the end of 1990, four months after the merger was completed, the price was down to $15.63, which was about 72 percent of book value.

The problems were not life threatening, and the Virginia bank may have done as well as could be expected under the adverse circumstances, but if Citizens & Southern had not merged with Sovran, its stock price would have been a lot higher. SunTrust, the remaining, large independent bank in Atlanta had a stock that was still trading at about two times book. The Citizens & Southern board members and investors were well aware of this, and from their less-troubled

Atlanta base, they were not shy about letting their disappointment be known. Their concern was heightened by Bottorf being scheduled to replace Brown as CEO at the end of the year.[3]

The problem might have blown over as the economy improved if NCNB had not interfered. C&S/Sovran had a lot of company with its high level of NPAs among large banks on both coasts and not just in its home area. Wells Fargo, Barnett, Fleet, BankAmerica and most big New York City banks had high NPA levels and yet were to have their stock prices increase by multiples of three to four times over the next seven years. For all of these banks, 1991 and 1992 were trying years made much harder by worried regulators reading them the "riot act" and raising the specter of a possible failure.

C&S/Sovran's declining asset quality and stock price combined with a sharply divided board and regulatory concern was an opportunity for NCNB to accomplish what it had failed to do two years earlier. In May 1991, McColl placed another call to Brown. This time he was not rejected out-of-hand and negotiations began.[4]

This was not really a hostile takeover as the acquirer was willing to consider the offer, but the Virginia board members did not welcome the offer. They most likely felt they were victims of something that was beyond their control and they might not personally survive, but the key elements of a successful hostile takeover were in place. The buyer was a competent, well-respected bank. The target was underperforming no matter what the excuses were, and there were no white knights to come to the rescue. C&S/Sovran was the twelfth largest bank in the country; far bigger than any bank, other than NCNB, in the South; and the large banks in New York and California, who already had their own problems, were excluded from buying banks in the Southeast because of the regional restrictions on interstate banking that were still in place. NCNB was still not a buyer of choice, but this time the seller did not have choices.

In retrospect, this was a "done deal" as soon as NCNB decided to move forward, but like any transaction of this size, it had many internal machinations. The Virginia directors wanted to stay independent, and most of the Georgia directors, including Brown, wanted to as well. The latter, though, were not enthused about seeing leadership transferred to Sovran's Bottorf. From an Atlanta perspective, the CEO transfer would have looked like a sale in its own right. There were also the usual concerns about price and pride.[5]

In July 1991, an agreement was reached, and a deal was struck for $4.5 billion, almost twice what had been offered for Citizens & Southern two years earlier despite the asset quality problems, and it was a new high for a bank sale price.

Although one that would be eclipsed a month later by BankAmerica's purchase of Security Pacific. The only negative vote was from the Citizens & Southern side, and it was a symbolic vote against the disappearance of the C&S name.[6]

A new name, NationsBank, chosen for the combined institutions, would be the nation's third largest bank with assets of $119 billion. In the spirit of equality, Brown became chairman of NationsBank, but it was a victory for NCNB and McColl. There were now few doubters that NCNB, or NationsBank, would be one of the survivors of the consolidation process.

NATIONSBANK–MNC

NationsBank was not through taking advantage of the problems of others. Buying C&S/Sovran made it by far the biggest domestic bank not based in New York or California and gave it the largest market share in the traditional Southeast region of Florida, Georgia and the Carolinas, as well as in the Middle Atlantic States to the immediate north. All that it was missing in the latter was a strong position in Baltimore that was there for the taking, along with an increased market share in the Washington area.

MNC, whose primary subsidiary Maryland National was the biggest bank in Baltimore, was second in size to C&S/Sovran between New Jersey and the Carolinas. It had greatly enhanced its coverage in 1987 with the acquisition of American Security, the second biggest bank in the District of Columbia, and in 1989, it merged Baltimore's third largest bank, Equitable, into Maryland National. By the end of 1989, MNC had assets of $26 billion, including Equitable, and was similar in size to Sovran, Citizens & Southern and Wachovia. It still owned MBNA, which was the fifth largest bank-owned credit card company in the country. MNC was a bank on the move, and a much bigger bank holding company than the one I had left a dozen years before.

Unlike the newly formed C&S/Sovran, MNC was not geographically diversified, and, as a result, it had a larger percentage of its funds committed to commercial lending in the Washington area. Its subsidiary, American Security, was second to Riggs in asset size in the District of Columbia, but it was the largest lender in the city and had substantial loan exposure in the Dulles Corridor. When the commercial real estate markets collapsed, MNC was the region's most vulnerable large bank.

In fact, no large bank between Boston and Miami was hurt more than MNC by the downturn in the real estate markets. Its American Security subsidiary had 9.70 percent of its assets not performing by the end of 1990. A year later, that number was up to 18.28 percent. Its much larger Maryland National subsidiary was not in nearly as much trouble, but with NPAs equal to 7.68 percent of all assets at the end of 1991, it also was a troubled bank.

Baltimore and Washington Largest Bank Asset Quality, 1989 to 1992

	1990 Assets (In billions)	NPAs/Assets			
		1992	1991	1990	1989
Baltimore					
Bank of Baltimore	$ 4	9.37%	6.03%	2.39%	1.03%
Maryland National*	14	4.79	7.68	7.51	1.05
Union Trust**	4	3.00	4.75	4.92	1.88
First National**	7	1.77	2.22	2.05	2.03
Washington					
American Security*	$ 4	10.86%	19.62%	21.40%	8.49%
Chevy Chase	6	10.54	13.26	8.89	5.61***
First American-Va.	4	9.53	10.70	5.05	.93
Riggs	7	6.02	6.00	4.71	.75
MNC	$27	6.19%	10.83%	7.41%	1.08%

*MNC subsidiary.
**Bank level data.
***Excludes non-accrual assets, data not available.
Source: Ferguson & Company, Irving, Texas.

American Security and Maryland National had a larger percentage of assets not performing than any of the other large banks in their respective markets. NPAs as a percent of assets for the four largest banks in each market showed the depth of the loan quality problem in Washington and how much worse it was there than in Baltimore, just 40 miles away. In 1991, three of Washington's four largest banks had more than 10 percent of assets not performing. A fourth, Riggs, which had never been much of a commercial real estate lender, was at 6.57 percent. In Baltimore, Maryland National with NPAs at 7.68 percent of total assets at year-end 1991, led the way, but among the four largest Baltimore banks, it had by far the most coverage in the Maryland suburbs of Washington.

The situation at MNC was further complicated by a commercial paper liquidity crisis early in 1990 that had forced the sale of MBNA. MNC had issued more than $2 billion in commercial paper that came due in 1990, which it would have defaulted on if it did not come up with substantial amounts of new money. Its answer was to sell MBNA in a public offering that raised $992 million. This solved the liquidity problem, averted a possible failure and brought in much needed new capital, but this was at the expense of a major source of strength and future value. This sale was similar to what Citigroup did almost 20 years later when it sold its Smith Barney affiliate to Morgan Stanley to build its capital base.

MNC changed management in 1990, and the Chairman of the recently acquired Equitable, Al Lerner, assumed the CEO role. He was an astute entrepreneur who had built Progressive Insurance into a model for a property and casualty underwriter. The timing, though, of the Equitable sale to MNC was not one of his finer moments. It was a mistake, however, that was made more palatable by his purchase of an almost 10 percent share of MBNA when it was sold to investors. His investment would be worth more than $1 billion a few years later, and it helped Lerner finance his purchase of the new Cleveland Browns franchise in 1998.

The MBNA sale was only a temporary solution for MNC, and even though its prospects were improving by 1992, it was under pressure from the regulators to sell or raise new capital. Since there were no buyers for banks with MNC's problems at that time, it had to either find new capital or hope it could keep its regulators at bay until the local real estate market improved. In mid-1992, the latter course carried with it more risk than its board was prepared to accept.

For the creative NationsBank, this was an opportunity to solidify its position in the region by becoming as strong in Maryland and the District of Columbia as it was in Virginia. NationsBank, like other potential acquirers, was not yet ready to take on MNC's problems in 1992, but it sold the MNC board on accepting a $200 million investment that could be used as capital in return for a five-year buyout option at approximately $1.3 billion. This was a low price for a healthy MNC, and in 1993, NationsBank exercised the option.

With the C&S/Sovran and MNC deals, NationsBank had created a southern powerhouse with national potential. Its branch coverage stretched from Baltimore to El Paso, and it had about 10 percent of deposits in the South. It was first in deposit share in Georgia, Maryland, South Carolina, Texas and Virginia, second in the District of Columbia, third in North Carolina and fourth in Florida.

First Union

NationsBank's cross-town rival in Charlotte, First Union, could not match its moves, but First Union vastly improved its position during this period as others disappeared or sat on their hands. From 1989 through 1993, First Union would acquire four banks with combined assets of close to $40 billion. With these purchases, its assets grew to a little over $70 billion by 1993, and it had become the country's ninth largest bank. In the South, only NationsBank was larger. First Union's target markets were Florida and the Washington area, and by the end of 1993, it was in the top two in each.

Its Florida success was particularly noteworthy in that its acquisitions moved it up to second place in deposit share behind Barnett and gave it the largest deposit share on Florida's Gold Coast, stretching from Miami north to Palm Beach. In what had been the primary target state for NCNB, First Union had made the big gains.

First Union's first post-1988 acquisition was the Jacksonville-based Florida National, which was the third largest Florida bank behind Barnett and Southeast Banking. It had assets of $7.8 billion when acquired, and Florida National, alone, would move First Union into second place in the state.

Another Florida purchase by First Union, Southeast Banking, would make it number one in Florida's largest market, Miami, and First Union may owe this success to NCNB's pre-occupation with C&S/Sovran. Miami's Southeast Banking was southern Florida's biggest bank with assets of $13.4 billion, but its location and orientation toward commercial lending would be its undoing in a real estate-driven depression. By early 1991, its loan quality and supporting capital had deteriorated to the point that it was unable to raise new capital, sell or survive. In September 1991, Southeast Banking was taken over by the FDIC and put up for sale under the FDIC's assisted-sale program.

NCNB and First Union were among the most interested potential acquirers, but because Southeast Banking had failed, its buyers were not strictly limited to states in the southern interstate banking compact. It was an opportunity for New York banks to gain access to a market that had long been high on their "wish lists." It was an attractive acquisition with most of the risk taken away by the FDIC, and Southeast Banking's buyer would be the leader in Florida's biggest market.

Fate, though, would smile on First Union. The New York banks were in their own battle for survival; two of the most likely buyers within the region, NCNB and C&S/Sovran, were otherwise involved; and Barnett had too much of a market overlap to gain regulatory acceptance unless there were no other alternatives. NCNB was actively pursuing Southeast Banking at the same time it was going after C&S/Sovran, and considering its success in Texas buying failed banks, it had to be a favorite to win in Florida as well. When NCNB won its more desired prize to the north, however, it had to put aside other endeavors. In the end, First Union, SunTrust and Barnett bid on Southeast Banking, and First Union's offer was considered the best by the FDIC.[7]

NCNB's acquisition of C&S/Sovran, and then MNC, did not preclude it from making additional acquisitions in Maryland, Virginia and the District of Columbia, but the practicalities of integrating such large banks into its system were substantial; and, thus, First Union was a logical haven for other struggling banks in those states and the District of Columbia. In 1992, First Union bought the $8.6 billion asset Dominion in Virginia, and a year later, it acquired the deeply troubled First American in Washington, a holding company with banks in Washington, as well as its Maryland and Virginia suburbs. Each of First American's three largest subsidiary banks had more than 9 percent of their assets not performing at the height of the recession.

First American made First Union a leader in the Washington area, a dubious distinction at the time, but Washington was a large market with good growth potential, even as its banks faltered. After completion of the First American acquisition, First Union had about 9 percent of the area's deposits, which was second only to NationsBank.

First Union was one of the more active buyers of failed thrifts during this time. In 1992, it bought four thrifts with total assets of almost $10 billion. This included the two largest in Georgia with combined assets of $7.2 billion.

First American

The motivation for First American's sale to First Union was quite different from that of most bank sales. The troubles that forced its sale went far beyond the asset quality concerns of other banks in troubled times and showed that the regulators did not know everything about the banks under their control. In the early 1980s, First American had secretly come under control of the Bank of Credit and Commerce International, or BCCI, an international bank founded by Agha Hasan Abedi, which was not just another foreign bank.

A Senate Foreign Relations Committee report in 1992 stated "Unlike any ordinary bank, BCCI was from its earliest days made up of multiplying layers of entities, related to one another through an impenetrable series of holding companies, affiliates, subsidiaries, banks-within-banks, insider dealings and nominee relationships. By fracturing corporate structure, record keeping, regulatory review and audits the complex BCCI family of entities created by Abedi was able to avoid ordinary legal restrictions on the movement of capital and goods as a matter of daily practice and routine. In creating BCCI as a vehicle fundamentally free of government control, Abedi developed in BCCI an ideal mechanism for facilitating illicit activity by officials of many of the governments whose laws BCCI was breaking."[8]

"BCCI's criminality include fraud by BCCI and BCCI customers involving billions of dollars; money laundering in Europe, Africa, Asia and the Americas; BCCI bribery of officials in most of those locations; support of terrorism, arms trafficking, and the sale of nuclear technologies; management of prostitution; the commission and facilitation of income tax evasion; smuggling and illegal immigration; illicit purchases of banks and real estate; and a panoply of financial crimes limited only by the imagination of its officers and customers."[9]

The size and scope of BCCI's activities and involvement with a major American bank were sufficient to make its control of First American a front-page story, and it was a story that benefited from star power as well. First American's chairman, Clark Clifford, and president, Robert Altman, whose careers became closely tied to BCCI, were far from anonymous figures. Clifford was a well-known advisor to presidents and a former Secretary of Defense. Altman was not as high profile as Clifford, but was the husband of television star, Lynda Carter, of Wonder Woman fame. Prior to assuming their positions at First American in 1981, Clifford and Altman also represented Bert Lance, a well-known adviser of Jimmy Carter, in the sale of Lance's National Bank of Georgia to a BCCI affiliate.

Ironically, prior to the coming of Clifford, Altman and BCCI, First American, or Financial General as it was called then, had the inside track on being one of the biggest of the 1980 superregionals. It was one of just seven banks that had been "grandfathered" into being able to operate in multiple states prior to the arrival of interstate banking. It had sold banks in some of these states, but in 1980, it was still active in Maryland, New York, Tennessee, Virginia and the District of Columbia and could have acquired banks in any of those states when others could not. For reasons that were clearer in 1992 than they were then, First American chose to concentrate on its Manhattan office and international banking, and the interstate opportunity was lost.

Thrift Decline

The consolidation process in the Southeast driven primarily by the sale of banks like First American was also helped by a decline in the number of thrifts and thrift assets. Some of the fall-off was the clean-up of the thrift crisis of the 1980s, particularly in Florida, but much of it came from the region's larger thrifts moving into commercial real estate in the late 1980s and paying a steep price for doing so.

From the end of 1988 through 1993, about 180 of the thrifts in a Southeast region, defined to include also Maryland, Virginia and the District of Columbia, disappeared, but more importantly was the decline in thrift assets in this region. They were more than halved from $198 billion in 1988 to $93 billion in 1993. In Florida, the asset fall-off was from $89 billion to $33 billion, and by 1993, every one of these Southeast states, except Florida, had thrift assets of $17 billion or less.

Southeast Thrift Change, 1988 to 1993

	Number of Thrifts		Thrift Assets	
	1993	1988	1993	1988
			(In billions)	
Florida	79	145	$33	$89
Maryland	83	97	17	23
Virginia	43	63	14	30
North Carolina	86	133	12	21
South Carolina	38	48	9	12
Georgia	39	21	7	20
District of Columbia	2	5	1	3
Total	370	562	$93	$197
Mid-South	110	232	$17	$43

Source: FDIC: Historical Statistics on Banking.

In the rest of the South, other than Texas, thrifts were never much of a factor and became even less so during this period. In the Mid-South states of Alabama, Louisiana, Mississippi and Tennessee, the number of thrifts fell from 232 to 110 between 1988 and the end of 1993. The most thrift assets in any one Mid-South state in 1993 were the $6 billion in Tennessee.

The disappearance of just the large thrifts was even more dramatic. In the expanded Southeast, there were 44 thrifts at the end of 1988 with assets in excess of $1 billion. Five years later, there were just 15, and by the end of 1995, there were only six. Just two, Chevy Chase and BankAtlantic, were still around in 2005; and by 2012, they were gone. Florida was by far the most impacted by the sale of its large thrifts. It had 26 thrifts with assets over $1 billion in 1988 and only nine in 1993. The buyers were usually banks, but in Florida, some of the sales were to large West Coast thrifts. Many of these transactions were regulatory-assisted sales of failed thrifts.

THEN THERE WERE TWO

The change in the Southeast banking landscape caused by the real estate recession of the early 1990s was one of the biggest facilitators of the consolidation process. At the end of 1988, the region had seven banks—NCNB, SunTrust, First Union, Barnett, Citizens & Southern, Sovran and Wachovia—with assets between $20 and $30 billion, and two others, MNC and Southeast Banking, with assets in excess of $15 billion. Five years later, NCNB, by then NationsBank, had acquired three of these nine banks; had almost $160 billion in assets; and was the country's third largest bank. First Union was a distant second in the Southeast with assets of $71 billion. It was, though, the only other big southeastern bank that was able to increase its size significantly during these five years.

Largest Southeast Banks, 1993

	Assets		Rank 1988	Eventual Owner
	1993	1988		
	(In billions)			
1. NationsBank	$158	$30	1	Bank of America
2. First Union	71	29	3	Wells Fargo
3. SunTrust	41	29	2	SunTrust
4. Barnett	38	26	4	Bank of America
5. Wachovia	37	22	7	Wells Fargo
6. Crestar	13	10	-	SunTrust
7. Signet	12	11	10	Wells Fargo
8. Central Fidelity	10	5	-	Wells Fargo
9. BB&T	9	4	-	BB&T

Source: American Banker, April 11, 1990 and April 14, 1994.

SunTrust, Barnett and Wachovia were still around in 1993, but with assets in the $35 to $45 billion range, they had done little more than grow with the rate of inflation. They were still substantial banks and made some acquisitions during this period, but they had fallen into a banking second tier regionally, as well as nationally, and looked more like sellers than buyers. NationsBank would acquire Barnett in 1998, and First Union bought Wachovia in 2001 and took the Wachovia name.

The remainder of the top ten in the Southeast in 1993 was composed primarily of Virginia banks with assets of less than $15 billion. Crestar, Signet, Central

Fidelity and First Virginia had survived a bank-damaging recession that had hit close to home, but three of the four would sell within four years and the fourth a couple of years later. Signet and Central Fidelity became part of First Union and eventually part of the Wells Fargo banking network; Crestar was acquired by SunTrust; and First Virginia was bought by BB&T. The latter made its first appearance in the Southeast top ten in 1993 while on its way to bigger things.

CALIFORNIA DREAMING

In 1989, it was hard to imagine that the economic problems that bedeviled the East Coast banks would soon become an equally negative force in California. Some of the larger banks in that state, particularly BankAmerica, had been hit hard by loans to developing countries, the earlier discussed LDC crisis, but California, and the entire West Coast, was benefiting from a burgeoning Japanese economy and President Reagan's defense build-up. At the time, it seemed like California and its largest city, Los Angeles, were riding an unstoppable wave of growth that would give its large banks and S&Ls national as well as regional preeminence.

In one of my banking reports in 1988, I was enamored enough to write that "it is inevitable that when barriers are removed, money flows to where the action is, and the combination of Japan, the strong economies of the region, the banking weaknesses in other parts of the nation are moving banking in the Far West to the head of the class. The regional allure has drawn eastern banking organizations such as Citicorp, Chase Manhattan and KeyCorp and every major Japanese bank … helping to transform Los Angeles into a banking center that threatens to rival New York and London, if not Tokyo."[1]

Today these statements sound ludicrous, but in 1988 and 1989, it was a logical assumption. Of approximately 70 banks and thrifts with assets in excess of $10 billion, 17 were in California—ten in Los Angeles alone—and just 13 in New York. Of the 15 highest bank or thrift capitalizations, five were in California and four were in New York. BankAmerica, Security Pacific, First Interstate and Wells Fargo ranked 3rd, 5th, 9th and 12th in size among banks, and the country's eight largest S&Ls, led by Ahmanson and Great Western, were in California. All of these institutions, except BankAmerica and Wells Fargo, had their headquarters in the Los Angeles area.[2]

Three years later, Japan's economy was faltering; the rising star of Far West banking, Security Pacific, was forced into a sale to BankAmerica; and five of the eight largest California banking organizations had more than 5 percent of their assets not performing; and a sixth just missed. What had looked so promising in 1988 and 1989 seemed ages ago, and any California dreams of domestic banking pre-eminence were over.

When economic conditions began to improve in California in 1994—the real estate-driven recession that began a year later than on the East Coast also ended a year later—among the big banks, only Security Pacific was gone, but those that remained were hurt. BankAmerica doubled its size with the Security Pacific acquisition, but along with that purchase came far more bad loans than anticipated. The local S&Ls were hit even harder. Of California's 13 S&Ls with assets in excess of $10 billion at the end of 1988, seven were gone by 1994.

A DIFFERENT LOCAL BANKING INDUSTRY

California's rapid descent from such heights was a sad turn of events for a local banking industry that had been at the forefront of banking trends for so many years. The state's size, rapid growth, geographic detachment from the rest of the country and early elimination of in-state prohibitions on branching allowed banks and thrifts to develop the economies of scale that spurred innovation and put California banks years ahead of banks in the rest of the country in retail banking. From the 1920s forward, the original Bank of America was the "poster child" for progressive banking with its large branch network and its pioneering of the bank credit card in the 1960s, but it was only the most visible part of a vibrant California banking industry.[1*]

Right up through the 1970s, when the ranks of the largest banks were dominated by New York and Chicago money center institutions, Bank of America, Security First, Western Bancorporation, Wells Fargo and Crocker National were the only retail banks that were regular members of the top 25 banks nationwide. They had branch networks in the 1930s and 1940s that banks elsewhere would not match until the 1970s. Transamerica, the Bank of America holding company,

*The continual usage of both Bank of America and BankAmerica in the text is confusing, but is factually correct. Bank of America was the name of the biggest California bank from 1930 until its sale to NationsBank in 1998. In 1968, a holding company formed as the parent of Bank of America that was called BankAmerica. In 1998, BankAmerica and Bank of America were bought by NationsBank, which chose to use the Bank of America name instead of NationsBank for both its holding company and lead bank.

owned so many banks outside California that when its banks, other than Bank of America, were spun off into a new entity, Western Bancorporation; it immediately became one of the country's largest bank holding companies with banks in eleven western states.

The rapid growth of California also created an in-state S&L industry that dwarfed what existed elsewhere. In 1980, the country's eight largest S&Ls were in California, and the state's S&Ls had about 20 percent of S&L assets nationwide. By the end of 1988, the twelve largest S&Ls were in California, and they held 31 percent of the national S&L assets.[3]

California Bank Deposits by Type of Bank, 1982 to 1986

	Total Deposits		Percent of Total	
	1986*	1982	1986*	1982
	(In billions)			
Big Four				
BankAmerica	$ 53	$ 58	27%	37%
Other **	72	46	37	29
Subtotal	$124	$104	64%	66%
Foreign Banks				
Japanese	$ 21	$ 8	11%	5%
British	-	21	-	13
Other	2	3	1	2
Subtotal	$ 23	$ 32	12%	20%
Local Banks	$ 46	$ 21	33%	134%

*Includes all mergers completed or in process to date.
**Security Pacific, First Interstate and Wells Fargo.
Source: FDIC Data Book, Operating Banks and Branches, June 30, 1982 and 1986.

The immense size of the market and interstate banking prohibitions also gave California banking an international flavor in the 1980s, as foreign banks flocked to a market that was off-limits to out-of-state domestic banks. Standard Charter, Lloyds, Midland and Barclays came from England. Bank of Tokyo, Sumitomo, Mitsui and almost every other large bank in Japan were among the foreign entrants, and banks came to California from Korea, Hong Kong, Italy, France, Canada and Mexico. Some of the foreign banks were serving their own ethnic populations, but others had bigger goals. In 1981, Midland bought 57 percent of Crocker National, which was the 13th largest bank in the country. Another English bank, Standard Charter, owned Union Bank with 1980 assets of $7 billion and was California's sixth largest bank. Bank of Tokyo and Barclays had California assets of $4 billion and $3 billion, respectively, in that same year.

The foreign invasion of California banking peaked around 1982 with 20 percent of statewide deposits with the British banks holding 13 percent. In the next six years, the British banks left California with Midland's sale of Crocker National to Wells Fargo and Standard Charter selling Union Bank to the Bank of Tokyo leading the way. By the late 1980s, the foreign share of California banking had dipped to 12 percent, almost all of which was Japanese.

The purchase of Crocker National by Wells Fargo was a major step in consolidating California banking in that it changed a big five into a big four, but this acquisition only maintained the big four's statewide deposit share at around 64 percent. Crocker National being acquired by Wells Fargo and smaller acquisitions by Security Pacific merely offset the lost share of a struggling BankAmerica.

Another dimension in California banking growth was the opening of a plethora of new banks. From 1980 through 1989, the number of banks in the state increased from 281 to 479, and in the four years between 1982 and 1986, the local banks' statewide deposit share increased from about 14 percent to 33 percent. This explosion of new banks was another manifestation of the state's booming economy in the 1980s.

DARK CLOUDS GATHER

It is convenient to pair the corresponding decline of the California and Japanese economies because of the coincidental timing and combined negative impact on the euphoria that had built up about the Pacific Rim, but the California decline had more to do with domestic events than Japan. Southern California had an even bigger stake in the American defense industry than New England, and, like in New England, the Reagan defense build-up of the 1980s was the primary source of southern California's economic boom. The region's major employers included Northrup, Hughes, Lockheed, TRW, Rockwell, McDonnell-Douglas and General Dynamics. When the Berlin Wall fell in 1989 and the Cold War ended, there was a substantial drop-off in defense spending and southern California was a big loser.[4]

The percentage of total defense-oriented jobs was never that high in southern California, but the rapid increase in defense-related employment fueled a growth in home and office building, much as the oil and gas boom had done in Texas. Between 1980 and 1990, available square footage of office space in Los Angeles County grew from 68 million to 148 million. When the basis of this growth, the defense industry, began downsizing, the office vacancy rate rose rapidly, and the only good news for local banks was that Japanese banks held about half of the commercial real estate loans. On the housing side, the high demand for living quarters, accompanied by a rapid increase in housing prices, created a high vulnerability of mortgage defaults if home values were not sustained.[5]

Despite the many negative indicators, belief in the California dream was slow to die. The state had been in a perpetual boom for decades, and all previous downturns had been mild. The feeling then was that this would be the case one more time. No one thought that when employment peaked at the end of 1990, California would lose 752,000 jobs in the next four years—most of which would be in southern California—or that the unemployment rate would reach 9.5 percent in September 1992. This just was not supposed to happen in California.[6]

While the reasons for the 1980s' economic boom in California were unraveling, the state's big banks were just starting to enjoy a welcome revival. A very competitive market and their ventures into money center activities, particularly LDC loans to Mexico, had resulted in BankAmerica losing money from 1985 through 1987, along with First Interstate and Security Pacific reporting losses in 1987. Wells Fargo had lost money in 1983 and 1984. From 1988 through 1990, though, all four were highly profitable and enjoying the best overall earnings of the decade, but they continued to carry relatively high levels of NPAs—above 2.5 percent of all assets. BankAmerica had more than 4 percent of its assets not performing.

In 1991, NPAs were rising and earnings declining for most banks in the state, and for some, much more than others. Security Pacific suffered the most among the large banks. It was the biggest bank in Los Angeles and had far more of its assets committed to southern California than the other large Los Angeles bank, First Interstate, a new name for what was once Western Bancorporation. Security Pacific's NPAs rose from 2.75 percent of all assets at the end of 1989 to 6.44 percent at the end of 1991, resulting in a loss that year of $775 million. First Interstate, which had almost two-thirds of its assets outside of California, also lost money in 1991, but much less than Security Pacific—albeit still a substantial $288 million. The San Francisco-based Wells Fargo and the Bank of Tokyo-owned Union Bank had big year-to-year increases in NPAs in 1991, but they continued to make money.

California Bank and Thrift Asset Quality, 1987 to 1992

	NPAs/Assets				
	1992	**1991**	**1990**	**1989**	**1987***
California					
Banks	4.79%	4.46%	2.78%	2.53%	3.56%
Thrifts	3.74	3.99	2.82	2.10	3.41
Banks					
Union**	5.53%	4.45%	2.71%	2.13%	2.15%
Wells Fargo	5.38%	4.79	2.82	2.63	3.90
BankAmerica	3.71	3.44	3.21	4.48	6.13
First Interstate	1.58	3.39	3.55	3.75	3.35
Security Pacific	-	6.44	3.77	2.75	3.45
Thrifts					
Ahmanson	5.07%	4.68%	2.67%	2.18%	1.38%***
GlenFed	4.62	3.31	2.15	1.86	1.51***
Golden West	1.60	1.47	1.02		
Great Western	1.33	1.24	.89	.45	.65

*1987 when available to accentuate improved asset quality of three of the four largest banks between 1987 and 1989.
**Bank of Tokyo subsidiary.
***1988.
Source: FDIC: Historical Statistics on Banking and SNL Financial Services Inc., Charlottesville, Virginia.

BankAmerica fared much better than its chief in-state rivals after 1990. Its 3.44 percent of assets not performing at year-end 1991 was up marginally from the previous year-end, but this was well below its 6 percent plus of the mid-1980s. This was not good asset quality nevertheless BankAmerica had raised its annual income above $1 billion in 1989, and kept it at least that level, or better, during the entire four years of economic problems.

The large California S&Ls generally came into the 1990s with better asset quality than the banks, and the largest among them had hardly been touched by the 1980s' S&L crisis. In fact, they had been buyers of failed thrifts in Florida and other states. By 1991, however, most of them were experiencing a rapid increase in NPAs. California's, and the country's, largest thrift, Ahmanson, the holding company for Home Savings, had 2.67 percent of assets not performing at the end of 1990, 4.68 percent a year later and then moved above 5 percent in 1992. GlenFed, California's and the nation's third largest S&L, followed the same trend from a slightly lower base.

There were some exceptions, however, to the rapid decline of asset quality. Great Western, which was only slightly smaller than Ahmanson, never had NPAs reach 2 percent of total assets, and Golden West, parent of World Savings, was totally committed to home mortgages and had minimal loan quality problems.

SECURITY PACIFIC

The big story in California banking during these years was the rapid decline of Security Pacific. It was the rising star of West Coast banking in the 1980s, and in 1989, it seemed likely to eclipse BankAmerica. Security Pacific's assets had increased from $28 billion in 1980 to almost $80 billion by the end of 1988. It was based in Los Angeles where the action was; its losses related to LDC loans were far less than for BankAmerica; and it was the fifth largest bank in the country. Security Pacific seemed to be the right bank, at the right place, at the right time.

Security Pacific began as Farmers & Merchants Bank in Los Angeles in 1871 and grew rapidly with its market. In 1929, it became Security First National Bank, and in the 1950s, Security First merged with Pacific National Bank in the northern part of the state and took the name Security Pacific. It had become one of California's largest banks by the 1920s, and since 1940, it was close to, if not in, the top ten nationally. By 1960, only BankAmerica and Western Bancorporation had larger branch networks.[7]

In the 1980s, Security Pacific was aggressively taking advantage of opportunities that came with interstate banking. In 1986, it bought Arizona BancWest, the third largest bank in Arizona. A year later, it bought Rainier National, the second largest bank in Washington, and Oregon Bank, the third largest bank in Oregon. In 1989, it added the second largest bank in Nevada, Nevada National. As a result, by 1989, it had 20 percent of its assets outside of California. This was less than the more than 60 percent non-California assets of cross-town rival, First Interstate, but Security Pacific had become more than just a California bank. It had also aggressively expanded into international banking.

The man responsible for this dramatic growth and diversification in the 1980s, Richard Flamson III, would hand the reins over to Robert Smith in 1990, who had promised to boost the stock price and push Security Pacific into a fresh round of acquisitions. Unfortunately, Flamson left behind a slew of problems, and Smith was soon into damage control rather than expanding. Along with a $200 million write-off in 1991, he closed down the international lending and securities trading operations. Meantime, loans on several highly-leveraged deals were going bad, and its bad real estate loans stretched from Great Britain to Arizona—and this was before California's real estate market began its sharp descent.[8]

By the second quarter of 1991, California real estate loans were about half of Security Pacific's $658 million nonperforming loans, and this was only the beginning of the rapid deterioration of its real estate loan portfolio. There was speculation that looming loan problems had ended merger talks with Wells Fargo—negotiations that presumably would have at least had Security Pacific as a nominal equal partner.[9]

In August 1991, BankAmerica was willing to tread where Wells Fargo was not and traded loan quality risk for franchise enhancement. It paid $4.7 billion for a faltering Security Pacific, and the size of the acquiree lifted BankAmerica's assets to a level just below that of Citicorp, but it was not all roses for the buyer. Security Pacific had $1.4 billion in losses in the three quarters prior to consummating the deal and BankAmerica would eventually charge off $3.6 billion of the purchase price against goodwill.[10]

BankAmerica paid far too much for a bank that would have been close to failing a year later, but the purchase reduced California's big four to a big three and combined what in 1988 had been the third and fifth largest banks in the country. It was another major step in the consolidation process, but the high cost in terms of price paid and losses incurred may have helped put BankAmerica in the secondary position when it merged with NationsBank in 1998.

Security Pacific was the only large bank forced to sell because of the real estate problems in California, but the number of banks in the state was greatly reduced. Between 1990 and 1994, there were 47 bank failures and 59 acquisitions, many of which were the result of the threat of failure. The largest of these smaller, forced bank acquisitions was First Interstate's purchase of the $2.2 billion San Diego Financial, parent of San Diego Trust & Savings.

S&L IMPACT ON CONSOLIDATION

There was no single deal remotely resembling the disappearance of Security Pacific on the thrift side of the California banking industry, but, collectively, the damage done to the S&Ls in the state during this period was substantial. In 1988, there were 13 S&Ls in the state with assets in excess of $10 billion, and five with assets over $25 billion—Ahmanson, Great Western, Cal Fed, First Nationwide and GlenFed. The latter were as large as NCNB, First Union, Fleet, Bank of New England and Bank One at the time. By the end of 1994, there were just six independent California S&Ls with assets of more than $10 billion and three with assets of more than $25 billion.

Largest California S&Ls, 1988

	Assets (In billions)	Net Income (In millions)	Percent of Assets		
			Tangible Capital	NPAs	Reserves/ Loans
1. Ahmanson	$40	$203	3.74%	.92%	.13%
2. Great Western	33	248	5.33	1.56	.36
3. Cal Fed	28	135	2.93	2.21	.46
4. First Nationwide	26	(3)	2.40	-	-
5. GlenFed	25	189	1.69	2.43	.86
6. HomeFed	17	111	4.60	3.27	.58
7. Golden West	17	138	3.34	1.10	.11
8. Great American	16	50	2.60	2.37	.32
9. American Savings	15	(1)	1.79	-	-
10. Gibraltar	13	(63)	2.33	-	-
11. Coast Savings	13	48	1.92	1.73	.25
12. Columbia Savings	13	65	5.31	.67	.20
13. Imperial	12	15	1.65	3.69	.72

Source: Thrift Securities Handbook, Kaplan Smith, April 1989.

Some of the California S&L situation was a carryover of the 1980s thrift crisis, which was both good and bad. On the good side, American Savings had been acquired by Robert Bass in a 1988 FSLIC-assisted deal and was moving forward with new capital and a cleaned-up and greatly reduced balance sheet. Not so good was Los Angeles-based Gibraltar Savings, which would be taken over by the FSLIC in March 1989. All of the other large S&Ls, except one, were profitable in 1988. That one, First Nationwide, lost only $3 million and was owned by Ford Motors whose "deep pockets" kept it from being a regulatory concern. The largest S&Ls, Ahmanson and Great Western, each earned more than $200 million in 1988.

Despite having survived the thrift crisis and producing strong earnings in 1988, California's S&Ls were far more vulnerable to a real estate-driven economic downturn than the banks. Eight of the 13 largest California S&Ls had 1988 tangible capital of less than 3 percent of assets—below 6 percent of assets was the threshold of regulatory concern. Their reserves were only slowly working their way up from the

.10 percent of loans that was the norm against home mortgages even though much of their lending was now in far riskier commercial real estate. In other words, many of these California S&Ls did not have much of a cushion for dealing with adversity.

Because of their size, the elimination of risk-free FSLIC deals and the real estate problems of the most likely buyers, there were no ready buyers for these large S&Ls when their loan portfolio put their survival at risk after 1988. Their size also made it very expensive for the RTC, which had replaced the FSLIC as the repository for failed S&Ls, to close an S&L and pay off the depositors. Thus, the normal RTC procedure for dealing with failing S&Ls in California after 1989 was for them to continue to operate under RTC receivership until a buyer could be found.

Between 1990 and 1992, three of California's largest S&Ls followed Gibraltar Savings into receivership. All three—Great American, HomeFed and Imperial— were in San Diego, a city that also lost its largest bank in a rescue acquisition by First Interstate during this period.

When economic conditions improved in California, Ahmanson, Great Western and Golden West were still standing with assets in excess of $25 billion, and they were in a position to be consolidators of what remained of the California S&L industry—a role briefly played by the first two. Golden West was the real success story having come through the bad times without any real loan problems, and, as a result, was able to go from seventh to third in asset size in the state while raising assets from $17 million to $31 million. Cal Fed and GlenFed, two other California S&Ls with assets over $25 million in 1988, had survived, but they were much smaller in 1993 than in 1988 and struggling.

Another survivor was First Nationwide, which was sold in 1994 by Ford Motors to MacAndrews & Forbes, a holding company controlled by Ronald Perelman. This was the same Perelman that had purchased First Gibraltar, the largest Texas S&L, from the FSLIC in one of the controversial Southwest plan deals in 1988, which he later sold to BankAmerica. He would subsequently buy control of Cal Fed in 1996 and GlenFed in 1998, both of which would become part of a holding company called Golden State. In 1998, Perelman had a controlling interest in what ten years earlier were three of California's largest S&Ls—First Nationwide, Cal Fed and GlenFed. Golden State was acquired by Citigroup in 2002.

CONSOLIDATION IMPACT

Unlike the Southeast during the early 1990s, the primary impact on the consolidation process in California, and all of the Far West, was not who made the gains, but rather the failure of any of the region's larger banks to materially improve their positions. The region had no NationsBank or First Union coming out of this difficult environment much stronger than when they went into it. BankAmerica had doubled its size because of the Security Pacific acquisition, but that only brought it back in relative size among big banks to where it had been a few years earlier and with Security Pacific came many problems. Wells Fargo and First Interstate were still big banks, but First Interstate had $6 billion fewer assets in 1993 than it did in 1988, and Wells Fargo had not grown much in these five years. These banks were still in the SunTrust-Barnett size category rather than keeping pace with NationsBank and First Union. Bank of Tokyo's deep pockets allowed Union Bank to make it through this period, but with 1993 assets of $17 billion, it was strictly a local player.

Among the thrifts, Ahmanson and Great Western had each moved up a position in size among banking organizations in California when Security Pacific was sold, allowing them to keep pace with Wells Fargo and First Interstate. They had also been major buyers of thrifts in other states. In mid-1994, Great Western had the largest deposit share of any thrift in Florida and Ahmanson was second. If there were to be any California thrifts playing a role in the national consolidation process, they were the prime candidates.

Largest Western Banks and Thrifts, 1993

	Assets		Rank	Eventual
	1993	1988	1988	Owner
	(In billions)			
1. BankAmerica	$187	$95	1	Bank of America
2. Wells Fargo	53	47	4	Wells Fargo
3. First Interstate	52	58	3	Wells Fargo
4. Ahmanson	51	41	5	JPMorgan
5. Great Western	36	31	6	JPMorgan
6. Golden West	28	16	-	Wells Fargo
7. US Bancorp	21	14	-	U.S. Bancorp
8. GlenFed	17	24	9	Citigroup
9. Union Bank*	17	15	-	Mitsubishi UFJ
10. American Savings	16	-	-	JPMorgan

*Bank of Tokyo subsidiary.
Source: American Banker, April 11, 1990.

On a regional basis, the prospects looked much more positive as the California banks still dominated banking throughout the western part of the country. The only non-California banks in the Far West top ten at the end of 1993 were U.S. Bancorp in Portland, Oregon and Bank of Tokyo, whose American operation is primarily the California-based Union Bank. California banks and S&Ls had been slowed by the economic downturn, but it seemed possible, and even likely, that they could use their positions in what was still one of the fastest growing parts of the country to regain their momentum.

In retrospect, the California banks and thrifts had lost their momentum for good, and they were ready to sell if the right offers came along. Within five years, BankAmerica would be sold to NationsBank; Wells Fargo would buy First Interstate and then sell to Norwest; and Washington Mutual would roll-up American Savings, Great Western and Ahmanson, all of which would become part of JPMorgan when Washington Mutual failed in 2008. Golden State held on until 2004 when it was bought by Citigroup.

It would not be a total loss for California, though, for after acquiring Wells Fargo, Norwest would move its headquarters from Minneapolis to San Francisco and keep the Wells Fargo name. The lure of the California market was enough to have kept one of the four dominant domestic trillion dollar banks of today headquartered there—even if that bank cannot claim to be homegrown.

NEW YORK BANKING
AT A CROSSROADS

The 1989 to 1992 recession played no favorites based on size and reputation, and New York was certainly no exception. It was the financial capital of the world in 1989, and its banks were the icons of the industry—at least that was the perception. To most, the term "big bank" meant Citicorp, Chase Manhattan, Chemical, Manufacturers Hanover, J.P. Morgan and one well-known bank on the other coast, BankAmerica. They had been the biggest banks as long as most could remember—albeit their names might have been a little different in earlier days. The advent of interstate banking had legislators shaping the banking laws of their states to slow the entry of these behemoths forever, if possible, but at least until local banks had a chance to solidify their positions within their state and region. Even if banks hit a "rough patch," as would happen in 1989, periods of change historically have enhanced the position of the big banks at the expense of their smaller rivals, and there was no reason to think it would be any different this time around.

This perception, though, could not have been more wrong, and for New York and its banks, the real estate woes that began in 1989 could not have come at a worse time. Since the late 1970s, its big banks had been struggling with nonperforming, or at least underperforming, international loans, most of them to Latin American countries. This slowed their growth throughout the 1980s, and it was these loans, even more than the regional interstate banking compacts, that had kept most of them on the sidelines during the early years of interstate banking. When New York banks were allowed to buy banks in New Jersey in 1989, only Chemical made the effort, and that was a relatively small purchase in the southern part of the state.

The international waters had not only been inhospitable to New York bank loan portfolios in the 1980s, but they had also lost their international preeminence. By 1990, not a single New York bank ranked among the top twenty in the world in assets, and they would have fared no better if the rankings had been based on earnings or market capital. From 1987 through 1992, profits and stock prices were not their strong points.

The decline in the relative size of the money center banks in New York and elsewhere compared to all banks was nothing new. In Chapter 2, the large banks' loss of deposit share was discussed in the context of the rapid growth of retail banking after World War II. Only the California banks, because of the immense size of the state and its liberal branching laws, however, approached the absolute size of the New York banks.

Despite the post-World War II deposit share decline, Citicorp, Chase Manhattan and BankAmerica were still the big three of American banking, and in most of those years, Manufacturers Hanover, Chemical, J.P. Morgan and Bankers Trust held the next four places. Charter—which would later change its holding company name to Irving—Marine Midland and Bank of New York were usually just outside the top ten. The dominance of the money center banks was further bolstered by the frequent inclusion among the leaders of Chicago's two money center banks—First National Bank of Chicago and Continental.

Ten Largest Banks by Location, 1940 to 1988

	NY	CA	Chicago	Total	Percent of Total
Assets (in billions)					
1988	$562	$231	-	$860	27%
1980	374	144	$71	589	31
1960	34	21	3	59	22
1940	11	2	3	16	23
Number of Banks					
1988	7	3	2	10	
1980	6	2	2	10	
1960	6	3	1	10	
1940	7	1	2	10	

Sources: SNL Financial, Charlottesville, Virginia; Polk's Bank Directory; and FDIC: Historical Statistics on Banking.

The perception of potential banking dominance flowing from the streets of Manhattan across the United States was still supported by bank numbers as 1989 began. Seven of the ten largest banks were in New York, and the largest, Citicorp, was the country's biggest bank and more than twice as large as number two, Chase Manhattan. J.P. Morgan and Chemical had each moved up a position in the rankings since 1980 to fourth and seventh, respectively. Manufacturers Hanover fell in asset size from fourth to eighth, but was still in the top ten. Bankers Trust was number nine, and Bank of New York, fresh off its hostile takeover of Irving, had moved into tenth place. With seven top ten banks in 1988, New York had one more bank in the top ten than it had in 1980, and the other top ten banks were more than 3,000 miles to the west in California.

The enhanced rankings of the New York banks in 1988 had more to do with the troubles of others rather than their own performances. Between 1980 and 1988, a struggling BankAmerica's assets fell from $112 billion to $95 billion, and, in 1984, Chicago's Continental was bailed out by the government because of excessive loan losses.

A couple of other numbers, though, tell a different story. Seven New York banks in the top ten may have been one more than in 1980, but it was a long way from 1940 when only Bank of America (as BankAmerica was called then) kept New York from having all of the ten biggest banks. More telling was the shrinkage of the ten largest banks' share of domestic banking assets from 31 percent in 1980 to 27 percent in 1988. They were still the biggest, but they were losing ground.

Thus, when the real estate markets in the greater New York area fell upon hard times, the banks that held the largest portion of the commercial real estate loans were in no condition to shrug these loans off as short-term problems. To make matters worse, their national reach brought them troubled real estate loans from around the country.

The negative impact of this recession on New York's large banks was the area's big banking story from 1989 to 1993, but the widespread decline in real estate values also hit New York's suburbs. This eliminated any chance New Jersey's banks had of keeping pace with NationsBank and First Union. That state's biggest banks, First Fidelity and Midlantic, would survive, but like so many of their larger brethren in New York, they were weaker in 1993 than they were in 1988—and it was only a matter of time before they were sold.

It was the New York banks during this troubled period, though, that would alter the direction of consolidation in the dramatic fashion that only their size could produce. Manufacturers Hanover was the lone large New York bank to disappear, but by 1993, Citicorp's once insurmountable size advantage over other banks had greatly diminished; Chase Manhattan was in a state of decline; and J.P. Morgan, Bankers Trust and Bank of New York had already diversified, or would be diversifying, out of mainstream banking. Only Chemical among these banks maintained anything like its previous status, and that was almost by default. New York City would still have skyscrapers filled with bankers, but, unlike the past, many of those bankers would be working for companies headquartered elsewhere or for investment banks like Goldman Sachs, Morgan Stanley and Merrill Lynch.

In 1989 and the early 1990s, the declining economic fortunes of banks in the greater New York area—money center and otherwise—unlike in most other negatively affected areas, was only tangentially impacted by defense industry cutbacks after the fall of the Berlin Wall. What drives New York City's real estate markets, commercial and retail and spills over into its suburbs is not manufacturing, but rather the fortunes of financial services companies, brokerage and investment banking firms as well as the banks. Beginning with the drop in stock prices in late 1987, the bread and butter of much of the area's financial industry—stock trading and deals—fell sharply, and with them bonuses and employment. This drove high-end housing values down and commercial real estate vacancies up. Ironically, the impetus for the declining economy came from some of the very same firms that would suffer so badly from the results.

An inevitable result of the weakening economy was that the balance sheets of several of the biggest New York banks, still feeling the negative effects of their international loans, went from bad to worse. The added jolt was enough to force Manufacturers Hanover into a sale and raise concerns as to whether Citicorp, Chase Manhattan and Chemical, the first, second and sixth largest banks in the country, would survive.

Asset Quality Decline by Numbers

The negative impact of falling real estate values beginning in 1989 hit Citicorp, Chase Manhattan and Manufacturers Hanover the hardest. By the end of 1990, Citicorp and Chase Manhattan had more than 6 percent of their assets not performing, and Manufacturers Hanover was just a step behind with 5.80 percent of assets not performing. Chemical, Bankers Trust and Bank of New York with NPAs between 4 percent and 5 percent of all assets were doing only marginally better, but this was enough for them to have superior outcomes.

Large New York Bank Asset Quality, 1988 to 1992

	NPAs as a Percent of Assets				
	1992	1991	1990	1989	1988
Citicorp	6.85%	6.93%	6.55%	4.63%	4.08%
Chase Manhattan	5.79	5.87	6.04	4.26	4.70
Chemical	4.65	4.73	4.78	4.79	5.28
Bankers Trust	3.51	4.74	4.30	2.58	2.31
Bank of New York	2.82	4.11	4.00	2.94	2.36
J.P. Morgan	.54	.67	1.18	1.29	1.89
Manufacturers Hanover	-	-	5.80	5.39	5.65

Source: SNL Financial, Charlottesville, Virginia.

J.P. Morgan was virtually untouched by real estate problems, but this reflected a corporate strategy that made it look as much like an investment bank as a commercial bank. It still made commercial loans, but almost exclusively to large corporate customers—and it made few commercial real estate loans. Much of its income came from securities offerings, securities trading and financial advisory services, including merger assistance. There were legal limits as to how much of this J.P. Morgan could do, but it made good use of the limited investment banking-type activities allowed.

MANUFACTURERS HANOVER[1]

New York's biggest recession casualty was Manufacturers Hanover, which was acquired by Chemical in 1991. It was the first bank sold while in the top ten nationally since the 1930s, but this was a sign of the times and of how an economic recession had pushed consolidation into high gear. Only months later, the nation's fifth largest bank, Security Pacific, was bought by BankAmerica, and the twelfth largest, C&S/Sovran, was acquired by NCNB.

Unlike the other large 1991 acquirees—C&S/Sovran and Security Pacific—Manufacturers Hanover had been on a downward spiral since the mid-1980s and was particularly hard hit by the 1987 suspension of LCD debt payments by Latin American countries. In that year, it made a $2.2 billion contribution to loan loss reserves and had a loss in excess of $1.1 billion. Latin American loans were problematic for all of the big New York banks, but Manufacturers Hanover's contribution to reserves was even higher in dollars than that of the much larger Citicorp. While it was profitable in 1988, the deterioration of the local commercial real estate market sent it back into the red in 1989 with a loss of $518 million.

192 ARNOLD G. DANIELSON

Manufacturers Hanover was marginally profitable in 1990, but with the deterioration of the real estate markets, loan losses continued to mount. By the end of 1990, almost 6 percent of its assets were not performing. This was a lower percentage of assets than for either Citicorp or Chase Manhattan, but it had neither the size nor determination to persevere. In July 1991, Chemical bought Manufacturers Hanover.

Chemical-Manufacturers Hanover, theoretically, was another of those supposedly equal mergers in which the CEO of the acquired bank became the CEO of the combined entity for a year or two after which time the leadership mantle was passed permanently to the CEO of the acquiring bank, which in this case was Walter Shipley of Chemical. This was the plan in Fleet's "equal" merger with Norstar and Sovran's with C&S. In this case, though, there was no attempt to include the acquiree's name.

It was a sad ending for one of the great names of New York banking—one that could trace its heritage back to 1812, when Manufacturers Trust first opened its doors. John Jacob Astor was a founder, and Albert Gallatin, Secretary of the Treasury under both Jefferson and Madison, was its first president. Throughout most of the 19th and 20th centuries, Manufacturers Trust was one of the country's banking elite. In 1960, it was the seventh biggest bank in the country, and a year later it merged with Hanover Bank, which was the 14th largest. Following this merger, the new Manufacturers Hanover, or Manny Hanny as it was often called, would be the fourth largest bank nationally in asset size.

Manufacturers Hanover's 1960's post-merger strategy followed the money center mantra of the time of pursuing international loans rather than domestic retail banking. In 1967, 20 percent of its operating income came from international businesses, and by 1977, it had risen to 60 percent. In the 1980s, this international concentration would become its Achilles heel and not only result in the $1 billion plus loss of 1987, but also reduce its credit rating to almost junk bond status.

In the early 1980s, Manufacturers Hanover attempted to reduce its international dependence by diversifying into nonbank businesses. It bought First Pennsylvania's mortgage banking operation, and for a portion of the decade, it was the nation's largest mortgage banker. In 1983, it acquired CIT Financial, a commercial finance company for $1.5 billion—at the time, the largest price paid by a bank for an acquisition. This was to no avail and with loan losses rising and its capital declining, Manufacturers Hanover sold 60 percent of CIT to a Japanese bank for $1.3 billion. This was one of many asset sales preceding the merger with Chemical.

CHEMICAL

That Chemical would be the only New York bank to retain its position as a national leader without an ownership change would not have been expected prior to 1990. It was not nearly as well-known as Citicorp, Chase Manhattan and J.P. Morgan, and as the 1980s began, Chemical still trailed Manufacturers Hanover in asset size. It did not cover itself with glory in the 1980s either. In 1987 and 1989, Chemical lost a combined $1.3 billion, but among the large New York banks, only J.P. Morgan and Bankers Trust came through the decade less damaged, and they, unlike Chemical, had shown little interest in commercial real estate loans.

Chemical was an active international lender in the 1970s and 1980s, like its money center brethren, but it differed from the others in its greater interest in retail and branch banking. In 1975, it made the largest bank acquisition of the decade when it bought the Security National Bank on Long Island. In 1982, it agreed to purchase Florida National contingent on interstate bank approvals. This was not to happen, but in 1986, a similar agreement with Horizon Bank in New Jersey became a reality in 1989 when interstate mergers were permitted between New York and New Jersey banks. Chemical's major interstate move was buying the troubled Texas Commerce in 1987 that made it a banking leader in Texas.

When Chemical and Manufacturers Hanover agreed to join forces in 1991, it was a merger based on the assumptions that the cost savings would make the combined entities more profitable than either would be on its own, and that the economy would improve. This was the rationale for the ill-fated Texas merger of Republic and InterFirst four years earlier, but in this case, the economic conditions improved in time for the cost savings to make a difference.

Chemical also used the momentum from the Manufacturers Hanover merger to raise additional capital and enhance its status in Texas. It added $1.5 billion in new capital that facilitated the acquisition of the failed First City Bank of Houston in 1993. The First City acquisition combined with the earlier Texas Commerce purchase made Chemical the biggest bank in Texas.

The Manufacturers Hanover acquisition had also made Chemical the third biggest bank in the country, ahead of a faltering Chase Manhattan—a bank it bought in 1996. It would lose that third position to NationsBank in 1993, but it was the second biggest bank in New York behind Citicorp and a market leader in Texas—positions it would not relinquish.

CHASE MANHATTAN

The downward slide of Chase Manhattan, even without an immediate sale, had almost as big an impact on the direction of consolidation as the sale of Manufacturers Hanover. Its slide would culminate in its falling out of its perennial position among the top three of American banking, and the slide was as unexpected as Chemical's ascendancy. It was unexpected, primarily because of its well-known name since Chase Manhattan had been struggling for many years and had large losses in 1987, 1989 and 1990.

The aura of Chase Manhattan was a product of its storied history. Its roots went back to the Bank of Manhattan that formed in 1799, and it became Chase Manhattan when it merged with Chase Bank in 1955. The latter founded by, and bore the name of, Salmon Chase, Lincoln's Secretary of Treasury and a one-time presidential candidate.

Long before the Chase merger, though, Bank of Manhattan was a big force in the banking business. Bank of Manhattan had greatly increased its size in the 1920s, and in 1930, it bought Equitable Trust, the eighth largest bank in New York City, from John D. Rockefeller. That acquisition made it the biggest bank in the country.

Becoming the biggest bank would magnify the impact of Bank of Manhattan and put it in an unfavorable light in the 1930s, when its CEO, Albert Wiggins, made a $4 million profit on a "short" sale on the bank's stock.[2] This was a "bet" that its stock price would decline, and a type of profiteering that did not sit well with politicians or the public in the midst of the Great Depression. This incident would contribute to Wall Street being blamed for the Great Depression and the passage of the Glass-Steagall Act that was to separate commercial and investment banking for the next sixty years.

With Wiggins' downfall, Bank of Manhattan's leadership moved to the Rockefeller family and its close associates. Winthrop Aldrich, a brother-in-law to John D. Rockefeller, Jr., replaced Wiggins and led the bank until the end of World War II. After the merger with Chase, David Rockefeller, one of John D. Rockefeller's sons, would take the helm of Chase Manhattan and hold it until 1981.

Rockefeller further raised Chase Manhattan's profile with his interest in international affairs, but local leadership was lost to First National City, the Citibank predecessor. By 1980, it was a distant second behind Citicorp, and it was downhill after that. From 1988 to 1993, Chase Manhattan's assets only increased by about $5 billion, and it fell from second to sixth nationwide. Then in 1996, it too was acquired by Chemical, which was well on its way to becoming today's JPMorgan Chase.

CITICORP

Citicorp fared better than Chase Manhattan did, but 1989 to 1992 were difficult years for the country's biggest bank. It had done much better than most of the New York banks in the 1980s, particularly in the early part of the decade when it expanded into California, Florida, Illinois and the District of Columbia with thrift acquisitions, and it had left BankAmerica and Chase Manhattan far behind in the battle for national leadership. Between 1980 and 1989, Citicorp's assets grew from $115 billion to $231 billion, and by 1989, it was larger than BankAmerica and Chase Manhattan combined.

By 1991, though, rumors were rampant that capital was a problem and Citicorp could fail. From 1989 through 1991, it contributed more than $9 billion to its loan loss provision; in 1991, it lost $457 million; and from 1989 to 1993, Citicorp's assets fell by $15 billion. Instead of being twice the size of the second largest domestic bank, its assets were only $30 billion more than those of BankAmerica in 1993, and NationsBank was coming on fast.

Citicorp, however, had more than size going for it. Its international coverage went far deeper than the troublesome Latin American loans, and it had the biggest bank-owned credit card. It needed assistance, but these strengths plus its past reputation helped it raise the capital it needed including a $643 million capital contribution—15 percent of total capital—from a Saudi Arabian prince, Alwaleed bin Talal.[3]

From a consolidation perspective, Citicorp was no longer the threat to local banks in other states it once was, nor was it still head-and-shoulders above all other financial services institutions. Its hold on the number one spot in the national banking pecking order was far from secure, and it was no longer "too big to be bought." Citicorp's acquisition in 1998 by the Travelers was a surprise, but this surprise was made possible by the slowed momentum in the late 1890s and early 1990s.

J.P. MORGAN, BANKERS TRUST AND BANK OF NEW YORK

J.P. Morgan had few loan problems and Bankers Trust and Bank of New York had relatively minimal asset quality problems compared to the other big New York banks, and all three were profitable every year from 1989 to 1993. This suggests that they should have gained at the expense of others and improved their national status.

They had done better, but two of them, J.P. Morgan and Bankers Trust, did so because they already had diversified away from mainstream banking. Bank of New York would move in that direction shortly after 1993. Thus, these banks, in effect, withdrew from being part of the full-service regional and national banking scene.

For J.P. Morgan, this withdrawal was consistent with its past. It was one of the most important banks in the world in the 1920s, but had lost its investment banking capabilities as part of the Glass-Steagall separation of banking powers in the 1930s with the spin-off of Morgan Stanley. It continued to be a banking leader thereafter, but its focus was on lending to the very best corporate customers across the nation. Unlike its major competitors in the post-World War II era, J.P. Morgan did not try to be a broad-based bank. It did not have branches and made few commercial real estate loans.

This proved to be a good decision, but in the late 1980s, "J.P. Morgan was widely thought to be dead in the water. Compared with rivals then eagerly building up loan portfolios, it appeared to have become a sluggish also-ran. Critics said Morgan was too set in its pinstriped ways to survive the rough and tumble of the changing marketplace."[4] What it was doing was becoming more of a hybrid commercial and investment bank, which was a decision that looked much better in 1993 than it did in 1988. It too, was sold to Chemical, but on relatively equal terms that preserved its name, if not management control.

Bankers Trust was a smaller version of J.P. Morgan without the long list of crème de la crème clients, and unlike other big New York banks, it did not date back to the nation's early days. Bankers Trust opened in 1903 to help other banks with their trust operations. In the 1920s, it broadened its horizons and became a multi-purpose bank, and by 1940, it was one of the ten largest banks in the country. In the 1980s, it fortuitously moved away from general purpose banking to concentrate on large corporate customers, its trust operation and a securities business. As a result, Bankers Trust was not as heavily committed to commercial real estate lending in the late 1980s as most other large banks.[5]

Bank of New York's history rivaled that of J.P. Morgan, but differed in that it was still a general-purpose bank in 1989, albeit a conservative one. This was consistent with its status as one of the oldest names in American banking having been formed by Alexander Hamilton in 1784. Bank of New York is also unusual among big banks in that it has kept its original name.

In the early 1900s, Bank of New York had fallen behind its New York money center rivals, but it almost made it into the top ten in the late 1980s. This was primarily the result of a hostile takeover of a mid-sized New York money center bank, Irving Trust, in 1988, but Bank of New York had made several smaller purchases to improve its retail coverage as well, particularly on Long Island and in the suburbs north of New York City.

After having survived the trials and tribulations of the 1989 to 1992 recession, Bank of New York would soon move its emphasis away from traditional banking. In 1995, it bought trust services, securities processing and bond administration businesses—and became a leader in each. In so doing, it would become a profitable financial services company, but would no longer be a major factor in traditional banking or play a role in the bank consolidation process other than through the sale of its New York banking offices to JPMorgan in 2006.

ACROSS THE RIVER

While the problems of New York's large banks understandably attracted the most attention in this real estate-driven recession, they were far from alone in their suffering in the New York metropolitan area. The negative impact of the real estate woes went well beyond New York City, and this clearly could be seen across the Hudson River in New Jersey. NPAs in that state jumped from 1.30 percent of total assets at the end of 1988 to 2.31 percent a year later, and by the end of 1990, more than 5 percent of New Jersey bank assets were not performing. By year-end 1991, the percentage was 5.60 percent, which was more than a percentage point higher than New York banks.

Middle Atlantic State Bank Asset Quality, 1988 to 1992

	Banks		Thrifts			
	N.J.	N.Y.	Pa.	N.J.	N.Y.	Pa.
	NPAs as a Percent of Assets					
1992	4.28%	4.22%	1.75%	2.53%	4.78%	1.60%
1991	5.60	4.52	2.31	4.92	5.84	2.94
1990	5.23	4.54	2.17	4.80	4.42	3.30
1989	2.31	3.43	1.34	3.53	2.88	2.59
1988	1.30	3.28	1.41	2.46	1.95	2.46

Source: FDIC: Historical Statistics on Banking.

Thrifts in New Jersey suffered a similar asset quality decline. Some of this was a carry-over from the 1980s' thrift crisis that had lifted collective NPAs of New Jersey thrifts to almost 2 percent of all assets at the end of 1988. By 1990 and 1991, though, it was commercial real estate loans that had almost 5 percent of the state's thrift assets not performing. During these years, its largest thrift, Howard Savings, would fail despite having few NPAs going into the period.

Trends were similar, but in more modest proportions beyond the New York metropolitan area in Pennsylvania. Bank NPAs in that state were in the 1.30 percent to 1.40 percent of assets range in 1988 and 1989 and rose to 2.31 percent of assets by the end of 1991. The thrifts had NPAs climb above 3 percent of total assets in 1990. These were statewide totals and banks and thrifts from Philadelphia north to the Poconos experienced a spillover effect from New York and New Jersey, and they had asset quality numbers that were much worse than the statewide averages.

New Jersey's two largest banks, First Fidelity and Midlantic, had differing results during this period, but the end result was the same—a loss of momentum and a sale in 1995. Asset quality suffered at both banks, but the larger of the two, First Fidelity, never had more than 4 percent of its assets not performing. Midlantic was not so fortunate and had over 7 percent of its assets not performing at the end of 1990, and in 1991 and 1992, the number was above 10 percent. It was still around in 1993, but this was primarily because of a lack of buyers in the area with the strength to take on its problems.

Large New Jersey and Pennsylvania Bank Asset Quality, 1988 to 1992

	NPAs as a Percent of Assets				
	1992	1991	1990	1989	1988
New Jersey					
Midlantic	10.16%	10.89%	7.10%	2.69%	1.57%
First Fidelity	2.70	3.56	3.46	2.07	1.70
Pennsylvania					
PNC	3.77%	5.03%	3.11%	1.52%	1.24%
CoreStates	2.67	3.24	2.11	.55	.56
Mellon	2.19	3.41	2.88	2.31	3.15

Source: SNL Financial, Charlottesville, Virginia.

First Fidelity's relative success reflected the strong actions taken by a new CEO, Anthony Terracciano. He ruthlessly cut costs and took his losses early. The result was a loss of momentum that was disappointing for a bank that was as big as NationsBank and First Union going into the period and was in a position to do in the Northeast what those banks would accomplish in the Southeast. Instead, New

England's Fleet benefited from the disorientation of the New York banks in the 1990s to acquire the Northeast's largest retail deposit share.

The loss of momentum would result in First Fidelity's sale in 1995 to First Union, but at least the sale was done from the much-improved position produced by Terracciano, and it was the best outcome for shareholders. Its $5.6 billion price tag was about four times that of MNC, a bank of similar size in 1990 that sold out of weakness in 1993. Midlantic sold to PNC for $3 billion that same year.

Pennsylvania's largest banks were outside the New York metropolitan area, but they were lending into the same market and all of its biggest banks had over 3 percent of their assets not performing by the end of 1991. The largest of these, PNC, had NPAs in excess of 5 percent of total assets. As with First Fidelity, the decline in asset quality slowed PNC's momentum in the early and mid-1990s, but PNC, and Pennsylvania banks, in general, fared better than the big banks to the north in New York and New England and those to the south in Maryland and Virginia.

Savings Bank Decline

Other big losers during the region's time of troubles were the once-powerful savings banks, but they had already been hurt badly in the thrift crisis. By 1988, they were only a pale imitation of what they once had been. There were just six savings banks or S&Ls in New York, New Jersey and Pennsylvania with assets in excess of $10 billion at year-end 1988, and three of these—Goldome, Empire of America and City Federal—had negative tangible capital. A fourth, Meritor, had tangible capital under 1 percent of assets, and another, Crossland, had tangible capital of less than 3 percent of assets. Only New York's Dime Savings was truly viable with tangible capital at almost 6 percent of assets, but it also had 5 percent of its assets not performing.

Largest Northeast Thrifts, 1988

	Assets (In billions)	Net Income (In millions)	Percent of Assets		
			Tangible Capital	NPAs	Reserve/ Loans
1. Meritor	$17	$(210)	.27%	3.68%	.87%
2. Crossland	15	15	2.83	2.10	.35
3. Goldome	15	(119)	(1.74)	2.86	.48
4. Dime Savings	12	80	5.97	5.39	.25
5. Empire of America	11	(57)	(5.15)	5.98	.82
6. City Federal	11	(12)	Minus	N/A	N/A

Source: Thrift Securities Handbook, Kaplan Smith, April 1989

By 1992, all but Dime were gone, and the region's thrifts had become primarily local banking organizations with minimal outreach. Some like Astoria Savings and Queens County Savings (which would change its name to New York Community Bank), found niches in mortgage servicing and multi-family lending—by-and-large thrifts would not be challenging the large banks in traditional banking. An exception to this much reduced role was Pennsylvania's Sovereign as it picked up the pieces others had left behind in New England, New Jersey and its home state, to grow to over $80 billion in assets by 2006 when it was sold to the Spanish Banco Santander, but in 1993, it had assets of less than $5 billion.

Aftermath

The impact of the recession and declining fortunes of so many of the large banks and thrifts in the New York area was felt on both a regional and national basis. Regionally, the big New York banks remained much larger than other Northeast banks, but their inability and unwillingness to move across state lines was an opportunity for others. As to national preeminence, by 1993, they had clearly lost their pre-1989 status.

Largest Northeast Banks, 1993

	Assets		Rank	
	1993	1988	1988	Eventual Owner
	(In billions)			
1. Citicorp	$217	$208	1	Citigroup
2. Chemical	150	67	4	JPMorgan
3. J.P. Morgan	134	84	3	JPMorgan
4. Chase Manhattan	103	98	2	JPMorgan
5. Bankers Trust	92	58	6	Deutsche Bank
6. PNC	62	41	8	PNC
7. Fleet	48	29	13	Bank of America
8. Bank of New York	46	47	7	Bank of New York
9. Bank of Boston	41	36	9	Bank of America
10. Republic	40	25	-	HSBC
11. Mellon	36	31	11	Royal Bank-Scotland*
12. First Fidelity	34	30	12	Wells Fargo

*Retail branches only.
Source: American Banker, April 11, 1990 and April 14, 1994.

Despite this lost national position, in a Northeast that includes New England, the New York banks—Citicorp, Chemical, J.P. Morgan, Chase Manhattan and Bankers

Trust—still towered over all other banks in 1993 in relative size, but this size advantage was misleading as to their true regional status. J.P. Morgan and Bankers Trust did not offer retail branch banking. Citicorp and Chase Manhattan increased assets by less than 6 percent in the preceding five years and had only marginally moved into neighboring states. Bank of New York survived relatively unscathed, but had fewer assets in 1993 than in 1988. Only Chemical with its Manufacturers Hanover acquisition was a larger regional factor in 1993 than it was five years earlier, and it was busy merging two big banks.

From a Northeast perspective, besides Chemical, the winners were PNC and Fleet—banks far removed from New York City. PNC increased its assets from $41 million to $62 million during this period and moved from eighth to sixth in the Northeast in asset size. It also moved into the top ten nationally for the first time. Fleet's acquisition of Bank of New England moved it from 13th to seventh in assets passing Bank of New York, Bank of Boston, Mellon and First Fidelity in the process.

Nationally, the New York slippage was more noticeable. Citicorp's minimal growth between 1988 and 1993—it actually lost assets after 1989—may not have cost it the number one position, but others were closing the gap. BankAmerica had narrowed much of the difference with its purchase of Security Pacific, and NationsBank and Chemical were each almost three-fourths of Citicorp's size. Chase Manhattan had fallen from second to sixth; Manufacturers Hanover was gone; and Bank of New York was no longer in the top ten.

The old order of dominance by New York banks, with the only banks of comparable size being in Chicago and California, was over by 1993. New York's top ten members were cut from seven to five; BankAmerica was the only representative from California; and Chicago was not represented at all. With NationsBank in third place and First Union in ninth in 1993, North Carolina had more top ten banks nationally than California.

The negative impact of real estate problems on New York area banks not only allowed BankAmerica, Fleet and the North Carolina banks to cut into the New York banks' once dominant position, but it also opened the door for banks in the Midwest. That part of the country had its problems in the early 1990s, but since it did not have a building boom in the 1980s because of a lack of attractive opportunities, there would be no real estate bust. This permitted Midwest banks to continue to grow and acquire in the early 1990s without concern over their own or potential acquiree's asset quality, and one Midwest bank, Bank One, had become the eighth largest in the country by 1993.

MIDWEST'S CHANGING
OF THE GUARD

Despite its stability in real estate values, the Midwest was hit as hard in the early 1990s by the national economic downturn as any part of the country. Jobs were lost and corporate earnings were down, but since the area had struggled economically through much of the 1980s, there was not only no commercial building boom, but also no rapid rise in property values. What did not go up would not come crashing down at the first sign of economic problems; and, as a result, there was no dramatic increase in real estate-related nonperforming loans.

Some Midwest banks had problems during this period, but in most cases, the problems came from out-of-area lending. Chicago's two largest banks, First Chicago and Continental, were still burdened with the after-effects of their heavy Texas involvement in the 1980s, and in the case of First Chicago, international loans. Michigan National and one of Ohio's largest banks, Ameritrust, also had balance sheets that looked as bad as those of any northeastern bank. For most of the Midwest banks, though, the recession years only resulted in NPAs moving toward, or slightly above, 2 percent of total assets. A couple of years earlier this would have been ample cause for concern, but compared to what was happening elsewhere in the early 1990s, 2 percent, or even 3 percent, of a bank's assets not performing was within the realm of acceptability.

This relative calm in Midwest banking allowed the consolidation pattern that was expected from the introduction of interstate banking to continue with little concern about out-of-region interference. Problems elsewhere kept BankAmerica and the New York banks home. The banks in Midwest states accepting interstate banking early on—Ohio, Michigan and Minnesota—moved ahead of those in states that had not, which included Illinois. In fact, the latter's belated acceptance of interstate banking would occur before fully accepting in-state branching, but this did not lessen the out-of-state interest in the Chicago market.

The biggest changes in Midwest banking between 1988 and 1993 would be the continual slide of the large Chicago banks, First Chicago and Continental, and the rapid growth of Bank One, KeyCorp and Norwest. The Chicago banks were one-two in asset size in the region in 1988. Five years later, First Chicago would be third and Continental would barely make it into the top ten. Meanwhile, Bank One and KeyCorp, both Ohio banks, had more than tripled in size, and the Minneapolis-based Norwest was not far behind. These rising regional forces also went well beyond the Midwest with their expansion. Detroit's NBD, although not growing as fast as the others, was also of a size by 1993 to be a major player in the next round, and it wanted a significant presence in the Chicago area.

Midwest banking's main attention-grabber in the early 1990s was the spectacular growth of Bank One. Sharing the spotlight with Bank One, albeit in a lesser way, were the consolidation in Cleveland; the opening of the Chicago market to all comers; and the quiet emergence of a Minneapolis bank, Norwest, whose historic focus had been on the farm states in the north central part of the country. It would be Norwest, not Bank One or a Chicago-based bank, that would become one of four banks that would dominate American banking by acquiring Wells Fargo—whose name it took—and then Wachovia.

BANK ONE

While no longer with us, the role played by Bank One in the banking consolidation in the 1990s cannot be overlooked. It had some down days in the mid-1990s, but over the entire decade, it surpassed First Union, Fleet and Norwest in total number of mergers, and by 1999, Bank One had become the fourth biggest bank in the country. Only Citigroup, Chemical (with its Chase Manhattan name) and Bank of America were larger.

This was quite an accomplishment for Bank One, a family-run bank since 1933 and a newcomer to the ranks of big-time banking. In 1935, the Reconstruction Finance Corporation—sort of the RTC of its day—installed John H. McCoy as president of a recapitalized City National Bank & Trust Company in Columbus, Ohio. City National was a small bank in a mid-sized city whose banking was dominated by Huntington and Ohio National, but McCoy was successful in overcoming the odds by countering the bank norm of the time to concentrate on retail rather than commercial banking. In the 1950s, McCoy's son, John G. McCoy, joined City National, and in 1958, he would replace his father as its CEO and driving force.

City National grew rapidly after World War II, and in 1967, formed a holding company, First Bank Group, but it was still a small factor in the overall Ohio banking market. In 1970, it had assets of about $500 million and was among the 200 largest banks in the country, yet it was just the eleventh largest bank in Ohio and third largest in Columbus.

In the 1970s, First Bank Group made numerous acquisitions in Ohio, and by 1980, it had $3.2 billion assets and a place in the top hundred banks nationwide. It also had become the fifth largest bank in Ohio; number two in Columbus; and was ready to move onto the center stage. In 1979, the holding company name was changed to the much simpler Banc One. The term Banc initially was used rather than Bank for the holding company because of legalities relative to the use of "bank" in a holding company name. When permitted the name was changed to Bank One, which is the nomenclature used throughout this book.

Bank One made a series of acquisitions in Ohio in the early 1980s, but it was not until the arrival of interstate banking—and a new McCoy, that it moved ahead of other banks in the state. In 1985, John B. McCoy became the third generation to head up this dynamic banking organization, and in 1987, it bought one of the largest banks in Indiana. A year later it acquired a mid-sized bank in Wisconsin and one of the Texas banking leaders, M-Corp, from the FDIC. By 1988, Bank One had assets of $25 billion and was the third largest Midwest bank behind First Chicago and Continental. It had almost $4 billion more assets than the second largest Ohio bank, National City.

The meteoric rise of Bank One under the second McCoy through 1988 was only the beginning. In 1989 and 1990, it made three small acquisitions, and two of them were in Illinois. In 1991, Bank One picked up the pace with three Illinois acquisitions and one in Kentucky with combined assets of about $5 billion. It also bought PNC's southwest Ohio banks, and at the end of the year, Bank One bought a $2.8 billion asset bank in Colorado. Its earlier acquisition of M-Corp in Texas was no longer an isolated expansion beyond the Midwest.

This was all a prelude to 1992 and 1993, when Bank One followed up the Colorado acquisition with the purchase of Valley National, the largest independent bank in Arizona with almost $11 billion assets, and four more acquisitions in Texas. Bank One also acquired the largest independent bank in Kentucky and the second largest bank in West Virginia.

This was a frenetic pace, and by the end of 1993, Bank One was the largest Midwest bank with assets of almost $80 billion and the eighth largest bank in the country. It had not matched the growth of NCNB, but Bank One was bigger than the other high-growth banks of his period—First Union, Wells Fargo and Fleet. It had come a long way in a short time.

KeyBank and the Cleveland Consolidation

Bank One's move from its humble Columbus beginnings to being the Midwest's biggest bank overshadowed the jockeying for position in Ohio's biggest city and financial center, Cleveland, but banks in that city would play a major role in Midwest and national bank consolidation; a much bigger role than would have been expected of banks in a "rust belt" city that had seen better days. Prior to 1980, five of Ohio's six biggest banks—Cleveland Trust, Central National, National City, Society and Union Commerce—were in Cleveland, and the largest, Cleveland Trust, had long been one of the biggest banks outside of New York, Chicago and California.

That Society would emerge from among these five to be Cleveland's biggest bank and second largest in the Midwest by 1993 was as improbable as Bank One's rise a decade earlier. Society's roots went back to 1844, but as a mutual savings bank, not as a commercial bank. It remained Society for Savings and a thrift, until 1955 when it converted to a bank charter and became Society National Bank. In 1980, Society was fourth in Cleveland behind Ameritrust—the new name for Cleveland Trust that was intended to give it broader geographic appeal—National City and Central National, and it was not much ahead of Union Commerce in total assets.

Society took a big step forward in the battle for preeminence in the Cleveland area in 1981 when it acquired Central National. By 1985, it had surpassed a faltering Ameritrust and was second locally only to National City. Society also had become a much more important bank throughout northern Ohio, but in 1988, it was just barely in the top ten of Midwest banks and well behind Bank One and National City.

In the early 1990s, Society was not nearly as acquisitive as Bank One, but two of its mergers were larger than any of those of its Columbus rival. In 1991, Society bought Cleveland's one-time banking leader, Ameritrust, and in 1993, it agreed to an equal merger with an Upstate New York bank, KeyCorp. The Ameritrust acquisition gave Society near parity in size with National City and the bulk to deal with KeyCorp on an equal basis.

The KeyCorp-Society merger was unusual in that it really was a near equal sharing between partners. Technically, Albany-based KeyCorp was the acquirer, and its CEO, Victor Riley, became the CEO of the combined banks without a set date as to when he would pass the reins over to a Society person. That, plus the Society name disappearing, suggested that Society had been the acquired bank. The *quid pro quo*, though, was that the main office would be in Cleveland, and, if nothing else, this made the new KeyCorp a Midwest bank. Headquarters also usually determines the winner in an equal merger as CEOs move on, and even when they are slow to do so, they become part of the city in which they live.

Merging with KeyCorp made Society more than just a Midwest bank, as well. When Riley took over at National Commerce Bank in Albany—the KeyCorp predecessor and an institution that had been around since 1825—he had ambitions that went far beyond Upstate New York. Riley changed the name to the much catchier KeyCorp and was only a step behind his Albany neighbor, Norstar, in announcing a Maine acquisition in 1982, which also made him an interstate banking pioneer. When it was blocked by the New England regional interstate banking compact from following up the Maine expansion with bank acquisitions in southern New England, Riley jumped to the other end of the continent and bought two banks in Alaska in 1985. In 1990, KeyCorp greatly increased its size by buying two failed, but large, thrifts in Upstate New York, and then in 1992, resumed the western adventure with a series of mergers in Idaho, Oregon and Washington.

The KeyCorp-Society combination announced in late 1993 not only created the second largest bank in the Midwest, but it also resulted in the tenth largest bank in the country with branches stretching from Maine to Alaska. This was an unusual Snowbelt strategy that was in sharp contrast to the Sunbelt strategies of Bank One and others; but there are pluses in going where the competition is less intense.

National City was the only other large Cleveland bank still around in 1993, and it also had spread its coverage beyond Ohio. It bought banking leaders in Kentucky and Indiana, and by 1993, National City was the sixth largest Midwest bank with $31 billion assets.

NORWEST

Norwest, unlike Bank One and KeyCorp, managed to stay out of the limelight with smaller acquisitions, but despite its quieter approach, it was not as much of a surprise in its move toward the upper echelons of regional and national banking. It was a large regional bank going back to the 1920s, and certainly did not start as a thrift like Society, and it had the benefit of having operated in multiple states for over sixty years. Nevertheless, it would not have been anticipated that Norwest would become one of today's four dominant banks after buying Wells Fargo and taking its name. In so doing, it gave one of the national banking leaders roots in the Plains states.

As discussed earlier, Norwest was formed in the 1920s as a protective association for troubled farm banks in Minnesota, Nebraska, Iowa, Montana and the Dakotas. These states were still its main market in the 1980s and the focus of its acquisition activities. Norwest made 23 acquisitions in nine states with combined assets of $18.5 billion from 1989 through 1993, and the majority of them were in these core states.

Norwest was also looking beyond these states, but its acquisitions outside its home area usually were natural extensions into neighboring states like Wisconsin, Colorado and Wyoming. The only real geographic jumps were eastward into Indiana and westward into a Sunbelt state, New Mexico. Its biggest acquisitions were in Colorado and New Mexico.

By the end of 1993, Norwest was the Midwest's fourth largest bank with $51 billion assets and was not far behind Bank One and KeyCorp. It was only warming up its acquisition machine as it would buy 16 banks in 1994, and all but two were in Arizona, Colorado, New Mexico and Texas. Norwest was going south and west into faster growing markets.

CHICAGO'S DIMINISHING ROLE

The enhanced status of Bank One, KeyCorp and Norwest coincided with the declines of First Chicago and Continental as well as Chicago as a banking center, but the introduction of interstate banking in Illinois had out-of-state banks tripping over themselves to get into the Chicago market. This paradox was the result of downstate legislators protecting their local banks at the expense of the Chicago banks by limiting in-state branching.

Illinois, like Texas, had held out against branch banking longer than other large states. It had a strict prohibition against bank branches until 1976 when banks were permitted to establish a second facility within 3,500 yards. In 1985, this was expanded to five banking facilities with one within 500 yards of the bank, which essentially was permission to build a detached drive-in facility; a second within 3,500 yards; and the remaining three had to be in the same county unless the branch was within ten miles of the main office. In 1990, the number of branches allowed was increased to ten in the home county and five in contiguous counties. Not until 1993 were all limitations on in-state branching dropped. This was about twenty years after most other large states had removed their in-state branching barriers.

The use of holding companies and autonomously-operating acquired banks provided some branching relief, but even using Illinois' 1985 branch expansion rules, First Chicago and Continental had less than 20 branches each, excluding drive-in facilities, in the mid-1980s. By then, BankAmerica and First Interstate had more than 1,000 full-service banking offices; and Citicorp and Chase Manhattan, even with their money center cultures, had more than 300 branches. Banks in other Midwest states were hampered by local branching regulations, but not nearly to the extent of the banks in Illinois. Society had more than 200 banking offices in Ohio by 1985, and this was long before its purchase of Ameritrust.

The inability to provide full coverage within their home market was a two-fold problem for First Chicago and Continental. It limited their ability to serve consumers and businesses in their own market, and it forced them to look beyond Chicago and retail banking for growth. This is why they sought loans in the oil patch with disastrous results and First Chicago followed the New York banks into Latin America. The expansion restraints at home not only closed off normal, and generally safer, avenues of growth, but they also slowed the development of any semblance of a retail culture.

As if that was not enough, when interstate banking came to Illinois in the late 1980s, First Chicago and Continental did not have much of a head start in their home market. Bank of Montreal and the Dutch-owned ABN AMRO had already used the international immunity from interstate banking prohibitions to buy the third and fourth largest Chicago banks, Harris and LaSalle; and Citicorp used a failed thrift acquisition in 1984 to give it access to Chicago. When interstate merger prohibitions were removed, banks in Ohio, Michigan, Wisconsin and Minnesota banks were quick to acquire banks in the Chicago area. As a result, by 1993, ABN AMRO was second only to First Chicago in Chicago area deposits. Continental, Bank One, Citicorp, NBD and two smaller Michigan banks, Old Kent and First of America, were among the area's ten largest.

Under these circumstances, it was not surprising that First Chicago and Continental had lost their leadership positions in the Midwest by 1993, and that this loss of momentum led to their being sold shortly thereafter. Continental was acquired by BankAmerica in 1994, and Detroit's NBD effectively took control of First Chicago in 1995.

Other Interstate Winners

Besides Norwest and the three Ohio banks—Bank One, KeyCorp and National City—there were other Midwest banks that used interstate banking to greatly enhance their positions from 1989 through 1993. Most prominent among these were NBD and Comerica, both based in Detroit, and St. Louis' Boatmen's National Bank. Similar in size, but not doing as well in the early stages of this period, was the other Minneapolis banking leader, First Bank System—the future U.S. Bancorp.

NBD was in the forefront of these banks during the early 1990s. Its assets went from $24 billion to $41 billion between 1988 and 1993, which was enough to move it from ninth to fifth in size in the Midwest. It was already Michigan's biggest bank, and after three Indiana acquisitions in 1991 and 1992, including that state's largest bank, Indiana National, NBD became the biggest bank in Indiana. In Illinois, a series of acquisitions made NBD one of the five largest banks in the Chicago area.

Comerica, the second largest Detroit bank, grew even faster than NBD during these years. It almost tripled in size between 1988 and 1993, and its 1993 assets of $31 billion were enough to move it from outside the top ten in the region to number seven. Most of the increase came from a merger with the third biggest bank in Detroit, Manufacturers National, but Comerica also began a Sunbelt strategy by acquiring three banks in Texas with combined assets of $2 billion and three in California that were, collectively, almost as large as its Texas acquisitions.

Boatmen's was the most aggressive of the St. Louis banks in the early 1990s. It almost doubled its assets from 1988 to 1993 with ten acquisitions, and with $27 billion assets, Boatmen's was the eighth largest Midwest bank. It, like Norwest, NBD and First Bank System, used the elimination of the interstate banking barriers to move into faster growing markets. Five of Boatmen's ten acquisitions during this period with combined assets of about $1.5 billion were in Oklahoma, which hardly qualifies as a fast growing state, but its biggest acquisition, Sunwest, was New Mexico's largest bank with assets of $3.2 billion.

First Bank System, the future U.S. Bancorp, did not keep pace with other banks of its size during these years and fell far behind its Minneapolis rival, Norwest. In the late 1980s, it had serious asset quality and securities problems; lost momentum; and looked more like a takeover candidate than a buyer. Between 1987 and 1991, its assets fell by about $10 billion. By 1992, though, First Bank System was making up for lost ground with two Colorado acquisitions of more than $5 billion in combined assets and one in its home state of Minnesota with $1.2 billion assets. In 1993, First Bank System also joined the crowd in Chicago with an acquisition of a bank in that city with assets of almost $2 billion. By the end of 1993, First Bank System had its assets almost back to the $27 billion it had in 1987, but it had fallen into the Midwest's second tier of banking leaders.

Changing of the Guard

Even though the Midwest had not been surfeited with the bad loans that were plaguing banks on the two coasts, the changing of the guard that took place from 1989 to 1993 was still influenced by asset quality problems, but the problems originated prior to 1989. Continental never fully recovered from the Penn Square loans that had precipitated its FDIC bailout in 1984, and both First Chicago and First Bank System had very difficult years from 1987 through 1989. The branching restrictions in Illinois were a problem for Continental and First Chicago, but more because they forced them to look beyond their home market for loans rather than their inability to maximize coverage in the Chicago area.

Largest Midwest Banks, 1993

	Assets		Rank	Eventual
	1993	1988	1988	Owner
	(In billions)			
1. Bank One	$80	$25	3	JPMorgan
2. KeyCorp*	60	15	9	JPMorgan
3. First Chicago	53	44	1	JPMorgan
4. Norwest	51	22	6	Wells Fargo
5. NBD	41	24	5	KeyCorp
6. National City	31	22	7	PNC
7. Comerica	30	11	11	Comerica
8. Boatmen's	27	15	8	Bank of America
9. First Bank System	26	24	4	U.S. Bancorp
10. Continental	23	31	2	Bank of America

*Includes Society-KeyCorp merger announced in 1993.
Source: American Banker, April 11, 1990 and April 14, 1994.

With First Chicago, Continental and First Bank System—the region's first, second and fourth largest banks in 1988—licking their wounds when Midwest interstate banking moved into high gear, the door was left open for others to gain the upper hand in the battle for regional leadership and survival. It was also an opportunity to play a bigger role beyond the Midwest, and Bank One, Society, KeyCorp and NBD, in particular, would take advantage of that opportunity.

Bank One was by far the most aggressive in number of acquisitions, and replaced First Chicago as the region's biggest bank, but it was not alone in moving past or close to First Chicago in size by 1993. Society was more creative in doing so with its willingness to take on the problems of Ameritrust and give up its name and management preeminence in exchange for geographic diversification and keeping its home in Cleveland. Bank One and Society took different routes, but by 1993, the biggest Midwest banks were in Ohio, not Illinois, and Minnesota's Norwest and Michigan's NBD were not far behind.

The shift of Midwest banking leadership from Chicago to Cleveland, Detroit and Minneapolis in the early 1990s was only the beginning of radical restructuring of Midwest banking. The entry of revitalized banks from the two coasts began in 1994 when Continental was acquired by BankAmerica. A year later, First Chicago would merge with NBD, which was technically a First Chicago acquisition that preserved the Chicago base, but management would come from the Detroit bank. Three years later, Bank One would buy a combined First Chicago and NBD to create a regional leader that in 2004 would deliver this status to Chemical, or as it was then known, JPMorgan.

EVERY OTHER MONDAY

Interstate banking and national recessions played major roles in the consolidation of American banking. The economic downturn from 1989 to 1992, coming so soon after the advent of interstate banking, was the single biggest determinant of which banks won and which banks lost in the 1990s, but it was the large mergers that were the primary vehicle for change. During these years, the 1,500 bank and thrift failures were disturbing, and a regional leader, Bank of New England, being among these failures had a direct impact on New England banking concentration, but it was the billion-dollar recession-driven acquisitions by Chemical, NCNB, BankAmerica and First Union that had the national impact. The collapse of Texas banking in 1986 and 1987 was another major direction-altering event, and it was large acquisitions of failed or failing Texas banks by Chemical, NCNB, Bank One and First Interstate that had made Texas so important to the consolidation process.

Prior to the changes wrought by the widespread economic problems from 1989 to 1992, bank consolidation was more a matter of perception than reality when measured by bank assets controlled by the largest banks. The failure of so many small banks in the Great Depression caused a big jump in the share of bank assets held by large banks in the 1930s, as they were better able to withstand the pressures of an economic downturn in an era when banks were not supported by federally insured deposits. This big bank share increase, though, rapidly eroded in the 1940s and throughout much of the 1950s by the return of public confidence in banking in general and an explosion of branches, few of which outside of California were operated by the nation's largest banks.

In the 1960s and 1970s, the large bank share of bank assets was again growing when measured against banks only, but the gain of the ten largest—they went from under 23 percent of bank assets in 1960 to about 31 percent in 1980—overstated what was really happening. Savings and loans were not included—and S&Ls were growing faster than banks. In addition, much of the large bank growth was funded by borrowed money and included large amounts of foreign loans.

The rise of the big bank asset share during the 1960s and 1970s would be reversed in the 1980s as foreign loans became a burden rather than an opportunity—a 31 percent share of bank assets of the ten largest banks in 1980 fell to less than 26 percent in 1990—but no one was talking about decentralization of banking. Interstate banking was rapidly moving forward, and banking changing locally from dominance by single state banks to dominance by large regional banks, or the superregionals, as they were then called. Small states like Kentucky, Maine, Oregon and South Carolina whose local banks were bought by multi-state banks based in Ohio, Massachusetts, California and North Carolina were experiencing consolidation no matter what the numbers said about the market shares of a few banks in New York and California. The reduced share of big banks in the 1980s also was influenced by the problems of a single large institution, BankAmerica.

Large Bank Asset Share, 1960 to 1996

Dec. 31	Share of Bank Assets		Total Bank Assets (In billions)
	Five Largest	Ten Largest	
1996	26.1%	38.3%	$ 4,582
1994	22.7	33.1	4,011
1992	20.6	29.3	3,506
1990	16.2	25.4	3,390
1980	21.2	30.6	1,856
1970	18.1	26.7	570
1960	15.4	22.7	256

Sources: FDIC: Historical Statistics on Banking, Sheshunoff Banking Organization Quarterly, Federal Reserve 1980 Bank Holding Company Report, Polk's World Bank Directory Spring 1961 and 1971 and SNL Financial.

Thus, while the seeds of bank consolidation go back to the pressures to cross state lines in the 1970s, the thrift crisis and the advent of interstate banking in the mid-1980s, statistically a nationwide increase in the share of bank assets held by a handful of large banks does not show up again in the national numbers until after 1990. What moved the numbers then were big mergers resulting from recession-driven asset quality problems. The most important of these were the two large mergers announced in late 1991 and consummated in that same year—NCNB-C&S/ Sovran and Chemical-Manufacturers Hanover—and the BankAmerica-Security Pacific merger announced at about the same time, but closed in 1992.

These acquisitions were of a size not previously seen in banking. In one year, the acquisitions of the fifth, eighth and twelfth largest banks were announced. Occurring during a recession when bank asset growth was slow, this resulted in the asset share of the five largest banks jumping by more than four percentage points in two years—from 16.2 percent to 20.6 percent—and the ten largest by a little less than four percentage points—from 25.4 percent to 29.3 percent. It was an extraordinary two year share gain, and consolidation had become more than a perception.

MEGAMERGERS OF 1995

The big mergers of 1991 were just a warm-up for the mega-mergers of 1995 that provided a second major spurt in the consolidation process. In 1995, there were fifteen bank acquisitions announced with individual deal values in excess of $1 billion. This was more billion-dollar bank sales than in all preceding years. It was a big year for mergers of all sizes, but where it differed dramatically from other years was in the number of large ones. Take off one month at the beginning of 1995, and add January 1996, and the number of large mergers goes up by only one, but that one, the $12.3 billion acquisition of First Interstate by Wells Fargo, providing a fitting finish to a truly amazing twelve months.

The merger frenzy of 1995 was so intense in the summer that from May through September, it seemed like there was a big merger announced every other Monday. Mergers of this size are usually finalized over a week-end when stock markets are closed and secrecy is easier to maintain and then announced on Monday, or Tuesday at the latest. Ten of 1995's billion-dollar bank sales were announced during these five months.

This big merger splurge began innocuously enough on February 5th with a foreign bank, National Australia, announcing the purchase of one of the lingering problems of the earlier recession, Michigan National, and it ended with the California blockbuster, Wells Fargo, buying First Interstate. In between those two deals, the bulk of the big merger activity was in the northeastern states—the most noteworthy being Chemical's purchase of Chase Manhattan. There was headline-grabbing action in the middle of the country as well with First Chicago and NBD joining forces.

The sudden surge in large mergers was a bit of a surprise since there was only one bank sale in 1994 with a price tag over $1 billion, and that was in January. Thus, for a full year prior to the Michigan National acquisition, there had been no billion-dollar bank sales. In the preceding years, 1992 and 1993 combined, there were just three such sales.

Large Bank Mergers, 1986 to 1996

	Bank Mergers		
	Over $1 Billion*	**Unassisted**	**Assisted**
1996	2	554	5
1995	15	609	6
1994	1	548	11
1993	2	481	35
1992	1	428	73
1991	5	447	85
1990	-	393	141
1989	1	411	175
1988	-	598	173
1987	3	543	136
1986	2	341	101

*Deal Value.

Source: SNL Financial, Charlottesville, Virginia and FDIC: Historical Statistics on Banking.

Even the over billion-dollar merger in 1994, BankAmerica's acquisition of Chicago-based Continental, was ten years in the making and not a harbinger of what was to come. After being bailed out by the FDIC in 1984, Continental never regained its momentum, but its ability to sell had first been hampered by Illinois' resistance to interstate banking. Then, after the interstate barriers were gone, banks big enough to buy Continental were not interested either because of their own problems or because of better opportunities closer to home. When sale conditions improved, Continental was ready to sell, and it gave BankAmerica its second big acquisition of the first half of the 1990s as well as entry into Chicago.

Why the sudden surge in large bank mergers in 1995? The reasons were enabling legislation, rising stock prices, better asset quality and board fatigue that, collectively, had created a merger environment equivalent of the "perfect storm." This was a term made famous in a best-selling book of that name by Sebastian Junger in 1997. It was made into a popular movie in 2000 about a fishing boat, the

Andrea Gail, which sailed out of Gloucester, Massachusetts in the autumn of 1991 and was caught in a rare combination of meteorological conditions that created what was referred to as a perfect storm. Since then the term has been used as a description of conditions coming together to create unusual and extreme circumstances, favorable and unfavorable.

The enabling legislation was the Riegle-Neal Interstate Banking and Branching Efficiency Act of 1994 (Riegle-Neal). This was national banking legislation that overrode state restrictions on interstate bank mergers and let national banks operate branches across state lines starting in June 1997. This allowed a single bank to have branches in multiple states, which was more cost efficient than a holding company having separate banks in every state. States could opt out of the branching part of Riegle-Neal, but only Montana and Texas chose to do so. If a state did not opt out, then interstate branching was allowed, but in many states entry was only permitted by merger as individual states could still prevent out-of-state banks from opening a branch in their state without it first buying a bank in the state.

Another part of the perfect storm creating a favorable large merger environment was better asset quality. Economic conditions had improved rapidly after 1992, but some bank balance sheets had bad loans long after the recession ended. This was a merger impediment as buyers were reluctant to add loan problems and wanted to get their own asset quality concerns behind them. By 1995, enough time had elapsed to make buyers more comfortable acquiring the loan portfolios of others.

Most important of all to the increased merger activity was rising stock prices. Since the dog days of 1990 through 1995, bank stock prices rose almost 26 percent per annum, and in 1995 alone, the increase was 50 percent. These were good years for stocks in general, but better for bank stocks than others. The corresponding stock price gains for the S&P 500 were 13 percent and 34 percent, respectively. The much-improved stock prices made it easier for buyers to pay a price that sellers would find attractive.

The stock price gains from 1990 through 1995, however, had annual variations that added to the strong sale climate in 1995. Bank stock prices rose rapidly from 1990 to 1993 as the Federal Reserve lowered the Fed Fund rate from a high of 9.75 percent in 1989 to 3 percent in 1992. This made bank loans more affordable and bank funding less costly, which investors like. In 1994, though, inflation became a concern, and the Fed Funds rate gradually increased until it reached 6 percent in February 1995. This upward movement of rates took away the market momentum in late 1993 and 1994, and in the second half of 1994, bank stocks as a group lost about 10 percent of their value.

Stock Price Index Gains, 1990 to 1995

	Bank Index	S&P 500 Index
Dec. 31, 1995	315	187
Dec. 31, 1994	209	139
Dec. 31, 1993	221	142
Dec. 31, 1992	208	132
Dec. 31, 1991	156	126
Dec. 31, 1990	100	100

]Source: Bank Securities Monthly, SNL Financial

These declining stock prices lowered acquisition activity in 1994 and early 1995 as it reduced the price buyers would pay while sellers expected the earlier values. As a result, many sales were put on "hold" until a more favorable merger environment returned in 1995 when stock prices were once more rapidly rising.

Last, but not least, in this perfect storm causing a sudden surge in big merger activity in 1995 was board fatigue. Banks on both the coasts suffered badly from loan problems in the 1989 to 1992 economic downturn, and accompanying the asset quality problems were regulators that could make life uncomfortable for bank directors. The regulators, themselves, were under pressures from legislators and the media for banking problems, particularly coming on the heels of a thrift crisis, and they could be brutal in how hard they came down on individual banks. In many cases, they were unduly pessimistic, but for directors, who in most cases were not bankers, these were scary times. So scary, in fact, that if they could have done so, many would have voted to sell their banks in the early 1990s. Bad loans and reduced earnings, though, made a sale either impossible or imprudent at the time. Thus, when sales at good prices were again possible, many bank directors were ready to move.

Bank Sale Price Increases

By mid-1995, the good sale prices had arrived. The $5.6 billion paid for New Jersey's First Fidelity in June 1995 was a new record high topping what BankAmerica had paid for Security Pacific in 1991. Two months later, Chemical more than doubled that price by paying $11.4 billion for Chase Manhattan. This seemed like a record that would stand for some time, but it lasted only five months. In January 1996, Wells Fargo paid $12.3 billion to acquire First Interstate. These were offering prices, and since they were all stock transactions, if the buyer's stock price subsequently increased, which was generally the case in this good economic climate, the closing price could be much higher.

Record High Bank Sale Prices*

	Deal Value (In billions)	Date Announced
Travelers/Citicorp	$82.5	5/9/98
First Union/CoreStates	17.1	11/18/98
NationsBank/Barnett	15.5	8/29/97
Wells Fargo/First Interstate	12.3	1/24/96
Chemical/Chase Manhattan	11.4	8/28/95
First Union/First Fidelity	5.6	6/19/95
Sovran/Citizens & Southern	2.1	9/26/89
Bank of New York/Irving	1.5	9/25/87
Fleet/Norstar	1.3	3/18/87
Chemical/Texas Commerce	1.1**	12/15/86
Wells Fargo/Crocker National	1.1	2/7/86

*Since first bank sale with announced deal value of $1 billion or more.
**Higher than preceding deal.
Source: SNL Financial, Charlottesville, Virginia.

The Wells Fargo-First Interstate transaction was almost ten years to the day after the first billion-dollar bank sale, which was also a Wells Fargo acquisition. In February 1986, Wells Fargo bought Crocker National from England's Midland Bank for almost $1.1 billion. Later that year, Chemical's purchase of Texas Commerce would be the second billion-dollar transaction.

In 1989 and 1991, the size of bank deals moved to a new level. In the first of those years, Sovran's merger with Citizens & Southern crossed the $2 billion threshold, a level reached by the Chemical acquisition of Manufacturers Hanover in 1991. A sign of what was to come in pricing came only a week after the Chemical-Manufacturers Hanover deal was announced with NCNB paying $4.5 billion to buy C&S/Sovran. Three weeks later, BankAmerica upped the ante to $4.7 billion with its acquisition of Security Pacific. This price stood as the highest bank sale price for almost four years until surpassed by the 1995 First Union purchase of First Fidelity.

The price paid by Wells Fargo for First Interstate in January 1996 would be the highest for more than a year-and-a-half. It was topped by a few billion dollars in late 1997 in acquisitions by NationsBank and First Union, but this was to be expected with the steady rise in stock prices during this period. What was not expected was that this gradual increase in bank sale prices would be followed by an almost $83 billion offer to buy Citicorp in 1998, but that is a story for another chapter.

A majority of the large bank sales in 1995 being in the Northeast—nine of the fifteen—was a logical reaction to the perfect storm. The region's banks suffered extensively from the extreme adverse economic conditions in the early 1990s, and there were more large banks in the Northeast than in other parts of the country. As a result, there were also more large banks in the region suffering from board fatigue. The region's 1995 large mergers were wide spread and left no major Northeast submarket untouched. In most of these mergers, it was not hard to see the impact of the early 1990s recession as a reason for the sale.

New England

Two of the large 1995 Northeast mergers were in New England—Fleet's purchase of Shawmut and Bank of Boston acquiring BayBanks—and they were among the most likely to have been at least partially motivated by board fatigue. Shawmut and BayBanks had struggled mightily during the 1989 to 1992 recession and had witnessed up close Bank of New England's failure. The larger of the two deals, Fleet-Shawmut, was announced early in the year when the troubles of the past were still a fresh memory and before the 1995 stock price surge was in full swing.

Fleet's acquisition of Shawmut was the first big 1995 merger from a consolidation perspective since a foreign bank acquiring Michigan National had no consolidation impact. This merger combined the first and third largest New England banks; made Fleet by far the biggest bank in the six-state area; and moved Fleet to within one position of being in the top ten nationally.

Bank of Boston's acquisition of BayBanks came ten months later, and may have been motivated by Bank of Boston trying to keep from falling too far behind Fleet and a failed effort to merge with Philadelphia's CoreStates. In the late summer of 1995, Bank of Boston and CoreStates had agreed on an equal merger that would create a $75 billion bank only to receive such a strong negative investor reaction that the merger had to be abandoned. Unlike the Fleet-Shawmut combination that involved banks of similar size in the same market, a Bank of Boston-CoreStates merger would have had far less cost savings and either Boston or Philadelphia would have lost a bank headquarters.

Another one-time Boston banking leader, State Street, had moved away from traditional retail and commercial banking, and this combined with all the bank mergers meant a once banking rich area had in a little over a decade seen more well-known names disappear than survive. Connecticut banking leaders, Hartford National and CB&T, along with Boston's Bank of New England, Shawmut and BayBanks were memories and, State Street was no longer a traditional branch-oriented bank.

All that remained of New England leading banks were Fleet and Bank of Boston, and they towered over the local competition. Two banks being so much larger than all others would prove to be an opportunity for the Royal Bank of Scotland's affiliate, Citizens, but in 1995, Citizens was still a long way from challenging them. Fleet had assets of $85 billion by year-end 1995, and with the acquisition of BayBanks, Bank of Boston was close to $60 billion assets. Citizens' assets in 1995 were only $10 billion.

CHEMICAL-CHASE MANHATTAN

In 1995, New York City only had one large merger, but it was by far the Northeast's most important from a consolidation perspective. Chase Manhattan had slid a long way from being one of the big three of banking, but it was still one of the biggest names in the industry and its acquisition by the less well-known Chemical was humbling.

Despite its reputation, Chase Manhattan had been sliding down the ranks of the national leaders for some time and seemed to lack any sense of where it was going. In the 1970s, it was hurt by international loans and the diminishing importance of correspondent banking, which was providing services for other banks. In 1981, David Rockefeller handed the reins over to his handpicked successor, Willard Butcher, and the loan problems continued, particularly international loans, but Penn Square and its oil and gas loans were also a major problem. When Thomas Labreque took over in 1990, the situation was such that his first move was to cut expenses, reduce the international coverage and sell its banking offices in Arizona, Florida and Ohio.

Thus, as others were expanding, Chase Manhattan was retrenching and had become a declining factor on the American banking scene. In 1988, it was the country's second biggest bank; by the end of 1994, it was number six; and before the Chemical merger consummated in early 1996, it was number eight. Chase Manhattan's loan problems were by then in the past, but its once sterling reputation was history as well.

In banking, though, names count, and Chase Manhattan could take some solace out of the fact that although bought by Chemical, the combined banks would bear the Chase Manhattan name. Not only that, but upon consummation of the merger, the new Chase Manhattan was America's biggest bank.

PENNSYLVANIA AND NEW JERSEY

It was in two almost forgotten states in the consolidation process up to this point, Pennsylvania and New Jersey, that most large merger activity would occur and provide the biggest regional direction shift in 1995. Five of the nine large bank mergers in the Northeast involved banks in these states.

The biggest and most important was the first to be announced—First Fidelity's sale to First Union. It was New Jersey's biggest bank; had a large market share in the Philadelphia area; and before it was slowed by 1989 to 1992 loan quality problems, First Fidelity was bigger than its buyer and almost as large as NCNB. It had lost momentum, however, and presumably had some director fatigue as well, and its sale brought one of the North Carolina banks destined to be a national leader north of the Mason-Dixon Line in a big way. The First Fidelity acquisition gave First Union a leadership position in a big Northeast state and a substantial stake in the Philadelphia area—a stake it would turn into dominance three years later when it bought CoreStates.

In 1995, board fatigue as a motivation to sell went well beyond First Fidelity in New Jersey. A much-diminished Midlantic sold to PNC in that year, and the British-owned National Westminster exited New Jersey with the sale of its United States banking business to Fleet. When the dust finally settled in New Jersey, First Union, PNC and Fleet—all out-of-state banks—had three of the state's four largest deposit shares.

The other major New Jersey merger that year, UJB's acquisition of Summit, was an in-state transaction, but it had long-term consolidation implications. With this acquisition, UJB replaced First Fidelity as both the biggest New Jersey bank and as number one in statewide deposit share. UJB would take the Summit name after the merger, continue to expand and then sell to Fleet in 2001, which three years later was sold to Bank of America.

In the Philadelphia area, the large 1995 mergers radically changed the local banking structure. The local banks had their problems with the early 1990s recession, but the only significant structural change in the area during that period was Mellon's acquisition of a failed thrift, Meritor, from the FDIC. Thus, as 1995 began, Philadelphia's leading banks—CoreStates, Mellon, Meridian, First Fidelity, PNC and Midlantic—were the same as five years earlier. Before the year ended, CoreStates had announced the acquisition of Meridian, PNC had a deal to buy Midlantic and First Union had purchased First Fidelity—and three of the six were gone.

The CoreStates-Meridian merger looked good on paper, as it appeared to create a stronger bank and to provide Philadelphia with at least one bank with a chance to be a major player. CoreStates was the holding company for Philadelphia National, the area's biggest bank, a position it had solidified a few years earlier by acquiring First Pennsylvania, which in the 1970s had been among the nation's twenty largest banks. In 1994, CoreStates had $29 billion assets, and acquiring Meridian raised its assets to about $44 billion. This did not lift it into a class with First Union or Fleet as the rejected Bank of Boston merger would have done, but CoreStates was still a big bank. The numbers, though, were better than the reality, and the Meridian acquisition was the beginning of the end.

CoreStates was not a skilled acquirer, and the Meridian merger did not proceed smoothly. It was a classic cultural mismatch in which a bank with a money center mentality acquired a retail-oriented bank, and the management battles took away all of the seeming pluses of the combination. The battle raged and the competition had a field day at CoreStates' expense. In 1998, CoreStates would be acquired by First Union and become a major stepping stone in that North Carolina bank's ascent.

MIDWEST

In the Midwest, 1995 was a big year for large mergers as well with the NBD-First Chicago equal merger and First Bank System, National City and Boatmen's continuing to spread beyond their home states with billion-dollar deals. First Bank System bought an Idaho bank holding company, West One, with bank affiliates in Oregon, Washington and Utah as well as Idaho. National City acquired the third largest bank in Pittsburgh, and Boatmen's bought the largest bank holding company in Kansas.

The NBD-First Chicago merger was the centerpiece of the Midwest 1995 merger activity. First Chicago had lost its number one position in the region to Bank One, but it was still the big bank in Chicago and, as such, remained a powerful force in the Midwest in which almost any substantial merger would restore its former regional preeminence. First Chicago had been rumored to be talking merger with a number of banks, and in July 1995, it announced a $5 billion equal merger with NBD that would regain the top spot regionally and move it back into the top ten nationally.

The new First Chicago NBD had the largest market share in Illinois, Michigan and Indiana, and with $122 billion assets and ranking seventh in size nationally, it was capable of playing a major role in the consolidation process. In 1995, First Chicago NBD would have been an obvious answer to a hypothetical question posed in an earlier chapter as to who were the most likely banks to be among the four or five that would dominate banking in the early years of the next century.

First Chicago and NBD were a curious mix, however, and how well they would mesh was uncertain. *Business Week* summed it up pretty well in stating, "Apart from being Midwestern bankers, their banks might have been from different planets. Although hurt in the 1980s and early 1990s by lending and trading problems, First Chicago had long been regarded as the preeminent international bank between the two coasts. First's execs viewed their Detroit sidekicks as little more than rubes running a second-tier outfit. NBD saw their new colleagues as East Coast-style gunslingers. And they had very different agendas: NBD wanted to expand beyond its region, while First Chicago wanted to avoid being taken over. Such cultural differences had capsized many mergers."[1]

In its efforts to not be taken over, First Chicago agreed to give a bank two-thirds its size an almost equal amount of shares and equal numbers of board seats, and it was initially viewed as the buyer since the headquarters remained in Chicago and the NBD name came second—and was likely to be dropped in articles and discussions. Fleet/Norstar, FleetBankBoston and JPMorgan Chase are ample evidence of a tendency to drop the last part of cumbersome bank names in conversation and in media reports.

It was NBD's management, though, that prevailed. The president of First Chicago resigned as a result of the merger, and part of the agreement was that NBD's chairman and CEO, Vernon Istock, would be president and CEO of the combined banks and then replace the First Chicago chairman when he retired. This would happen just six months after the merger was consummated. With NBD's Istock running the show, the perception was that NBD was the buyer regardless of who legally bought whom.

What made the First Chicago-NBD merger important from a consolidation perspective was that it worked well up to a point, but not well enough to maintain its independence for more than three years. In 1998, the same scenario would be rerun with Bank One and First Chicago NBD agreeing to an equal merger with the headquarters again remaining in Chicago. This time around, the First Chicago NBD name disappeared, and Bank One was running the show from day one.

WELLS FARGO–FIRST INTERSTATE

The Wells Fargo-First Interstate merger in the Far West was almost a rerun of the First Chicago-NBD merger and had the same end result. The acquired, First Interstate, like First Chicago, appeared well-positioned to be one of the top banks in the United States long before interstate banking became accessible to all banks. When divested by Transamerica in 1954, it was the fourth largest bank holding company in the country with banks in eleven western states. Only BankAmerica had more branches, and First Interstate, or Western Bancorporation as originally called, had none of First Chicago's branching constraints. With this starting point in the fastest growing part of the country, First Interstate had a franchise to be envied.

First Interstate, though, never lived up to its potential. In 1970, it was still the sixth largest bank in the country, but by 1980, it had fallen to ninth, and it was far behind BankAmerica and only marginally larger than three other California banks—Security Pacific, Wells Fargo and Crocker National. It fared no better in the 1980s even as its home base in southern California benefited from sunshine, defense spending and a strong Japanese economy. By 1990, its cross-town rival, Security Pacific had left it far behind, and Wells Fargo had surpassed it in asset size with its purchase of Crocker National. As First Interstate struggled in the 1980s, it had even tried a "Hail Mary" pass with a hostile bid to acquire a larger BankAmerica at its low point, but this came to naught.

When the early 1990s recession hit California, First Interstate fared better than its Los Angeles counterpart, Security Pacific, but it had its share of bad loans and was vulnerable to a takeover. First Interstate's size, the problems of the most likely buyers and an unfavorable sale environment, however, had allowed First Interstate to move into 1995 without any undue pressure to sell. Wells Fargo had been interested in acquiring First Interstate since 1992, but First Interstate dismissed the thought of a merger at least until it had its "house back in order."[2]

By 1995, First Interstate had left its bad days behind, but it was still vulnerable to a takeover. As a result, in October 1995, after being rebuffed by First Interstate management, Wells Fargo, which was smaller in assets, but slightly bigger in earnings and market capital, put a hostile offer of $141 per share, or about $11 billion, on the table. This unwanted offer was turned down by First Interstate in favor of a friendlier, but lesser, offer of $136 per share from First Bank System.[3] First Bank System was, in effect, a "white knight" in that it had not precipitated the sale of First Interstate. In addition, as a primarily Midwest bank, it would not have much overlap and would make fewer personnel cuts. Wells Fargo, however, did not give up, and in January 1996, it offered $152 per share, or $12.3 billion. This was "too rich" not to be accepted by First Interstate. By the time the transaction closed, a rising stock market had lifted the price to $174 per share, or a little over $14 billion—a nice pay-off for a reluctant seller.

Wells Fargo was the winner, but it was a victory with a bad aftertaste. It not only had cultural problems—Wells Fargo was cold and efficient while First Interstate was more people-friendly—but even as a buyer that had overpaid, Wells Fargo was still viewed by First Interstate's management as a hostile acquirer. The result was management defections, unenthusiastic employees, computer glitches and branch closings that led to considerable customer dissatisfaction and a merger nightmare.[4]

Despite the merger problems, an expanded Wells Fargo had assets in excess of $100 billion; was the only large bank with broad coverage on the West Coast other than BankAmerica; and was right behind First Chicago NBD in the national rankings at eighth place. From a numbers perspective, the Wells Fargo–First Interstate merger looked like a success. Wells Fargo had been weakened to the point, though, that like First Chicago NBD, in 1998, it was acquired by a smaller Midwest bank. In Wells Fargo's case, it was Norwest.

Big Bang Outcome

One periodical referred to 1995 merger activity as banking's "big bang," and until 1998 came along, it was a merger year that went far beyond any other. Some of the names remained, but with Chase Manhattan, First Chicago and First Interstate disappearing within a few months of each other, 1995 was a year worthy of the "Big Bang" appellation. On the East Coast, the disappearances of Shawmut and First Fidelity had almost as much of a shock effect as the sales of the aforementioned three.

In a single year, the sixth, eleventh and thirteenth largest banks disappeared; a bank other than Citicorp or BankAmerica was the country's biggest; First Union as the sixth largest bank in the country gave North Carolina two banks among the top six; a Chicago bank was back in the top ten, but with Detroit management; Wells Fargo had rekindled some of its old glory; and Fleet was just one merger away from being in the top ten. It was a new era in banking with some new players with high ambitions and a lot of momentum behind them.

Largest American Banks, 1995

	Assets December 31,		Rank 1994	Eventual Owner
	1995*	1994		
	(in billions)			
1. Chase Manhattan	$304	$171**	3	JPMorgan
2. Citicorp	257	251	1	Citigroup
3. BankAmerica	232	216	2	Bank of America
4. NationsBank	195	170	4	Bank of America
5. J.P. Morgan	185	155	5	JPMorgan
6. First Union	132	77	9	Wells Fargo
7. First Chicago NBD	122	47	17	JPMorgan
8. Wells Fargo	108	53	14	Wells Fargo
9. Bankers Trust	104	104	7	Deutsche Bank
10. Bank One	90	89	8	JPMorgan
11. Fleet	85	49	16	Bank of America
12. PNC	74	64	12	PNC

*Includes mergers in process and early 1996 Wells Fargo-First Interstate merger.
**Assets of Chemical.
Source: SNL Financial, Charlottesville, Virginia.

The impact of these big 1995 bank mergers on the asset share of the large banks was substantial, but since so many of the deals closed in the following year, the impact was spread over two years. Between year-ends 1994 and 1996, the asset share of the ten largest banks jumped by five percentage points from about 33 percent to a little more than 38 percent. The share increase of the top five, which came almost totally from the Chemical-Chase Manhattan merger, was not as much, but the gain from a little less than 23 percent to almost 25 percent was previously surpassed only by the 1990 to 1992 gain.

1998: THE SUPERBANKS COMETH

The sudden surge in large bank mergers in 1995 was at least partly a race for survival, and it was reasonable to expect that the mega-merger mania that surfaced in that year to continue into 1996. The conditions that had fueled the 1995 merger activity had not changed. Bank stock prices were still rising—up 35 percent in 1996 and 48 percent in 1997;[1] the economy was in high gear; asset quality was no longer a problem; and banks were enjoying a windfall—the elimination of the FDIC charges for deposit insurance. It looked a lot like 1995, but after the Wells Fargo-First Interstate announcement in January 1996, large bank merger activity slowed to a crawl.

What was different in 1996 and early 1997, was that the most aggressive acquirers were busy digesting what they had already bought and the banks that most wanted "out" after the tough times a few years earlier, had been sold. The only notable acquirer omissions from the 1995 mega-merger activity were NationsBank and BankAmerica, and the latter was struggling with its early 1990s acquisitions of Security Pacific and Continental. BankAmerica, in fact, looked more like the sellers of 1995 than an acquirer, but it was seemingly almost too large to sell.

The "too busy digesting" line of reasoning was reinforced as 1996 moved on when NationsBank, and only NationsBank, moved into action. It could not stay on the sidelines for long, and in August 1996, it announced the year's only billion-dollar bank purchase, other than the Wells Fargo-First Interstate transaction, when it paid almost $10 billion for the St. Louis-based Boatmen's.

This acquisition took NationsBank's coverage north from Texas into Oklahoma, Missouri and southern Illinois and west into New Mexico, but it was an isolated event. Banks making billion-dollar acquisitions in 1995 were not only non-acquirers in 1996, but they remained inactive through the first half of 1997.

Early 1997 showed a rise in large bank merger activity with three acquisitions announced with deal values in excess of $1 billion, even with the 1995 acquirers on the sidelines, but except for one, these were mid-sized regional deals. The only one of any size, First Bank System's acquisition of U.S. Bancorp in Portland, was by another bank that had not made a major acquisition in 1995—but was of more than passing interest as it gave First Bank System a new, and lasting, name.

It would be late 1997 before the frenetic mega-merger pace of 1995 would begin again and by then the debilitating economic impact on banks of the 1989 to 1992 recession was in the distant past. In late 1997, and particularly in 1998, the wave of large mergers that totally transformed the industry structure was driven primarily by prices too good to be refused by investors and the strong feeling that size was vital to the long-term survival of large banks.

The large merger hiatus ended in August 1997 when NationsBank struck again and announced it was buying Barnett, Florida's largest bank, for $15.5 billion. It was a new high in bank pricing and made NationsBank the largest bank in the country's fastest-growing high-population state. Coming so close on the heels of the Boatmen's acquisition, the Barnett deal was a reminder to other large banks that if they sat still for too long, the bankers from North Carolina would be leaving them behind. Some of the large bank merger activity that followed may have been at least partially a response to the purchases of NationsBank and those of its North Carolina compatriot, First Union.

First Union went back into action in the latter half of 1997. In November, it would "one-up" NationsBank and set another new high for bank sale pricing when it paid a little over $17 billion for CoreStates, Philadelphia's biggest bank. A few months earlier, it had announced that it was buying Signet, a $12 billion bank with offices in Virginia, Maryland and the District of Columbia. In late 1997, First Union spent more than $20 billion for banks with about $60 billion in total assets and became far more than just another regional bank.

The acquisitions by NationsBank and First Union in the second half of 1997 began a period of large bank acquisitions that radically altered the structure of American banking and took bank consolidation to another level. The largest mergers during this period were announced in 1998, and, as a result, it is the year most associated with this particular merger surge, but this merger wave began in earnest in the third quarter of 1997 and ran through the first four months of 1999. When it was over, the dominance of a few—the new superbanks—was readily apparent, and the share of banking assets controlled by four or five banks was well on its way to 50 percent.

The actual number of large mergers in 1998 was not that high—there were six fewer billion-dollar deals than in 1995 or 1997—but it was the size of the 1998 acquisitions and what happened in just seven days in April that made the year a watershed for bank consolidation. Between April 6th and 13th, Citicorp was bought by a slightly smaller, but ambitious insurance company, Travelers, for about $83 billion, or almost five times the previous highest bank sale price; NationsBank, the country's third largest bank, continued its furious acquisition pace and nearly matched the Citicorp sale price when it bought BankAmerica for $66 billion; and Bank One paid almost $30 billion to buy First Chicago NBD. In one week, the sales of the country's second, fourth and ninth largest banks with assets of almost $700 billion were announced.

Two months later the consolidation march continued when Norwest announced that it was buying Wells Fargo for almost $35 billion. This was the fourth bank among the nation's ten largest whose acquisition was announced in just two months, and it was not the end.

In November 1998, the sale of Bankers Trust, the nation's seventh largest bank, was announced. Since the buyer, Deutsche Bank, was a foreign bank, this transaction had little impact on consolidation, but with this announcement, half of America's ten largest banks had been sold in one year.

Large Bank Merger Value, 1994 to 1999

	Bank Mergers			
	Deal Value Over		All	Large Deal Value (In billions)
	$1 Billion	$10 Billion		
1999	7	2	428	$ 46
1998	9	4	567	245
1997	9	1	602	62
1996	2	1	559	22
1995	15	1	615	47
1994	1	-	559	2

Sources: SNL Financial, Charlottesville, Virginia and FDIC: Historical Statistics on Banking.

Some of these sale prices were not only record highs for American banks, but for companies of all types worldwide. The prices for Citicorp, BankAmerica and Wells Fargo ranked one, two, three in sale values up to that time, and the $30 billion offer for First Chicago NBD was the fifth highest right behind the ill-fated 1998 acquisition of MCI by WorldCom.

The combined announced deal value of 1998's nine billion-dollar bank sales was $245 billion. This was about four times the $62 billion combined value of the nine large acquisitions in 1997 and more than five times the $47 billion of the fifteen announced in 1995.

There were seven more billion-dollar bank mergers in the following year, including two with deal values in excess of $10 billion. Total 1999 transaction values of $46 billion, however, would pale beside the $245 billion of 1998, and none of the acquired banks in 1999 was among the ten largest.

The impact of these deals on bank consolidation was immense. Between year-ends 1996 and 1998, the share of bank assets controlled by the ten largest banks increased from 38.3 percent to 45.3 percent. This was by far the largest two-year increase since the concentration numbers began to rise in 1991.

Large Bank Asset Share, 1990 to 2000

Dec. 31	Share of Bank Assets		Total Bank Assets (in billions)
	Five Largest	Ten Largest	
2000	36.1%	47.2%	$6,246
1998	32.9	45.3	5,443
1996	26.1	38.3	4,582
1994	22.7	33.1	4,011
1992	20.6	29.3	3,506
1990	16.2	25.4	3,390

Sources: FDIC: Historical Statistics on Banking and Sheshunoff Banking Organization Quarterly.

As large as the asset share gain was for the ten biggest banks, it understated the 1998 impact on consolidation. In that year, it was not just the gains by the ten largest banks, but rather what was happening among the five largest banks that would change the banking structure. By the end of 1998, it was apparent that domestic banking was likely to be dominated by four or five large banks, not ten or more. Between 1996 and 1998, the share of bank assets held by the five largest went from 26.1 percent to 32.9 percent. In 1998, the five largest banks held almost as much of the banking assets as the ten biggest had at the end of 1994.

TRAVELERS-CITICORP

It was hard to say which was the more transformative merger in 1998—Travelers buying Citicorp or NationsBank's purchase of BankAmerica. The Travelers-Citicorp deal was priced higher; was more of a surprise; and the end result was the biggest American financial institution measured by assets, market capital and earnings. When measured by deposits, loans and banking offices, though, the NationsBank-BankAmerica deal was larger and had the greater direct impact on bank consolidation. The number of combined banking offices was more than 3,000, and this dwarfed Citicorp's less than 400 banking offices.

Travelers-Citicorp, though, was not only a big deal, but also a landmark bank acquisition in that it challenged the last remaining barrier for mergers between firms in different parts of the financial services industry—and won. A merger between a bank holding company and an insurance underwriter was not allowed in 1998, as it was not permissible for a commercial bank to have more than 25 percent of its revenues generated by products not allowable for commercial banks based on Glass-Steagall and the Bank Holding Company Act of 1970. This transaction violated the tenets of both of these legislative acts, and if it was approved, the rules for bank expansion would be dramatically changed.

This began a major congressional debate, but in the end, what Citicorp wanted Citicorp got. In November 1999, the Gramm-Leach-Bliley Act was passed, and, with its passage, mergers between financial services companies of all types were allowed. Thus, by the end of 1999, Glass-Steagall was history and the barriers separating banks from these other financial firms were gone.

The passage of Gramm-Leach-Bliley created a new holding company type referred to as a financial holding company to accommodate Citicorp (soon to be called Citigroup), and it also opened the door for large nonbanks to establish bank or thrift subsidiaries as part of financial holding companies. Merrill Lynch, MetLife and others were soon operating financial holding companies with newly created banking affiliates holding assets of more than $50 billion, and, in some cases, more than $100 billion. In 2008, this allowed the Federal Reserve to give "bank" status to Goldman Sachs and Morgan Stanley to avoid "runs" on these investment banks that would have made the financial debacle occurring at that time much worse.

Whether or not the elimination of all product barriers between banks and other financial firms was a good thing, will long be debated—including whether it played a significant role in the real estate excesses of the early 2000s that led to the financial crash that reached its peak in late 2008. There is no question, though, that it accelerated the consolidation process not only in traditional banking, but also in the delivery of financial products and services of all types. While non-traditional bank acquisitions did not directly affect the share of bank assets held by large banks, they increased their overall size and market power, and greatly influenced the consolidation process.

NATIONSBANK-BANKAMERICA

Citigroup notwithstanding, no bank had as much of an impact on the consolidation of banking, or financial services, in general, as NationsBank; no CEO played a bigger role than Hugh McColl; and NationsBank's acquisition of BankAmerica was the culmination of a more than 25-year march by that bank into national preeminence.

- In the 1970s, NCNB, as NationsBank was known then, was one of the two or three most aggressive bank holding companies in moving across state lines with non-bank acquisitions, and its 1972 acquisition of a Florida trust company gave it a head start on interstate banking.

- In 1982, NCNB used its head start when its trust company acquisition allowed it to circumvent Florida's laws against interstate banking. It created a loophole through which NCNB was able to buy a Florida bank and, in effect, make interstate banking in the Southeast a reality, albeit it took another couple of years to get all the legal approvals.

- In 1988, NCNB made an innovative use of tax credits to buy the failed Republic and InterFirst banks in Texas, and with this transaction, it became more than a regional bank. When its Texas acquisitions were consummated in 1989, NCNB was the country's 7th largest bank.

- In the early 1990s, NCNB used the troubles of C&S/Sovran and MNC to further enhance its status. After the C&S/Sovran deal was finalized, it took the more expansive name of NationsBank; and when both of the acquisitions were completed, it had taken another big step forward and temporarily became the country's third largest bank. In 1995, Chemical's acquisition of Chase Manhattan would push it back to fourth.

- The only part of the consolidation process NationsBank missed was "the every other Monday" of 1995, but it more than made up for that in 1996, 1997 and 1998 with the purchases of Boatmen's, Barnett and BankAmerica. With these acquisitions, it became the country's largest bank in terms of domestic loans and deposits, and second largest in overall assets.

The choice of the NationsBank name in 1992 might have been a tip-off to what would happen in 1998. It was an inversion of the BankAmerica name, and NationsBank was well on its way to nationwide coverage. In the mid-1990s, there was considerable speculation that there could be a merger between NationsBank and BankAmerica with McColl in charge. Thus, the only real surprise when this merger was announced was that it came so soon after the Barnett deal, but there was little time to wait in a frenzied merger climate or BankAmerica might have gone elsewhere.

The BankAmerica acquisition put NationsBank over the top. It had regained the third position after the Boatmen's and Barnett purchases and moved beyond its southern roots. Barnett was an in-region merger that solidified its position in Florida, and Boatmen's was its first major venture into the Midwest. With the addition of BankAmerica, it had become number one in the Far West and South as well as nationally; gained a presence in Chicago; and added more offices in Florida and Texas. NationsBank was clearly a national bank and a giant even among the large banks.

When the NationsBank-BankAmerica merger was announced, there was no question as to who was the acquirer—the headquarters was to be in Charlotte and Hugh McColl would be in charge. BankAmerica's David Coulter would be the president and CEO of the bank, but it was clearly a secondary position. The name was to be decided later, but even that delay appeared to be a NationsBank call.

The decision to use Bank of America as the name for both the holding company and consolidated bank was a bit of a surprise, but it made good marketing sense. The NationsBank name was retired after just six years, and arguably, the best known name in banking, Bank of America, was not only kept alive, but also raised to new heights.

For Hugh McColl, it had been quite a ride. He had played a major role in the rise of NCNB in the 1970s, as an executive vice president, and from 1983 on, he was the CEO and primary decision-maker. When he took command, NCNB was the 26th largest bank in the country with assets of $12 billion. Upon completion of the BankAmerica merger and at the end of the 1990s, he was running the nation's biggest bank with assets of $633 billion.

NATIONSBANK, FIRST UNION AND THE SOUTH

By 1999, the acquisitions by NationsBank, as well as those of First Union, were being viewed relative to their national impact, but it was only a few years earlier that there were questions about whether either would even be the leader in the South. Even after the Texas banks disappeared in the mid-1980s, there were nine Southern banks with assets between $15 and $30 billion. NationsBank was the largest and First Union was third, but there was no certainty that either would move away from the crowd to become the biggest bank in the South with far more than a regional content.

Largest Southern Banks, 1999

	Assets		Rank	Eventual
	1999	1996	1996	Owner
	(in billions)			
1. Bank of America	$633	$186	1	Bank of America
2. First Union	253	140	2	Wells Fargo
3. SunTrust	95	52	3	SunTrust
4. Wachovia	67	47	4	Wells Fargo
5. BB&T	43	21	8	BB&T
6. AmSouth	43	18	10	Regions
7. SouthTrust	43	26	6	Wells Fargo
8. Regions	43	19	9	Regions
9. Union Planters	33	15	-	Regions

Source: SNL Financial, Charlottesville, Virginia.

After the early 1990s recession and the 1995 merger spree, there were still five large banks in the South—NationsBank, First Union, SunTrust, Barnett and Wachovia—but by then it was a big two of NationsBank and First Union and three others. NationsBank assets were over $180 billion and First Union was up to $140 billion. SunTrust, Barnett and Wachovia had assets between $40 and $50 billion, and Sovran, Citizens & Southern, MNC and Southeast Banking were long gone. By the time 1998 was over, NationsBank had bought Barnett.

    With NationsBank, or as it was now called Bank of America, over $600 billion assets at the end of 1999 and First Union past the $250 billion mark, it was hard to even imagine that ten years earlier these two banks had assets of less than $30 billion and were similar in size to SunTrust, Barnett and Wachovia. SunTrust was still a strong regional factor in 1999 with $95 billion assets—enough to be a third southern bank in the national top ten—and Wachovia at $67 billion was still a highly-respected, multi-state banking operation, but they were increasingly being viewed as acquisition targets, not as buyers.

There were other large southern mergers during this period, but they had little impact on the regional or national banking structure. Three billion-dollar 1998 acquisitions, however, created a bit of a stir in the Mid-South, which had been left out of the earlier periods of consolidation. Even after these mergers, though, the acquirers—Birmingham's Regions, Memphis-based Union Planters and First American in Nashville—were still relatively small banks, even when compared to SunTrust. The largest of the three, Regions, had assets of $43 billion.

NORWEST-WELLS FARGO

Norwest in 1998 was no Bank of America and was not generating the headlines of First Union, but it was about to move into the big leagues. When it announced that it was acquiring Wells Fargo less than two months after the NationsBank-BankAmerica agreement, it took a big step toward being one of the four or five banks that would dominate American banking—a position it would cement a decade later when it bought First Union, which by then had taken the Wachovia name.

This acquisition also seemed like a sad ending for a once vibrant California banking industry, with little chance that the state would be the base for a national or multi-regional bank with the stature of NationsBank and First Union or even of a SunTrust. Wells Fargo, BankAmerica, First Interstate, Security Pacific, Crocker National—giants of California banking two decades earlier—had all been sold. To make matters worse, in March 1998, the state's largest thrift, Ahmanson, was acquired by another out-of-state banking organization, Washington Mutual.

The Norwest-Wells Fargo merger, though, was a "more equal" merger than most that claimed that status. Wells Fargo was the bigger of the two banks, but the troubles that flowed from its turbulent 1995 takeover of First Interstate had hurt its reputation and market value. Thus, it was not surprising that Norwest was the buyer or that its management team headed by Richard Kovacevich would be in charge, and it also made sense that the Wells Fargo name was kept and that the headquarters was in San Francisco. Thus, Wells Fargo may have been sold, but California still had a bank almost as large as First Union.

Initially, the survival of a San Francisco headquarters was somewhat muted by much of the Wells Fargo management continuing to work in Minneapolis, but as time went by and personnel turned over, management gravitated toward the city by the bay. Today, only the purists think of Wells Fargo as the successor of Norwest and anything but a California-based bank.

Regardless of who bought whom, Norwest-Wells Fargo was a merger with a major consolidation impact. The new Wells Fargo had more than $200 billion assets and 3,000 branches in 21 states. It ranked in the top three in deposit share in most of the states west of the Mississippi River, and, along with Bank of America, it was one of the two dominant banking forces in the western half of the country.

The interest that Norwest and Wells Fargo had in generating and servicing residential mortgages resulted in a national mortgage banking operation with more than 800 offices in 50 states. It was one of the three largest mortgage banks, which was a business that would grow rapidly in the housing boom that was to come.

Unlike the Wells Fargo-First Interstate merger, Norwest-Wells Fargo would not experience cultural problems. Kovacevich was a highly respected, competent leader; the overlaps were minimal; and the management that survived the turmoil of the Wells Fargo-First Interstate consolidation did not want to see a repeat of that situation. The new Wells Fargo would continue the Norwest historic pattern of small in-region mergers that allowed them to be one of the winners in the industry meltdown from 2007 to 2009.

WASHINGTON MUTUAL

Wells Fargo was not alone among western banking organizations to come out of 1998 much enlarged and with a national reach. In that year, Washington Mutual, the nation's largest thrift, acquired San Francisco-based Ahmanson, the second largest, which made it the lone thrift to climb into the upper echelons of domestic banking. Ahmanson's purchase did not come cheaply, it had a price tag of almost $10 billion, but it raised Washington Mutual's assets to $165 billion at year-end 1998, and for a few months, it was the country's seventh largest banking organization. The Norwest-Wells Fargo merger and Fleet's purchase of Bank of Boston would push it back to number nine, but Washington Mutual had come a long way and was far from done.

Washington Mutual at the time was a success story rivaling those of Bank One, Fleet, First Union and Norwest. In 1980, it was a small S&L in Wenatchee, Washington known as Columbia Federal with assets of less than $300 million. In

1988, it changed its name to Washington Mutual and in 1992 moved its home office to Seattle. It was still, however, a relatively small S&L with assets of $9 billion and 17 offices. It also was a virtual nonentity in a West Coast thrift industry dominated by large California S&Ls, but its location spared it the loan problems of those S&Ls in the early 1990s. It also had the courage to venture into that huge market when the opportunity arose.

Washington Mutual did not move into California until 1996, but when it finally did, it raised a few eyebrows with the purchase of American Savings. With assets of $20 billion, American Savings raised Washington Mutual's total assets to more than $44 billion as of year-end 1996. In 1997, it followed up the American Savings deal with the acquisition of one of the biggest California S&Ls, Great Western. This not only gave Washington Mutual the largest thrift deposit share in California, but also expanded its presence to Arizona and Florida. By the end of 1997, Washington Mutual's assets were almost $97 billion. In 1998, it completed its California "trifecta" with the Ahmanson acquisition.

With its S&Ls roots and large California base, Washington Mutual was challenging the big commercial banks, particularly BankAmerica and Wells Fargo, but it was doing so with a model based totally on mortgage banking. It was already in 1998 one of the largest originators and servicers of home mortgages, and over the next few years it would take its mortgage business nationwide and become part of a mortgage banking big three that included Wells Fargo and another mortgage specialist, Countrywide.

This was a model different from most of the big commercial banks, Wells Fargo being an exception, but it was a model that depended on the generation of deposits to fund its mortgage banking business. As a result, Washington Mutual was competing with banks of all types in pursuing deposits as well as mortgage loans. By 2005, it had almost 2,000 banking offices in 15 states and one of the two largest deposits shares in California, Oregon and Washington. It also had a significant presence in Florida, and modest coverage in New York and Chicago. Unfortunately, four years later it was gone as one of many victims of the subprime mortgage debacle.

Bank One-First Chicago NBD

While Norwest was moving westward in 1998, other big Midwest banks continued the regional consolidation that began in the late 1980s. The Midwest, though, was still a fragmented banking market, and despite Bank One's acquisition of First

Chicago NBD in 1998, it would remain so. That acquisition, though, made Bank One much larger than any other bank in the region, and many of the other Midwest banks that looked like potential consolidators after 1995 were gone by the end of 1998—First Chicago NBD and Boatmen's; had moved its base out of the region—Norwest; or had lost momentum—KeyCorp. Only First Bank System, or U.S. Bancorp as it was now called, and National City made even modest efforts to keep pace with Bank One in the Midwest and the large buyers elsewhere in the country.

Bank One's purchase of a larger First Chicago NBD, without corresponding moves by others, created a Midwest banking leader with the size to play on the national stage. It more than doubled its assets between 1996 and 1999 from $102 to $269 billion; was about three times the asset size of the second largest bank based in the Midwest—National City; and it was the fifth largest bank in the country.

Bank One had become far more than just another Midwest bank. It was among the leaders in Texas, Louisiana, Colorado and Arizona and seemed well-positioned to join Bank of America as a truly national bank. It was already there with its credit card operation, First USA, which was one of the three largest issuers of credit cards.

The acquisition of First Chicago NBD was the culmination of Bank One's rise from a second-tier bank in Columbus, Ohio to national prominence. Despite some stumbling in the mid-1990s, by 1998, Bank One was back to being a high performer. First Chicago NBD had put most of its cultural problems of the 1995 First Chicago-NBD merger behind it, and joining forces with Bank One made good sense to new management in that it created a regional giant with access to a wide variety of markets. Thus, for the second time in four years, First Chicago was bought by a bank from another Midwestern city, and for a second time, the appeal of Chicago kept the headquarters there.

Largest Midwest Banks, 1999

	Assets		Rank 1996	Eventual Owner
	1999	1996		
	(in billions)			
1. Bank One	$ 269	$ 102	2	JPMorgan
2. National City	87	51	5	PNC
3. KeyCorp	83	68	4	KeyCorp
4. U.S. Bancorp	82	36	6	U.S. Bancorp
5. Firstar	73	10	-	U.S. Bancorp

Source: SNL Financial, Charlottesville, Virginia.

Two other Ohio banks, National City and KeyCorp, along with U.S. Bancorp and Firstar, had assets in the $70 to $90 billion range and were still in the race for size and presumably survival. They were, though, much smaller than Bank One. Nevertheless, with all the large banks that had disappeared since 1995, this was enough size to place them at or near the bottom of the national top ten. Of these banks, only Firstar made a 1998 or 1999 acquisitions of significant size.

FIRSTAR

Milwaukee-based Firstar's 1998 merger with Star Banc involved two mid-sized banks. This merger, however, triggered a series of mergers that helped create one of today's leading banks.

Firstar-Star Banc was another of those equal mergers that was based on one partner, Star Banc, having management control and the other the headquarters, but, in this case, Firstar not only had the headquarters, but it also kept its name. Neither name nor the headquarters location, however, would be of long duration.

For a brief time, though, Firstar had its day in the sun. The Firstar-Star Banc merger was consummated in November 1998, and the new Firstar had assets of $38 billion and was the fifth largest bank in the Midwest. Five months later, it bought Mercantile Bancorp in St. Louis, and with that merger, it more than doubled its size. By year-end 1999, Firstar had assets of $78 billion.

Firstar was a secondary player on the national stage, but it was moving fast, and its president, Jerry Grundhofer, was the older brother of Jack Grundhofer, the president of U.S. Bancorp. In 2000, Firstar and U.S. Bancorp would have a family reunion in another equal merger. Firstar technically was the buyer, but it was the U.S. Bancorp name that was utilized and the headquarters was in Minneapolis, not Milwaukee.

FLEET

In New England there was little room for further consolidation as its banking elite was effectively down to just two—Fleet and Bank of Boston, or BankBoston as the holding company was then called. State Street was still around, but it was a specialty bank with only six banking offices, and the Citizens affiliate of Royal Bank of Scotland was growing rapidly, but still far behind the big two. Short of a Fleet-Bank of Boston merger or the takeover of one of the two by either the Royal Bank of Scotland or a large, out-of-area bank, the New England role in bank consolidation had pretty much run its course, or so it seemed.

By the second week-end in March 1999 another chapter in New England bank consolidation was about to be written, and another big merger in this mega-merger wave was about to take place. A telephone call from the *Boston Globe* that weekend wanted my views on an impending merger of Fleet and Bank of Boston. Fleet was completing its improbable run of directly, or indirectly, absorbing almost every bank of any size in New England. By the time it was through, Bank of Boston, Bank of New England, Shawmut, BayBanks, CB&T, Hartford National, Society for Savings, Boston Five and almost every other substantial New England banking organization was part of the Fleet franchise.

With the acquisition of Bank of Boston, Fleet almost doubled its size in a year. With assets approaching $200 billion, it had moved from eleventh to eighth in size nationwide. Fleet would have to divest some of its New England branches and deposits, but the next largest New England banking organization, Royal Bank of Scotland's Citizens affiliate, was a distant second with regional assets of just $23 billion in 1999.

As the 1990s wound down it was a bit unfair to think about Fleet as just a New England bank. It started its move to prominence back in 1987 with an equal merger with Norstar, which made it a leader in Upstate New York and gave it offices in the New York metropolitan area. In 1995, Fleet bought NatWest's New Jersey franchise and became one of the leading players in New Jersey. Even with the purchase of Bank of Boston, Fleet was still a lot smaller than Citigroup and Chase Manhattan and trailed J.P. Morgan as well, but it was a solid fourth in asset size among banks headquartered in the Northeast. It also was number one in deposit share if large bank main office deposits, which tended to be corporate or government deposits from outside the immediate area, were excluded.

CHANGING NORTHEAST STRUCTURE

The changing structure in the Northeast during the late 1990s flowed from the large mergers by some big banks—Fleet-Bank of Boston being the latest—and a loss of momentum by others. Citigroup and Fleet more than doubled their size through mergers in 1998 and early 1999; while the combined Chemical-Chase Manhattan, which was the biggest bank in the country in 1996 and 1997, was busy trying to put together two very complex organizations, had stalled. As a result, the new Chase Manhattan was not much bigger in 1998 than in 1996 and 1997. J.P. Morgan and PNC were other Northeast banks that did not grow much in the late 1990s.

Largest Northeast Banks, 1999

	Assets		Rank 1996	Eventual Owner
	1999	1996		
	(in billions)			
1. Citigroup	$717	$310	1	Citigroup
2. Chase Manhattan	406	366	2	JPMorgan
3. J.P. Morgan	261	222	3	JPMorgan
4. Fleet	191	86	5	Bank of America
5. PNC	75	73	6	PNC
6. Bank of New York	75	56	8	Bank of New York
7. Mellon	48	43	11	Mellon*
8. Summit	36	23	12	Bank of America
9. M&T	22	13	13	M&T

*Branch network only.   Source: SNL Financial.

The major Northeast bank losses by acquisition during these twenty months of frenzied merger activity centered upon 1998 were Bankers Trust, Bank of Boston and CoreStates. This did not leave much of a second tier behind Citigroup, Chase Manhattan, J.P. Morgan and Fleet in a region that included New York City, Philadelphia and Boston. The other Northeast banks with assets above $50 billion in 1998—PNC, Bank of New York, Mellon and Republic—were second-tier players with either little momentum or little appetite for traditional banking—and by the end of 1999, Republic was gone via a sale to HSBC.

The sale of Bankers Trust to Deutsche Bank was not only a sale, but it was also Bankers Trust's final step in a move away from traditional banking. Deutsche Bank, even in Europe was more of an investment bank than a full-service bank, and much of its base in the United States came from its 1996 acquisition of Alex. Brown & Sons, a Baltimore-based investment bank. As part of Deutsche Bank, Bankers Trust would fit into that same mode.

NATIONAL LEADERS

The merger activity in 1998 had created two superbanks, Citigroup and Bank of America, and left eight banks and a thrift much larger than all other banking organizations. Mergers announced or completed in 1998 and early 1999 had more than doubled the asset size since 1996 of Citigroup, Bank of America, Bank One, Wells Fargo and Fleet. The smallest of the eight, Fleet, upon completion of its Bank of Boston acquisition, was more than twice as large as the ninth biggest, SunTrust.

Largest American Banks, 1999

	Assets December 31,		Rank 1996	Eventual Owner
	1999	1996		
	(In billions)			
1. Citigroup	$717	$281	2	Citigroup
2. Bank of America	633	186	5	Bank of America
3. Chase Manhattan	406	336	1	JPMorgan
4. Bank One	269	102	10	JPMorgan
5. J.P. Morgan	261	222	4	JPMorgan
6. First Union	253	140	6	Wells Fargo
7. Wells Fargo	218	80	11	Wells Fargo
8. Fleet	191	86	10	Bank of America
9. SunTrust	95	52	16	SunTrust
10. National City	87	51	18	PNC

Source: SNL Financial, Charlottesville, Virginia.

Gone were the original California-based BankAmerica, Bankers Trust, First Chicago NBD, the original Wells Fargo, Barnett, CoreStates and Bank of Boston. Citicorp was also acquired. Citicorp, or Citigroup as it was now called, was far from gone, though, and the driving force behind the acquiring Travelers, Sandy Weill, saw Citicorp, not Travelers, as the focus of this financial conglomerate. It was not a stretch to say that Citicorp was both the acquired and the survivor, and this would be made quite clear a few years later when Citigroup sold the insurance business of Travelers with little, if any, negative impact on earnings.

After the mega-merger mania of late 1997, 1998 and early 1999, American banking was heading into the new millennium, with four or five banks well on their way to controlling half of all American banking assets. Citigroup and Bank of America were well-positioned to be among the elite banks. On size and reputation, Chemical, now bearing the Chase Manhattan name, and J.P. Morgan, were logical candidates, but they had no momentum at the time, and the latter had not yet moved toward a full-service banking mode of operation. Bank One, First Union, Wells Fargo and Fleet had momentum, but still had a long way to go to be ultimate survivors—and were small enough to be bought by Citigroup, Bank of America or Chase Manhattan.

BEYOND TRADITIONAL BANKING

From the perspective of 2000, the big banking story in the 1990s was the incredible growth of a few banks through a series of mega-mergers, but looking at those years today, this was clearly only half the story. The other half—and one that received a lot of attention later—is how these banks that had become so large during those years had at the same time regained the powers big banks had in the 1920s along with an accompanying enhanced level of risk by the repeal of the 1933 Glass-Steagall Act. Whether this caused the near collapse of a broadly defined financial services industry in 2008 may be arguable, but today's banking giants are as much a product of expanded powers gained in the 1990s as they are of the mega-merger boom.

The passage of Gramm-Leach-Bliley in 1999 that in effect repealed Glass-Steagall, which was passed to separate banks whose purpose was to gather deposits and make loans from banks in more complex businesses such as investment banking, securities sales and trading, and also took bank consolidation to a new level. A few big banks were no longer just moving toward holding about 50 percent of bank assets, but rather 50 percent, or more, of all financial services. By 2013, just four big banks had a larger share of all financial services, other than insurance, than they did of only bank assets. This commercial bank move beyond traditional banking in the late 1990s was a key element in consolidating financial services, but it also played a role in the financial excesses of the early 2000s.

The pressure to eliminate, or at least roll back, the prohibitions of Glass-Steagall had been building even before the 1990s, but it took a political will for deregulation and banks big enough to use the opportunity to make it a reality. The political will came to the fore in the 1980s with the election of Ronald Reagan and rose to a fever pitch in the go-go years of the 1990s when banks were large enough to take advantage of the opportunity.

In the 1990s, Glass-Steagall constraints were being chipped away long before the Travelers-Citicorp merger, but it was that 1998 transaction that took it down totally. This merger made Sandy Weill, CEO of Travelers and then Citigroup, one of the most important, as well as controversial, banking leaders.

With the elimination of Glass-Steagall, investment banking defined to include underwriting securities, securities transactions and merger assistance; selling and underwriting insurance; and an aggressive use of trading desks were no longer off-limits for commercial banks. This was a major change in bank powers, and it ushered in an entirely new set of dynamics and the potential for a much broader approach to one-stop shopping for financial services. It added risk to banks that chose to go in that direction, but these broader powers were used primarily by large banks.

The expansion into previously off-limit segments of financial services coincided with a segmenting of some of what were once normal bank products into sub-industries of their own. Mortgage banking, credit cards and asset management had long been bank services, but they had increasingly become sub-industries of their own with complications and economies of scale that favor the large, but it was only in the 1990s that banks had become large enough to fully exploit these economies. In mortgage banking, one of those complications was the introduction of the securitization of home loans that allowed the mortgage process to move a step beyond what Glass-Steagall envisioned.

The emergence of sub-industries within the broad financial services industry was a more gradual process than the disappearance of Glass Steagall. Banks and thrifts had been originating and servicing mortgages for decades, and they continue to originate and book home mortgages as well as offer trust services and credit cards. By the end of the 1990s, though, small and mid-sized banks, as well as thrifts, were reduced to operating on the fringes of these once traditional banking businesses that were increasingly being dominated by large banks and specialty boutiques.

ONE-STOP SHOPPING

The expansion of bank powers to include investment banking; the sale and underwriting of securities; and insurance transactions initially received a lot of attention as a major step toward one-stop shopping for financial services. For most banks, this was the primary reason for getting rid of Glass-Steagall, not the ability to market exotic, high risk products. It was the one-stop shopping benefits that made Weill want to bring into a single organization a commercial bank, investment bank, insurance firm and securities brokerage. It may not have worked as well as anticipated on the retail side, at least partly because Citigroup did not have much branch coverage beyond New York City, but one-stop shopping remains a major banking objective relative to retail as well as commercial customers.

The one-stop shopping concept involving traditional bank products being sold with other financial services was not new, but some earlier efforts were by outsiders that were not restrained by Glass-Steagall. In the 1980s, Sears was moving in that direction; the installation of banking offices in grocery stores was a possible step toward one-stop shopping; and BankAmerica's acquisition of Charles Schwab & Co. and its discount brokerage activities was another, albeit directly involving a commercial bank. To many these movements were viewed in the 1980s as being as much of a competitive threat as an opportunity.

Sears, in particular, was of concern to bankers since in the 1980s, it still carried the perception of a retail giant. As such, its owning a savings and loan, real estate brokerage, insurance company and credit card brought forth a vision of a powerful marketing force that would have people flocking to Sears to put their money into CDs, buy insurance, make credit card payments, visit an ATM and check out home prices in adjoining kiosks. Only later was it realized that Sears was a rapidly fading force in retailing activities of all types and not capable of doing much to promote these many businesses in combination with one another.

Bank branches in grocery stores were seen as an expansion of the bank delivery system and not as nearly the threat to traditional banking as the Sears one-stop shopping concept. There was concern, though, these store branches could morph into the stores owning the branches—a threat that seemed even more ominous with the rising power of Wal-Mart.

Combining the original, California-based BankAmerica's large branch network with the Schwab discount approach to trading securities, which was relatively unique—albeit still quite small—at the time, was clearly a step in the direction of one-stop shopping for financial services. Being part of a bank, though, kept it within the confines of the banking industry.

Customer resistance and problems at Sears and BankAmerica reduced any lasting trend toward one-stop shopping long before the 1980s ended. Sears was only a shell of its former self, and the loan problems of BankAmerica during the mid-1980s caused a rift between it and the previous owner of Schwab that ended with Charles Schwab buying the business back. Grocery store branches would continue to exist, but their ownership stayed with banks and thrifts.

Resuscitating interest in the one-stop shopping concept came with the emergence of the Internet in the late 1990s. It was widely believed, as the decade wound down, that the Internet would make it a viable concept activated from home or work and not be dependent on the personal contact of a banking office. Like much that had to do with the Internet, however, one-stop shopping on the retail side via Internet was an over-hyped idea whose primary contribution to bank consolidation may have been the damage it did to one of its prime adherents, Bank One. Bank One's commitment to—and the losses from—its Internet banking subsidiary, Wingspan.com, might have been the difference between it being a survivor and its eventual sale to JPMorgan. Whether one-stop shopping using the Internet was over-hyped or just ahead of its time, though, was, and remains, an open question.

Unanswered or not, just the probability of one-stop shopping being a deciding factor in which direction bank customers would go was a strong enough concern in the late 1990s to make it an integral part of planning for banks of all sizes, but particularly the large ones. Deep pockets, thousands of branches and large advertising budgets were marketing realities and strong incentives for the big banks to get rid of the Glass-Steagall prohibitions and expand their product base.

Fall of Glass-Steagall

When interstate banking barriers fell in the 1980s and rendered the 1920s' McCarran Act obsolete, the 1930s' Glass-Steagall Act was the next constraint the banking industry wanted to see gone. Over the years, the prohibitions had been modified slightly in areas where there were no apparent, or at least minimal, conflicts of interest, but these modifications were so minor that as the 1990s began, financial services and products that went much beyond lending and deposit-gathering were still not readily available to banks.

It seemed, however, a virtual "given" in the early 1990s that Glass-Steagall would go the way of the McCarran Act. Lending credence to this was a 1989 Federal Reserve ruling that a bank holding company could own an investment bank if no more than 10 percent of its revenues came from services and products not allowable for commercial banks. This permitted bank holding companies to buy or set up specialized investment banking subsidiaries. The 10 percent revenue limitation was too restrictive for an investment bank subsidiary to have much of an impact on a bank holding company's overall earnings, but it was a start.

The next step came in late 1996 when the Federal Reserve increased the limit for investment banking activities to 25 percent of bank holding company revenues. This provided much more flexibility, and in early 1997, several banks were looking to totally circumvent Glass-Steagall and test the Federal Reserve's willingness to let this 25 percent of revenues ruling be its access to a broad-based investment banking effort.

In April 1997, the test case came with Bankers Trust announcing that it was acquiring Baltimore's Alex. Brown & Sons. The $1.7 billion price alone was eye-catching, and Alex. Brown was far more than just a regional investment bank. It ranked sixth in the nation in securities underwriting in 1996.1 Thus, this proposed transaction had the nation's seventh largest bank buying the sixth largest securities underwriter, and if allowed, it would be a major step in the total elimination of Glass-Steagall constraints.

In July 1997, the Federal Reserve ruled in favor of Bankers Trust, and in the go-go business environment of the late 1990s, a rush by commercial banks to buy investment banks was anticipated. It would be almost a year before the Travelers-Citigroup merger proposed combining a commercial bank and investment bank larger than Bankers Trust and Alex. Brown, but there were numerous bank holding company acquisitions of investment banks announced starting in June 1997.

BankAmerica and NationsBank did not wait for the Bankers Trust-Alex. Brown decision before announcing the acquisition of two of the West Coast's hot, new investment banks. BankAmerica reported its plans to buy Montgomery Securities almost simultaneously with NationsBank's announced purchase of Robertson Stephens in 1997. Before the year ended, Fleet, Wachovia, SunTrust, U.S. Bancorp, First Chicago NBD and Fifth Third were among banks that had deals in place to buy investment banks or securities brokerages. The largest of these was Fleet's acquisition of Quick & Reilly, a nationwide discount broker with more than a million clients.

There was no Morgan Stanley, Merrill Lynch, Goldman Sachs or Salomon Brothers among the to-be-acquired investment banks, but because of the nature of their business, most of the investment banks that were being bought by bank holding companies were well-known, at least locally, and their sales garnered far more attention than their size may have warranted. This was partly because this was an industry fueling the bull market and contributing to the dot-com frenzy of the late 1990s.

All of the bank holding company acquisitions of investment banks in 1997 and 1998 combined, though, did not have the immediate consolidation impact of the

1997 merger between an insurance company and an investment bank—a merger that did not involve a commercial bank. In September 1997, Travelers Insurance announced it was buying Salomon Brothers. It was one of the giants of investment banking that would be even more powerful when combined with Travelers' Smith Barney securities brokerage operation.

The Travelers-Salomon Brothers transaction was completed in November 1997, and with this acquisition, the merger-oriented Sandy Weill, Travelers' CEO, had the size and prestige to consider combining with Citicorp. Five months later, the Travelers-Citicorp merger was announced, and with this move, Weill had dramatically altered the direction of the financial services industry.

SANDY WEILL

No one was more enthralled with the positive possibilities of one-stop shopping for financial services than Sandy Weill, even before he added Travelers Insurance to his stable of businesses. After buying Salomon Brothers in 1997, his primary objective was to fill the void in his collection and add a large commercial bank to his holding company. Citicorp was his first choice—he saw no reason not to start at the top—and if Weill had been rebuffed there, he undoubtedly would have found another commercial bank partner. He was not rebuffed, however, by Citicorp, and with that deal, not only did he change the direction of the financial services business, but he also turned himself into a banking and corporate legend—albeit one whose reputation would be hurt by the troubles of Citigroup and the banking industry that began in late 2007.

Unlike other bankers who played leading roles in the consolidation of banking, Weill was not readily identifiable with a single company. Walter Wriston and John Reed were Citicorp; Hugh McColl was NationsBank; and Ed Crutchfield was First Union. Weill would spend just eight years with Citigroup, and his primary contribution to that firm and the industry's future was the initial act of buying it. That alone, though, was enough to make him a major player in the consolidation process.

Weill was a well-known figure in financial circles long before 1998 and the Citicorp merger. His career began as a runner for Bear Stearns in 1955, and five years later at the age of 28, he was one of four partners in the newly formed Carter, Berlind, Potoma & Weill brokerage firm. In 1970, his firm acquired the better-known Hayden Stone, and in 1973, Weill became CEO of the combined firms. In the next five years, Shearson Hamill and Loeb Rhoades would be added to Weill's growing network of securities brokerage offices. After the last acquisition, what was then called Shearson Loeb Rhoades was second in size only to Merrill Lynch among securities brokerages.[2]

In 1981, Weill took his first step toward one-stop financial services shopping when he agreed to merge his firm with American Express, and in so doing, he was willing to take the second spot behind the American Express CEO, James Robinson. The combination of American Express and Shearson would create a diversified financial services company that was the leader in travelers' checks and credit cards and second in securities sales, but it was not a happy marriage for Weill who resigned in 1985. It seems playing "second fiddle" to Robinson was not as easy as he had thought.

Weill, though, was far from through, and after failing to gain control of BankAmerica, he took over a failing Baltimore business finance firm, Commercial Credit, which would be his new vehicle for buying companies. In 1988, he made a key move when he bought a struggling Primerica, which the year before had acquired Smith Barney, Harris and Upham, a securities brokerage firm.

Commercial Credit, Primerica and Smith Barney were only the start of Weill's second career. In 1992, Primerica made a 27 percent investment in the country's eighth largest insurance company, Travelers, and a year later bought Shearson back from American Express *and* the remaining 73 percent of Travelers. With the latter, the Primerica name changed to Travelers. In 1997, Travelers added Salomon Brothers to the mix.

The new Travelers was primarily a collection of once struggling companies, but by 1997, it was a large financial firm with revenues of about $38 billion and net income of $3.1 billion—and one of the 50 largest companies in the United States. If it had been a bank, it would have ranked as the largest in revenues and second largest in profits. Only Citicorp had higher earnings. To his credit, Weill had accomplished this the hard way by buying firms with problems and then making the necessary improvements. He had done this very well, and what he wanted next was a large commercial bank.

Travelers–Citicorp

Citicorp was a big target for Weill, but after the Salomon Brothers purchase, Travelers was about the same size. In 1997, Citicorp had revenues of $30.3 billion, earnings of $3.6 billion and market capital as of the end of February of $56 billion. Corresponding figures for Travelers were $37.6 billion, $3.1 billion and $64 billion. In Weill's favor was the *Business Week* performance ranking of S&P 500 firms for 1996 that had Travelers fifth behind Intel, Microsoft, Dell and Cisco—heady company at the time. A year later, Travelers fell to 16th, but Citigroup, which was in 86th place in 1996, had slipped to 245th in 1997. Thus, when Weill approached Citicorp about a merger in February 1998, he was not coming with hat-in-hand.[3]

That Citicorp, the country's largest bank with a long and illustrious history, would be receptive to overtures from a financial services firm that had been cobbled together in just ten years was far from certain, but its CEO, John Reed, was thinking about the benefits of size and one-stop shopping. He was intrigued by the possibility of joining forces with Travelers. In fact, Reed was so intrigued that a merger between Citicorp and Travelers would be announced five weeks later to a generally stunned audience.[4]

Business Week's perception of the transaction was that "perhaps, the best way to describe the Citicorp-Travelers Group Inc. merger is audacious. John S. Reed, America's top banker, and Sanford I. Weill, America's top financial services dealmaker, on April 6 proposed a $70 billion merger that defies existing law. Banks such as Citicorp can't own property & casualty insurers such as Travelers, and are limited in their ability to acquire brokerages. No matter: Reed and Weill believe that by acting aggressively, they can persuade legislators to knock down Glass-Steagall barriers and create a new kind of global financial paradigm."[5]

"In addition to chutzpah, Reed, 59, and Weill, 65, are propelled by their shared desire to go out in a blaze of glory. Both are nearing the end of their careers and seem intent on making history by creating the first successful, fully-integrated financial services behemoth. Says a clearly ecstatic Weill: 'The last major thing we are going to do is make this happen.' Adds Reed: 'We don't have to do this. We wanted to create this great enterprise together.'"[6]

Not only was it audacious in challenging existing banking law, but also Travelers-Citicorp was the biggest merger in corporate history up to that point. The announced price was $83 billion, not the $70 billion reported in the *Business Week* article. The price took a "hit" as bank stock prices headed down in late 1998, but within two years of closing, two financial firms that had a combined market value of about $120 billion prior to the merger had a consolidated market value of $256 billion.

The approval risk for a merger that clearly violated existing banking laws was somewhat mitigated by the Federal Reserve not having to approve or disapprove the merger based on its status relative to Glass-Steagall. It could, and did, decide based on normal bank merger criteria, which was contingent on divesting activities that violated banking law if after two years the bank was still in violation of that law. This put the risk on the merging parties, and the Federal Reserve approved the transaction in October 1998.

The risk was there, but relatively slight as Glass-Steagall no longer had many supporters, and 1998 and 1999 was a time when business and mergers were viewed positively by regulators and legislators. Citicorp and Travelers had a lot of legislative power, and the banking industry was behind them as most banks wanted the flexibility of being free of the Glass-Steagall constraints.

The result was the passage of the Financial Services Modernization Act, or as it was technically entitled the Gramm-Leach-Bliley Act, in November 1999. This act created a new type of holding company called simply a financial holding company that in addition to traditional banking could engage in insurance and securities underwriting and sale, merger advisory, merchant banking and other formerly nonbank financial activities. With this legislation, Citicorp and Travelers were home free, and others were encouraged to follow their path.

For Citicorp and Travelers, one of the intended outcomes of the merger was one-stop shopping, but an immediate, positive result was an enhancement of Citicorp's competitive status relative to corporations and affluent bank customers. The holding company name was changed, but only slightly, from Citicorp to Citigroup, and Weill, who was to be one of the co-CEOs—Reed being the other— despite coming in as the head of Travelers, was not an insurance man. The reality was that this merger was as much between Citicorp and one of the country's largest investment bank/brokerage operations, Salomon Smith Barney, as it was between Citicorp and an insurance company.

For Weill and Reed, it was a rocky marriage personally as co-CEOs. Reed may have assumed because of age that Weill would be gone not too long after the merger was finalized, and that he would be running the show. This was not to be, and in 2000, Reed would retire, leaving Weill in total control, which made the obvious—Weill being in charge—official.

GRAMM-LEACH-BLILEY

An immediate reaction to Gramm-Leach-Bliley was that there would be many more mergers between commercial banks, insurance companies, investment banks and securities brokerages that would create a new Citigroup, or at least mini-versions of it. The numerous merger announcements of banks buying small brokerages and investment banks in 1997 and 1998 made it clear that Citicorp and Travelers were not the only ones thinking along these lines, but the outcome was not what was initially expected.

The Citicorp-Travelers merger and Gramm-Leach-Bliley created a new set of dynamics for commercial banks and other financial services companies, but it did not result in a deluge of mergers between banks, insurance companies and investment banks. Its primary effect was to help the largest banks grow and increase their "deep pockets" advantage over everyone else. The only banks to take much advantage of the new law were Citicorp, JPMorgan, Bank of America and Wachovia.

Several years after the passage of Gramm-Leach-Bliley, it appeared that:

- Banks had little interest in acquiring insurance underwriters, presumably because of the risks and relatively low growth rates of that business.

- Insurance companies were not buying banks despite banking being perceived as a better business, which may reflect an inferior investor status that made them noncompetitive as buyers.

- The biggest banks could expand in these newly allowed areas of opportunity without major acquisitions.

Relative to the last point, this changed dramatically in 2008, but this was more of a response to opportunities resulting from the economic calamity that devastated the investment banking industry and created some "easy pickings" for JPMorgan, Bank of America and the London-based Barclays with the collapse of Bear Stearns, Merrill Lynch and Lehman Brothers. These, though, were easy pickings that had large, unexpected costs to the buyers.

Even before 2008, Citigroup had become a leader in investment banking with the acquisition of Salomon Smith Barney in the Travelers merger, and with all its corporate connection, JPMorgan was not far behind, but without a substantial securities brokerage business. Bank of America and Wachovia were moving in this direction, but were still far behind the investment banking leaders. JPMorgan and Bank of America were big enough to buy one of the large independent investment banks—Morgan Stanley, Merrill Lynch, Goldman Sachs and Lehman—but up until then, they either did not feel a need to do so or were just not interested.

SECURITIES BROKERAGE/ASSET MANAGEMENT

Areas often considered part of investment banking where the commercial banks had a strong interest in the late 1990s were the buying and selling of stock for customers and asset management. The securities brokerage business has been commonly grouped with investment banking, as its leaders have typically been investment banking power houses, with Merrill Lynch and Salomon Smith Barney being recent examples. Underwriting securities and their subsequent sale are not only two different businesses, but the conflict between doing both is such that regulatory authorities insist that when underwriting and sales are done within the same company, there should be no communication between the sections that do one part and those that do the other—the proverbial Chinese Wall.

The reality, though, is that successful securities underwriting requires a strong sales element, and it is easier and more profitable to get this sales assistance "in-house." Chinese Wall or not, there is a tendency—and usually with good intentions—for brokers to "suggest" stocks to their customers that their firm is bringing to market. The excesses of the late 1990s' Internet and technology boom, though, brought with it a heightened regulatory concern over this process. Combining commercial bank lending power with securities underwriting and the sale of securities could be viewed as having actually increased the conflict of interest and enhancing the ability of large banks to gain customers at the expense of others.

Selling securities was not new to commercial banks in 1999, as Glass-Steagall had not totally closed the door on their selling stocks. If it had, then BankAmerica could not have bought Charles Schwab in the 1980s, and in the late 1990s, banks of all sizes were experimenting with stock sales, particularly via mutual funds, through their branches. Prior to 1998, though, they were fringe players in this business, but the Travelers-Citicorp merger changed that.

With the announcement of Travelers' acquisition of Citicorp, much of the attention was on combining insurance and securities underwriting with the traditional banking activities of a large bank, an obvious violation of Glass-Steagall. That Travelers also owned one of the country's largest securities brokerages, Smith Barney, went relatively unnoticed. Unnoticed or not, with the completion of the Travelers-Citicorp merger, the newly-formed Citigroup became one of the largest brokers of securities of all types.

Securities brokering did not appeal to all large banks, but one that would follow the Citigroup lead was Wachovia. In 2003, it merged its securities sales business with the extensive brokerage business of Prudential, a large insurance company. Wachovia owned 62 percent of the combined venture, and it was, in effect, a Wachovia subsidiary operating under the Wachovia name. In 2007, it added to its securities brokerage business by paying almost $7 billion for the St. Louis-based brokerage, A.G. Edwards.

Citigroup and Wachovia were not alone among the banks that had brokerage businesses, but even alone, they were enough to put commercial banks at the forefront of securities sales. In 2006, Merrill Lynch was still number one, but Citigroup and Wachovia were second and third in net revenues from the sale of securities and in size of sales force. The domestic leaders included a foreign bank, Switzerland's UBS, which in 2000, bought Paine Webber, a large American securities brokerage. Wachovia with its A.G. Edwards 2007 purchase moved past Citigroup, at least in number of brokers, into second place.

The sale of securities is part of a much larger asset management business since the stockbroker who sells securities at least loosely manages the assets of the clients for which he was trading stocks, and often it was more than just "loosely." Firms that managed assets included mutual fund companies, bank trust operations and private banks for the wealthy. Merrill Lynch, Citigroup and Wachovia did all of this, but taking asset management beyond securities sales brought in the likes of Fidelity and Vanguard with their mutual funds; Bank of New York, State Street and Northern Trust with their trust operations and related businesses; and the private banking of JPMorgan and others.

Ranking the leading asset managers by amount of assets managed is complex, but a listing in *Barron's* in 2004 for United States put Merrill Lynch first, followed by Citigroup, Fidelity, UBS, Wachovia, JPMorgan and Bank of America. Northern Trust was number nine, and Wells Fargo eleventh.[7] These rankings showed that not long after the enactment of Gramm-Leach-Bliley, the commercial bank role in asset management went far beyond their trust department origins.

Events in 2008, even with Bank of America assuming Merrill Lynch's number one position, did not immediately increase commercial bank control of the securities brokerage business. Offsetting this was Citigroup in its need for capital, having to sell its Smith Barney affiliate to Morgan Stanley.

MORTGAGE BANKING

Unlike investment banking, mortgage banking did not need Glass-Steagall to disappear in order for the big commercial banks to take over a business that had once been dominated by independent mortgage banks and thrifts. In the 1970s, the Amendments to the Bank Holding Company Act opened the door for commercial banks to either buy or internally establish a mortgage banking subsidiary that operated across state lines. Citicorp, Wells Fargo, Norwest, First Union and others had bought their way into the top ten in mortgage banking in the 1970s. Being one of the top ten at the time, though, meant having national market shares of less than 2 percent. Thrifts, not one of which ranked among the leading mortgage companies at that time, collectively held and serviced about 50 percent of home mortgages.

What would change mortgage banking in the 1980s and 1990s was the securitization of mortgages that allowed banks and others to originate home loans and sell them to mortgage pools such as Fannie Mae and Freddie Mac. The originator of the loan needed little funding to do this, which opened the door for mass loan originations over a broad geographic region by mortgage banking specialists. This greatly increased the dollar amounts involved and the share of mortgages originated and serviced by the market leaders.

Securitization also brought Glass-Steagall constraints to mortgage banking as the packaging of home mortgages, and then turning them into mortgage-backed securities and their sale thereafter, was not a business available to commercial banks when Glass-Steagall was in effect. This created a large intermediary business for investment banks, and even after the 1999 fall of Glass-Steagall, it was a process that they continued to dominate.

This increase in the size of the mortgage business of a few operations was dramatic in the 1980s on a percentage basis, but the big gains in dollar amounts took place after 1990. In 1980, the largest servicer of residential mortgages was Lomas & Nettleton, a boutique not aligned with a bank that was servicing about $7 billion of mortgage loans. A decade later, Lomas & Nettleton was still among the leaders servicing $24 billion of mortgage loans, but it had fallen far behind Citicorp and Fleet that were then servicing $63 billion and $46 billion in mortgages, respectively.[8] These numbers seemed big at the time, but 17 years later, Wells Fargo and Countrywide were servicing residential mortgages valued at more than $1.4 trillion, and Citigroup, Washington Mutual and JPMorgan were servicing more than $700 billion each.

Historic numbers are not as readily available on mortgages originated, but the growth of a handful of originators in the ten years leading up to 2007 was equally astounding. The 1995 origination leaders were Countrywide and Norwest with $35 billion and $34 billion in home mortgages originated, respectively, and they were still the leaders in 2007, albeit Norwest was by then bearing the Wells Fargo name. The difference between 1995 and 2007 was that in the latter year, Countrywide was originating $408 billion in home mortgages—almost a twelve-fold increase—and Wells Fargo $272 billion, and these numbers were down from 2005 and 2006.[9] The size and scope of mortgage banking in the early 2000s favored the large banks, and the only interloper in their dominance of the business was Countrywide, an aggressive mortgage banking specialist with a thrift charter. It was the leader in mortgages originated and serviced in 2007 with $408 billion and $1.5 trillion, respectively.

Countrywide and Wells Fargo were by far the biggest mortgage bankers in 2007 with about 30 percent of the country's mortgage originations and 32 percent of the mortgages serviced between them in 2007. Citigroup was third in mortgages serviced with 9 percent, and fourth in mortgages originated with 7 percent. Washington Mutual, JPMorgan and Bank of America rounded out the top six in both home mortgages originated and serviced. Wachovia was eighth in servicing and seventh in originations.[10]

The impact of the mortgage banking concentration on the overall bank consolidation was substantial. In 1995, Countrywide, Washington Mutual and four banks—Wells Fargo, JPMorgan, Citigroup and Bank of America—collectively, originated only $102 billion in residential mortgages. By 2007, their combined originations were more than $1.4 trillion and 46 percent of all home mortgage originations, which created a much greater access to a broad customer base than they would have had without this real estate presence.[11]

The numbers on the servicing side were even bigger. In 1995, these same six institutions were servicing $452 billion in home mortgages, and twelve years later, were up to almost $5.8 trillion. This was about 62 percent of all home mortgages serviced.[12]

There is a big difference, though, between mortgages owned and serviced. Countrywide and Wells Fargo owned very few of the $1 trillion plus of the mortgages they each serviced. They, in effect, were managing these loans and collecting fees for receiving mortgage payments and forwarding them to the owners and occasionally foreclosing when mortgage payments were not forthcoming. To the borrower, though, the servicer was who they dealt with, and in "bad times" when foreclosures became commonplace, they became the "face of evil" in the mortgage banking process.

Unlike most other areas of banking, the rise of a handful of firms into dominant positions in mortgage banking was accomplished primarily by internal expansion. The mortgage bankers, themselves, are a fluid employee group, and periodically changed jobs without their previous employer being sold. This makes it relatively easy for a well-heeled mortgage bank to enter new markets by just acquiring originators.

Nevertheless, mergers have played a significant role. Wells Fargo's 2007 position owed a lot to the combination of Norwest and Wells Fargo, each of which had a large mortgage banking business. Bank of America's move into the top six was facilitated by combining the mortgage banking operations of NationsBank, the original Bank of America and Fleet.

CREDIT CARDS

Credit cards followed the same path as mortgage banking from being a traditional bank product to a business dominated by the few, but with an even greater level of concentration. Unlike mortgage banking, after the Bank of America purchase of MBNA in 2005, the credit card business no longer had an independent specialist along the lines of Countrywide competing with banks at the top and owed much more to mergers in its consolidation process.

The origin of the bank credit card goes back to the original Bank of America and the BankAmericard in the late 1950s, and in the early years of the card, the bank portion of it was aligned with two card systems, Visa and MasterCard. This made it possible for banks of all sizes to have their own card using their own name. The bank card also had early competition from American Express and retail store cards, including the Sears card, which would eventually become the Discover card and whose ownership moved from Sears to Dean Witter to Morgan Stanley that spun it off to its shareholders under the name Discover Bank.

The credit card, though, benefited more from scale economies than most bank products, and by the time the 1990s began, a few bank cards had become much larger than all others. Citicorp led the way, and other banks among the leaders were Chase Manhattan, BankAmerica, Wells Fargo, First Chicago and MNC with its MBNA subsidiary. The number of non-bank cards also expanded to include specialists like First USA and finance company cards issued by Household Finance and Advanta.

By the time the 1990s ended, the big bank dominance of the business was greatly increased. Much of the gain came from mid-sized and small banks selling their portfolios, but some of the increase came from the exiting of a few large players. Bank One bought First USA in 1997, and a year later, Fleet took over the credit card business of Advanta. Bank share gains at the expense of nonbanks was somewhat mitigated by a corresponding success of two bank spin-offs—MBNA from MNC and Capital One from Signet. By 2000, MBNA had become part of a credit card "big three" with Citigroup and Bank One.

Like many financial services in the early 2000s, credit cards would be dominated by the nation's largest banks. Citigroup was already there, and when JPMorgan bought Bank One, it added what was once First USA to its own card business and replaced Bank One as part of the credit card top three. In 2003, Bank of America took a big step in that direction when it announced the purchase of Fleet and its substantial card business. Then in 2005, it bought MBNA—the boutique equivalent of Countrywide in credit cards without the baggage. This gave Citigroup, Bank of America and JPMorgan well over half of the domestic credit card outstandings.

INSURANCE

The combination of banking and insurance did not play out quite as expected after the Travelers-Citicorp merger. There were no other major bank-insurance underwriter mergers, and in 2003 and 2005, Citigroup sold its Travelers' insurance underwriting operations. Banks continued, though, to show a strong interest in the sale of insurance, if not underwriting, as retail banking is generally a distribution business.

The mass sale of insurance had long been a local mom-and-pop business, even more so than banking before the interstate era. Underwriters like State Farm had numerous captive insurance agencies and three large insurance agencies—Marsh & McLennan, Aon and Willis Group Holdings—dominated corporate insurance sales. The bulk of retail insurance sales, however, were made by small, local firms, and these firms had myriad of state laws protecting them from bank competition.

Banks had long seen the potential for selling insurance through bank branches as a natural adjunct to their banking business, and in some European countries, banks sold most of the insurance. Even before 1999, American banks were trying to get around the legal constraints, and by the early 2000s, most of the more serious constraints had been removed.

Even after these constraints were removed, customers did not flock to banks to buy insurance, and the most successful banks selling insurance bought agencies and let them continue to operate as they always had. As banks acquired multiple agencies, though, they began to combine them and sometimes gave them the bank name.

Wells Fargo and BB&T were the most aggressive banks in purchasing insurance agencies, and by 2007, ranked fourth and sixth in insurance sales revenues behind the three agencies mentioned above that specialized in corporate sales. The revenues, however, were small when compared with other non-bank businesses that banks have entered. Wells Fargo had about $1.3 billion in insurance revenues in 2007, and BB&T had insurance revenues of a little over $800 million, numbers and rankings that have changed little since then.[13]

According to an American Bankers Insurance Association survey, in the early 2000s, bank insurance revenues were growing at about 20 percent a year, but accounted for just 7 percent of commercial insurance sales and 3 percent of personal lines. In addition, about two-thirds of the revenues banks reported as insurance fees were annuities, a product for which banks accounted for two-thirds of all sales. Annuities, though, are as much an investment product as an insurance product.[14] Banks have a long way to go before they become major factors in the sale of insurance, and it does not appear that they have a big interest in doing so.

POST-1999 NONBANK EXPANSION SUMMARY

The impact on the consolidation of banking and the broader financial services business from the expansion of the largest banks into related areas such as investment banking, securities sales and asset management after the fall of Glass-Steagall in 1999 was extensive. Citigroup and JPMorgan had investment banking revenues that clearly placed them among the leaders in this business by 2007. Wachovia and Citigroup ranked right behind Merrill Lynch, which was a year away from being acquired by Bank of America, in securities sales as well as in overall asset management.

The fall of Glass-Steagall had little to do with bank expansion in credit cards and mortgage banking, but the growth of the large banks in these two businesses coincided rather closely with what was happening in investment banking, securities sales and asset management. The post-2000 credit card purchases by Bank of America and JPMorgan put Citigroup, Bank of America and JPMorgan far ahead of all others in that business. Mortgage banking was not totally dominated by the big banks in the early 2000s as Countrywide and Washington Mutual were still among the leaders, but the industry was just two acquisitions away from having a structure similar to that of the other major nonbank financial businesses. This was taken care of by Bank of America buying Countrywide and JPMorgan acquiring Washington Mutual in 2008.

By 2007, banks had gone far beyond gathering deposits, making loans and using the bricks and mortar to sell traditional products and services, and it took a lot of resources for them to move beyond traditional banking. Once that step had been taken, though, those that had made the move had a competitive advantage in brand identification, "deep pockets" and gaining access to all the banking needs of businesses and individuals, particularly affluent individuals.

The fall of Glass-Steagall was a trigger that helped move commercial bank consolidation beyond traditional banking in the late 1990s and early 2000s. It was, though, the desire of the big banks to be as dominant in these specialty businesses as they were in their existing businesses—and where possible concentrate as many of a customer's financial needs in one place—that made it happen.

THE 1990S IN RETROSPECT

The 1990s were like the fourth act of a five act play, as banking moved from a localized industry that had existed from the mid-1930s until the late 1960s that culminated in the 2008 meltdown of the financial service industry. In many ways, the 1990s' mega-mergers, large increase in concentration, elimination of Glass-Steagall and growth of what at the time were called superregionals at the expense of money center and small banks, could be considered nothing more than a natural evolution of banking to meet the demands of an interconnected world. It also set the stage for some of the not so pleasant events that were to follow.

In looking at the 1990s in retrospect it may be helpful to step back and briefly summarize the first three acts that preceded these years to put the go-go atmosphere of the 1990s into the proper perspective—and suggest how some of what occurred would play a major role in creating the problems that arose late in the next decade. This includes the growth of securitization and loss of direction by the OTS in the 1990s, which may have had as much, if not more, to do with the 2008 problems as banks getting bigger and elimination of Glass-Steagall.

The evolution of banking from the highly localized business that existed after the Great Depression and into the 1940s began with banks moving from one office operations by opening branches at a rapid rate in the 1950s and 1960s. The major cause of this was the natural desire of a business to follow its customers to the suburbs as the automobile and the rise of shopping malls changed the retail habits of the country. In many states, this led to statewide branch networks that made moving across state lines, something that was prohibited at the time, a natural next business move.

This desire to cross state lines had become a major aim of many banks by the 1970s, a decade that is best known for a lengthy economic recession that combined with high interest rates to create a difficult business environment. Thus, while banks were trying to expand geographically, they were also dealing with a bad economic environment that resulted in some significant bank failures and the beginning of the end for much of the thrift industry. This combination of banks wanting to expand and the worst economic conditions since the Great Depression created an environment that made interstate banking and a much-changed banking industry structure inevitable in the 1980s.

The 1980s represented a watershed for the once localized banking industry whose only large banks were in the biggest cities and/or states—New York, Chicago and California. From a banking perspective, the decade is known primarily for the arrival of interstate banking and collapse of the thrift industry, particularly the S&Ls, but it was also a period of stress in many areas as the thrifts were not the only ones to suffer. Troubles in the oil patch virtually wiped out the large and mid-sized banks in Texas, money center banks were plagued by loan defaults in Latin America and in 1989 a real estate-driven recession began that in a four-year period would result in more than 2,500 bank and thrift failures.

This created the potential for massive industry consolidation if the economy and regulators co-operated—and co-operate they did. Deregulation had become the cure-all for all business problems by the mid-eighties and when the 1989 to 1992 economic downturn was in the rear view mirror, the American economy went into an economic upswing, fueled by the Internet, which went beyond anything that had been seen before. Merger mania was a major part of this, and banks benefited not only from the booming economy, but also as big players in enabling the merger process for all industries. From an industry that was struggling with failures as the 1990s began, as the decade ended, banking became the center of the business universe with financial services firms accounting for about 40 percent of market capital on the major stock exchanges.

To show the extent of the change from the 1980s to the 1990s without going into many pages of text, a few numbers do quite well.

- In the 1980s, the highest sale price for a bank was $2.1 billion. This was a long way from the $83 billion that was paid for Citicorp; $66 billion for BankAmerica; and $30 billion for First Chicago NBD in the 1990s.

- In these ten years, the share of bank assets held by just five banks rose from 16 percent to 36 percent and the ten largest from 25 percent to 47 percent.

- Merger mania was so prevalent in the 1990s that despite the opening of almost 1,200 new banks, the number of commercial banks fell from 12,347 to 8,582—a drop of 3,765, or 30 percent. Coincidentally, the number of thrifts fell from 2,815 to 1,642—a drop of 1,173, or a 42 percent decline.

- Most astounding of all was that of the 13 largest banks in 1990, only two had not been sold by the end of 2000.

There were good reasons why it was out with the old and in with the new, but it would have been hard to imagine in 1990 how in just ten years that eleven of the country's thirteen largest banks could be sold with nine of them eventually becoming part of just three banks—JPMorgan, Bank of America and Wells Fargo. It would have been equally hard to imagine that fifteen years later there would be three banks with assets in excess of $1 trillion. In 1990, the thirteen largest banks combined had assets of only a little over that number.

Largest American Banks, 1990

	Assets		
	1990	2000	
Bank	(In billions)		Eventual Owner
1. Citicorp	$217	Gone	Citigroup
2. BankAmerica	111	Gone	Bank of America
3. Chase Manhattan	98	Gone	JPMorgan
4. J.P. Morgan	93	Gone	JPMorgan
5. Security Pacific	85	Gone	Bank of America
6. Chemical	73	715	JPMorgan**
7. NCNB	65	643	Bank of America***
8. Bankers Trust	64	Gone	Deutsche Bank
9. Manufacturers Han.	62	Gone	JPMorgan
10. Wells Fargo	56	Gone	Wells Fargo****
11. First Interstate	51	Gone	Wells Fargo
12. C&S/Sovran	51	Gone	Bank of America
13. First Chicago	51	Gone	JPMorgan

*Citicorp acquired by Travelers and changed its name to Citigroup.
**Chemical took this name after acquiring J.P. Morgan.
***NCNB took this name after acquiring BankAmerica.
****Norwest took this name after acquiring Wells Fargo.
Source: American Banker, April 20, 1982 and February 8, 1991.

This change, however, was more than megamerger mania as it reflected a shift away from money center banks to large retail banks and economic problems in California early in the 1990s. Six of the large banks that were sold were money center banks—Citicorp, Chase Manhattan, J. P. Morgan, Bankers Trust, Manufacturers Hanover and First Chicago—and four were in California—BankAmerica, Security Pacific, Wells Fargo and First Interstate. The exception was C&S, a Virginia-based regional that would not have been sold if it had not faced a hostile takeover in a period of weakness. Using fifteen banks instead of thirteen would have added PNC, which is still around, but number fifteen, BankBoston, was also among those gone by the end of 2000.

The eventual owner did not always reflect their 2000 status. First Chicago was bought by NBD that was later bought by Bank One, and the latter was still independent in 2000. The purchase of J.P. Morgan by Chase Manhattan was announced in 2000, but was not completed until 2001. The combined entity was then renamed JPMorgan Chase. For the purist, Chase Manhattan had been bought earlier in the 1990s by Chemical that then took the more familiar Chase Manhattan name.

A major change in the 1990s that primarily affected the big banks was the disappearance of Glass-Steagall. This would have a major impact going forward, particularly in 2008, but it did not occur until 1999, so its impact in the 1990s did not go much beyond the acquisition of Citicorp by Travelers.

Beyond the Large

Merger mania was something that went far beyond the large banks in the 1990s as there were over 5,000 non-assisted bank sales compared to about 3,500 in the 1980s and a little over 1,300 in the 1970s—and this was from a smaller number of banks in total. There were only about half as many government-assisted mergers, though, with 429 in the 1990s compared to 804 in the more recession-plagued 1980s.

Bank Mergers in the 1990s

Year	Mergers			New Charters
	Unassisted	Assisted	Total	
1995-99	2,742	22	2,764	833
1990-94	2,297	407	2,704	348
Total	5,039	429	5,468	1,181
1980-89	3,467	804	4,271	2,700
1970-79	1,316	50	1,366	2,224

Note: There were 28 banks closed in the 1990s, 226 in the 1980s and 50 in the 1970s.
Source: FDIC: Historical Statistics on Banking.

Despite the big drop in the number of commercial banks, they were still able to increase their share of assets held by depository institutions. In the 1980s, a troubled thrift industry limited its share decline to two percentage points as those that survived grew rapidly in an effort to reduce their dependence on low-yielding fixed-rate home mortgages. The bottom fell out of this strategy as the 1980s came to an end. In the 1990s, the thrift share of depository institutions fell from 27 percent to 15 percent. Conversely, the bank share went up from 68 percent to almost 80 percent, and the credit union edged up from 5 percent to 6 percent.[1]

An under-reported story about this decline in the thrift role in banking is the impact of the competition that thrifts were having from mortgage bankers outside the bank regulatory system and the efforts of the thrift regulator, the OTS, to maintain its status and as an independent regulator. The outside threat had greatly reduced the thrifts' reason for existence as the securitization of loans and the ability to sell them immediately allowed lenders to make home loans with only minimal funding. This process was as much a 1980s' story as a 1990s' one, but it was the continuation of the process in the later decade that helped bring about the subprime mortgage crisis.

Holders of Home Mortgage Debt, 1990 and 2000

	Home Mortgage Debt				
	2000	1990	2000	1990	Annual Increase
	(in billions)		(share of total)		
Mortgage Trusts	$2,916	$990	56.1%	36.8%	11.4%
Comm. Banks	967	427	18.6	15.9	8.5
Thrifts	505	611	9.7	22.7	(1.9)
Individual	478	402	9.2	14.9	1.7
Other	329	261	6.4	9.7	2.2
Total	$5,195	$2,691	100.0%	100.0%	6.8%

Source: Federal Reserve Bulletin, May 1991 and May 2001.

Quite simply, prior to the 1980s and 1990s, thrifts made and held most home mortgages and incurred all the risk when things went bad—as they did when funding costs rose higher than the yields on the long terms loans they held. There was no way prior to securitization for loans to be made and immediately sold with little risk to the originator. This changed dramatically with securitization, but initially the only damage was to the thrift role in mortgage lending as the amount of residential mortgages they held fell from more than 50 percent in the 1970s to less than 10 percent in 2000.

Another 1990s problem was the concern of the OTS as to its future and the jobs of those that worked for it as the thrift role in delivering financial services diminished. In so doing, it took a much more relaxed attitude in regulating its members and was considered much more favorable in attitude toward "going that extra step" in mortgage lending. This would be carried to the extreme in 2007, when the mortgage crisis was becoming increasingly evident, the OTS still approved the conversion of Countrywide from a bank to a thrift.

Product Mix

The 1990s did not have the dramatic change in product mix as in previous decades, particularly relative to checking accounts and MMDAs. The move away from demand deposits and toward MMDAs continued, but at a much reduced rate.

The downward trend of dependence, and availability, of demand deposits was still a problem, but the decline from 1990 to 2000 from 20 percent of deposits to 15 percent was much less than the decline from 36 percent to 20 percent in the 1980s.

Bank Deposit Mix by Type, 1970 to 2000

	Percent of Deposits			Deposits/ Assets
	Demand	Savings*	CDs	
2000	15%	45%	40%	67%
1990	20	34	46	78
1980	36	17	47	80
1970	51	21	28	85

* Includes MMDAs, NOW accounts and regular savings.
Source: FDIC: Historical Statistics on Banking.

The increase in MMDAs is somewhat obscured in the accompanying table as they are included in "other savings," but by 1990 they had become most of that category. By 2000, regular savings had passed CDs as the primary time deposits. The customer interest in these products was influenced by interest rates, but it was the MMDA that had the bigger impact on the decline of checking accounts.

A noticeable change on the asset side of bank balance sheets was the decline of deposits as a percent of assets falling from 78 percent to 67 percent. Banks were making greater use of borrowed funds than in the past, which probably reflected the much increased share of assets held by large banks that were comfortable with non-deposit funding.

The major change of the loan side in the 1990s was banks holding more home mortgages in their portfolio and fewer consumer loans. The rapid rise in commercial real estate as a percent of all loans that occurred in the 1980s was not continued.

Bank Loan Mix by Type, 1970 to 2000

	Percent of Loans					Loans/ Assets
		Other Real Estate	Comm. & Ind.	Consumer		
	Home Mtg.			Credit Card	Other	
2000	24%	19%	28%	7%	9%	61%
1990	19	19	29	6	13	62
1980	14	11	38	3	19	55
1970	14	10	38	2	16	52

Source: FDIC: Historical Statistics on Banking.

Also not continuing was an increase in loans as a percent of assets that had been going on since well before 1970. It appears to have peaked in the 60 percent to 65 percent of assets range, but this, as the other changes in product emphasis, are technical and not changes that will have anything resembling the future impact of increased concentration, elimination of Glass-Steagall or securitization.

AND THEN THERE WERE FIVE

The opportunities offered by the disappearance of Glass-Steagall had changed banking, and as the new millennium began, industry consolidation had reached a level that left few doubts about the degree of dominance of a handful of large banks. The number of banking organizations with more than regional aspirations was down to eight commercial banks—Citigroup, Bank of America, Chase Manhattan, J.P. Morgan, Bank One, First Union, Wells Fargo and Fleet—and a single thrift, Washington Mutual, and they, like all banks and thrifts, now had the freedom to go beyond traditional banking.

This concentration of so much power in so few hands came only eighteen years after interstate banking was introduced; sixteen years after it became a legal reality; nine years after the concentration of assets in the hands of the large banks began to gather momentum; and one year after the fall of Glass-Steagall. By 2000, it was apparent that in a few years, five or fewer banks could control more than half of the nation's banking and financial services business.

These 2000 banking leaders had survived a winnowing process, but in 2000, they were far from equal. Citigroup and Bank of America had momentum and, with the exception of Chase Manhattan, were much larger than all of the others. Chase Manhattan with the Chemical management in charge had size, but not momentum. Fleet, Wells Fargo and Washington Mutual were the smallest of the group, but going into 2000, they were the stars in performance and momentum. Not doing as well were J.P. Morgan, Bank One and First Union, and each had a different weakness.

J.P. Morgan had an identity problem. It was a bank, but had stayed with the money center model of being primarily a banker to corporations and governments.

Thus, it had a competitive disadvantage in a role that put it somewhere between large, full-service banks that offered more options and aggressive investment banking firms that were not closely regulated. It was one of the most respected names in banking, but it was only moderately profitable and not growing at near the rate of its competition.

Bank One had a spectacular run in the 1980s and 1990s, but its rapid growth and high ambitions brought with them challenges that appeared to be beyond its management capability. It still had an expensive cost structure, and in 2000, Bank One was starting to experience asset quality problems as well. To make matters worse, it, more than any other large bank, was committed to Internet banking, and a free-standing Internet-banking subsidiary, Wingspan.com, added more in costs than it was producing in revenues.

First Union's problems were a result of rapid growth and, in its case, a flawed acquisition program. In an effort to keep pace with the other emerging banking leaders, particularly its Charlotte neighbor, NationsBank, First Union made some questionable acquisitions, and its execution was not the best with its quality purchases. Its acquisition of The Money Store in 1998 was a disaster. It was closed two years after being acquired, and as part of the closing, First Union took a $2.8 billion charge.[1] By 2000, it was not benefiting the way it should have from the good market position it had assembled in Pennsylvania and New Jersey through the acquisitions of First Fidelity and CoreStates.

With the consolidation of banking having come so far by 2000 and the economy showing signs of weakness as the long stock market rise came to an end, this was no time to be falling behind. J.P. Morgan, Bank One and First Union looked vulnerable as the new millennium began. In addition, Fleet began to feel the pain of the acquired BankBoston's commitment to Argentina, investment banking in the Silicon Valley and national corporate lending.

J.P. Morgan did not even make it out of 2000 as it was acquired by Chase Manhattan, but its name survived in the new JPMorgan Chase, and by 2001, the gap between the haves and have-nots among the banking elite was immense. Citigroup, Bank of America, JPMorgan and Wells Fargo had the look of winners while it seemed to be only a matter of time before Bank One, First Union and Fleet followed J.P. Morgan out the door. Washington Mutual was doing well, but size and being a thrift constrained its ability to keep pace with the others.

Another 2000 merger brought a new challenger to the fringes of the banking elite—U.S. Bancorp. By combining with Firstar in 2000, it was almost as large as Fleet, Bank One, First Union and Wells Fargo. U.S. Bancorp, though, did not make another major bank acquisition in the next few years, and by 2007, was the leader of a second tier of regional banks that included PNC, SunTrust, Capital One, National City, Regions and BB&T, rather than a laggard in the first tier.

With the elimination of so many of what was already a small group of banks controlling such a large part of the banking industry, it would not be long before the new millennium would begin to take on the aura of being a post-consolidation era. This era had not quite arrived in 2000 as the merger-mania of the late 1990s still had a year to run, and in 2000, there were eleven billion-dollar bank mergers. These included the sale of J.P. Morgan to Chase Manhattan and the merger of U.S. Bancorp and Firstar. The $81 billion in collective deal value for 2000's large mergers was surpassed up to that time only by the $245 billion of 1998.

Large Bank Merger Value, 2000 to 2007

	Bank Mergers			Large Deal Value (in billions)
	Deal Value Over			
	$ 1 Billion	$ 10 Billion	All	
2007	9	2	294	$ 53
2006	6	2	309	37
2005	3	-	270	9
2004	9	3	266	106
2003	2	1	227	53
2002	-	-	282	0
2001	6	1	362	24
2000	11	2	462	81

Source: SNL Financial, Charlottesville, Virginia and FDIC: Historical Statistics on Banking.

By 2007, bank consolidation was even more extreme, but along lines that might have been expected in 2000. The early years of the new millennium, though, were not without surprises. The survival of First Union was one, and Chase Manhattan continuing to add size by acquiring J.P. Morgan and Bank One was another. The latter's changing its name to JPMorgan Chase was a plus, but its earnings would continue to lag behind Citigroup, Bank of America, Wells Fargo and even First Union, which was by then called Wachovia.

After 2001, the number of large mergers and their total deal value dropped sharply, and the cumulative large deal value from 2001 to 2003 was less than in 2000 alone. The low point was the post-recession year of 2002 when there was not one billion-dollar merger involving independent banks. M&T bought Allfirst for $2.9 billion, but the Baltimore-based Allfirst was an affiliate of an Irish bank. The quiet period continued through the first nine months of 2003 when there was only one fairly small billion-dollar sale announced—BB&T acquiring First Virginia.

A rise in bank stock prices and the lagging momentum of a couple of big banks reignited the megamerger activity in late 2003, and for about ten months, it looked like 1998. In October 2003, Bank of America announced the acquisition of Fleet, and less than three months later, JPMorgan agreed to acquire Bank One. These two mergers had a combined deal value of $108 billion and created a banking "big five" that left everyone else far behind. By August 2004, eight more billion-dollar bank sales had been announced with a collective value of $47 billion.

This surge in large bank mergers temporarily ended in August 2004. In the last four months of 2004 and through all of 2005, there were just three large bank sales with a total deal value of less than $10 billion. This slowdown in the midst of an economic boom reflected the dramatic reduction in the number of large buyers and that some of those remaining were busy with recent deals.

The slowdown in large merger activity, though, was temporary, and even though 2006 did not match 2004, it was a busy acquisition year. There were six bank acquisitions with deal values in excess of $1 billion, and two of them, Capital One's purchase of North Fork and Regions' acquisition of AmSouth, had values in excess of $10 billion. The total deal value for the six large bank mergers was $37 billion, which was more than four times the $8.6 billion of the previous year.

Adding to consolidation activity in 2006 was JPMorgan's acquisition of Bank of New York's branch system. This added 338 branches in the New York City area with more than $30 billion deposits and eliminated a major local competitor.

In 2007, the number of bank acquisitions in excess of $1 billion in deal value matched 2004, and the total value of these large deals was up to $53 billion. As in 2006, two had price tags above $10 billion—Bank of America's purchase of Chicago-based LaSalle bank from a Dutch bank, ABN AMRO, and Spain's Banco Bilbao's purchase of Compass Bankshares, an Alabama bank with a branch network in Texas. Another foreign bank, the Toronto-based, TD Banks, bought the rapidly growing Commerce Bank in New Jersey for more than $9 billion.

CONCENTRATION IMPACT

The consolidation impact of merger activity from 2000 through 2007 was greater than the number of mergers would suggest as fewer large banks magnified the concentration impact of those that occurred. Because of the much larger starting base, though, it was virtually impossible for the asset share increase from 2000 to 2007 to match the approximate doubling of the share of bank assets held by the five largest banks in the 1990s. Nevertheless, by 2007, a lot of headway was made in that direction as the five largest banks' share went from about 33 percent to almost half of all bank assets.

Large Bank Asset Share, 1990 to 2007

Share of Bank Assets			
Dec. 31	Five Largest	Next Five	Bank Assets (in billions)
2007	49.2%	7.9%	$11.2
2005	43.7	8.8	9.0
2003	36.2	13.1	7.6
2001	35.6	12.6	6.6
2000	33.2	13.7	6.3
1990	16.2	9.3	3.4

Source: SNL Financial, Charlottesville, Virginia and FDIC: Historical Statistics on Banking.

Most of the asset share increase occurred after 2003 from the acquisitions of Fleet by Bank of America and Bank One by JPMorgan. The combining of four of the eight largest banks lifted the five bank asset share from about 36 percent in 2002 and 2003 to almost 44 percent in 2005—a jump of more than seven percentage points in just two years—but the momentum did not stop there. With smaller acquisitions, internal growth and some shifting of their thrift assets into bank assets, the five largest banks had a 5.5 percentage point gain between 2005 and 2007.

The growing importance of five rather than ten banks on the national scene was readily apparent in the diminishing share of banks ranked sixth through tenth. Between 2000 and 2007, their share fell from almost 14 percent of all bank assets in 2000 to less that 8 percent in 2007, with most of the decline coming after 2003. This was less than in the early 1990s when concentration ratios first began to rise. Put another way, the ratio in asset size of the top five banks to the second five rose from 1.7 to 1 in 1990 to 2.4 to 1 in 2000 to more than 6 to 1 in 2007. This suggests the increase of market power of a very few banks grew much faster from 2000 to 2007 than it did between 1990 and 2000.

The growth of the top five at the expense of the second tier of large banks was a continuation of the pattern of the very largest banks buying the biggest banks available. In 1998, five of the ten largest banks were sold. When this big-buying-big type of merger activity occurred after 2000, the concentration impact was greatly enhanced by the increased sizes of both the buyers and sellers. When eight banks leave all others behind, and then in the next five years, three of the eight—J.P. Morgan, Bank One and Fleet—are bought by two of the three largest banks, Bank of America and JPMorgan, a large concentration gain is inevitable.

It was clearly mergers, not organic growth, driving this consolidation. That was evident in the asset share change of the five largest banks in the quiet merger period from the end of 2001 through 2003, which did not include Bank of America's purchase of Fleet that was announced in 2003, but completed in 2004. Their share of bank assets increased in each of these years, but by the end of 2003, their share was only about a half-of-a-percentage point more than it was two years earlier.

The problems that were to surface from the subprime mortgage excesses in the early 2000s may have had little to do with these five banks, but come 2008 at least three of them were front center in the rescue operation—and whether they deserved it or not, they became the recipients of considerable political and public abuse. Four of the five—JPMorgan, Bank of America, Citigroup and Wells Fargo—had built formidable financial franchises come 2008, albeit not quite so formidable that Citigroup could survive $35 billion in losses in 15 months without help. The fifth, Wachovia, made a valiant effort to make the best of a bad start, but it had not done quite enough.

JPMORGAN CHASE

The first large bank out of the blocks with a big acquisition in 2000 was the one with the least recent momentum, Chase Manhattan. It was the product of early and mid-1990s' mergers that brought Chemical, Manufacturers Hanover and Chase Manhattan under the same roof with Chemical's management and the Chase Manhattan name. They were all struggling New York money center banks when they merged and were still struggling in 2000.

The new Chase Manhattan was different from its component banks in size only. It was still a New York bank specializing in national corporate lending with little in the way of retail coverage beyond New York, and the holdings that Chemical had in Texas. Each of the original banks had suffered badly from their 1970s and 1980s expansion into international lending, and by the late

1990s, even combined they did not begin to match Citigroup's international operations. Bigger it was, though, and in 1996 and 1997, Chase Manhattan was the country's largest bank measured by assets. At the end of 1999, even with its lack of momentum, it was still the country's third largest—and much larger than number four, Bank One.

The announcement in September 2000 that Chase Manhattan would acquire J.P. Morgan sounded like more of the same—a fourth large New York money center bank being added to the other three, and this time with no retail coverage at all. J.P. Morgan, however, had an elite national commercial customer list and more investment banking expertise than its acquirer. Chase Manhattan wanted the merger badly enough to put J.P. Morgan front and center in the holding company name. The new bank, though, would operate as Chase Bank. This merger created substantial size, and upon completion, the new JPMorgan may not have been as big as Citigroup in total assets or Citigroup and Bank of America in earnings, but it had a semblance of parity with these banks in a national big three.

While the combination of Chase Manhattan and J.P. Morgan created a third domestic bank of tremendous size, its formation coincided with the downside of the 1990s' stock market and merger boom to the detriment of JPMorgan and other large banks. The Enron, WorldCom and similar, lesser mishandlings of corporate accounting were exposed along with the role of the big banks. The losses from their involvement would be in the billions of dollars, and JPMorgan did not have the earnings of Citigroup or Bank of America to handle easily this type of reversal. The losses did not threaten JPMorgan's survival, but they contributed to its earnings being less than those of its primary competitors in the early 2000s. Citigroup earned more than $13 billion each year from 2000 through 2004 while JPMorgan maxed out at $6.7 billion in 2003.

In February 2004, JPMorgan took a big step toward gaining greater parity with Citigroup and Bank of America when it acquired Bank One. This merger reduced the emphasis on large commercial loans; made it a more complete full-service bank; and, most importantly, increased its earnings potential. The Bank One acquisition was totally outside of its past mode of adding money center banks to the fold and overnight, JPMorgan became one of the country's largest retail banks. Bank One had almost 1,900 branches spread across the midsection of the country and the largest deposit share in the Midwest. It was one of the three biggest credit card issuers, although the quality of its credit card portfolio may not have matched the standards of the other leaders, Citigroup and MBNA. The credit card had been part of Bank One's problems in recent years.

The Bank One acquisition had interesting management implications in that part of the deal was that the Bank One president, Jamie Dimon, would succeed JPMorgan's William Harrison as president and CEO after two years. Dimon had been number two behind Weill at both Travelers and Citigroup before he moved on to take the job at Bank One. This merger brought him back to New York as Weill's counterpart at one of Citigroup's biggest competitors. This attracted a lot of media attention, but direct competition between the two never materialized as Weill stepped down from his leadership position shortly after Dimon was in full control at JPMorgan.

JPMorgan made another big move in 2006 with the purchase of the retail operation of one of its biggest rivals in the New York metropolitan area, Bank of New York. This took Bank of New York out of the ranks of second tier American retail banks, and left New York City with only two locally-based banks in the first *and* second tier of banking leaders.

With the Bank One and Bank of New York purchases, JPMorgan had become one of three American banks with assets of more than a trillion dollars, with Citigroup and Bank of America being the others. It would lag behind the other two in earnings through 2006, but was closing the earnings gap in 2007; was second only to Bank of America in domestic deposits; and was ready to become the industry leader come 2009.

BANK OF AMERICA

Bank of America was the other big buyer in the post-2000 era, but it was a little slower than JPMorgan to swing into action. The 1998 merger between NationsBank and BankAmerica, which instigated the name change, was a big one, and there was a lot of consolidating to be done. Also in 2001, the man who built this banking empire, Hugh McColl, stepped aside and the reins passed to his longtime number two, Ken Lewis. Whether Lewis would be as active an acquirer as McColl was yet to be seen.

It would be only a matter of time, though, before Bank of America would be back on the acquisition trail. The NationsBank-BankAmerica merger was hailed as having created the first true national bank with banking offices stretching from the Atlantic to the Pacific Ocean, but this was an overstatement. Bank America had no coverage in the Northeast, and its Midwest banking franchise did not go much north of Missouri. Bank of America was also a secondary player in credit cards, mortgage banking and investment banking.

In October 2003, Lewis showed he was going to continue along the path of McColl when he announced the acquisition of Fleet. It was a pricey $49 billion deal that had some initial criticism, but Fleet was more than just the seventh largest bank in the country. It was the one acquisition that could fill the biggest gap in Bank of America's franchise as it had the best retail banking coverage in the Northeast. Fleet was number one in deposit share in New England and New Jersey; had the fourth largest deposit share in New York; and some coverage in eastern Pennsylvania.

There was not a comparable acquisition alternative to Fleet in the Northeast. If Fleet had been bought instead by Citigroup or JPMorgan, Bank of America might have found other ways into the region. It talked about opening ten to fifteen offices in major metropolitan areas in which it did not have a presence, but this would have taken a long time and the end result would have been far less than what it achieved by acquiring Fleet.

With the purchase of Fleet, Bank of America was close to the 10 percent cap on national deposit share that was part of banking regulation and a constraint relative to future large bank acquisitions. At this point, though, the only gap in Bank of America's national branch coverage was in the slowest-growing part of the country, the Midwest, and even there it was already the market leader in Missouri and had a modest position in the Chicago area.

Bank of America, however, was not through buying. In June 2005, it bought MBNA, the country's largest independent credit card company and one of the three largest bank card issuers. This added to its existing card business and made Bank of America a challenger for the top spot in a fast growing segment of the financial services industry.

By the end of 2006, Bank of America had assets of about $1.5 trillion, and in terms of profitability, it stood with Citigroup and the London-based HSBC far above all other financial services companies. Only GE and a couple of large oil companies were in the same earnings class. McColl had built a banking powerhouse, and Lewis had taken it to a higher level.

In 2007, Bank of America continued to expand. It purchased the LaSalle Bank affiliate of ABN AMRO that was among the deposit share leaders in Chicago and Detroit. This partially filled the Midwest void in Bank of America's coverage, and raised its assets to about $1.7 trillion.

Bank of America had reached new heights with best banking franchise in the United States. Lewis was off to a good start, but 2008 and 2009 would not be kind to Bank of America or Lewis.

CITIGROUP

Citigroup did as much selling as it did buying in the early 2000s, but this did not slow its momentum. It increased its assets from $717 billion to almost $1.9 trillion between year ends 1999 and 2006, and its earnings rose from $13.5 billion in 2000 to a little over $21 billion in 2006—and this was even with the sale of Travelers' insurance businesses. Citigroup had long since moved beyond being just a New York money center bank, and in the early 2000s, it was arguably the most important financial institution in the world.

This is not to say that everything went smoothly for Citigroup during these years. Its size was both a blessing and a curse in that its head did not always know what its arms were doing, which was complicated by a geographic sprawl that left little of the world untouched. Citigroup was front and center with its involvement in Enron, WorldCom and other large corporate accounting scandals, and was accused by Japan and Great Britain of wrongdoings in its financial activities in those countries. Citigroup took an after-tax charge of $5 billion in 2004 for just the WorldCom shareholder suits.[2] In 2004, the Federal Reserve went so far as to prohibit Citigroup from any large acquisitions until it had its house in order.

These problems took more of a toll on management than on earnings and resulted in Weill turning over Citigroup leadership to its chief counsel, Charles Prince, and relinquishing his chairman's role. This was not early retirement as Weill was 73 when he stepped aside in 2006. Some of the top management that had come into Citigroup from Travelers with Weill also left the firm during this period.

The accusations and management changes kept Citigroup in the news, but did little to slow its momentum. A billion-dollar fine was less than two week's pre-tax earnings by 2005, and from 2000 to 2006, Citigroup was in the top two in earnings among all domestic corporations.

The earnings comparisons with its leading competitors were not only favorable, but the contrast in the early 2000s with JPMorgan was extreme. Citigroup earned $13.5 billion in 2000, and by 2003, its earnings had grown to $17.9 billion. They fell slightly in 2004, the peak year for fines and charge-offs from WorldCom and other similar ill-fated involvements, but in 2005, its earnings were up to $24 billion and almost three times its local rival's $8.3 billion. Bank of America was far behind Citigroup as the 2000s began, but was closing the gap even before buying Fleet and MBNA. By 2006, Bank of America's earnings were more than $21 billion and only slightly below those of Citigroup.

Citigroup, though, did not look like its large domestic competitors. It only had about 1,000 branches, almost all in the New York City area and California. Its strengths were in international banking and a myriad of specialty financial businesses with investment banking, securities sales and credit cards being the most prominent.

Under Weill, Citigroup had shown more willingness to expand its branch network than in the past, but its movement in that direction remained relatively modest. Fleet and Bank One made as much sense for Citigroup to acquire as they did for Bank of America and JPMorgan, but instead it chose to buy a $54 billion asset thrift in California, Golden State; a $15 billion asset bank in the New York City area owned by a consortium of European banks, EAB; and a small savings bank in Texas. This put Citigroup on the potential buyer list for second-tier banks, but the acquisitions did little to change its overall corporate profile.

WELLS FARGO

For Wells Fargo there were few big acquisitions, but it was an active buyer during this period having bought sixteen banks, but only the $22 billion, Utah-based First Security went much beyond being a local, community bank. Good internal growth and the numerous acquisitions, though, were enough to raise Wells Fargo's assets from $218 billion in 1999 to about $500 billion in 2006. It had slipped behind Wachovia to fifth in asset size, but that understated its real position.

Wells Fargo loomed larger than its asset size primarily because it was the most consistent earner among the nation's five largest banks in the early 2000s. It earned $4 billion in 2000, increased earnings in each subsequent year and reached $7.8 billion in 2005. This was almost as much as the far bigger JPMorgan. It did not keep pace with JPMorgan's large earnings gain in 2006, but its earnings continued their strong upward pace and exceeded $8 billion.

The growth momentum of the markets Wells Fargo served, particularly the Southwest and West Coast, helped to generate the good performance, and its commitment to the housing market, a business that was sizzling at that time, also helped. By 2007, Wells Fargo was the second largest originator and servicer of mortgage loans in the country.

The steady performance was well-received by investors, and Wells Fargo's stock outperformed the other large banks during this period. Its market value in 2007 made it the seventh most valued bank in the world, and it was ready for bigger things.

FIRST UNION/WACHOVIA

By size, First Union was a long way from being in the JPMorgan, Bank of America or Citigroup category in 2000. It was not a total surprise that it fell by the wayside, but it deserved an A for effort before and after 2000. It had been one of the shooting stars of the 1990s, but by 2000, First Union's acquisition program had not only run out of steam, but was threatening its ability to survive. First Union was losing customers in the Philadelphia area after mishandling its acquisitions of CoreStates and First Fidelity, and the only positive thing said about its Signet acquisition in Virginia was that there were fewer customers to lose. Its $2 billion purchase of The Money Store, a specialty lender, in 1998 had gone beyond losing customers and had cost First Union large amounts of money prior to and as part of its closing. After earning about $3 billion in both 1998 and 1999, First Union reported earnings of just $92,000 in 2000.

It had become an unpopular bank with investors, particularly after cutting its dividend in half in 2001, and First Union's stock dropped from an adjusted high of almost $66 per share in 1998 to less than $24 per share in late 2000. After the dividend cut, investor thinking was not "When will First Union return to its previous earnings level?" but rather "What buyer will come to the rescue?" The problem with the latter scenario was that there were not many banks large enough to buy First Union. Of the few that were big enough, some either had troubles of their own, like Bank One; were busy digesting an earlier merger as JPMorgan was doing; or, in the case of Bank of America, had too much overlap to be an acceptable suitor from an antitrust perspective. Citigroup and Wells Fargo were the only realistic buyers.

Being relatively safe from an unwanted takeover, First Union showed a boldness that surprised almost everyone when it announced in April 2001 that it had agreed to buy Wachovia for $12.7 billion. Wachovia had a long and revered history and was the bank in North Carolina when First Union and NCNB were just beginning their rise to prominence. To many in the state, Wachovia was still considered a step above its two much larger rivals. Wachovia, like First Union was stumbling in 2000 and early 2001, which made it susceptible when First Union came calling with a cozy in-state deal in which Wachovia would be treated as a near-equal partner with the new entity operating under its name and with equal board representation. The headquarters, though, was in Charlotte where First Union was based, not in Wachovia's Winston-Salem home, and Ed Crutchfield's successor at First Union, Ken Thompson, would be the CEO.

Since the joining of these two struggling banks was not greeted with much enthusiasm outside of North Carolina, an Atlanta-based SunTrust thought it had a chance to win Wachovia away from First Union. In May 2001, it made a $13.6 billion hostile bid for Wachovia—$900 million more than the Wachovia offer. SunTrust hoped a higher offer and its better financial condition would carry the day. It was more money, but it was also a more complete takeover as the Wachovia name would not survive and the headquarters would be in a much more distant Atlanta. The hostile bid forced First Union to raise its price to $14.6 billion, which SunTrust bettered with a $15.3 billion offer, but how much better was blurred by the true values of the stocks being offered in exchange for Wachovia stock. In the end, First Union prevailed, and in September 2001, the merger was completed and the First Union name was retired in favor of Wachovia.

A "done deal," though, was different from a widely acclaimed deal, and there were more doubters than believers in the future of the new Wachovia. Earnings of $1.6 billion in 2001 were a big improvement over the near breakeven of 2000, but it was still well below what a much smaller First Union had earned a couple of years earlier.

First Union had learned a lot from its previous mistakes, and the merging of the two banks went smoothly. It was easier to integrate an acquisition in markets in which it was not viewed as an outsider. Yet, it was more than that. By 2002, its performance had improved in the markets to the north, particularly the Philadelphia area, and earnings were on the upswing. In 2003, the new Wachovia earned $3.6 billion, and a year later, its net income topped $4 billion.

By 2004, Wachovia was ready to move on, and that year, it bought the Birmingham-based SouthTrust for $14.4 billion. SouthTrust had assets of $53 billion, 726 branches stretching from Virginia to Texas and fit well with Wachovia. SouthTrust and the old Wachovia acquired by First Union were much smaller than Fleet or Bank One, but they were two of the four largest bank acquisitions since 2000.

In 2006, Wachovia continued its national expansion by acquiring Golden West, a California-based S&L and the second largest thrift in the country. Golden West had $128 billion assets and was a family success story—it was almost wholly-owned by the Sandler family—and the last large California S&L.

There was the usual investor furor over the Golden West purchase that accompanied so many of the Wachovia acquisitions, particularly since it occurred during a period of declining real estate values, which raised questions as to the short-term earnings impact. The immediate effect, however, was that in 2006, the new Wachovia had assets of $716 billion; earned $7.8 billion; and when measured by market capital or earnings, was among the dozen largest banks in the world. Not bad for a bank given up for dead by so many only five years earlier, and it had begun to look like a survivor. Unfortunately, two years later it would be gone with Golden West and its subprime mortgage loans being a primary reason.

How Far They Had Come

That five banks had left all others behind was evident in the numbers, and it was amazing how far they had come in 26 years. Citigroup, Chemical and Wells Fargo were big banks by the standards of the time in 1980, but those numbers pale beside what they would be in 2007. Citigroup raised its assets from $115 billion in 1980 to almost $2.2 trillion in 2007; Chemical, or JPMorgan as it was now called, jumped from $41 billion to almost $1.6 trillion assets; and Wells Fargo increased its assets from $24 billion to $575 billion.

What was truly astounding, though, was just how far the two North Carolina banks, Bank of America and Wachovia, had come. In 1980, what was then NCNB had assets of $7 billion, which was a long way from the $1.7 trillion assets of Bank of America at the end of 2007. Despite its relatively small size, it was a well-known bank in 1980 because of its nonbank activities that went beyond the borders of its home state of North Carolina. No one at the time, though, could have imagined that 27 years later, NCNB would be using the Bank of America name and be the largest bank in the country measured by branches or deposits and one of the two biggest banks in the world, based on earnings and market capital.

Wachovia was not nearly as large as Bank of America in 2007, but it had journeyed a long way since 1980 when its predecessor bank, First Union, had only $3 billion in assets and was number three in North Carolina. By 2007, it was the fourth largest domestic bank with assets of almost $800 billion and in the top fifteen worldwide in earnings and market capital.

There were eight other domestic banks—U.S. Bancorp, SunTrust, Capital One, Regions, National City, BB&T, PNC and Fifth Third—with assets of more than $100 billion and extensive branch networks in 2007. Of these only U.S. Bancorp had assets above $200 billion, and just barely so. The growth of most of these second-tier banks was just as explosive as that of Bank of America and Wachovia. In 1980, U.S. Bancorp had assets of $13 billion, PNC $6 billion, National City $5 billion, SunTrust $3 billion and Regions, BB&T and Fifth Third were in the $1 to $2 billion range.

Large Bank Growth, 1980 to 2007

	Assets				
	2007	1999	1993	1988	1980
	(in billions)				
Big Five					
Citigroup	$2,187	$716	$217	$208	$115
Bank of America	1,716	633	158	30	7
JPMorgan	1,562	406	150	67	41
Wachovia	783	253	71	22	31
Wells Fargo	575	218	53	47	24
Subtotal	$5,884	$2,226	$649	$374	$218
Second Tier					
U.S. Bancorp	$238	$82	$26	$24	$13
SunTrust	177	95	41	29	3
Capital One	151	13	-	-	-
National City	150	87	31	22	5
Regions	141	43	11	5	2
PNC	139	69	76	42	6
BB&T	133	43	9	4	1
Fifth Third	111	62	17	5	1
Subtotal	$1,240	$494	$211	$165	$31
Washington Mutual	$328	$187	$16	$1	-

Source: SNL Financial, Charlottesville, Virginia and American Banker, April 20, 1982 and April 11, 1990.

Capital One, the nation's eighth largest bank, did not even exist in 1980. It was founded as a credit card operation through a spin-off from a mid-sized Virginia bank, Signet, in 1996, and prior to 2005, would not have even been considered among the second tier banks. With the acquisitions of Hibernia in New Orleans and the Long Island-based North Fork Bank in 2005 and 2006, respectively, with a combined $80 billion assets, Capital One became more than a credit card bank.

Washington Mutual was still a thrift, but in 2007, it was larger than any of the second-tier banks with assets of $328 billion, but because of its balance sheet mix, it was closer in market strength—earnings and market capital—to U.S. Bancorp than to Wells Fargo and Wachovia. Washington Mutual had traveled a particularly long way. In 1980, it was Columbia Federal, a mutual thrift with assets of less than $300 million in the small Washington town of Wenatchee.

A Prelude to Disaster

While the incredible, continued growth of a few large banks was a big story in the early 2000s, it, unfortunately, would not be the biggest banking story of these years as negative events took over the headlines. Banking in the early 2000s will be most remembered for a housing pricing boom and collapse and the rapid growth of subprime mortgage lending—and the disastrous effect this had on the banking business and economies worldwide. The large banks were generally bystanders in this process, but they too would pay a big price.

HOUSING BUBBLE AND SUBPRIME MORTGAGES

In my previous book, *Consolidation of Banking*, published in late 2007, there was little coverage of, and certainly no chapter committed to, a housing bubble and subprime mortgages. The latter had become a problem by early 2007, but the commercial banks were not heavily involved, and it did not seem likely that these mortgages would play a major role in future direction of the industry. Of course, one could have said the same thing about the imminent collapse of the S&Ls in the 1980s relative to the 1989 to 1992 real estate-driven recessionary conditions, and for a second time, it was learned in a big way that commercial banks are part of a much larger financial services industry. If something bad happens in one segment, the rest is not immune to the results. The big commercial banks also learned that if something bad happens in any part of the industry, they can expect to be blamed by the politicians and the public for the negative results.

The primary cause of the 2008 financial collapse was a rapid rise in housing prices that began in 1999 and reached irrational levels from 2003 to 2006 that ended with a much larger subsequent decline than expected. The initial increase in housing prices may not have been driven by subprime mortgage lending, but when the bubble burst, these mortgages made the result much worse. The trigger for both the unsustainable rise in housing prices and subprime mortgages was a reduction in 2003 of the Federal Reserve's key interest rate to 1 percent. This made housing relatively inexpensive and more readily available to a wider group of potential buyers. It also made subprime mortgages more feasible and increased their originations from a little over $300 billion in that year to almost $700 billion in 2005 and, unfortunately, with accompanying lowered lending standards.[1]

While there may be some debate about the responsibility for what went wrong in the residential real estate market, what happened relative to subprime mortgages is not complicated—and came in five parts. These were:

- Mortgage bankers, most of whom were nonbanks, made loans to subprime borrowers that did not meet sound lending principles, particularly relative to home values and the ability of borrowers to make payments.

- Packagers of loans, primarily investment banks, bought the subprime loans from mortgage banks and turned them into mortgage-backed securities that were sold to investors.

- Rating specialist firms provided unrealistically high ratings for mortgage-backed securities that facilitated their sale.

- Banks, and others, purchased these securities on the assumption they were of a high quality despite, in many cases, providing unrealistically high returns.

- The entire process assumed a continuing increase in home values.

HOUSING BUBBLE

From a 2014 perspective, much of the emphasis on what went wrong in the early 2000s to cause the financial collapse in 2008 is on subprime mortgages. There, however, would not have been a subprime mortgage problem if there had not been a housing bubble that led investors and borrowers to make bad decisions based on a false belief that a rapid increase in home values was sustainable. The rationale was similar to that of the technology bubble in the late 1990s in that this was a new environment with new rules and the starting base was low. Rational observers did not believe this, but enough people did to drive prices higher for a number of years and invite in those who wanted to profit from this phenomenon.

To understand just how irrational this belief in sustainable increases of housing prices was in the early 2000s, two numbers tell the story. Historically, housing prices have grown slightly better than inflation, and the annual rate that was generally considered normal was about 3 percent per annum. From 1999 to 2006, housing prices *doubled* according to Case-Shiller Home Price Indices, and about 70 percent of that increase occurred from 2003 to 2006.[2] It might also be noted that after the recession from 1989 to 1992, the annual increase through 1999 was close to the historic 3 percent per annum.

This rapid rate of increase would have been manageable if prices had just stalled at the top, but that was not to be the case. By the end of 2005, prices stopped rising and remained close to their peak through 2006, but 2007 saw a better than 8 percent decrease. Then in 2008, the nationwide decline was 23 percent, and this is what put so many mortgages written since 2003 with little, if any, down payment under water.

These numbers understate the problem as they are national in scope and the level of increase and subsequent decline were much greater in the so-called "hot" markets. In states like Florida, Arizona, Nevada and California, housing prices had more than doubled from 1999 to 2006 and fell much more than 23 percent in 2008.

THE RESPONSE

Needless to say, a pricing boom in a market that represented about half of all domestic debt provided ample opportunities for those that financed housing, most of which were primarily interested in short-terms gains. In all fairness, it is likely most of those who saw these opportunities did not see the danger at the end or there would not have been so many failed participants in 2007 and 2008.

The mortgage bankers that saw the opportunities and made the subprime mortgage loans that would turn a "bubble" into a disaster, represented a wide variety of financial firms. Two of the three largest subprime lenders during this period, Ameriquest and New Century, were unregulated mortgage brokers. Others among the top ten were two thrifts—Washington Mutual and Fremont General; a large British bank, HSBC, through its Household Finance subsidiary; a subsidiary of the tax accounting firm, H.R. Block; a big bank, Wells Fargo; GE; and two players that are hard to classify—the biggest subprime lender of all, Countrywide, and First Franklin.

Among the leaders, Countrywide, Ameriquest, New Century, First Franklin, Washington Mutual and Fremont either failed or were saved by acquisition. HSBC, Wells Fargo, GE and H.R. Block were large and diversified enough to survive the debacle, and they had stopped making subprime mortgage loans by 2008.

With the exception of Wells Fargo, the large commercial banks were not among the top ten in subprime lending based on the numbers collected by The Center for Public Integrity and the very large banks, collectively, accounted for only about 9 percent of all subprime loans made from 2005 through 2007. The 25 leading subprime lenders of all types accounted for about 72 percent of all subprime mortgage loan originations.[3]

Top Subprime Mortgage Lenders, 2005 to 2007

	Company	Subprime Mtge. Loans (In billions)	Eventual Outcome
1.	Countrywide*	$97	Bank of America
2.	Ameriquest**	81	Failed
3.	New Century**	76	Failed
4.	First Franklin*	68	Bank of America
5.	Washington Mutual*	65	JPMorgan
6.	H&R Block**	65	Closed business
7.	Fremont General*	62	Failed
8.	Wells Fargo	52	Wells Fargo
9.	HSBC	50	Closed business
10.	GE**	50	Closed business

*S&L in 2007.
**Non-bank.
Source: The Center for Public Integrity, "The Subprime 25," Washington, D.C., May 6, 2009.

Wells Fargo was in the top ten in subprime mortgage loan originations, but it was toward the bottom of that group at number eight, and JPMorgan, Citigroup and Wachovia were well back in the second ten. Bank of America did little, if any, subprime mortgage lending. Subprime mortgage originations accounted for about 13 percent of Citigroup's total mortgage originations from 2005 to 2007, and they were less than 8 percent of total originations for Wells Fargo and JPMorgan.

Ironically, Bank of America suffered the most from subprime mortgages. This was because it took on the subprime mortgage loan problems of Countrywide and Merrill Lynch, which had bought National City's First Franklin mortgage lending subsidiary in December 2006, and did so without any protection against future litigation. The extent of the future cost of doing this was not imaginable in 2007 or 2008.

The primary packagers of the subprime loans were four of the largest investment banks—Goldman Sachs, Merrill Lynch, Lehman Brothers and Bear Stearns—and Citigroup. Among the investment banks, only Goldman Sachs had not bought an originator of subprime loans to increase their packaging volume. Citigroup originated mortgage loans of all types and used its investment banking affiliate that came with the Travelers merger in the late 1990s for packaging.

The large banks would become further involved with subprime mortgages through their servicing operations. In 2006, six financial institutions—JPMorgan,

Bank of America, Citigroup, Wells Fargo, Countrywide and Washington Mutual serviced 60 percent of all mortgages.[4] This was the four largest banks plus two of the leading subprime mortgage originators that were acquired in 2008 by Bank of America and JPMorgan. Through their servicing operations, these four banks were the ones primarily responsible for the foreclosing and restructuring of existing mortgages whether they had originated them or not. They had not anticipated this downside and became the "bad guys" as they were overwhelmed and not prepared for the task.

Where banks of all sizes got involved was in buying these toxic securities for their portfolios. By law, banks, except in a couple of states, were not allowed to buy corporate equities and had been urged by politicians and regulators to buy mortgage-backed securities to support home ownership and provide what was usually good liquidity. Since the banks, like everyone else, relied heavily on the rating agencies in their purchasing of mortgage-backed securities, they ended up with subprime mortgage assets that resulted in billions of dollars in losses.

Subprime mortgage lending was not something that came out of nowhere in the early 2000s, it had just changed its format. In most large urban markets there were thrifts that, for years, had made lending to subprime borrowers a major part of their business. If done well, it was quite profitable based on funding the loans with cheap, local savings deposits and lending to borrowers with subpar credit who were willing to pay a premium for a 30-year fixed-rate loan. The key was to know the market well; be tough enough to foreclose when, and if, the payments stopped; and housing values increased. It was a business serving a positive need, and in most of those years in the late 1990s, subprime mortgages accounted for between 10 percent and 13 percent of home mortgages originated. In no single year, though, were subprime mortgage originations above $160 billion.[5]

What changed in the early 2000s was a much larger mortgage market with subprime mortgage loans accounting for 20 percent or more of all mortgage originations. In 2004, subprime mortgage originations were in excess of $500 billion, and a year later, they were approaching $700 billion. This level of originations lasted through 2007. This lending was no longer done primarily by local thrifts that knew the market and kept the loans in their portfolios, nor were they long-term fixed-rate loans. Instead, most of them were adjustable rate mortgages, often with initial teaser rates, originated by loosely regulated mortgage bankers that cared little about the borrower's ability to pay or what happened later. The loans were then sold as soon as possible to packagers of mortgage-backed securities, and the originator pocketed the proceeds.

Countrywide, Ameriquest and New Century

The largest originators of subprime residential mortgage loans were clearly driven by greed. They were not alone in this, though, and could not have existed without enabling investment bank packagers, rating agencies and compliant or overloaded regulators, but they were the start of the process—and also not a well-regulated group.

First, and foremost, was Countrywide, the most illustrious and largest originator of subprime mortgage loans as well as the largest originator and servicer of mortgages of all types. It looked for the regulator that would be most favorable to the way it did business, albeit that part did not begin until 2001.

Countrywide was founded in New York City in 1969 by Angelo Mozilo and David Loeb under the name of Countrywide Credit Industries. Its business was mortgage lending, and it would soon relocate to California. As a nonbank mortgage lender, it grew rapidly—by 1980 it had 40 offices in eight states—and it was generally considered a reputable firm that was able to compete on equal terms with the banks and thrifts.[6]

By the start of the 2000s, it was already the country's preeminent originator of all types of mortgage loans when it took advantage of the Gramm-Leach-Bliley Act that allowed companies with more than 90 percent of revenues in financial businesses to become financial holding companies to be regulated by the Federal Reserve and own a bank with FDIC-insured deposits. Countrywide bought a small bank in the District of Columbia in 2001 with assets and deposits of a little more than $100 million; moved it to Virginia; and began soliciting deposits across the nation to support its mortgage lending. By 2006, it had assets of $93 billion, deposits of $60 billion and was the 12th largest bank in the country. The holding company had assets of $200 billion and market capital of $24 billion.[7]

While it had become the nation's largest subprime lender in the early and mid-2000s, this was still a small part of its mortgage business. During the years from 2004 to 2007, subprime mortgage loans originated were generally just 10 percent to 15 percent of its total originations.

Countrywide's regulatory status was particularly interesting after it moved into the banking system. The holding company was supervised by a Federal Reserve that was not in the business of supervising large mortgage portfolios, but the bank was supervised by the OCC that was supposed to oversee mortgage activities. Its rapid growth and method of operation, or at least connection to an affiliated mortgage banking operation, though, did not fit well with OCC thinking. This prompted Countrywide, bank and holding company, to apply for conversion to an OTS regulated savings and loan charter. This was granted in 2007 even as the subprime mortgage situation was deteriorating, and this said a lot about the OTS's leniency toward subprime mortgage lenders.

By 2007, the good days were over for Countrywide despite its relatively small percentage of subprime mortgage loans. In August 2007, to alleviate concerns, it raised capital of $2.7 billion by selling 16 percent of the company to Bank of America. In the third quarter of 2007, it reported a $1.2 billion loss. In January 2008, a sale for $4 billion in cash to Bank of America was announced, which was a long way from market capital of $24 billion of 2004.

This, of course, was no bargain for Bank of America and not good news for Countrywide's founder, Mozilo. Bank of America would pay legal claims upward of $50 billion in the next five years stemming from its purchase of Countrywide. Mozilo, who was the CEO of Countrywide during these years and became the poster boy for the mortgages abuses of this era, was fined $67 million by the Securities and Exchange Commission; albeit that has to be measured against the estimated exit fee of $115 million he received with the sale to Bank of America.

Mozilo, also in conjunction with David Loeb, had started Countrywide Mortgage Investment in 1985 that was spun-off to create Independent National Mortgage Corporation in 1997, better known as IndyMac. This firm acquired a thrift franchise in California in 2000 and became a leader in subprime mortgages.[8] It grew rapidly over the next few years internally and by acquisition, but experienced hard times in 2007. In 2008, IndyMac became the fourth most expensive failure of a domestic banking organization.

Ameriquest and New Century, which ranked second and third in originating subprime mortgages from 2004 to 2007, differed from Countrywide in that the emphasis of their lending was primarily on subprime mortgages right from the start. They also stayed clear of bank or thrift regulators in the 2000s.

The former's history is hard to follow with its name changes and affiliates, but Ameriquest's interconnections put it at the heart of the subprime mortgage problem. It began in 1979 in California as Long Beach Savings & Loan, but converted to a nonbank mortgage lender in 1994 and was renamed Long Beach Mortgage. Three years later, part of its business was spun-off under the Ameriquest name, and in 1999, the nation's largest thrift, Washington Mutual, bought what was still called Long Beach Mortgage.

Ameriquest in the 2000s became one of the best known names in subprime mortgage lending. It was a national advertiser as the "proud sponsor of the American dream" and put its name on the Texas Rangers stadium. The end result, though, was Ameriquest filing for bankruptcy in 2007 and its loan servicing unit being sold to Citigroup in 2008.

As to the Long Beach Mortgage sector that was sold to Washington Mutual, it was the basis of its buyer's subprime lending business, which from 2004 to 2007 was the fifth largest in the country. In 2008, Washington Mutual failed and was acquired by JPMorgan in a federally-assisted transaction.

New Century was the "shooting star" of subprime mortgages and prided itself on making mortgages available to those ignored by traditional banks. It opened in 1996 and by 1998 had over 1,000 employees, 111 offices and originated $2 billion in mortgages. In 2004, it was listed on the New York Stock Exchange and originated $42 billion in mortgages. A year later its originations were up to $56 billion, and in 2006, it was second in subprime originations. On April 7, 2007, it too filed for bankruptcy.[9]

A leading subprime lender that could even top Ameriquest for complicated interrelationships was First Franklin Financial, which was founded in California in 1981, but did not become primarily a subprime mortgage lender until 1994 when it was bought by Donaldson, Lufkin & Jenrette. It was subsequently sold to National City in 1999 who in turn sold it to Merrill Lynch in 2006. In 2008, National City and Merrill Lynch, poisoned by their First Franklin connections, were forced under distress to sell to PNC and Bank of America, respectively.

THE INVESTMENT BANKS

The packagers of subprime mortgage loans were the same investment banks that packaged all mortgage loans, and the change in the early 2000s was that this had become such a big business that these investment banks pursued it with a much greater zeal and creativity than in the past. These large firms should have known better, but it was their willingness to package subprime loans with prime loans that made the process possible with disastrous end results.

The primary packagers were Goldman Sachs, Merrill Lynch, Lehman, Bear Stearns and Citigroup. The other big investment bank, Morgan Stanley, was late to the game, as its management turmoil limited entering or expanding new activities in the early 2000s. These investment banks, Morgan Stanley initially excluded, were so eager that three of them—Merrill Lynch, Lehman and Bear Stearns—bought subprime mortgage originators to enhance their flow of securitized mortgage. Citigroup, of course, already had a mortgage originating operation.

The result, for the packagers was not much better than it was for the originators. Merrill Lynch, Lehman and Bear Stearns either failed or were forced into a sale. Citigroup was quasi-nationalized, albeit this was primarily the result of trading losses, not subprime mortgages. Goldman Sachs and Morgan Stanley were more fortunate, but still needed to convert into bank holding companies to get the protection of the Federal Reserve.

RATING AGENCIES AND BUYERS

As to the rating agencies and buyers of the tainted mortgage-back securities, the former were embarrassed, but suffered no real setback, and the latter were left holding unwanted assets. This included not only domestic banks, but also foreign banks, insurance companies, pension funds, endowments funds and many others. They were stuck with their losses with most of the perpetrators they would like to have sued for compensation being long gone.

The exceptions were Bank of America and JPMorgan. Bank of America had assumed the liabilities of Countrywide and Merrill Lynch, with the former alone accounting for more than $40 billion of losses through 2012 and more to come. JPMorgan was not hit quite so hard with its acquisitions of the liabilities of Bear Stearns and Washington Mutual, but by 2013, its losses related to these acquisitions were climbing into the tens of billions.

Unfortunately, the aftermath was much broader than a lot of bad assets in the wrong places and two large banks paying very high prices for their purchases. The subprime mortgage disaster caused a near collapse of banking systems worldwide and an economic recession that was the worst since the Great Depression.

THE YEAR THE MUSIC STOPPED

For banking, in particular, 2008 was "the year the music stopped" as the American and world economies fell into the worst economic recession since the Great Depression, and ironically, this led to an even greater domination of financial services by a handful of banks. It was a crisis that without government aid could have brought down *all* of the big investment banks and at least two of the country's largest commercial banks.

Even with the government assistance, three of the five biggest investment banks—Merrill Lynch, Lehman Brothers and Bear Stearns; one of the largest commercial banks, Wachovia; the only thrift with assets in excess of $200 billion, Washington Mutual; the largest originator and servicer of mortgage loans, Countrywide; and the government-sponsored enterprises that held or guaranteed most of the nation's home mortgages, Fannie Mae and Freddie Mac—either failed, were rescued by acquisition or were nationalized in 2008. In addition, Citigroup, the country's largest bank going into the year, and AIG, one of the nation's largest insurance firms, were quasi-nationalized, and they, in all likelihood, would have failed if this had not occurred.

When looking back at 2008, it is almost easier to enumerate who was left rather than who disappeared. Among the largest commercial and investment banks, the only true survivors were Bank of America, JPMorgan, Wells Fargo, Goldman Sachs and Morgan Stanley. "Surviving" differed from prospering as their stock prices fell dramatically and there were times in 2008 and early 2009 when Bank of America, Goldman Sachs and Morgan Stanley seemed close to joining the ranks of their less fortunate brethren.

294 ARNOLD G. DANIELSON

For the survivors, though, increased size and strength was the end result, albeit much of it at the expense of shareholders. Bank of America acquired one of the largest investment banks and securities brokerages, Merrill Lynch, and the biggest originator and servicer of home mortgages, Countrywide. JPMorgan absorbed one of the big investment banks, Bear Stearns, and the largest savings and loan, Washington Mutual. Wells Fargo reduced a banking "big five" to a "big four" with its purchase of Wachovia, and Morgan Stanley became a co-leader in the securities brokerage business by acquiring Citigroup's Smith Barney brokerage operation.

How could so much happen so fast, catch the regulators by surprise and create a worldwide economic downturn the likes of which had not been seen since at least the 1970s, and as far as banking was concerned, the 1930s? There was a lot of finger-pointing, many theories and some who would even say it was not a surprise, but there are a few items about which there was not a lot of debate. These were that the primary causes were very low interest rates, the misuse of subprime residential mortgages and unrealistically high housing prices in the early 2000s, and if what happened was not totally a surprise, the extent of the negative impact was.

In 2007, and even 2006, it was readily apparent that as a result of a housing pricing bubble, the large number of subprime mortgages and irrationality of their terms that there were major economic problems ahead. By the second half of 2007, the impact of these problems was being felt in bank earnings and stock prices. Except for doomsayers that are always present, especially in the academic community, though, no one expected that what was a growing problem in 2007 would become a national calamity the following year.

That, however, is what happened. In those difficult days in the autumn of 2008, it appeared that "runs" on Morgan Stanley and Goldman Sachs were almost certain after Lehman Brothers failed, and only actions of the Treasury Department and the Federal Reserve kept this from occurring. If they had gone, who knows what the status of JPMorgan, Bank of America and Wells Fargo— and the nation's banking system—would have been.

Even the large commercial bank survivors—JPMorgan, Bank of America and Wells Fargo—that had improved their competitive status by just surviving 2008 were not without major problems going into 2009. Bank of America and Wells Fargo were not only the leading banks in the most troubled of real estate markets—California, Arizona, Nevada and Florida, but they added to the concern with merger rescues of Merrill Lynch, Countrywide and Wachovia with the latter two having no government assistance. These were "rescues" of which some may look good from a competitive perspective in the future, but Countrywide badly hurt Bank of America investors with an eventual $40 billion plus in losses. These were not easy days for JPMorgan either, but it had limited exposure in the states most impacted by the housing crisis.

From a concentration perspective, the mergers in 2008, all of which were endorsed by regulators, did more to move the process forward than the four years from 1989 to 1992 that resulted in more than 1,800 bank and thrift failures. Not only did it reduce a commercial bank "big five" to a "big four" with Citigroup's problems threatening to turn it into a "big three," but it also resulted in a much diminished second tier falling even further behind. The combined assets of the banks ranked five through fifteen in 2009 were about the same as just those of the third largest bank, Citigroup. For better or for worse, events in 2008 had greatly expanded the coverage of a big four—and really just a threesome of Bank of America, JPMorgan and Wells Fargo—in other parts of the financial services industry including investment banking, mortgage banking, securities sales and wealth management.

Bank consolidation in the 1990s, and even the early 2000s, was a natural evolution toward a normal industry structure, but what happened in 2008 went beyond normal. Four dominant commercial banks may be a couple less than ideal, and if there is concern about banks being too big to fail, these four certainly were and are.

As noted earlier, the 2008 financial collapse was caused by a rapid increase in housing price and then a sudden drop with the increase being the result of a reduction in 2003 of the Federal Reserve's key interest rate to 1 percent. This was a major reason the value of subprime mortgages originated grew from a little over $300 billion in that year to almost $700 billion in 2005 with accompanying lowered lending standards.

Who to blame for this financial crisis will long be debated, but, in general, it was one of those "perfect storms" that combined many contributing factors that added up to disaster. Interest rates were kept too low too long and many mortgage lenders were essentially unregulated and others were given far too much latitude by the regulators, particularly the OTC. Greed held sway over good sense with the Wall Street investment banks in their introduction of many complicated new investment products and their packaging of faulty mortgage-backed securities. Rating agencies, in an effort to maintain fees from investment banks and others, were overly lenient in the ratings they gave to mortgage-backed securities and banks blindly bought defective products, often with yields so high that they should have known there could be a problem. Meanwhile, investors, politicians and the public did what they always do, bought into the "good times" and saved their complaints until things went bad.

Meltdown Timeline

Signs of a coming financial meltdown first surfaced in early 2006 when it became increasingly obvious housing prices were a problem. The first quarter of 2006 saw the first decline in home prices in years, and by August, the national home construction index was down over 40 percent from a year earlier. Rumors were rampant about the possible failures of home builders and lenders. These rumors became a reality in April 2007 when one of the largest subprime lenders, New Century, filed for bankruptcy.

By 2007, it was increasingly obvious that the country was heading into recession and the financial services industry was in trouble, although the extent of what would eventually occur was beyond the thinking of most. In June 2007, Bear Stearns sounded an alarm by closing redemptions at two of its mutual funds. In July, the stock market peaked with the Dow Jones Industrial Average above 14,000 before starting its long slide downward, and bank stocks, in particular, felt the negative impact of what was happening. Bank stocks began to slip in the first half of the year with the SNL bank index down about 5 percent, and by year-end 2007, bank stocks were off December 31, 2006 levels by 25 percent. In August, Ameriquest closed its doors, and Countrywide narrowly averted filing for bankruptcy by taking out an $11 billion loan from a consortium of banks. Then, in October, Merrill Lynch reported an $8.4 billion loss related to subprime mortgages.

The stage was set for an extremely difficult 2008. It began with Bank of America taking over the struggling Countrywide in January, and then in March, JPMorgan acquired Bear Stearns, the smallest of "big five" investment banking firms in a "fire sale" with the Federal Reserve providing $30 billion to cover Bear Stearns losses. In July, the OTS-regulated IndyMac Bank failed at a tremendous loss for taxpayers.

These were just warm-ups for six weeks in September and October that would greatly alter the shape of the financial services industry and came close to creating a financial calamity that could have rivaled the Great Depression. During those six weeks, the banking headlines approached those of the closing days of a presidential election, and, if what was happening in banking did not change the election result, it certainly widened the margin of Obama's victory.

The six disastrous weeks began on September 7, 2008 with the government takeover of Fannie Mae and Freddie Mac. These government-sponsored, but not owned, agencies held or guaranteed about half of the nation's $12 trillion mortgage loan principal and were a vital cog in the way the mortgage market worked. There was no way they could be closed, and the government by nationalizing them had become a major player in the financial services industry.

A week later, the government tried desperately to find a buyer for the fourth largest investment bank, Lehman Brothers. It was in the midst of a liquidity crisis that if not solved, threatened to take down Merrill Lynch, Morgan Stanley and Goldman Sachs in that order, with Citigroup and the nation's biggest insurance company, AIG, likely to be part of the debacle. With JPMorgan already having taken over Bear Stearns, the only potential buyers were Bank of America and the British Barclays Bank. In a weekend filled with drama, the leaders of the largest banks were ordered to New York to assist in a government-induced rescue, but it only highlighted the helplessness of the regulators and administration. The interest of Bank of America was lukewarm at best, and then on Sunday it announced that it was buying Merrill Lynch instead. That same day, the Bank of England nixed any rescue of Lehman by Barclay's. The result was on Monday, September 15, 2008, Lehman filed for bankruptcy.

This was not what anyone wanted to happen, and the rest of that week was a "scramble" by regulators to contain the fall-out. These were trying times for the three key regulators—Secretary of the Treasury, Hank Paulsen; Federal Reserve Chairman, Ben Bernanke; and president of the New York Federal Reserve Bank and soon to be Treasury Secretary, Tim Geithner—that had the primary charge for keeping a financial crisis from becoming a total economic collapse.

They had to act quickly, and hardly a day went by over the next couple of weeks without a major financial headline. On Wednesday, just two days after the Lehman failure, the government lent AIG $85 billion to keep it operating, which was a quasi-nationalization of that large insurance company. On Thursday, Paulsen and Bernanke met with key legislators to push a $700 billion emergency bailout fund that would be formally called the Troubled Asset Relief Program, or TARP, to get through the financial meltdown. Sunday, September 21, Goldman Sachs announced that the Federal Reserve had approved bank holding company status for itself and Morgan Stanley, providing them with the protection of the Federal Reserve along with the deposit insurance status of banks.

The following week more "dominos" began to fall. On September 25, the FDIC seized the $300 billion Washington Mutual—the nation's largest thrift and sixth largest banking organization—and sold it to JPMorgan. The following weekend, the FDIC took effective control of Wachovia and with Bank of America and JPMorgan otherwise occupied, looked to Wells Fargo or Citigroup as a buyer. Of the two, Wells Fargo was in much better shape, but after showing some interest, it said it would not proceed. As a result, on Monday, the FDIC announced the sale of Wachovia to Citigroup in a federally-assisted transaction. From a consolidation perspective, these two transactions would have combined the third largest bank, JPMorgan, and the largest thrift, Washington Mutual, as well as the largest and fourth largest banks, Citigroup and Wachovia.

The rationale for letting a deeply troubled Citigroup buy a failed Wachovia was solving two problems with one move and something Geithner seemed to want very much.[1] This merger would have reduced Citigroup's overdependence on bought funds because of its modest branch network and relatively few domestic deposits. Wachovia, on the other hand, had a large branch network and a majority of its liabilities were domestic deposits. Thus, with this merger, the regulators would have had a home for Wachovia while providing Citigroup with a much needed injection of cheap funds.

Unfortunately for Citigroup and the regulators' hopes, later that week Wells Fargo changed its mind and made an offer to buy Wachovia for $7 per share without any federal assistance. The change of heart on Wells Fargo's part was based on a change in accounting rules on Tuesday that would let Wells Fargo use Wachovia's past losses against its future income creating billions in cost savings. The FDIC could not refuse this offer because of the extent of the taxpayer cost of the Citigroup transaction. Losing Wachovia left Citigroup in a precarious position, but the consolidation impact was little changed, as it was still two of the five largest banks being combined.

While the Citigroup/Wells Fargo contest for Wachovia was taking place, Congress approved the $700 billion in TARP bailout funds, and shortly thereafter the government injected $125 billion of that money into the nine largest banks, whether they wanted it or not. The intention was not to differentiate between the weak and the strong banks, and several of the banks were emphatic about not needing the funds. At a minimum, though, these funds gave the regulators more control over these banks and leverage to make them raise additional private capital.

This wrapped up a hectic six weeks, but there were two more crisis-related events that occurred before the end of 2008. The first was the agreement in late October by PNC to acquire a faltering National City to create a new number five in bank rankings based on size. The other was Bank of America realizing in mid-December that it was overpaying for a much weaker Merrill Lynch than expected and was considering backing out of the transaction. Pulling out, though, was frowned upon by the regulators, and Bank of America proceeded with the deal, but with government loan guarantees and more TARP funds.

In retrospect, this could be viewed as the regulators putting Bank of America at risk. If it had pulled out, Bank of America would have been subject to some shareholder lawsuits, but nothing that would have been overly concerning—and the last thing the regulators wanted was a failed Merrill Lynch back on their hands with no buyers. As things turned out, it was Countrywide and not Merrill Lynch that put Bank of America at risk.

Bernanke also made it easier for a struggling banking industry with the first of the Federal Reserve's "quantitative easing" policies. In late November 2008, it started by buying $600 billion in mortgage-backed securities, and by March of 2009, it had close to $2 trillion in bank debt, mortgage-backed securities and Treasury notes on its balance sheet. These purchases helped keep rates low, boost the economy and make cheap funding available for the banking industry.

For a more in-depth overview of what happened in the run-up to the collapse in 2008 and the events in fall of that year, three books stand out. *All the Devils Are Here* by Bethany MacLean, a writer for *Vanity Fair* and *Fortune*, and Joe Nocera, a columnist for *New York Times* and formerly a writer for *Fortune*, provides exhaustive background on what led up to the 2008 collapse. For details on the fall of 2008 that almost brought down the financial services industry, there is no better book than *Too Big to Fail* by Andrew Ross Sorkin of the *New York Times* and CNBC. Last but not least is *After the Music Stopped* by Alan Blinder, a former vice chairman of the Federal Reserve that carried the story through to 2012.

DID THE REGULATORS ACT CORRECTLY?

As would be expected after a financial collapse as substantial as this one, questions and criticisms came from all corners. There were those that thought Lehman should not have been allowed to fail. Conversely, there were as many, or even more voices, calling for letting more large banks fail or more to the point be nationalized as had effectively happened in England. Giving the banks taxpayer money as a limited bailout also had its critics.

Letting Lehman fail may have been a dangerous risk, but in hindsight, it appears that other actions by the Federal Reserve averted what could have been a much worse situation. Lehman's failure could have resulted in a "run" on Morgan

Stanley and, perhaps, Goldman Sachs, that might have brought them down and given Bank of America more reason to back away from its Merrill Lynch purchase. The Federal Reserve's action five days later giving Morgan Stanley and Goldman Sachs bank holding company status and FDIC deposit insurance solved the liquidity problems of these investment banks, and the hard line taken with Bank of America about backing out of its Merrill Lynch commitment kept that troubled investment bank from becoming a potential start of another "run" situation.

As to not letting a large bank fail or be nationalized, this was primarily Citigroup's situation. Bank of America, JPMorgan and Wells Fargo in 2008 were profitable and not remotely close to failing. They were instead considered sources of strength by the regulators and allowed to assume the assets of a troubled Merrill Lynch, Washington Mutual and Wachovia. Wachovia, which was the fourth largest bank at the time, was on the brink of failure, but was rescued in an unassisted purchase by Wells Fargo. Bank of America would have its problems later on, but the extent of the legal problems that flowed from its early 2008 purchase of Countrywide was not part of the 2008 and 2009 thinking.

Citigroup lost almost $28 billion in 2008, because of a $26 billion trading loss and—without a large capital infusion—it probably would have failed, if not in 2008, then in early 2009. There was a chance Citigroup might have attracted funding from a private group in the Mideast, or elsewhere, as it had done earlier or that it could have been taken over and sold in parts—the domestic operations possibly to JPMorgan and its extensive foreign business to HSBC or a Chinese bank. These, though, were outcomes that would not be popular, and there was not a lot of time to waste. The decision was to bail out Citigroup and the results suggest it was by far the best of some bad choices.

THE 2009 AFTERMATH

Turning the calendar to a new year by no means ended the problems for the banking industry, and it was not until April 2009 that the worst of the crisis was over. Investors did not accept TARP funds as real capital, and many felt Citigroup and Bank of America would be joining Wachovia, Lehman, Washington Mutual and others, as failed companies. There were those that thought both should be nationalized before things got worse. These feelings were so prevalent that the two banks whose stocks a couple years earlier had been trading at more than $50 per share fell to about $1 per share in the case of Citigroup and $3 per share for Bank of America.

Bank stocks, in general, had fallen sharply since 2006 with the SNL Bank Index being down by 59 percent at the end of 2008, but the first quarter of 2009 was worse. On March 9, 2009, an average of actively traded bank stock had only 17 percent of the value it had at the end of 2006. Optimists could point to 230 percent gains from that low point over the rest of the year, but by the end of 2009, bank stocks still had only 40 percent of their 2006 value.

Despite the abysmal stock performance, surprising first quarter profits by most of the largest banks and capital insertions prompted by government "stress tests" eliminated the likelihood of additional large bank failures and investor confidence prompted the above-mentioned upswing in stock prices. By year-end, every large bank except Citigroup had paid back its TARP funds, albeit, in some cases, with additional capital insertions that further diluted already heavily diluted shareholders. Citigroup was widely viewed as a survivor by year-end 2009, but only after converting its TARP funds into equity capital and thereby giving the government 27 percent ownership.

CONSOLIDATION

Consolidation was on hold in 2009 as the largest banks were in no condition to expand further and the balance sheet risk of sellers was a major sale deterrent. The only significant acquisition by a first or second tier bank was BB&T's purchase of Alabama's $26 billion asset Colonial BancGroup in a federally-assisted deal.

Even with the good news after 2009's first quarter relative to survival, the big bank balance sheets continued to be plagued by bad assets that created real risk if there was a setback in what was, at best, going to be a slow economic recovery. Capital seemed more than adequate for most of the large banks, but Citigroup and some second tier banks had less certain safety nets.

Mergers were the primary drivers of bank consolidation, but in a recession as severe as what began in late 2007, listing bank acquisitions with deal values in excess of $1 billion as was done in early chapters, was far less meaningful in 2008 and immediately following years. In 2008, there were only two such acquisitions— Wells Fargo buying Wachovia and PNC's acquisition of National City—and they had sharply lower pricing than what would have occurred in better times. In 2009, there were no billion-dollar bank sales, and the transaction value of all bank sales was not much over $1 billion. These listings do not include federally-assisted transactions such as the aforementioned BB&T's purchase of Colonial BancGroup that would have been a $1 billion plus deal in normal times.

Also excluded are the acquisitions of financial services firms that were not commercial banks and these types of acquisitions were having a growing impact on the consolidation process. In 2008, they included Bank of America's purchase of Merrill Lynch and Countrywide as well as JPMorgan buying Bear Stearns and Washington Mutual with the first three having deal values well above $1 billion.

The only acquisition impacting the asset share of the five largest banks between 2007 and 2009 was Wells Fargo's purchase of Wachovia. This pushed the share of bank assets held by five banks from just under 50 percent at the end of 2007 to almost 52 percent in 2008—a percentage that changed little in 2009. This was a long way from the 16 percent share of the five largest in 1990, or even the 33 percent in 2000.

Large Bank Asset Share, 1990 to 2009

	Five Largest	Next Five	Assets (in billions)
Commercial Banks			
2009	51.5%	7.7%	$11,895
2007	49.8	7.6	11,176
2000	33.2	13.7	6,246
1990	16.2	9.3	3,390
Five Largest	**Asset Share**	**Dep. Share**	
JPMorgan	14.9%	9.7%	$1,768
Bank of America	14.0	12.4	1,664
Citigroup	10.6	4.7	1,263
Wells Fargo	9.7	11.3	1,155
PNC	2.3	2.8	278

Source: SNL Financial, Charlottesville, Virginia and FDIC: Historical Statistics on Banking.

Bank asset concentration change in 2008 and 2009 was more meaningfully measured, though, if done using just four banks. With Wachovia gone, just four large banks at the end of 2009 had about 49 percent of all bank assets, which was not much less than what five banks had in 2007. The fourth largest, Wells Fargo, also had an asset share more than four times that of number five, PNC, even after the latter had bought National City.

Asset share is just one way of measuring concentration, and it may not be as meaningful to the competitive situation relative to other banks and bank customers as deposits. The five leaders had a smaller 41 percent share of domestic deposits, but this hides the true position of just three banks. Bank of America, Wells Fargo and JPMorgan had about one-third of domestic deposits between them in 2009.

The deposit shares also spoke to the future direction of consolidation and suggested that the consolidation process in traditional banking may have run its course, at least as driven by inter-industry mergers. A statute barring acquisitions that took a bank's deposit share above 10 percent nationally was still in effect, and with the intense political concern over bank size, it would be many years, if ever, before acquisitions—except in emergency situations—would be approved that allowed banks already holding more than 10 percent of bank deposits to buy another large bank. This would keep Bank of America and Wells Fargo from making further significant healthy bank acquisitions and limit any sizeable bank purchases by JPMorgan.

This may have been a moot point in any event, as these banks were of a size in 2009 that further bank acquisitions were of little interest at least to two of them. Bank of America had virtual national coverage, and the large cities in which it did not have banking offices, such as Cleveland, Pittsburgh, Buffalo and Minneapolis, were not overly significant in a national scenario and could be easily covered by internal expansion. Wells Fargo's situation was similar with its coverage gaps being in most of New England and the slow-growing Rust Belt. JPMorgan was different in that it had minimal coverage in the Southeast, an area of prime interest to a bank with national aspirations.

The reasons for concerns by regulators and politicians about the largest banks in 2009 being too big to fail, and also possibly too large from a competitive perspective, could readily be seen in asset totals. Four banks—Bank of America, JPMorgan, Citigroup and Wells Fargo—had assets in excess of $1 trillion, and two of them, Bank of America and JPMorgan, were over $2 trillion.

What had really changed from 2007 to 2009 was not just the absolute size, but also the gap between the four largest banks and all others. Wells Fargo, the fourth largest, was almost five times as big as number five, PNC, and the assets of banks ranked from five to fifteen were, collectively, similar to the assets of the number three, Citigroup, by itself. Bank of America and JPMorgan had each added about $500 billion in new assets during these two years while the combined banks ranked five through fifteen had lost $200 billion in assets—and this included three specialty banks—Bank of New York, State Street and Northern Trust—that were concentrating on trust operations and had few, if any, branches. This was a big shift in relative sizes of the 15 largest banks, much of which had occurred in 2008 with regulatory approval and frequently regulatory encouragement.

Large Bank Financial Summary, 2009

	Bank	Assets 2009	Assets 2007	Net Income	Domestic Deposits	Banking Offices
		(In billions)				
1.	Bank of America	$2,251	$1,716	$4.7	$901	6,161
2.	JPMorgan	2,041	1,562	9.2	626	5,182
3.	Citigroup	1,888	2,188	(1.7)	311	1,052
4.	Wells Fargo	1,228	575	6.9	764	6,769
5.	PNC	271	139	1.1	187	2,669
6.	U.S. Bancorp	265	238	2.0	151	3,056
7.	Bank of New York	212	198	(1.6)	59	51
8.	SunTrust	173	180	(1.7)	118	1,745
9.	Capital One	169	151	(.9)	114	985
10.	BB&T	165	133	1.0	95	1,861
11.	State Street	163	143	(2.1)	21	1
12.	Regions	140	141	(6.7)	94	1,884
13.	Fifth Third	111	111	(1.3)	78	1,357
14.	KeyCorp	97	98	(1.7)	67	1,018
15.	Northern Trust	78	65	.3	24	799
	Banks 5 to 15	$1,844	$2,159*	$(11.6)	$1,008	15,426

*Includes Wachovia and National City.
Source: SNL Financial, Charlottesville, Virginia.

Domestic deposits showed a similar situation with one added element—a "big four" turning into a "big three." Citigroup, with year-end 2009 domestic deposits of a little over $300 billion, had only a little more than one-third the domestic deposit base of Bank of America and Wells Fargo and less than half that of JPMorgan. It was still a big bank, but Citigroup's branch network was far from being national as it was focused almost entirely on the New York City area with modest coverage in California and Texas.

The disparity between Bank of America, JPMorgan, Wells Fargo and all others, including Citigroup, was readily apparent in 2009 earnings, albeit even with their earnings being way below earlier standards. These three banks were profitable in 2008 and 2009, and in the latter year earned a combined $21 billion. In 2009, Citigroup lost almost $2 billion, and the collective loss of banks five through fifteen was close to $12 billion.

CHAPTER

THE RECOVERY

The post-crisis recovery was muted at best, as poor economic conditions continued into 2010 through 2013, and in the last of those years, banks were still struggling, but the worst was over. Industry-wide earnings in 2013 were above 2006 record levels, and no large bank was in danger of failing. JPMorgan and Wells Fargo were doing better than when the bad times began. The new emphasis on higher capital, though, kept shareholder returns industry-wide well below pre-crisis levels, and 2013 bank stock prices remained far below historic levels.

The after-effects of the subprime mortgage problem that created a massive foreclosure situation were a continuing problem for banks, big and small, serving the southeastern and southwestern parts of the country. There were 440 banks and thrifts that failed from 2009 through 2012 and another 24 failed in 2013. Subprime mortgages caused massive losses during these years for Bank of America, as a result of its Countrywide purchase, which was a perception problem for the industry and a real problem for the bank.

In early 2008, Bank of America acquired—without government assistance—the nation's leading mortgage lender and servicer, Countrywide, which was also the leading originator of subprime loans in the years preceding the crisis. Most of the leading subprime mortgage originators had failed and if subsequently bought, as was the case with Washington Mutual, it was with some government protection against future liability. Bank of America, thus, was pretty much alone as a "deep pocket" target for lawsuits relative to faulty subprime mortgages. From 2010 through 2013, it had credit crisis and mortgage-related settlements of more than $40 billion, most of which were the result of the Countrywide acquisition.

This was an enormous number, with $22 billion of it coming in a single year, 2011, and it kept Bank of America's name in the headlines in an unflattering way. For a bank that generated $25 to $30 billion in pre-tax income in a normal year, this did not threaten its survivability, but was a public relations disaster, a regulatory concern and created a need for large amounts of new capital to the detriment of existing shareholders. These losses and being one of the two largest banks in the country helped fuel the widespread anti-big bank feeling.

Citigroup did not have Bank of America's legal problems, but a $28 billion loss in 2008—following a $7 billion loss in 2007's fourth quarter coming almost entirely from trading losses, created capital needs that were equally devastating for shareholders. This forced the sale of one of its most valuable assets, the Smith Barney brokerage business, to the detriment of its future competitiveness.

Despite all having dominating positions regionally and/or nationally, the trillion dollar banks—JPMorgan, Bank of America, Citigroup and Wells Fargo—differed greatly by 2012, both in earnings and market value change. Citigroup was unique with its decline in investment banking and few domestic deposits.

It was the earnings and stock price declines that really separated the initial winners and losers among the big banks. JPMorgan did the best with net income of about $21 billion by 2012 with Wells Fargo not far behind at $19 billion while Bank of America and Citigroup earned less than $10 billion. These, though, were modest differences compared to how shareholders fared.

When 2006 ended, Bank of America and Citigroup were trading in the $54 to $57 per share range and only slightly more than the just under $49 per share for JPMorgan, but the similarity ended there. All three stocks dropped sharply in 2008 and early 2009, but JPMorgan's $15.90 per share yearly low price in 2009 looked a lot better than the $3.14 per share for Bank of America and $1.02 per share for Citigroup. These were a 94 percent and 98 percent decline in value. Wells Fargo's slide was roughly similar to that of JPMorgan.

Most of this reflected performance, but some of the precipitous drop on the part of Bank of America and Citigroup reflected 2006 inflated values. JPMorgan's stock was trading at a substantial 256 percent of tangible equity at the time, but the equivalent ratios for Bank of America and Citigroup were approximately 400 percent and 451 percent, respectively. The 2006 prices were clearly inflated to begin with, but as the economy collapsed, the extent of the decline in a little over two years was astounding.

Tale of Four Banks, 2006 to 2012

	2012	2009*	2006*
	Stock Price		
JPMorgan	$40.53	$15.90	$48.95
Wells Fargo	33.04	8.12	36.81
Bank of America	9.33	3.14	54.90
Citigroup**	3.65	1.02	56.41
	Book Value Per Share		
JPMorgan	$50.17	$39.88	$33.45
Wells Fargo	27.10	20.03	13.57
Bank of America	20.40	22.45	29.75
Citigroup**	6.36	5.35	22.71
	Tangible Book Value		
JPMorgan	$36.91	$26.76	$19.13
Wells Fargo	20.00	12.78	10.06
Bank of America	13.42	11.52	14.12
Citigroup**	5.34	4.27	12.52

*Stock prices are the yearly highs in 2006 and yearly lows in 2009.

**Citigroup's 2011 numbers are without its 10 for 1 reverse split.

Source: SNL Financial, Charlottesville, Virginia.

For Bank of America the price decline was substantial, but not quite as catastrophic as for Citigroup with common equity falling from $29.75 per share to $22.45 and tangible book from $14.12 per share to $11.52. Citigroup's common and tangible equity was only in the $4 to $5 per share range.

JPMorgan and Wells Fargo's stock dropped precipitously as well, but this reflected market attitudes, not capital losses and solvency concerns. JPMorgan's stock fell from almost $50 per share in 2006 to a low just under $16 per share in early 2009, but its common and tangible equity were up about $6 per share. Wells Fargo's stock dipped from a high of about $37 per share in 2006 to a low of $8 per share in 2009, but thanks to accretion from the Wachovia purchase, its capital per share was up about 50 percent to around $20 per share, although a much lower $13 per share on a tangible basis.

By 2012, solvency was no longer a concern for any of these banks, but a pricing disparity in favor of JPMorgan and Wells Fargo continued and was justified by capital levels. At the end of 2012, JPMorgan was trading around $50 per share and Wells Fargo's stock at $35 per share, which was close to 2006 levels. Bank of America and Citigroup stock prices were improved, but in late 2012, it was around $12 per share for the former and about $4.50 per share for the latter, discounting the 1 for 10 reverse stock split. This was about 10 percent of the JPMorgan stock price.

JPMorgan and Wells Fargo came through the recession looking better than they did before, while Bank of America and Citigroup had irreparably hurt their shareholders and were at a short-term competitive disadvantage—albeit by 2013 the gap was closing. The primary reasons for the latter two's problems were Citigroup's disastrous 2008 and Bank of America's Countrywide liabilities, but it requires a closer look at each to fully understand the varying results and where about 50 percent of the banking business stood in 2013 and 2014.

JPMorgan

In 2006, JPMorgan would not have been the obvious choice to be the bank that would come out of a severe financial recession as the country's largest and the most profitable in all but one year from 2009 to 2013. In the late 1990s and the early 2000s, it was still struggling with the consolidation of three of the largest and most troubled of New York City's money center banks—Chemical, Manufacturers Hanover and Chase Manhattan. The addition of J. P. Morgan in 2000 helped, but it still could not match the earnings of Citigroup and Bank of America.

With a combination of superior management and a little luck, by 2010, JPMorgan had become the biggest and strongest bank in the United States—and arguably in the world. The "luck" was that it had minimal exposure to the nation's most troubled housing markets in the Southeast and Far West, but still had a substantial, cheap deposit base to provide the needed liquidity. Bank of America was a market leader in the troubled areas, and Citigroup did not have a large enough domestic retail deposit base to provide liquidity in case of problems. A real difference between JPMorgan and its East Coast rivals, Bank of America and Citigroup, though, was management, particularly the decision-making of its president, Jamie Dimon, in a financial crisis.

Dimon first showed up in banking in 1998 as number two to Sandy Weill at Travelers when it merged with Citicorp to form what would be called Citigroup in the merger that changed the direction of banking and created what was then by far the largest banking organization in the country. Shortly thereafter, however, he left Citigroup. Two years later he reemerged as president of Bank One, the nation's fifth largest bank with an extensive branch network in the Midwest. In 2004, after the purchase of Bank One by JPMorgan, he became the latter's president and chief operating officer. He became chairman and chief executive officer in 2006.

Under Dimon, JPMorgan made it through the 2007 to 2013 period without experiencing a loss in any year; had earnings above $10 billion in all but one year; and made its two key acquisitions with regulators limiting any significant loan loss possibilities. In March 2008, it acquired Bear Stearns with the Federal Reserve assuming the loss risk for assets up to $29 billion. Then in September, right after the Lehman bankruptcy, it acquired the nation's largest thrift, Washington Mutual, from the FDIC. This gave it more than 2,000 West Coast and Florida branches—areas in which it had had little if any coverage—and made it one of the largest servicers of home mortgages, albeit the last was a mixed blessing. Washington Mutual had been one of the leading subprime lenders, but buying it from the FDIC sheltered JPMorgan from most legal risks related to prior actions.

JPMorgan still did not have the retail franchise of Bank of America. It had no branches in the Southeast outside of Florida and was a non-factor in such major East Coast cities as Boston, Philadelphia and Washington, but it also did not have Bank of America's legacy problems. What it did have was a $7 billion trading loss in London in 2012, but even with that, it was able to report annual earnings of $21 billion. It had a rocky 2013 with what appeared to be politically-motivated lawsuits, but its earnings were still almost $18 billion.

WELLS FARGO

Wells Fargo was the other winner among large banks in the industry shake-up that accompanied the 2008 financial collapse. Prior to 2008, it was just a large West Coast regional bank with a good reputation, but not remotely in the trillion dollar asset size class of Bank of America, JPMorgan and Citigroup. It was not even half their size, and its only pretense to national status was as a mortgage lender and servicer. It also had a greater commitment to subprime lending than these bigger banks.

All of this changed in 2008, when a slightly larger Wachovia became one of the casualties of the autumn financial calamity and Wells Fargo was the buyer. This more than doubled the size of Wells Fargo to about $1.3 trillion and created a fourth trillion dollar bank. With the merger accounting benefits and Wachovia's modest legal problems relative to its mortgage loans, Wells Fargo would not face much of a drag on earnings in these years. Its net income was $12 billion in 2009 and 2010, $15 billion in 2011, almost $19 billion in 2012 and more than $22 billion in 2013 when it out-earned JPMorgan.

BANK OF AMERICA

Bank of America had by far the country's best retail banking franchise in 2007 that was enhanced by the purchases of ABN AMRO's Chicago and Detroit banking offices late that year and Merrill Lynch's securities brokerage business in 2008, but instead of enjoying these successes, it became a symbol of big bank incompetence because of its Countrywide acquisition. As discussed earlier, that early 2008 purchase bought with it more than $40 billion in pre-tax losses related to legal claims through 2013. The Merrill Lynch purchase was much better and brought with it a valuable securities brokerage operation and investment banking skills, but it also had some mortgage problems from its 2006 purchase of National City's subprime mortgage operation.

The Countrywide acquisition was devastating to a Bank of America that in the first half of 2007 was riding high. The previous year, it had earned $21.1 billion and ranked fifth in the world in net income behind three oil companies and Citigroup. Through the first six months of 2007, earnings were on a pace to top $22 billion and later that year it announced the purchase of the Dutch-owned ABN AMRO's LaSalle Bank that filled the largest gaps in its national franchise. The franchise built from a small community bank in North Carolina in the 1950s, primarily by Hugh McColl, had come a long way, but it was about to experience its first serious setback.

The clouds began to gather in the second half of 2007, but with other banks experiencing similar problems, the extent of what was to follow was not readily visible. The first mistake occurred in August 2007, when Bank of America's president, Ken Lewis, announced a $2 billion investment in the deeply troubled subprime lender, Countrywide. By that time, the mortgage industry's problems were well known, and earlier that year, one of the largest of the subprime lenders, New Century, had filed for bankruptcy. This was a move that raised eyebrows from the start.

The big mistake, though, was Bank of America's decision in January 2008 to spend $4 billion to purchase a failing Countrywide. The rationale was that combining Countrywide's mortgage platform with Bank of America's would solve the problem and give Bank of America the nation's best mortgage platform and supposedly add substantial servicing income. The skeptic view was that Bank of America spent $4 billion to protect its earlier $2 billion investment. Whatever the rationale, this may have been the worst acquisition in corporate history.

Despite these missteps, when the national financial crisis peaked in the early fall of 2008, Bank of America was, along with JPMorgan, one of the two financial firms that were considered sources of strength by the regulators. Citigroup was sinking fast, and large investment banks had liquidity problems that had made their survival questionable. Wells Fargo was doing fine, but this was prior to its buying Wachovia, and it did not have the size or capability to take on a large investment bank with problems. Thus, with JPMorgan having already rescued the failing Bear Stearns, Secretary of Treasury Paulsen was looking to either Bank of America or the British Barclays to take over Lehman to keep it out of bankruptcy. In that crucial weekend of September 16th and 17th as the crisis hit its peak, Bank of America said "no" to Lehman and then announced a $50 billion purchase of a struggling Merrill Lynch, but whose securities brokerage business made it a better fit for Bank of America.

The purchase of Merrill Lynch may not have been as disastrous as buying Countrywide, but its acquisition was handled poorly and initially did more to damage Bank of America's reputation. It was widely criticized immediately for paying too much for a company that was likely to be the next investment bank to fail and be available for purchase at fire sale prices with government guaranties.

Bank of America seemed unaware of the depth of Merrill Lynch's problems and the lack of other buyers when the deal was announced. It mistakenly assumed Goldman Sachs would be interested; a view that may have come from not being part of the New York banking scene, and that led to wrongly assuming it had to beat their possible bid.[3] Then in December after getting shareholder approval, its president, Lewis, said conditions at Merrill Lynch had deteriorated and implied that Bank of America might want to back out. This was not well-received by either Paulsen at Treasury or Bernanke at the Federal Reserve, and Bank of America reluctantly moved forward with some loan protection and additional TARP money.

By early 2009, Bank of America had moved from being a source of strength for the regulators to being a possible fatality of the crisis. A stock that had once been over $55 per share had fallen to $3 per share, and there was widespread talk about it being nationalized. It was in need of capital and Lewis' days were clearly numbered.

Capital concerns were alleviated by the sale of 1.3 billion shares of common stock in 2009 and asset sales, of which its holdings in Chinese banks were the most significant. This increased common equity from 3 percent of tangible assets at year-end 2008 to more than 6 percent by the end 2011.

Lewis was gone by the end of 2009, as was much of the board, in an effort to strengthen their Board's business background. Coincidentally, it removed all of its members with Carolina ties. Its new president, Bryan Moynihan, came with the acquisition of Fleet in 2004, and the new Chairman was a retired Chairman and CEO of DuPont. Also added to the board were a former Chairman of the FDIC; a former member of the board of governors of the Federal Reserve; and a one-time part of Morgan Stanley's Office of the Chairman. It was a very different board with strong New York and Washington connections.

By 2013, Bank of America was on its way back under Moynihan, had earnings in excess of $10 billion and had become one of the international leaders in investment banking as well as having the nation's best retail franchise. The future looked good, but it had come at great expense to long-time shareholders.

CITIGROUP

Citigroup was not a source of strength for the regulators going into the crisis and one of several candidates for failure. It had substantial losses in the three quarters prior to the September crisis with no end in sight—total losses for the five quarters ending December 31, 2009 would be $38 billion. For a bank of its size, this would not in and of itself be fatal, but unlike JPMorgan, Bank of America and Wells Fargo, it did not have a large pool of cheap deposits and, thus, had liquidity problems similar to the investment banks. In addition to the $25 billion in TARP money it received in October, it took an additional $20 billion a month later, and in February 2009, the government increased its holdings to 36 percent. This was at least quasi-nationalization, and without this capital injection, in all likelihood, Citigroup would have failed.

This was not Citigroup's first time in the near-failure position. In the financial recession of the early 1990s, it was rumored to be failing. These rumors did not stop until the injection of new capital by the Saudi prince, Alwaleed bin Talal, equal to 15 percent of total capitalization occurred.

Citigroup's problems led to a leadership change long before the crisis days of the fall of 2008. Disappointing results in the second half of 2007 led to the resignation of Charles Prince, a protégé of Sandy Weill, and he was replaced by Vikrim Pandit, a newcomer to Citigroup via its buying a hedge fund he operated after spending years at Morgan Stanley. He inherited a "bad hand" that was not made easier by the failure of his hedge fund, and there was pressure for him to step down as early as 2009—and in 2012, he left after a dispute with his board.

The capital needs and regulatory pressures resulted in a questionable move that hurt Citigroup's long-term prospects—the sale of Smith Barney. It was one of the two largest securities brokerages, Merrill Lynch being the other, and provided direct access to a large segment of the country's wealthiest people, which was why Bank of America was willing to pay a high price for Merrill Lynch. Despite the contact value, capital problems forced Citigroup to sell 51 percent of Smith Barney to Morgan Stanley and the option to buy the entire operation at a later date—an option that was exercised in 2013.

Like Bank of America, the worst was behind Citigroup and 2013 earnings were more than $14 billion, but it still had it doubters. The sale of Smith Barney had put it in the second tier in investment banking, and it still had a large commitment to potentially unstable foreign markets.

MERGER ACTIVITY

There was minimal bank merger activity in these post-crisis years for banks of any size. Just eight bank or bank asset sales had deal values of $1 billion or more, and five of the eight involved the exiting or reduction in size of three foreign banks—Royal Bank of Canada, the Dutch-based ING and HSBC. Royal Bank of Canada sold its 426 banking offices in southeastern United States with deposits of $19 billion to PNC. ING's American operation with about $80 billion in Internet-generated deposits was acquired by Capital One, and the latter also bought HSBC's $30 billion credit card portfolio. In addition, HSBC sold its 195 Upstate New York and Connecticut branches to First Niagara.

The most important of the domestic bank or thrift sales announced during these years, with a deal value over $1 billion and an American buyer, was M&T's 2012 purchase of Hudson City Bancorp. This was a merging of two of the 25 largest banking organizations in the country, and it, when finalized, would move M&T up the ranks of the lower end of the second tier banks. As of early 2014, though, it still had not received regulatory approval. The other billion-dollar bank deals were First Niagara's purchase in 2010 of a Connecticut-based thrift, NewAlliance, and a Midwest merger between Ohio-based FirstMerit and Citizens Republic in Michigan.

The overall impact of these deals on consolidation was slight, but the PNC and Capital One acquisitions lifted them into the top three of second tier banks behind, albeit far behind, JPMorgan, Bank of America, Citigroup and Wells Fargo. They had, though, along with U.S. Bancorp, put considerable distance between themselves and the next largest banks, SunTrust and BB&T.

Continuing poor economic conditions and public attitude limited what the biggest banks could do expansion-wise after a disastrous 2008 and early 2009. They faced a deposit cap limiting what they could acquire domestically, and the existing anti-bank feeling being what it was, large acquisitions by these banks would not have been well-received by legislators, regulators or the general populace.

This stalling of the consolidation process, however, came after the process had moved beyond what might have been considered the logical end point with four banks so much bigger than any others and having taken their dominance well beyond traditional banking. There was still room for JPMorgan, Citigroup and Wells Fargo to fill out their domestic coverage, but that would not greatly change the four largest banks' share of bank assets. What they had already done going beyond traditional banking suggested that future size increases beyond normal market growth might have to be accomplished in foreign markets. In 2009, four banks held 49 percent of banking assets. Four years later that number was down slightly to a little under 48 percent and not likely to be going up any time soon.

Non-bank Expansion

This stalling at close to 50 percent of bank assets, though, did not reflect what had happened in non-traditional banking activities, particularly those dominated by investment banks. JPMorgan buying Bear Stearns, Bank of America acquiring Merrill Lynch, Citigroup being forced to sell its Smith Barney securities brokerage business and Lehman failing gave a new look to the largest banks, and overnight, a broadly defined investment banking business had a "big four" of Goldman Sachs, Morgan Stanley, JPMorgan and Bank of America. What banks were at the top depended on how much weight was given to various components such as trading and securities sales. With trading income removed from the totals, Morgan Stanley, JPMorgan and Bank of America were the investment banking leaders. Citigroup was losing ground, and excluding trading income, by 2013, it had fallen behind Wells Fargo.[1]

Securities sales that were dominated pre-2008 by Merrill Lynch and Citigroup with Wells Fargo in third place was totally turned upside down by the 2008 deals. By 2012, Bank of America with the 2008 purchase of Merrill Lynch, and Morgan Stanley with its acquisition of Smith Barney were one-two in securities sales revenues with Wells Fargo still in third place.[2]

Mortgage banking is not really "beyond traditional banking," but events in 2008 shook up this large segment of financial services to the benefit of the big banks, albeit in at least one case it was a dubious benefit. Pre-2008, the big three of mortgage banking were Wells Fargo, Countrywide and Washington Mutual. Then, with Countrywide being bought before it failed by Bank of America and JPMorgan acquiring a failed Washington Mutual from the FDIC, this business was primarily in the hands of three large banks with Wells Fargo becoming a dominant number one because of Bank of America's problems with Countrywide. These problems forced Bank of America to reduce originations, but it is likely that in time, it will use its large mortgage platform to regain some of the lost ground.

Despite merger problems, the increased stature of three of the four banks—Bank of America, JPMorgan and Wells Fargo—that dominated traditional banking and other financial services since 2008 was substantial, and by 2013, they had gone well beyond where others could catch-up anytime soon. Citigroup was in their size class, but with its problems and the sale of Smith Barney that may have prompted its change in management in 2012, it seemed to have a much more difficult future than the others.

REGIONAL STATUS

Just how dominant the 48 percent of bank assets held by America's four largest banks—and really three when looking at retail banking—had become by 2013 can readily be seen in deposits in the four major geographic subdivisions in the United States—the Northeast, South, Midwest and Far West. JPMorgan had the largest deposit share in two of the four areas, and Bank of America and Wells Fargo in one each. JPMorgan was third in the two areas where it was not first, and Bank of America and Wells Fargo were either second or third in two of the four areas.

In the Northeast, JPMorgan had by far the most deposits, $445 billion in 2013, followed by Bank of America at $253 billion. These two banks were far ahead of everyone else in the region. The third member of the top three was a foreign bank, Toronto-Dominion, and it had less than half the deposits of the two leaders.

In the South, Bank of America and Wells Fargo were far ahead of all others with $405 billion and $300 billion deposits, respectively, and Wells Fargo's status came primarily from its 2008 purchase of Wachovia. JPMorgan was a distant third at $164 billion, and this was a one-two-three sweep for the largest banks.

The big three of retail banking were not nearly as dominant in the Midwest as in the rest of the country. In 2013, JPMorgan and Wells Fargo ranked first and third, but being at the top required regional deposits of less than $200 billion. U.S. Bancorp filled out the Midwest top three with deposits of $150 billion.

Deposit Share Leaders by Region, 2013*

	Deposits (in billions)		Deposits (in billions)
Northeast		South	
1. JPMorgan	$445	1. Bank of America	$405
2. Bank of America	253	2. Wells Fargo	300
3. Toronto Dominion	115	3. JPMorgan	164
Midwest		Far West	
1. JPMorgan	$160	1. Wells Fargo	$340
2. U.S. Bancorp	150	2. Bank of America	328
3. Wells Fargo	115	3. JPMorgan	146

*June 30, 2013 and excludes large credit card affiliates.
Source: SNL Financial, Charlottesville, Virginia.

The Far West was the most concentrated of the four regions, with Wells Fargo and Bank of America running far ahead of all others having combined 2013 deposits of $668 billion. JPMorgan, as a result of its 2008 federally-assisted purchase of Washington Mutual, was third with $146 billion—creating another one-two-three sweep for Wells Fargo, Bank of America and JPMorgan.

FOREIGN BANKS

There had also been pre-2008 expectations about foreign banks playing a bigger role in American banking and even becoming part of the top tier as several large European and Canadian banks either expanded an existing position or made an initial entry into the American market in the early 2000s. This included HSBC, Royal Bank of Scotland, Banco Santander, Banco Bilbao, BNP Paribas, ABN AMRO, ING, Toronto Dominion and Royal Bank of Canada. These were the biggest banks in England, Spain, France and the Netherlands and two of the largest in Canada. Another Canadian bank, Bank of Montreal, had long been present in the Chicago area. Not since the late 1970s and early 1980s has there been such a significant foreign bank presence in the country, and the foreign banks looked to have more staying power this time around.

This presence reflected nine good-sized American banks and thrifts being bought by foreign banks from 2000 through 2007. Go back one day to December 31, 1999 and add in HSBC's purchase of Republic of New York that closed on that day, and the number of big foreign bank purchases rises to ten. This did not include the 2002 purchase by HSBC of Household Finance that was not a bank, but it was a nationwide consumer lender.

HSBC, in particular, with American assets approaching $500 billion; almost 400 banking offices, mostly in New York; and numerous finance offices across the country in 2007, appeared to have the potential with the acquisition of a second-tier American bank, to challenge the likes of Bank of America and JPMorgan on their own turf. It was a potential acquirer whenever a large regional bank was being sold.

Royal Bank of Scotland, which at the time was the world's biggest bank, was the most aggressive of the foreign banks in the early 2000s with its purchase in 2004 of Charter One, a thrift with $41 billion assets and 571 branches focused on Ohio, Michigan and western New York. This helped lift its total number of banking offices to about 1,700 by 2007, which made it the eighth largest branch network in the country.

The early 2000 interest in American banking by these foreign banks was symptomatic of the rising globalization of the industry. In Europe, Canada and Japan, the limited size of the home market prompted banks to look to new markets for expansion. In the United States, Citigroup needed no prompting to do so, but as Bank of America and JPMorgan reached regulatory and geographic limits on their domestic expansion, they too seemed likely to want to expand into other countries to maintain their growth momentum as well as trying to keep pace with Citigroup.

This was before the world of banking changed in 2008, and some of the European banks were hurt as much, or more than, the American banks. Royal Bank of Scotland was hit particularly hard and was bailed out by the British government, and HSBC lost billions on its commitment to American subprime lending. In 2012, Royal Bank of Scotland was urged by regulators to sell its American operations, and in early 2014 announced the sale of its Charter One branches in the Midwest to U.S. Bancorp. HSBC sold most of its American branches, and by 2014, it was concentrating on high-end customers in a few large cities. The Dutch banks, ABN AMRO and ING, had abandoned their American efforts with the former doing so in 2007 because of problems that predated the 2008 financial collapse.

Countering this, Canadian and Spanish banks were net buyers, but this did not include the Royal Bank of Canada, which sold all of its branches in the United States to PNC in 2009. The Bank of Montreal bought Marshall & Illsley, a major Midwest regional, in 2010. Toronto Dominion acquired Commerce Bank in New Jersey in 2008 and South Carolina's South Financial in 2010. Banco Bilbao bought Compass Bancorp, an Alabama banking holding company with offices in Texas, in

2007, and Banco Santander bought Sovereign, the country's second largest thrift in 2008.

In 2013, Royal Bank of Scotland and Toronto-Dominion had more than 1,300 branches each and were similar in size to Fifth Third, Regions and other second tier domestic banks. Banco Santander, Banco Bilbao, BNP Paribas and Bank of Montreal had between 700 and 800 branches and were strictly regional operations in America. The Spanish banks had avoided the worst of the problems in Spain by not being large players in that country's real estate lending and had major positions in Latin America, but Spain's problems still limited their ability to expand in the United States.

HSBC was the largest foreign bank with multiple offices in the United States if measured by assets, but its commitment to retail banking was greatly reduced by the sale of its Upstate New York branches to First Niagara. In 2012, it had about 250 American banking offices.

STRUCTURAL CHANGES

Banking changes between 2008 and 2013 were more than a few big banks getting larger and increasing their share of the banking business and other financial services and a seeming end to the possibility of an enlarged position for foreign banks. At the opposite end of the spectrum, smaller banks and thrifts continued to disappear at a rapid rate.

The total number of domestic banks fell from 7,098 in 2008 to 5,937 in 2013, or a drop of about 16 percent. This included 391 failed banks. From 2010 through 2013, only seven new banks opened. This reflected an unofficial moratorium on regulatory approvals, but there was also a much reduced investor interest.

Thrifts had been a diminishing factor since the thrift crisis in the 1980s, and the latest economic crisis was not kind to them. In 2008, the nation's largest thrift, Washington Mutual, failed, and the second largest, Sovereign, was acquired by the Spanish-based Banco Santander. In 2011, the S&L regulatory agency, the OTS, was eliminated, and its regulatory responsibilities were shifted to the OCC that was responsible for regulating commercial and savings banks. In 2013, what had by then become the largest thrift, Hudson City Bancorp, was in the process of being acquired by M&T, a regional commercial bank. The total number of thrifts at year-end 2013 was 954, which was well below the 7,000 plus of the 1970s.

The rapid decline of thrifts and a negative aura surrounding big commercial banks was a plus for credit unions that operated in a non-profit environment much like thrifts did 50 years ago. Their growth in deposit share since 2008, though, was not that significant, rising only from 6 percent to 7 percent by 2013.

By 2013, competition between local banks and large banks also was much less than in days past. This was reflected in loan and deposit mixes of banks of varying sizes and type. This was particularly true relative to the big banks and small banks in urban areas in consumer banking and commercial real estate.

With their domination of credit cards, ATM and remote access banking, in general, consumer banking had become primarily a big bank business, particularly in urban areas. In an analysis done in 2012, consumer loans accounted for about 27 percent of the loans of the biggest banks; 23 percent for large regional banks; and less than 3 percent for local urban banks.

Loan and Deposit Mix by Type, 2012

	Loan Breakdown			
	Real Estate		Comm. & Ind.	Consumer
	Res.	Comm.		
Big Banks*	36%	7%	19%	27%
Large Regionals**	27	13	24	23
Local Banks				
Urban****	36%	45%	12%	3%
Country****	15	16	14	8
	Deposit Breakdown			
	Transaction	MMDA & Savings	CDs	
Big Banks*	16%	76%	8%	
Large Regionals**	16	70	15	
Small Banks				
Urban***	21%	42%	37%	
Country****	28	39	33	

*Bank of America, JPMorgan and Wells Fargo.
**BB&T, PNC and SunTrust.
***Maryland and New Jersey banks under $1 billion assets.
****North Dakota and South Dakota banks under $1 billion assets.
Source: FDIC: Historical Statistics on Banking and SNL Financial, Charlottesville, Virginia.

Going the other way were commercial real estate and business lending. In 2012, they were 45 percent of local bank loans, but only 7 percent of loans for the biggest banks and 13 percent for the large regional banks. The lending emphasis on commercial and industrial loans not secured by real estate did not show a similar difference, but there was not much overlap in competition there either as the size of loans small banks can make limited the type of the commercial businesses they can serve.

It is important to differentiate between urban and country banks as the latter face different dynamics because the big banks have limited interest in small town banking except for what is doable by remote access. To differentiate between these types of small banks, the accompanying chart used two of the most urbanized states, Maryland and New Jersey, and two without large cities, North and South Dakota. The latter are much more balanced in their lending, including a category not in the table, farm loans.

It is loans, not deposits, that best define the orientations of banks in different size and geographic categories, but there are clear differences on the deposit side as well. Banks, large and small, depend primarily on MMDAs and other savings for most of their funding, but the large banks have less interest-rate risk with deposits because of their much lower dependence on CDs. For the typical small banks, urban and country, CDs account for 30 percent to 40 percent of deposits. For the biggest banks, they are only 8 percent; and the large regionals, 15 percent. This differential can be important if interest rates rise significantly.

Changes in deposit and loan mixes of banks of all sizes in the recovery years reflected the normal reaction to economic conditions. An extended period of low interest rates drove money out of CDs with their time commitments and into checking accounts or MMDAs where it was essentially "parked" while looking for better investment opportunities. The down economy with minimal loan growth had loans falling as a percent of deposits and assets. The only loan type that grew faster than assets and deposits was the credit card.

There was a significant change, though, between 2008 and 2013 in who held the home mortgage debt that represented about half of all private debt. The vast majority was still held by Fannie Mae and Freddie Mac, but they were no longer quasi-private organizations, but rather wards of the federal government. Most of the rest was held by commercial banks that still had about one-third of the total. The once dominant thrift position had been greatly diminished long before 2013. This left big questions going forward as to the future direction of the domestic mortgage business.

CHAPTER

WHAT NEXT?

So what is next for big and small banks, after the turmoil of the last six years and extensive change over the last 35 years? Projecting the future is never easy, but industry trends and environmental conditions provide a good framework for what to expect, at least for the next ten years. In particular, banking in 2014 reflected the four major banking events since 1980 that will continue to play a major role. These were:

- The introduction of interstate banking in the mid-1980s;

- The passage of Gramm-Leach-Bliley in 1999;

- The unrestrained market excesses from 2002 to 2007; and

- The severe financial crisis in 2008.

The arrival of interstate banking allowed what was a local banking industry to finally go national like any other business—and go national it did. This released the natural business urge to grow and make money, and, more specifically, it set in motion the "merger mania" of the 1990s that ran through 2001. This resulted in seven banks—Citigroup, JPMorgan, Bank of America, Wells Fargo, First Union, Bank One and Fleet—becoming much larger than all others. This concentration was carried a step further in the next few years by the seven turning into four as a result of JPMorgan buying Bank One, Bank of America acquiring Fleet and Wells Fargo absorbing First Union, which in the interim had taken the Wachovia name. This gave us the four banks that in 2014 held almost 50 percent of all bank assets.

The Gramm-Leach-Bliley Act endorsed the Citigroup-Travelers merger in 1999 and ended the Glass-Steagall restraints that kept commercial banks from going beyond traditional deposit-gathering and lending and turned the biggest of them into what are often referred to as "universal banks" that provide all financial services, including investment banking, securities brokerage and securities underwriting. It instantaneously made Citigroup a leader in all these areas. It also meant that when the investment banking business fell on hard times in 2007 and 2008, JPMorgan and Bank of America were able to pick up the failing Bear Stearns and Merrill Lynch. With Lehman's failure, this left only Goldman Sachs and Morgan Stanley as freestanding, large investment banks.

The unrestrained market excesses from 2002 to 2007 had two parts—the sale and packaging of subprime mortgages and an increased emphasis by investment banks and the New York City commercial banks, collectively referred to as Wall Street, on profits generated by a trading desk. The subprime mortgages were sold by independent, and generally unregulated, mortgage banks; loosely regulated thrifts; and commercial banks. The majority and the worst of these loans, though, were made by the first two groups. The much-expanded subprime mortgage lending process, however, would not have been possible without the packaging and sale of these home mortgages by the investment banks.

In all fairness, the excesses of the early 2000s that caused so much trouble could not have happened without the Federal Reserve keeping interest rates unusually low and raising no concern about potential problems; the willingness of Fannie Mae and Freddie Mac to buy these loans; bond rating companies giving these subprime securities triple A ratings; and politicians from both sides of the aisle cheering on the process. There was plenty of blame to go around, but the result was the debilitating financial crisis of 2008.

For better or worse these four events—interstate banking, the elimination of Glass-Steagall, early 2000 excesses and 2008 financial crisis—left a banking system with four banks being far larger than all other commercial or investment banks. In 2014, there were still fifteen commercial banks besides the big four with assets in excess of $50 billion, but combined they had fewer assets than JPMorgan, Bank of America or Citigroup. There were still two large investment banks, Goldman Sachs and Morgan Stanley, but even they together were smaller than the biggest commercial banks.

Looking at the consolidation that occurred as a result of these determinants, it is easy to assume that the big banks will keep getting bigger and the overall number of banks will continue to fall. This has been the case since 1990 when the full impact of interstate banking began to be felt, but the spectacular growth in size of the largest banks goes back well beyond that. In 1990, the median size of the top five banks was $98 billion, which was almost an eleven-fold jump over the $9 billion of 1960. This was a big jump in 30 years, but a long way from the 20 times increase from 1990 to the $2 trillion median of 2014's big four.[1]

Coinciding with this rising dominance of a few banks was a steep decline in the number of banks that began in the 1980s with the advent of interstate banking. This was accelerated by numerous bank failures in the late 1980s and early 1990s. In that decade, the total number of banks fell from more than 14,000 to a little over 12,000. The decline continued in the 1990s when the number of banks fell by about 4,000, and another drop of about 2,300 since 2000 reduced the total at the end of 2014 to less than 6,000. During this same period, the number of savings banks and S&Ls, which were almost all local institutions, declined at an even faster rate, falling from about 7,000 to a little under 1,000.[2] This was a combined bank and thrift drop from about 21,000 to 6,900.

The almost 50 percent of bank assets held by the four large banks in 2013 did *not* mean local banks held the other 50 percent. About 30 percent of bank assets were held by regional banks with assets in excess of $50 billion, foreign banks and subsidiaries of other financial service companies, primarily investment banks and insurance companies. This left local banks, collectively, with about 20 percent of bank assets. This was a large amount of assets, but it was only about 25 percent more than what JPMorgan had on its own.

GOING FORWARD

So where does the industry go from here? There are other factors involved besides past trends, but even if the four largest banks grow at a rate of 5 percent per annum, a pretty conservative number, their median asset size would be $3.2 trillion in 2024, and the largest would be close to, if not above, $4 trillion. This level of growth might not increase the top four's share of bank assets, but it almost certainly would be accompanied by a decline in the number of banks to 4,000 or less.

Projecting what banking might look like in 2024, though, needs to consider some other factors and, in particular:

- A low growth economic environment in an interconnected world;
- Anti-bank sentiment and accompanying banking legislation;
- Another possible economic crisis; and
- Technological change.

These factors impact various bank types differently. All banks, however, will have to deal with a low growth economy, technological change and, if it occurs, another banking crisis. The anti-bank sentiment and global events primarily affect the large banks, and, although this was not the intent, banking legislation, ironically, will have a bigger negative impact on small banks.

GLOBAL ENVIRONMENT

When looking at the banking environment going forward, it is necessary to look globally. The financial world operates on an international basis, and as noted above, almost 50 percent of the domestic bank assets are held by four large banks, of which three operate extensively across national borders. The third largest, Citigroup, gets about 75 percent of its revenues outside the United States, and JPMorgan and Bank of America are among the leaders in investment banking worldwide. In the crisis years, there was a tendency of banks worldwide to concentrate on home markets, but in a slow growth environment, big banks have to go beyond their domestic markets if they expect to produce the growth investosrs want.

The countries or economic blocs that will have the most impact on American banks from an economic and competitive perspective are China, the euro zone and the United Kingdom. China, with an Organization for Economic Co-operation and Development ("OECD") estimate of a 2023 Gross National Product of more than $36 trillion would be the biggest national economy, with the United States next at $26 trillion. A northern European bloc inclusive of euro zone and other continental northern European countries was estimated to be at about $20 trillion and the United Kingdom at $3.5 trillion. The last is relatively small, but it, or at least London, historically has punched above its weight in banking. Based on what was happening in 2013 and 2014, though, the OECD projections seemed generous for China.

China, in particular, seems unlikely to come anywhere near the $36 trillion estimate by 2023, and that is not necessarily good news for other countries. A slow growing China would put a damper on economic growth everywhere, but on just numbers of people, it is still likely to be the world's biggest economy, albeit by a smaller margin.

Regional comparisons put in perspective just how favorable the global environment is for American banks compared to banks in the rest of world. By 2023, China will become the world's biggest economy, even if not by the margin projected by the OECD, but it would still have less than one-third the United States per capita income and almost no safety net for its rapidly aging population.

World's Largest Banks, 2013*

		Assets**	Market Capital	Net Income	Tang. Cap/ Assets
			(in billions)		
1.	HSBC	$2,436	$193	$18.2	5.88%
2.	JPMorgan	2,416	212	17.9	6.83
3.	Mitsubishi UFJ	2,356	86	12.7	5.39
4.	Bank of America	2,102	177	11.4	7.20
5.	Crédit Agricole	2,066	35	7.4	2.88
6.	BNP Paribas	2,044	99	7.3	5.00
7.	Citigroup	1,881	146	14.1	8.85
8.	Mizuho	1,739	49	8.5	4.24
9.	Barclays	1,602	72	2.0	5.82
10.	Societe Generale	1,593	47	2.5	5.11
11.	Banco Santander	1,576	96	2.9	3.67
12.	Wells Fargo	1,527	235	22.2	8.22

*Excludes China's state operated banks.
**Estimate derivative assets and liabilities netted out for foreign banks.
Source: SNL Financial, Charlottesville, Virginia and bank annual reports.

A region that may have as good economic prospects as the United States is northern Europe with its less expensive, in-place safety net and almost as high per capita income, but it is bound by the euro zone to a southern Europe, including France, that is unlikely to have significant growth over most of the next ten years.

Thus, even though the United States may have problems in funding its social needs, especially relative to an aging population, it is better positioned to deal with what are universal problems than most industrialized countries outside of northern Europe. The U.S. is wealthier, relatively under-taxed, and, unlike northern Europe, it does not have a southern sector to deal with that is overextended and either over-taxed or does not know how to collect taxes. The bad news is that the United States may have a lot of political turmoil. The good news for banks is that this does not have to have a large negative effect on them, and certainly not on American banks' ability to compete with banks from around the world.

America's largest banks, even as politicians talk about "too big to fail" and either breaking them up, limiting their growth or taking away the profit incentive by making them carry excess capital, look good when compared to banks elsewhere. They, along with HSBC, are the largest and strongest non-state banks on a global basis.

If balance sheets are made comparable by netting out derivative assets and liabilities of all banks as is done in the United States, JPMorgan was the world's second largest investor-owned bank in 2013. Bank of America was fourth, Citigroup seventh and Wells Fargo twelfth. London-based HSBC was first, but was ahead of JP Morgan by such a small margin that currency conversion changes could quickly reverse their positions.

Assets are only one way to measure comparative bank size and strength, and probably not the best way. Based on tangible capital, JPMorgan, Bank of America and Citigroup are the top three, and Wells Fargo was sixth. Only HSBC and Mitsubishi UFJ are even close to America's big banks in this category. The American banks also had higher tangible capital as a percent of assets. In earnings, Wells Fargo and JPMorgan were one-two, and Citigroup and Bank of America were fourth and fifth.

Take away HSBC with its heavy commitment to Southeast Asia, and the foreign banks are not even close to the American banks in balance sheet strength. Some like Mitsubishi UFJ, BNP Paribas, Crédit Agricole and Barclays are hurt by being based in countries with economies in worse shape than the United States. Deutsche Bank is in the right place and Germany's largest bank, but it had marginal earnings in 2013 and tangible capital of about 4 percent of assets.

When one looks at the future of these banks, it is likely that JPMorgan, Bank of America and Citigroup along with HSBC will be the largest privately-owned banks worldwide in 2024, and it is not a stretch to think Wells Fargo will move from its twelfth place in 2013 into the top five. This does not include the large state-owned Chinese banks, one of which, Industrial and Commercial Bank of China, may technically be the world's largest bank, but they are not comparable.

The presumption that the largest American banks will be the largest non-state banks in the world in 2024, and by a widening margin, further suggests that they will be too big to be allowed to fail, which they already are in 2014. It also can be argued with justification that they are and will be too big and diversified to fail in a way that the "hurt" goes beyond investors.

FINANCIAL CRISES

Most projections made for national environments and the impact on banking do not take into consideration unusual events. For banks, this could be another crisis, which is not unusual as every eight or nine years it seems to happen, but even if this occurs, the negative impact should not be as bad as in earlier financial crises. The causes of the banking crises in the past were different, but the results were usually the same—big banks got bigger; the number of banks was further diminished; and the public was mad at banking in general.

The part of the multiple economic crises of the 1970s that hurt banking the most was inflation and accompanying high interest rates. The commercial banks survived these high rates fairly well, but S&Ls and savings banks were devastated and never truly recovered as an industry from the resulting mismatched yields and cost of funds.

The late 1980s and early 1990s economic crisis was primarily caused by an overbuilding of commercial real estate. More than 2,500 banks and thrifts would fail, and it began the consolidation process that gave us JPMorgan, Bank of America and Wells Fargo as three of four dominant banks.

Compared to what happened in these economic crises and what was to come later, it is hard to put the downturn of the early 2000s in the same category as it was a loss of wealth caused by the bursting of a technology-driven stock market bubble, but had a minimal impact on banking. It did, however, hurt some banks more than others, and helped send Bank One and Fleet into the hands of JPMorgan and Bank of America.

There is little need to go over the causes and impact of the economic crisis that peaked in 2008 and 2009 as this is well-remembered by all. Of particular importance to the future of banking is that this latest crisis made four commercial banks much larger than other financial firms and created an environment that made it more difficult for small banks.

So when will the next financial crisis come? Moreover, how will it impact banking? History suggests it will arrive sometime in the 2015 to 2020 period, and a possible cause would be a rapid rise in interest rates, if only because rates have been so low for so long. With so many home loans having been written with fixed rates, or at least rates that do not adjust for up to seven years, in the 3 percent to 4 percent range, this would hurt Fannie Mae and Freddie Mac the most and other holders of these loans, but there would be a significant spillover on all banks.

Even if this was to occur, and in 2014, it was hard to see why interest rates would rise sharply in the near future, this should not be an economic crisis like 2008 or even 1989 to 1992. If it occurs, it should be more like what banks experienced in late 1994 when the primary result was lower bank earnings and a drop in bank stock prices.

A more likely cause of an economic recession in the next few years than banks is one caused by political differences. With an increasing elderly population that will not easily give up its social security and Medicare benefits and a growing segment of the population that will need more Medicaid and welfare assistance, there will be an increasing revenue shortage that will require adjustments that will not come easily—and possibly only when financial concerns force the issue. Even this, though, should do more harm to the economy than bank earnings.

ANTI-BANK SENTIMENT AND BANK LEGISLATION

The final outcome of the rules being discussed as part of Dodd-Frank were not known in early 2014, but after the 2008 and 2009 crisis there was a lot of anti-bank feeling that had not abated. One can quibble about the banks or bank types that caused the crisis—mortgage banks, thrifts, big commercial banks, investment banks—but to most outside the industry they are all banks, and there is a natural tendency to blame the big and somehow think one's own local bank is somehow better.

It appears, though, despite all the talk about "too big to fail" and the need to control the size and scope of big banks, the most likely impact of increased bank regulation will have been more capital and paperwork for all banks—a burden that falls disproportionately on small banks in added compliance costs. The political will does not exist to break up the big banks. The added paperwork connected with further attempts to regulate banking, by its very nature favors the big, for which it is just a nuisance, over the small—a burden that encourages them to exit. In other words, Dodd-Frank will do little to change the pattern of the big getting bigger and there being fewer banks.

This is not to suggest the new regulations are all bad. Higher capital requirements reduce the chances of bank failures even if some of the concern over "too big to fail" is either misguided or self-correcting. The concern over trading losses was real considering the $35 billion lost by Citigroup in late 2007 and 2008, but this type of trading was, and is, not part of the Bank of America and Wells Fargo DNA or that of any large regionals. JPMorgan's London trading loss of

$7 billion in 2012 was a reminder of the threat of trading losses to Wall Street's commercial banks, JPMorgan and Citigroup, but was a manageable concern for JPMorgan considering its size and diversity.

TECHNOLOGY

When looking at "what's next" for banking, technology, particularly remote access banking, is front and center. Its effects are already with us as people are able to pay their bills and transfer funds electronically with minimal impact on bank earnings, competitive position and ability to survive. This, though, was just the beginning, and the key elements driving technological change are:

- Banking being more adaptable to remote access than most other businesses;

- More customers understanding and utilizing remote access banking; and

- The affluent increasingly using brokerage accounts as their primary banking source.

This is hardly news to those that work for or deal with banks. Direct deposit of paychecks has been with us for a long time, and depositing of checks in an ATM machine or from a mobile phone has become commonplace. A growing number of people pay for even small purchases with a debit or credit card. If there is a need to borrow money, it can be done automatically through a credit card, home equity loan or line of credit. If cash is needed, there are ATMs on almost every corner, but even their usage has peaked as they represent the past more than the future.

So what is new about remote access? Primarily, it has become so much easier to utilize, and the number of technologically sophisticated users has grown by leaps and bounds. One cannot underestimate the importance of more customers being able to fully understand and utilize remote access banking every year—even if there were no further technological improvements. It is hard to pick a precise year, but, in general, people born from 1965 forward are likely to be more Internet savvy than those born earlier. This implies that the upper age limit of people with minimal person-to-person banking needs will be 50 years by 2015 and 60 by 2025.

Demographically, though, it is not just the young getting older that works in favor of remote access banking as older people are being dragged into the remote access process as well. An expanding senior citizen base has it social security retirement payments deposited directly into a bank account. This eliminates a big reason for going to a bank branch and depositing that check.

In addition, increasingly the primary bank account of the more affluent and most profitable banking customer is held with a securities brokerage firm. They can write checks against this account; make deposits directly into it; and transfer money from it into other banking accounts. In other words, it has the same functions as commercial bank accounts.

There will be a much-increased usage of technology to bypass banks using prepaid cards, point-to-point retail payments from nonbank sources and other processes still to be developed. This will get many headlines and talk of disaster for banking from trade associations, but the volume will be relatively minimal in overall scope of bank assets and will be used mostly by the least profitable bank customers.

This suggests less usage of bank branches; fewer of them; and being used differently by bank type. Large banks will have fewer branches, but those branches will be diversified offices that have asset management as well as traditional banking services. Branches of local banks in the future may look more like loan production offices—at least in urban areas.

There are lessons to be learned from the delivery of banking services in other countries as well. In Europe, branch traffic is far less than in the United States because of much greater use of direct payment, not because the customers are more Internet savvy, but because the largest recipients of checks—utilities, credit card companies and lenders—demand it. In time, this practice should become the norm in the United States on a voluntary or involuntary basis.

With the direct deposit of payroll or government checks, remote deposit of personal checks and automatic or computer bill paying, the competitive advantage goes to banks that can deliver the broadest array of these automatic services. This may not favor the largest banks over the large regionals, but it has already taken most small urban banks out of the consumer banking business.

What really favors the large banks in an increasingly "wired world" is the cyber threat. As remote access grows, so does the threat of financial accounts being hacked and security compromised. Through 2014, the large banks have been the primary targets of cyber-attacks, but as technology moves forward so will the target base, and small banks will be less able to afford the losses and protection costs—and far less willing to put up with the hassle.

A 2024 Scenario

So what will financial services look like in 2024? The names may not be that different, but it will be a very different industry. Three, and maybe four or five, banks will still be much larger than all others with assets at least twice what they are today, but they will be acting more like utilities than totally market-driven firms. There will be large regional banks providing competition to these very large banks, but fewer than the fifteen or so in 2014. In urban markets, there will be many fewer local banks, and those that exist will primarily be specialists serving local needs for commercial real estate and small business lending. In outlying markets, local banks will look much the same as today, but they may be doing more "franchise type" operations by selling at least some large bank products.

At the top, JPMorgan, Bank of America and Wells Fargo are not going away, and by 2024, the first two could have assets in excess of $4 trillion, and Wells Fargo will probably be over $3 trillion. They will be dominant in consumer and residential real estate lending, and with the increased use of remote access banking, probably more so than they are today. The more utility-like aspect is that they will be minimally involved in trading for profit; conform to well-defined rules in mortgage and consumer lending; *and* less leveraged than in the past.

Thus, they may be "too big to fail," but in reality, they will be "too risk-adverse and well-capitalized to be at risk of failing." This will come at the expense of the high returns on equity of the pre-2008 years, but investors will still like returns in the 12 percent to 14 percent range with dividend yields above 4 percent—and minimal risk.

Citigroup is an "iffier" situation as it does not have the traditional universal bank model of the others. It is, and will likely continue to be, more of a holding company for banks in various countries, and mostly in emerging nations, with minimal holding company liquidity—and with it, the threat of sovereign debt losses. It is still the same bank that essentially failed in 1990 and 2008, but it is likely to be far less vulnerable to trading losses.

There will likely be more than just the three universal banks "at the top" in 2024 even if the others are a bit smaller, but it is less certain who they will be. Citigroup, despite its riskier model, is certainly a candidate, but its sale of the Smith Barney brokerage business and primary dependence on foreign revenues makes it "no sure thing," but some substantial acquisitions could change this. Another possible number four or five could come from the largest second-tier banks—U.S. Bancorp, PNC or Capital One—buying their way into more prominent positions. They would be far smaller than the biggest banks and more regional in their coverage, but with similar service capabilities. Other possibilities include Morgan Stanley or a Canadian bank—Toronto Dominion or Bank of Montreal—adding a substantial domestic depository institution to its existing base.

Banks outside of North America are unlikely contenders. With the banks in Europe struggling the way they are and with HSBC, ING and presumably RBS selling much, if not all, of their American operations, it is unlikely they will have enough interest in the United States to be more than marginal factors.

Most of the regional banks with assets between $50 and $400 billion in 2014 will be around in 2024, partly because the banks big enough to buy them may not feel the need for added coverage and are constrained by regulatory and political pressure from making large in-market purchases. This is particularly true in a broadly defined Midwest where most of these regional banks are located. The most likely to be gone are those in the Southeast—BB&T, Regions and SunTrust—because of the attractiveness of their franchises to others.

Investment banking will be increasingly dominated by the large universal banks—JPMorgan, Bank of America and Wells Fargo. Morgan Stanley and Goldman Sachs may still be around and, perhaps, keeping pace, but the latter may have to abandon its banking charter if it wants to continue trading as aggressively as in the past to maintain a high return on equity.

There will continue to be hedge funds, mutual fund firms and venture capital specialists playing an increasing role at least partially outside of close regulatory supervision that will play an important role—and some of which, like BlackRock and Fidelity, will be as big, or bigger, than the largest regional banks. Their importance is likely to grow, as the big universal banks will not want to get the added scrutiny that goes with some of their businesses.

The steady decline of banks from more than 14,000 in 1980 to less than 6,000 in 2014 is not a positive sign for local banks, and by 2024, the number may be less than 4,000 of which the vast majority will be country banks serving markets that do not interest the big banks. This further reduction would not be surprising, or that much different from what was happening before.

The 1,000 or so local banks that are in urban areas will probably be reduced to less than 500, and most of those surviving will be boutiques with a specialized niche at which they are very proficient. In large markets with populations of two million or more, in particular, there will be a demand for banks specializing in local real estate and small business lending. This may not be that different from what existed in 2014, but there will be fewer such banks chasing the same loans.

Fewer local banks in urban markets will mean many local bank mergers and few new entrants. Those "wanting out" will not find the high sale prices of the past, as the likely buyers are other local banks that are not sufficiently larger than the seller to pay a substantial premium. Added regulatory compliance costs will also contribute to the small bank consolidation process.

The costs of greater regulation go beyond the local banks. The big banks will not be exiting, but they will have to adjust earnings expectations downward. Their having more capital than in the past will make returns on equity of 12 percent to 14 percent more realistic than their 16 percent to 18 percent of the past. Even at this lower level, they should still rank among the largest corporate earners in the world.

The differences in banking in 2024 from what it is today will be more noticeable to the banks themselves than the public. The names the public knows the best will still exist, and the gradual movement from direct contact to remote access banking is a continuation of an ongoing process. One thing that will not change is the need for financial intermediaries of which banks have been and will continue to be the primary vehicle, further technological changes notwithstanding.

Largest Banks or Bank Holding Companies, 1930 to 2012

	1930	City	Assets (In millions)
1.	Chase National Bank	New York	$2,697
2.	Guaranty Trust	New York	2,022
3.	National City Bank	New York	1,947
4.	Continental Illinois	Chicago	1,249
5.	Bank of America	San Francisco	1,162
6.	Irving Trust	New York	881
7.	Bankers Trust	New York	849
8.	Central Hanover	New York	835
9.	First National Bank	Boston	751
10.	Security First	Los Angeles	611
11.	First National Bank	New York	564
12.	Bank of Manhattan	New York	552
13.	First National Bank	Chicago	496
14.	Bank of America	New York	437
15.	Peoples Wayne County	Detroit	422

	1940	City	Assets (In millions)
1.	Chase National Bank	New York	$3,824
2.	National City Bank	New York	3,095
3.	Guaranty Trust	New York	2,718
4.	Bank of America	San Francisco	1,817
5.	Continental Illinois	Chicago	1,620
6.	Bankers Trust	New York	1,580
7.	Central Hanover	New York	1,368
8.	First National Bank	Chicago	1,238
9.	Manufacturers Trust	New York	1,050
10.	Chemical	New York	958
11.	First National Bank	Boston	940
12.	First National Bank	New York	935
13.	Irving Trust	New York	893
14.	Bank of Manhattan	New York	795
15.	JP Morgan	New York	773

	1950	City	Assets (In millions)
1.	Bank of America	San Francisco	$6,863
2.	National City Bank	New York	5,526
3.	Chase National Bank	New York	5,283
4.	Guaranty Trust	New York	2,940
5.	Manufacturers Trust	New York	2,773
6.	First National Bank	Chicago	2,598
7.	Continental Illinois	Chicago	2,591
8.	Bankers Trust	New York	1,837
9.	Security First	Los Angeles	1,824
10.	Central Hanover	New York	1,770
11.	Mellon	Pittsburgh	1,717
12.	Chemical	New York	1,714
13.	First National Bank	Boston	1,602
14.	National Bank of Detroit	Detroit	1,568
15.	Irving Trust	New York	1,360

	1960	City	Assets (In millions)
1.	Bank of America	San Francisco	$11,942
2.	Chase Manhattan	New York	9,260
3.	First National City	New York	8,668
4.	Western Bancorporation	Los Angeles	5,112
5.	Chemical	New York	4,540
6.	Morgan Guaranty	New York	4,424
7.	Manufacturers Trust	New York	3,974
8.	Security First	Los Angeles	3,594
9.	Bankers Trust	New York	3,430
10.	First National Bank	Chicago	3,136
11.	Continental Illinois	Chicago	2,886
12.	Wells Fargo	San Francisco	2,700
13.	Mellon	Pittsburgh	2,226
14.	Hanover Bank	New York	2,192
15.	Irving Trust	New York	2,104

	1970	City	Assets (In millions)	Banking Offices
1.	Bank of America	San Francisco	$29,366	955
2.	Chase Manhattan	New York	24,474	150
3.	First National City	New York	25,219	182
4.	Manufacturers Hanover	New York	12,665	102
5.	Western Bancorporation	Los Angeles	11,409	654
6.	Morgan Guaranty	New York	11,153	5
7.	Chemical	New York	10,979	145
8.	Bankers Trust	New York	9,930	155
9.	Continental	Chicago	8,812	1
10.	Security First	Los Angeles	8,038	398
11.	First National Bank	Chicago	8,028	1
12.	Marine Midland	Buffalo	7,638	261
13.	Charter	New York	6,309	82
14.	Wells Fargo	San Francisco	6,209	-
15.	Crocker-Citizens	San Francisco	5,917	280

	1980	City	Assets (In millions)	Banking Offices
1.	Citicorp	New York	$114,920	426
2.	Bank of America	San Francisco	111,617	1,207
3.	Chase Manhattan	New York	76,190	214
4.	Manufacturers Hanover	New York	55,552	NA
5.	JP Morgan	New York	51,991	21
6.	Continental Illinois	Chicago	42,089	-
7.	Chemical	New York	41,342	285
8.	Bankers Trust	New York	34,202	117
9.	First Interstate	Los Angeles	32,110	901
10.	First Chicago	Chicago	28,699	-
11.	Security Pacific	Los Angeles	27,794	607
12.	Wells Fargo	San Francisco	23,638	403
13.	Crocker National	San Francisco	19,074	382
14.	Irving Bank	New York	18,089	121
15.	Marine Midland	Buffalo	17,480	295

	1990	City	Assets (In millions)	Banking Offices
1.	Citicorp	New York	$216,996	-
2.	Bank of America	San Francisco	110,728	1,200
3.	Chase Manhattan	New York	98,064	342
4.	JP Morgan	New York	93,103	20
5.	Security Pacific	Los Angeles	84,731	550
6.	Chemical	New York	73,019	425
7.	NCNB	Charlotte	65,295	923
8.	Bankers Trust	New York	63,596	4
9.	Manufacturers Hanover	New York	61,530	221
10.	Wells Fargo	San Francisco	56,199	547
11.	First Interstate	Los Angeles	51,356	1,041
12.	C&S/Sovran	Norfolk	51,237	1,012
13.	First Chicago	Chicago	50,799	55
14.	PNC	Pittsburgh	45,333	535
15.	Bank of New York	New York	45,496	258

	2000	City	Assets (In millions)	Banking Offices
1.	Citicorp	New York	$902,210	199
2.	JP Morgan	New York	715,348	572
3.	Bank of America	Charlotte	642,664	4,390
4.	Wells Fargo	San Francisco	272,426	2,982
5.	Bank One	Chicago	269,300	1,810
6.	First Union	Charlotte	254,272	2,193
7.	Fleet	Boston	179,519	1,220
8.	SunTrust	Atlanta	103,660	1,174
9.	National City	Cleveland	88,619	1,132
10.	U.S. Bancorp	Minneapolis	87,336	1,179
11.	KeyCorp	Cleveland	87,270	940
12.	Firstar	Milwaukee	77,585	1,166
13.	Bank of New York	New York	77,114	359
14.	Wachovia	Winston-Salem	74,032	668
15.	PNC	Pittsburgh	69,921	717

	2012	City	Assets (In millions)	Banking Offices
1.	JPMorgan	New York	$2,359	5,707
2.	Bank of America	Charlotte	2,212	5,387
3.	Citigroup	New York	1,865	1,030
4.	Wells Fargo	San Francisco	1,423	6,293
5.	Bank of New York	New York	359	55
6.	U.S. Bancorp	Minneapolis	354	3,140
7.	Capital One	McLean, Va.	313	908
8.	PNC	Pittsburg	305	2,937
9.	State Street	Boston	222	1
10.	BB&T	Winston-Salem	184	1,839
11.	SunTrust	Atlanta	174	1,548
12.	Fifth Third	Cincinnati	122	1,369
13.	Regions	Birmingham	121	1,713
14.	Northern Trust	Chicago	97	71
15.	KeyCorp	Cleveland	89	1,058

Sources: 1931 Moody's Financial Directory, New York; 1951, 1961 and 1971 Polk's Bank Directory; American Banker, April 20, 1982; and February 8, 1992; and SNL Financial, Charlottesville, Virginia.

LIST OF TABLES

Notes and Sources

Chapter 1–Surprise or Business as Usual

1. SNL Financial Corporation, Charlottesville, Virginia and Federal Deposit Insurance Corporation., Statistics on Banking, Washington, DC: FDIC.

Chapter 2–The Early Years

1. "A Brief History of Central Banking in the United States," *From Revolution to Reconstruction*, Edward Flaherty, accessed March 6, 2003.

2. Board of Governors of the Federal Reserve System (U.S.), *All Bank Statistics 1896 to 1955*, "United States Summary," Washington, DC: Board of Governors of the Federal Reserve System, May 11, 2007, p.59.

3. Ibid., p. 59.

4. John R. Walker, "Depression-era Bank Failures: The Great Contagion or the Great Shakeout?" *Federal Reserve Bank of Richmond Economic Quarterly Volume 91/1*, Winter 2005, p.45.

5. Background on the original Bank of America comes from Gary Hector, *Breaking the Bank*. New York: Little Brown and Company, 1988.

6. FDIC, Historical Statistics on Banking.

Chapter 3–Uncharted Waters

1. "Forces Affecting Bank Expansion in the 1980s" presentation, Virginia Commonwealth University, Richmond, Virginia, March 10, 1980.

2. Carter H. Golembe and David S. Holland, *Federal Regulation of Banking—1981*, Washington, DC: Golembe Associates, Inc., 2003, p. 114.

3. Background on Citigroup comes from Phillip L. Zweig, *Wriston*, New York: Crown Publisher, Inc., 1995; Ron Chernow, *The House of Morgan*, New York: Atlantic Monthly Press, 1990, and *International Directory of Company Histories*, Chicago and London: St. James Press, Volume 59, pp. 121–127.

4. Phillip L. Zweig, *Wriston*, New York: Crown Publisher, Inc., 1995, p. 256.

5. Ibid., p. 362.

6. Background on NCNB comes from Ross Yockey, *McColl*, Atlanta, GA: Longstreet, Inc., 1999, and Howard E. Covington, Jr. and Marion Ellis,

The Story of Nationsbank, Chapel Hill, NC: The University of North Carolina Press, 1993.

7. *Managing the Crisis: The FDIC and RTC Experience*, "First Pennsylvania Bank, N.A.," Washington, DC: FDIC, 2003, p. 518.

8. *American Banker*, October 15, 1979.

CHAPTER 4–ECONOMIC TURMOIL AND BANKING

1. Data on interest rates and prime rates come from United States. Federal Reserve Board.

2. Background on Bank of Commonwealth comes from Irvine H. Sprague, *Bailout*, Washington, DC: Beard Books, 1986.

3. Ibid., p. 75.

4. Natalie Canavor, "1974: Franklin National Bank goes under," *Long Island Business News* Long Island, NY, August 27–September 2, 2004.

5. *Federal Reserve Bulletin*, November 1982, p. A.14.

6. The *Nilson Report*, Carpinteria, California, H S N Consultants, Inc., (January, 1982).

CHAPTER 6–THRIFT CRISIS: EARLY STAGES

1. '81 *Savings and Loan Sourcebook*, Chicago: United States League of Savings Associations, p. 38 and FDIC, Historical Statistics on Banking.

2. *Histories of the Eighties—Lessons for the Future*, "The Savings and Loan Crisis and Its Relationship to Banking." (Washington, DC: FDIC, 1997), p. 168.

3. *Business, Government and Society*, 8th Edition, 1997. "The Savings and Loan Debacle." Internet.

4. *Histories of the Eighties—Lessons for the Future*, "The Savings and Loan Crisis and Its Relationship to Banking." Washington, DC: FDIC, 1997, p. 169.

5. FDIC, Historical Statistics of Banking.

6. *History of the Eighties—Lessons for the Future*. "The Savings and Loan Crisis and its Relationship to Banking," Washington, DC: FDIC, 1997, p. 168.

7. *History of the Eighties—Lessons for the Future*. "The Mutual Savings Bank Crisis," Washington, DC: FDIC, 1997, p. 226.

8. Ibid., 226.

9. *Monthly Market Report*, SNL Financial, Charlottesville, Virginia, (January 1991), p. 5.

10. Sheshunoff Information Services, Inc., Austin, Texas.

11. *History of the Eighties—Lessons for the Future*, "The Savings and Loan Crisis and Its Relationship to Banking," Washington, DC: FDIC, 1997, p. 168.

12. Ibid., p. 181.

Chapter 7–Trouble in the Oil Patch

1. *History of the Eighties—Lessons for the Future*, Banking Problems in the Southwest," Washington, DC: FDIC, 1997, p. 291.

2. Ibid., p. 292.

3. Ibid., p. 291.

4. Ibid., p. 291.

5. *The Handbook of Texas Online*, Texas State Historical Society, October 10, 2004. Internet.

6. *Managing the Crisis: The FDIC and RTC Experience*, "Continental Illinois National Bank and Trust Company," Washington, DC: FDIC, 2003, p. 546.

7. Irvine H. Sprague, Bailout, Washington, DC: Beard Books, 1986, p. 113.

8. *Managing the Crisis: The FDIC and RTC Experience*, Continental Illinois National Bank and Trust Company," Washington, DC: FDIC, 1997, p. 560.

9. *History of the Eighties—Lessons for the Future*, "Continental Illinois and 'Too Big to Fail'," Washington, DC: FDIC, 1997, p. 237.

10. Ibid., p. 240.

11. Ibid., p. 242.

12. *Managing the Crisis: The FDIC and RTC Experience*, "Continental Illinois National Bank and Trust Company," Washington, DC: FDIC, 1997, p. 560.

13. *History of the Eighties—Lessons for the Future*, "Banking Problem in the Southwest," Washington, DC: FDIC, 1997, p.299.

14. Ibid., p. 303.

15. Ibid., p. 323.

16. Howard E. Covington, Jr. and Marion Ellis, *The Story of Nationsbank*, Chapel Hill, NC: The University of North Carolina Press, 1993, p. 214.

17. *Managing the Crisis: The FDIC and RTC Experience*, "First Republic Bank Corporation," Washington, DC: FDIC, 2003, p. 601.

CHAPTER 8–INTERSTATE BANKING GATHERS MOMENTUM

1. Ross Yockey, *McColl*, Atlanta, GA: Longstreet, Inc., 1999, p. 171.

2. Howard E. Covington, Jr. and Marion Ellis, *The Story of Nationsbank*, Chapel Hill, NC: The University of North Carolina Press, 1993.

3. Ross Yockey, *McColl*, (Atlanta, GA: Longstreet, Inc., 1999), p. 247.

4. *History of the Eighties—Lessons for the Future*, "LDC Debt Crisis," Washington, DC: FDIC, 1997, p. 191.

CHAPTER 9–THRIFT CRISIS: CHANGING THE LANDSCAPE

1. Cincinnati Enquirer, January 8, 2000. Internet.

2. Ibid.

3. James Ring Adams, *Big Fix: Inside the S&L Scandal*, New York: John Wiley & Sons, New York, 1990, p.176.

4. Cincinnati Enquirer, January 8, 2000. Internet.

5. James Ring Adams, *Big Fix: Inside the S&L Scandal*, New York: John Wiley & Sons, New York, 1990, p. 176 and Internet story.

6. Ibid.

7. *History of the Eighties—Lessons for the Future*, "The Savings and Loan Crisis and Its Relationship to Banking," Washington, DC: FDIC, 1997, p. 183.

8. Martin Mayer, *The Greatest-Ever Bank Robbery*, New York: Charles Scribner's and Sons, 1990, p. 14.

9. New York Magazine, 1989. Internet

10. Martin Mayer, *The Greatest-Ever Bank Robbery*, New York: Charles Scribner's and Sons, 1990, p. 14.

11. Ibid., p. 256.

12. S&L Bailout Costs, Franklin Mancuso, updated 1999. Internet

13. SNL Financial Corporation, Charlottesville, Virginia

14. *History of the Eighties—Lessons for the Future*, "The Savings and Loan Crisis and Its Relationship to Banking," Washington, DC: FDIC, 1997, p. 187.

CHAPTER 11–NEW ENGLAND "MIRACLE" ENDS

15. *Histories of the Eighties—Lessons for the Future*, "Banking Problems in the Northeast," Washington, DC: FDIC, 1997, p. 337.

16. *New England Banking Report*, Danielson Associates Inc., February 19, 1993, p. 2.

17. *New England Banking Report*, Danielson Associates Inc., November 15, 1990, p.1.

18. Chicago Tribune, Business Section, February 17, 1989.

19. Phillip L. Zweig, *Wriston*, New York: Crown Publisher, Inc., 1995, p. 868.

20. *Managing the Crisis: The FDIC and RTC Experience*, "Bank of New England Corporation," Washington, DC: FDIC, 2003, p. 641 and 648.

21. *Managing the Crisis: The FDIC and RTC Experience*, Seven Banks in New Hampshire," Washington, DC: FDIC, 2003, pp. 672, 674 and 679.

Chapter 12–Charlotte's Web

1. Ross Yockey, *McColl*, Atlanta, GA: Longstreet, Inc., 1999, p.429.

2. Howard E. Covington, Jr. and Marion Ellis, *The Story of Nationsbank*, Chapel Hill, NC: The University of North Carolina Press, 1993, p. 281.

3. Ibid., p. 293.

4. Ibid., p. 295.

5. Ibid., p. 296.

6. Ibid., p. 306

7. *Managing the Crisis: The FDIC and RTC Experience*, "Southeast Banking Corp.," Washington, DC: FDIC, 1997, p. 657.

8. *The BCCI Affair*, Report to the Committee on Foreign Relations, United States Senate, Senators John Kerry and Hank Brown, December 1992, Executive Summary.

9. Ibid.

Chapter 13–California Dreaming

1. *Far West Banking Report*, Danielson Associates Inc., April 2, 1988, pp. 1, 3 and 4.

2. Sheshunoff S&L Quarterly: December 1988 Ratings, Sheshunoff Information Services, Inc., College Stations, Texas, 1990, pp.19 and 39.

3. *History of the Eighties—Lessons for the Future*, "Banking Problems in California, Washington, DC: FDIC, 1997, pp. 382–384.

4. Ibid., pp. 387–350

5. Ibid., pp. 391 and 394

6. Ibid., p. 394

7. Background on Security Pacific comes from *International Directory of Company Histories*, (Chicago and London: St. James Press, Volume II), pp. 349-350.

8. *Business Week Online*, August 19, 1991. Internet.

9. Ibid.

10. *History of the Eighties—Lessons for the Future*, "Banking Problems in California," (Washington, DC: FDIC, 1997), pp. 409–410.

Chapter 14–New York Banking at a Crossroads

1. Background on Manufacturers Hanover comes from *International Directory of Company Histories*, Chicago and London: St. James Press, Volume 46, pp. 312–314.

2. Background on Chase Manhattan comes from *International Directory of Company Histories*, Chicago and London: St. James Press, Volume 13, pp. 145–148.

3. Economist.com, October 29, 2004. Internet.

4. *Business Week Online*, "Mighty Morgan," December 23, 1991. Internet.

5. Background on Bankers Trust comes from *International Directory of Company Histories*, Chicago and London: St. James Press, Volume 49, pp. 59–63.

Chapter 16–Every Other Monday

1. *Business Week Online*, "Is 'Nice Big Dull' Good Enough?" May 12, 1997.

2. *Business Week Online*, "First Interstate: Up for Grabs," September 18, 1995.

3. *Business Week Online*, "First Interstate Snubs Wells Again," December 4, 1995.

4. *Business Week Online*, "Why Wells Fargo is Circling the Wagons," June 9, 1997.

Chapter 17–1998: The Superbanks Cometh

1. Bank Investor, SNL Financial, January, 1996, 1997 and 1998.

Chapter 18–Beyond Traditional Banking

1. *TIME.com*, "Bankers Trust Acquires Alex Brown, April 7, 1997. Internet

2. Amey Stone and Mike Brewster, *King of Capital—Sandy Weill*, New York: John Wiley & Sons, Inc., 2002, pp. 44 and 119.

3. *Business Week*, "The Best Performers," March 24, 1997 and March 30, 1998.

4. Amey Stone and Mike Brewster, *King of Capital—Sandy Weill*, New York: John Wiley & Sons, Inc., 2002, pp. 224–225.

5. Business Week, "The Coca Cola of Personal Finance," April 20, 1998.

6. Ibid.

7. Barron's, September 15, 2004, p. 24.

8. *American Banker*, October 16, 1991.

9. *American Banker*, April 16, 1996 and *National Mortgage News*, Annual Data Report for 2008.

10. *National Mortgage News*, Annual Data Report for 2008.

11. Ibid.

12. Ibid.

13. *Business Insurance*, July 17, 2006 with Wells Fargo and BB&T numbers updated for 2007.

14. Financial Services Fact Book, Financial Services Roundtable, Washington, DC, 2006, p. 49.

CHAPTER 19–THE 1990S IN RETROSPECT

1. FDIC: Historical Statistics on Banking; 1988 Factbook of Savings Institutions; and 1990 Credit Union Report.

CHAPTER 20–AND THEN THERE WERE FIVE

1. CNNMoney, June 26, 2000. Internet

2. Citigroup 2004 Annual Report, p. 31.

CHAPTER 21–HOUSING BUBBLE AND SUBPRIME MORTGAGES

1. Inside Mortgage Finance, The 2007 Mortgage Market Statistical Annual.

2. Case-Shiller

3. The Center for Public Integrity, "The Subprime 25," Washington, DC, May 6, 2009.

4. *National Mortgage News*, Annual Data Report for 2008.

5. Inside Mortgage Finance, The 2007 Mortgage Market Statistical Annual.

6. Case Western University, Case 15 "Countrywide Financial Corporation and the Subprime Mortgage Debacle," Ronald W. Eastburn, The McGraw-Hill Companies, New York, 2011, p. 1.

7. Ibid., p. 1

8. "Too Good to Be True: The Fall of Indy Mac, John Devcik," September 22, 2009, p. 1.

9. "Rise and Demise of New Century Financial," Barry Neilsen, Feb. 26, 2009, p. 2.

Chapter 22–The Year the Music Stopped

1. Sheila Bair, *Bull by the Horns*, New York: Free Press, 2012, pp. 96, 99 and 105.

Chapter 23–The Recovery

1. SNL Financial Corporation, Charlottesville, Virginia

2. SNL Financial Corporation, Charlottesville, Virginia

Acknowledgments

Much of this book is based on my recollections from the last 40 years refreshed by articles and reports I had written years ago, the rereading of which was often painful, but occasionally gratifying. Over time, though, memory blurs, and often what seemed the case then, no longer seems quite the same now. Sometimes the earlier thoughts were just wrong.

Fortunately, the books and articles listed in the bibliography filled many of the gaps and improved the recollections. Of particular help were two studies by the FDIC available on the Internet—*History of the Eighties—Lessons for the Future and Managing the Crisis: The FDIC and RTC Experience*. They provided much-needed details on the crisis-laden 1980s when consolidation was in its early stages and my memory was being sorely stretched. The International Directory of Company Histories was invaluable in providing historical background on the banks that led the way in the consolidation process.

I also had the good fortune of having access to the SNL Financial data through my firm, Danielson Associates. SNL Financial has bank and thrift call report data and merger information going back to 1990. This provided statistical data for the later chapters and a quick reference for dates.

For older statistical information, there were the standard bank data sources such as the Federal Reserve Bulletin; the FDIC's Historical Statistics on Banking; Polk's Bank Directory; and Moody Financial Directory. I had kept copies of the annual Polk's Bank Directory since 1971, Federal Reserve Bulletins since 1978 and tables from the American Bankers from 1978 through the 1990s. The FDIC data, like so much other good information, is readily available on the Internet. When it came to the numbers, I also have to give thanks to John Putman, who understands the SNL database so much better than me.

The book also may have gotten written without the efforts of Laura Kozinski and my daughter, Diane Danielson, in the earlier edition and Jenna Lloyd this time around, but certainly not in such grammatically correct and readable form. Jenna Lloyd was also very helpful in getting the book ready for publication by the SDP Publishing Company.

Index

ABOUT THE AUTHOR

The impact of economic crises and consolidation on banking is something that Arnold G. Danielson witnessed beginning in the early 1970s from inside a bank holding company and from 1977 to 2007 from his firm, Danielson Associates, which was an advisor to banks and thrifts attempting to adjust to a continually changing banking environment. From 1985 to 2007 he wrote the regional and national Danielson Reports that described what was happening in the industry at the time. In 2007, he published his book, *Consolidation of Banking: or How Five Banks Bought 50% of America's Biggest Business*, of which this book is a revision of and updated to include the period from 2008 to 2013 and place a greater emphasis on the impact of economic crises on banking.

Today, Mr. Danielson is retired, and he and his wife, Vivian, split their time between homes in Potomac, Maryland and Nice, France. His time in France and love of history are reflected in a book far removed from banking, *A Traveler's History of Cote d'Azur*, published in 2012.

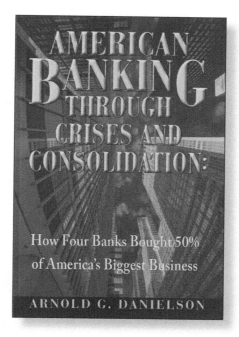

American Banking Through Crisis and Consolidation:

How Four Banks Bought 50% of America's Biggest Business

Arnold G. Danielson

www.ambfg.com

Also available in ebook format

TO PURCHASE:

Amazon.com

BarnesAndNoble.com

SDPPublishing.com

 **SDP Publishing**

www.SDPPublishing.com

Contact us at: info@SDPPublishing.com

CPSIA information can be obtained at www.ICGtesting.com
Printed in the USA
BVOW09s2336150914

366950BV00005B/16/P